3-00-64

DATE DUE

OCT 29 '71	
DEC 10 '71	
MAY 15 '72	
OCT 24 1994	
MAY 1 5 2000	

THE FAITH

of the

CHRISTIAN CHURCH

THE FAITH

OF THE

CHRISTIAN CHURCH

By GUSTAF AULEN

Translated from the fifth Swedish edition by
ERIC H. WAHLSTROM

THE MUHLENBERG PRESS
Philadelphia

Preface to the
Fifth (Swedish)—the Second (English)—Edition

Four earlier editions of this book have already appeared. The second edition, 1924, a year after the first, did not show any great changes; but the third edition, 1931, contained many additions and revisions. The fourth edition, 1943 (from which the first English edition was translated) also contained some changes, but the work of revision was not as extensive and complete as I would have desired. This edition appeared at a time when the duties of the episcopal office, other official functions, and work in connection with the war situation left only a limited time that could be devoted to the work. In the present fifth edition the following chapters have been entirely rewritten: 7, 8, 39, 45, and 50. Chapters 3, 11, 20, 21, 27, 41, 42, 43, and 44 have been largely reworked. In other chapters extensive additions, deletions, and revisions have been made.

A book of this kind is never finished. The gospel, the Christian message, and therefore the Christian faith as such, are indeed unchangeable. But the task of interpreting the Christian faith in the contemporary situation presents ever new problems to theology. All such attempts necessarily bear the marks of imperfection and incompletion. I am very well aware of the shortcomings of my presentation. At the same time I am deeply grateful for this opportunity to make a new attempt at improvement. The changes which have been made have to some extent indeed been occasioned by contact with modern theological research, which has gained new insights and sound new approaches to the old problems. But my intention has always been to develop more clearly, both in content and terminology, those fundamental motifs which have characterized my presentation of the meaning of the Christian faith.

Lund, December, 1956   Gustaf Aulén

Preface to the First English Edition

This book is a translation of the fourth revised edition of *Den allmänneliga kristna tron*. The Swedish word *allmännelig* is the word that is used in the Apostolic Creed: "We believe in one holy catholic (Christian) Church." Because the word "catholic" can easily be misunderstood, the title of the book has been translated: *The Faith of the Christian Church*. It is of course not my intention to assert that the statements of this book could be or ought to be accepted in all Christendom. The title does not imply a claim but indicates a most important direction which systematic theology cannot ignore without failing to fulfill its function.

Systematic theology has a special object—as does every science. The object of systematic theology is the Christian faith as a living reality. To explain the significance of this faith, to make clear what essentially belongs to it, and to bring to light, wholly and completely, its own characteristic viewpoints, is the task of systematic theology. Thus theology must reveal what the eyes of faith see. In other words, theology must conscientiously endeavor to set forth the meaning of Christian truth.

Therefore, theology must firmly adhere to the ecumenical perspective. Its endeavor must not become the private confession of a theologian. In that case theology would surrender its scientific-critical purpose in relation to its object. The same thing would happen if theology would confine itself to a narrow and self-satisfied confessionalism. That does not constitute a plea for indifference to confessional points of view. But it does mean that no doctrine can be accepted as truly Christian simply on the basis of its confessional relations; for instance, its relations to Luther, Calvin, or Thomas Aquinas. We do not refer to Luther as a final arbiter of truth, but only in so far as he helps us to see more clearly the soul of Christianity. In the measure that systematic theology is faithful to its aim, it must imply a self-examination. It must be thankful for the gifts received in our own confession and at the same time condemn every tendency toward being *incurvatus in se* as sinful.

In the nineteenth century as well as in the first decades of the twentieth century there has been a conflict between two main theological types, one known as the fundamentalist and the other as the modernist. The first has had a scholastic or a pietist character, and sometimes it has tried to combine both of these attitudes. The second type has reinterpreted Christianity according to the viewpoint of idealistic philosophy and a rather vague humanism. In reality both of these types have been equally incapable of accomplishing the theological task of understanding and explaining the Christian faith. In both cases the radical realism of Christianity has been obscured. The alternatives seemed to be either narrow-mindedness or a disintegrating misinterpretation.

Fortunately, it is not necessary to choose either of these alternatives. The theological outlook is in the process of changing. In that respect two factors have had a dominating influence: first, a new and deeper insight into the meaning and motif of the Reformation; second, and foremost, a new, fresh, and realistic approach to the biblical message. Above everything, the endeavors of theology must be to see Christianity as it actually is, according to its uniqueness. That is, one must liberate the Christian message from all that obscures its fresh colors and so let it appear in all its original power.

The Bishop's Residence,
Strängnäs, Sweden,
October, 1947

Gustaf Aulén

Table of Contents

Chapter 2 *The God Who Acts*

Part II THE ACT OF GOD IN CHRIST

Chapter 3 *The Victorious Act of Reconciliation*

Chapter 4 *The Broken and Restored Relationship with God*

Part III THE CHURCH OF GOD

Chapter 5 *The Nature of the Church*

Abbreviations

for Editions of Luther's Works

EA —*D. Martin Luthers sämmtliche Werk*
(Frankfurt and Erlangen, 1826-1857).

WA—*D. Martin Luthers Werke.* Kritische Gesamtausgabe
(Weimar, 1883-).

Introduction

FAITH AND THEOLOGY

1. The Task of Systematic Theology

1. *The project: to understand the faith.* Systematic theology has as its object of study the Christian faith. The intention of the discipline is to elucidate the content and meaning of the Christian faith with all the means at its disposal. The task is neither demonstrative nor normative, but analytical and critical. Its purpose is neither to furnish proofs for faith nor to determine what "ought to be believed." Everything is concentrated on the attempt to understand the faith and to present its meaning with the greatest possible clarity.

2. *"Systematic" theology.* Since the Christian faith is by its nature completely theocentric, and thus determined by the act of God in Christ, the presentation of its content must appear as one organic whole.

3. *Systematic theology and philosophy of religion.* Systematic theology is differentiated from philosophy of religion, which undertakes to investigate the place of religious experience in the life of the human spirit. It is entirely foreign to that kind of philosophy of religion which appears as rational metaphysics.

4. *Systematic theology and psychology of religion.* Since faith directs itself exclusively toward God, and its affirmations therefore concern *the relationship between God and man,* systematic theology is differentiated from psychology of religion which deals with the religious subject and is limited to an analysis of the religious consciousness.

5. *The "ecumenical" Christian faith: systematic theology and symbolics.* Since the function of systematic theology is to elucidate the meaning of the *Christian* faith, it cannot be bound by confessional limitations. It can be confessional only in so far as this is of assistance in the comprehension of that which is genuinely Christian. It is thus differentiated from symbolics, which interprets the various confessions and their relationships to one another.

6. *The scientific character of systematic theology.* The function of systematic theology is purely scientific in so far as its task is to explicate the meaning of the Christian faith. It can serve the Christian life only by performing this scientific task without any secondary purposes.

1. The Project: to Understand the Faith

In defining the task of systematic theology it is necessary first of all to emphasize that the object of study is the Christian faith as a given, objective reality. Systematic theology is therefore that theological discipline which has as its purpose the study and investigation of the Christian faith.

Faith is the only object of study that can be legitimately considered. God himself cannot be made the object of scientific investigation, so that theology in that sense should be a study of God. God is not a "thing" which can be scientifically investigated. As far as faith is concerned God is Alpha and Omega, but analytical theology can be concerned only with the elucidation of the nature of the Christian relationship between God and man and with the idea of God which is characteristic of Christian faith.

It must be emphatically stated that systematic theology is confronted with the same situation as are all other scientific disciplines, namely, that it is concerned with the study of a definite object. This insight is obscured if theology is presented as a kind of confession expressed in a "purified and scientific" form. Such an attempt would place theology in the same category as preaching. It would then be a confessional proclamation in a complete and logical form. One reason why such a conception of the function of theology has been presented from time to time is that theological expositions of the Christian faith have neglected essential elements in that faith and consequently have become misinterpretations. Such presentations are intended to protect the faith by emphasizing the confessional viewpoint. But even though the intention is good, the result is a tragic confusion of the viewpoints of the religious life and scientific research. The theological function as a science is of an entirely different nature from the confessional function which belongs to the religious life. In view of this fact, we must insist that systematic theology is concerned simply with investigating and elucidating a certain area of research. This study must be characterized by the greatest possible objectivity since the purpose is to express the genuine meaning of the faith. If theological interpretations of the Christian faith have sometimes become perversions and the real nature of faith has not been expressed, the remedy is not to be sought in a demand that theology should be given the character of a subjective confession, but rather the opposite, namely, in a purely scientific and objective approach. The guarantee that the interpretation will not become a misinterpretation and perversion lies in this objective attitude.

In maintaining this view of the function of systematic theology, the confusing discussion about the personal qualifications of the investigator disappears. Often in the history of theology an attempt has been made to transform the scientific discussion concerning the meaning of faith into a discussion about the personal faith of the theological investigator. When the task is defined as indicated in the previous paragraphs, there can be no other requirement than the demand to understand the subject under investigation. This is likewise the situation in all scientific research.

The function of systematic theology is, therefore, to elucidate the content and meaning of the Christian faith by the use of all available resources. The purpose of the study must continually be directed toward this one central point. The task is to unveil and reveal everything that is essential, to brush aside all nonessential and foreign elements, to remove all unnecessary accretions, and to bring out clearly the very heart of the matter. It is self-evident that such an approach must assume a critical character. The investigation cannot stop at the surface or with the most obvious formulations. By a critical analysis it must penetrate through shifting forms to the underlying and fundamental religious motifs and at the same time be continually mindful of that which is uniquely and essentially Christian.

But systematic theology must not be given either a demonstrative or a normative character. It does not seek to demonstrate "the truth" of faith or to provide rational grounds for faith, or to furnish proofs of the existence of God. Such attempts are as scientifically impossible as they are foreign to faith since faith is not conscious of being founded on any rational proofs. They are therefore also foreign to that scientific discipline whose only purpose is to understand faith. Even if rational arguments could be presented, they would have no reference whatever to faith. The god whose "reality" could be thus demonstrated would be of an entirely different nature from the God of faith. Systematic theology can discuss the question of the certainty of the Christian faith only in so far as it investigates the nature of this certainty.

Neither can the function of systematic theology be of a normative character. Theology does not write laws for faith, or act as lord over faith. It does not determine faith, but analyzes the Christian faith as it actually exists. Just as little as ethics can undertake to tell men what they ought to do, can systematic theology, which is directed toward a study of faith, presume to determine what ought to be believed. There is really no such "normative" science. Just as Christian ethics has to make clear the specifically Christian ethos, so theology must make clear and establish the unique character of Christian faith. But personal attitudes toward these factors are an entirely different matter, which must not be confused with critical research. Rather, systematic theology must focus its attention upon what is and what is not characteristically Christian. This critical examination is the principal concern of systematic theology because its task is to understand the *Christian* faith and to present the content, motifs, and viewpoints of faith itself with the greatest possible clarity.

In this connection it must be strongly emphasized that the specific problem with which systematic theology deals is the *content* and *meaning* of the Christian faith. Systematic theology is not a historical discipline. The problem is not to set forth the origin and development of Christian doctrines. This belongs to the history of dogma. The study of this history is of utmost importance as a prerequisite for systematic theology, but these two are distinct and separate disciplines. Systematic theology does not ask how faith in Christ originated and what elements may be regarded as having belonged to the confession of faith as it emerged in the primitive church. It asks rather about the essential import and meaning of such a confession.

Systematic theology has its own clearly defined function, but in performing this task it stands in close relationship to a number of scientific disciplines and must utilize all available resources. Its closest contacts, of course, are with all departments of religion and theology. But its associations extend far beyond the study of religion proper, especially toward philosophy and the humanities in general. In the following paragraphs the relation of systematic theology to these disciplines will be further defined. It is not isolated but is closely connected with a number of scientific disciplines, but none of these undertakes to treat of that which is the specific function of systematic theology: to expound the content and meaning of the Christian faith.

2. "Systematic" Theology

When systematic theology seeks to investigate the meaning of Christian faith, it does not deal merely with a multitude of disparate doctrines which, as in the so-called "loci theology," appear as unrelated statements. There is rather an inner, organic homogeneity in everything that constitutes the object of systematic theology. This unity is given in the completely theocentric character of faith. It is therefore a confusion of terms to speak of a "theocentric theology." This redundant expression is no doubt intended to enhance the theocentric character of faith, and this is indeed a point which cannot be overemphasized.

In the realm of Christian faith the question is always about God and man's relation to him. God is the only center of faith. Christian faith is faith in God and in him alone. Nothing can be equated with God. Faith cannot be divided so that it is directed partly to God and partly to other "objects." When we speak about faith in Christ, or in the Spirit, or faith in the forgiveness of sins, in the church and eternal life, and so on, it does not mean that a number of objects of faith have been introduced which might in a certain sense compete with God for attention. This mechanical and superficial viewpoint would completely obscure the living, simple, and immediate character of faith.

To speak about different objects of faith has significance only if thereby different aspects of God's activity in behalf of man are clarified, and it thus becomes apparent that in everything it is a question of faith in God. If we speak about Christ as an object of faith, we are talking about God revealed; if we speak of forgiveness of sins, we are referring to that God who establishes communion with men; if we speak about eternal life, we are talking about the eternal and life-giving God. If other "objects of faith" are placed by the side of God and compete with him, God has already lost that sovereignty which belongs to him in the realm of faith. There is nothing more obvious and inescapable to faith than that "we should trust God above all things," nothing less than this. Where it is a question of designating the "object" of Christian faith, the word of the Bible is appropriate: God is "the Alpha and the Omega, the beginning and the end" (Rev. 21:6).

If the Christian faith possesses this unitary, theocentric character, the presentation of systematic theology must become, if it does justice to its subject, an organic whole. It cannot be a "loci theology," which presents a series of more or less disconnected doctrines. The various pronouncements of faith stand in an inner organic relation to one another, and this fact must be reflected in the theological analysis. In reality there is only one subject, but it must be seen from various points of view. The analysis is concerned at all times with *the relationship between God and man* as this is determined by the act of *God* in Christ. Nothing must find a place in the analysis of the meaning of faith which is not connected with and does not express this relationship.

But this organic and systematic character of the theological analysis would be completely misunderstood if it be concluded that the theological presentation ought to appear as a rationally completed system. The unity in question is not a closed system of reasoning but rather a unity characterized by an inner tension. This fact will have to be noted time and again in our presentation. This tension cannot be eliminated by a rational compromise for in so doing faith is misinterpreted and perverted. On the other hand, in spite of the tension, this faith which is directed toward only one center has the character of an organic whole. The object of systematic theology is a most sensitive organism, in which one aspect stands in intimate relation to the other, and what happens on the periphery is reflected at once at the very center.

3. Systematic Theology and Philosophy of Religion

In view of the diverse interpretations of the function of philosophy of religion and the obscure conceptions of its relation to systematic theology, it becomes necessary to define this function and clarify the relation between these two disciplines. If, as we have seen, it is the intention of systematic theology to permit the content and meaning of the Christian faith to be expressed fully and completely, this can be accomplished only by letting the unique and vital viewpoints of faith itself be brought to light. But this cannot be accomplished if faith is examined and judged in accordance with perspectives which are external and foreign to faith. The task is to unveil and expose

7

that which is essential to Christian faith. Faith must be understood from its own center. If it is forced into conformity with a system foreign to itself, it is misinterpreted and perverted.

From this starting point we are now able to decide how the relation between systematic theology and philosophy of religion ought to be determined. It cannot be denied that there has often been a confusion between the functions of these two disciplines, and that philosophy of religion has often attempted to be a substitute for systematic theology. In doing so it has also claimed a certain superiority. It has been assumed that philosophy of religion should endeavor to create a common, primary delineation of the "essence of religion." Such a delineation would serve as a starting point and as a dependable, critical standard for the examination and evaluation of various historical religions, including Christianity. Philosophy of religion would then be able to deal with Christianity from a higher and more scientific point of view than "dogmatics," which is bound by confessional presuppositions and cannot assume as free and detached a position as can philosophy of religion.

This type of thinking nevertheless represents a warped view of the function of systematic theology, and it also misunderstands the function of philosophy of religion. It has become perfectly clear that this confusion of the functions of these two disciplines neither contributed anything to philosophy of religion nor furthered the study and elucidation of the Christian faith.

Religion exists only in historical manifestations. When philosophy of religion in one way or another constructs a certain "common religion" and then makes this idea the basis of its judgment of the Christian faith, the result is inevitably that the Christian faith is investigated and judged from the outside, from a point of view and by a methodology which is not its own. This cannot lead to clarity about the nature and meaning of Christian faith. The interpretation becomes a reinterpretation according to a previously arranged outline. In spite of all claims to scientific objectivity, this method becomes highly subjective and arbitrary. It generally happens that the investigator who makes the greatest claims to have found an objective, scientific, and safe basis of judgment turns out to be the most arbitrary and helpless. In substantiating this claim we can point to the attempts of the Enlightenment to reinterpret Christian faith in accordance with its "philosophical" common religion, and also to the nineteenth-century idealism with its philosophy of religion and theology. Here the Christian faith has been forced into foreign forms. The reinterpretations which inevitably appear cannot hide the fact that faith has been subject to a transformation which has obscured its nature, and that its own characteristic ideas have been only partially understood, if at all. Even Schleiermacher, who attacked the "philosophical" common religion and prepared the way for a better understanding of the function of theology by presenting the Christian faith as the proper object of the study of theology, was not able to liberate himself from the baneful influence of idealistic philosophy of religion. He was not able to develop the program he outlined for himself. In his celebrated treatise on the Christian faith he made theology dependent upon philosophy of religion because the criterion for determining the "essence of Christianity" was found in a religious idea whose content was characterized by the monistic philosophy of immanence. This idea exercised a tremendous influence on the subsequent presentation of the Christian faith and its content and rendered it impossible for him to permit the characteristic ideas of faith to appear.

If ability to discern and clarify the objects of a scientific study is evidence of scientific research, then the kind of philosophy of religion which has been described here has little reason to look condescendingly at that systematic theology whose function has been defined in these paragraphs. The scientific methodology claimed for the philosophy of religion influenced by rationalistic metaphysics is an illusion; it is not able to understand Christianity. Evidently it is not sufficiently free from its own presuppositions. It judges—and reinterprets—on the basis of postulates whose content it has not clearly examined. If it is at all possible to "understand" Christianity, to understand the content and meaning of the Christian faith, such a possibility can be actualized only by a study which intends nothing else than to allow the motifs and viewpoints of faith itself to appear in their rightful place, and which desires nothing else than to understand faith from within.

If, therefore, it can be established that a philosophy of religion which has been influenced by metaphysics cannot serve the positive study of the Christian faith, it can also be affirmed that the purely religio-philosophical function has not been understood in a scientifically satisfactory way. It is clear that the idea of religion obtained by such means is not achieved through scientific analysis but is based rather on highly subjective principles. It is nothing but a subjective conception of faith on which an attempt is made to superimpose the marks of objectivity and philosophical scholarliness. It is a "confession" which lays claim to being philosophical. But such a combination as a "philosophical confession" is a *contradictio in adjecto*. A personal confession, no matter how much it attempts to clothe itself with the robe of philosophy, cannot claim a proper place among scientific studies.

If philosophy of religion is to assume a really scientific character, it must free itself resolutely from all tendencies to create "philosophically" a commonly accepted religion which would be primary in relation to all historical religions. It must seek critically to explicate the area of religious experience and to determine its position in man's spiritual life, i.e., to examine its relation to the theoretical, ethical, and esthetic categories: the true, the good, and the beautiful. Philosophy of religion will then deal with a number of questions essential to the study of religion which systematic theology must leave untouched if it is to adhere strictly to its own task. When philosophy of religion engages in this important but currently neglected study, a fruitful co-operation between philosophy of religion and systematic theology can be established, provided that both retain their essential function. Philosophy of religion would have to abandon its critical character if it were to exercise a directive influence on the theological task, which consists in explicating the content of the Christian faith. This study must be governed exclusively by the material being investigated.

Although systematic theology is related to a critical philosophy of religion, it is completely differentiated from the "philosophy of religion" which appears as rational metaphysics. This is clear from what has already been said, but it deserves to be emphasized again, especially since such a rational metaphysics has again and again forced its way into theology. "Philosophical" metaphysics pretended to be able to offer a rationally motivated and outlined "doctrine of God and the supersensual world." Even in the primitive church rational metaphysics made its influence felt. Since that time all *scholastic* theology, both of the medieval and the post-Reformation period, has attempted to build upon such a philosophical metaphysics in order to parade as a so-called "natural theology." A distinction was made between *articuli puri*, which were rooted in revelation and had the character of affirmations of faith, and *articuli mixti*, which were based partly on revelation and partly on rational metaphysics. It cannot be denied that from one point of view this broader basis represented a certain protection for theology against exclusiveness during those times in which the function of systematic theology was conceived of in a rather narrow confessional and doctrinaire form. But on the other hand, it must be said that this wider perspective was purchased at too great a price. Nothing could obscure the difference in nature between the Christian faith and metaphysics more than this idea that the "doctrine about God" should appear in the form of *articuli mixti*.

The reason systematic theology does not want to have any part with rational metaphysics is not simply because such a metaphysic is suspect from a critical point of view, and that therefore a criticism of the metaphysics would be extended also to a theology containing this element. The reason is rather that faith has really nothing to do with rationalistic metaphysics. Christian faith in God is something else than a rational explanation of the universe. Theology has no other task than to inquire into that which is given in and is characteristic of faith. From the very beginning and in those periods when it has been most conscious of its own nature, Christian faith has testified boldly that the God about whom it speaks reveals himself only to the eye of faith and is not apprehended by any human wisdom (cf. Matt. 5:8, 11:25, John 7:17, I Cor. 1:17 ff., 2:10, etc.).

Our criticism has been directed against a philosophy of religion which appears as "natural theology." But this does not imply a completely negative attitude, rejecting something without substituting something else. Whenever this negative attitude has prevailed, the result has been that questions vital for theology have been neglected, and theology has become isolated. But we must not be maneuvered into a position where we have to choose between a complete acceptance or radical rejection of such a philosophy of religion. A philosophy of religion determined by metaphysics is untenable both from a philosophical and a theological point of view. But behind its unconvincing argumentation there are nevertheless tendencies and viewpoints which are significant for the Christian faith, especially with regard to the doctrine of creation and the universal aspect of revelation (cf. § 3, ¶ 3, and § 21). Philosophy of religion as natural theology testifies in an inadequate yet real way to God's sovereignty over man and the world. Scholastic, metaphysical philosophy of religion must be replaced by one of a different character. The Christian philosophy of religion must liberate itself from the tyranny of rationalistic metaphysics. It may do so by taking its starting point in the universal perspective of the divine revelation, where the center is the acts of the living God rather than man's rationalistic ideas about God.

4. Systematic Theology and Psychology of Religion

Psychology of religion, understood as a purely empirical and descriptive investigation of the religious consciousness as such, has a secure place and an important function within the science of religion. Such researches can in various ways become a preparation for and an assistance to the work of systematic theology. But the two cannot be identified. Just as there has frequently been a commixture of philosophy of religion and systematic theology, so there has been a similar mixture of the latter with psychology of religion. This confusion can really be traced back to Schleiermacher. We have already noted that he was not able to carry out his theological program because in his interpretation of the Christian faith he placed it under the pressure of religious concepts whose content was fixed and determined beforehand. And furthermore, he did not accomplish his purpose because he made faith practically identical with the religious consciousness as such, and in this way gave systematic theology a psychological direction. In view of the influence which Schleiermacher's method has had, it is important to point out that the task of systematic theology is in principle something else than that of psychology of religion, no matter how great an importance the latter may have for the former.

If the problem of systematic theology is to elucidate the content of the Christian faith, to understand the faith, then this elucidation must take into account the fact that faith always appears as an expression of a relation in which everything is concerned with God as the only "object." Faith cannot be "understood" without the realization that *every* affirmation of faith is a statement about God and his activity. If a statement is made about the meaning of the work of Christ, that here God was "reconciling the world to himself," then the question is not about an empirical history or a purely psychological affirmation, but rather a word about God and his activity. The same is true, if we take another example, in regard to what faith says about forgiveness of sins. It is a question here not simply about a variation in the religious consciousness, but a divine act through which a communion between God and man is established. The nature of faith is not revealed if we say with Schleiermacher that the Christian doctrines are "accounts of the Christian religious affections set forth in speech." [1] Precisely because all the affirmations of faith are statements about God and his activity, systematic theology must differentiate itself from psychology of religion in its attempt to understand faith. In the elucidation of the meaning of the Christian faith everything revolves around that relationship to God which is wholly defined by God's active revelation of himself. Psychology of religion concerns itself exclusively with *the religious subject*, while systematic theology deals with a *relationship* in which the revelation of God is the decisive factor. The attempt of theology to "understand faith" must be directed in the first instance toward a comprehension of the content of the divine revelation, an interpretation of the meaning of that revelatory context in which Christ is the center.

5. The "Ecumenical" Christian Faith—
Systematic Theology and Symbolics

The purpose of systematic theology is to investigate and elucidate the content and meaning of the *Christian* faith. This purpose would be distorted and limited if systematic theology were to start from and allow itself to be bound by a denominational or confessional conception of faith regarded as given once and for all. Systematic theology cannot assume as self-evident that a certain confession in every respect represents that which is perfect and genuinely Christian.

[1] Friedrich Schleiermacher, *The Christian Faith*, H. R. Mackintosh and J. S. Stewart (eds.) (Edinburgh: Clark, 1928), p. 76.

13

In that case the task would be to reproduce, arrange, and define those doctrines which have been presented in a certain set of confessional writings. When Schleiermacher in his encyclopedia says that the function of dogmatics is to present the doctrine accepted in a certain communion,[2] he obscures the fact that systematic theology is concerned with the task of understanding *the genuinely Christian*. It should also be pointed out that this statement of Schleiermacher contradicts what he asserts elsewhere: that the object of theology is not a certain limited, individual, or confessional "Christian consciousness," but rather "the Christian religious affections in general."

It is evident and quite understandable that an exclusive and doctrinaire confessionalism has given "dogmatics" a certain bad reputation. It cannot be denied that systematic theology would lose its scientific character if its investigation of the meaning of the Christian faith were from the beginning bound to a specific and authoritative conception in which the result is already given. This would mean that confessional writings are regarded as boundaries at which theological research is compelled to halt. The investigation of the Christian faith would then be governed by other purposes than the desire to understand, which is the truly scientific purpose. This closed and narrow conception of the function of systematic theology bears part of the blame for the supplanting of theology by the abortive "philosophy of religion" previously mentioned. Against exclusive confessionalism this "philosophy" could successfully maintain that the Christian faith must be viewed from a wider and more comprehensive perspective. It could say that the study of Christianity by "dogmatics" was in advance bound to certain restrictive forms, which prevented a free outlook and had to be defended at all costs. It could also point to the confessional polemic which emerged as a result. These criticisms were no doubt well founded. The trouble was that a "philosophy of religion" which looked at Christian faith from the outside and judged it from foreign points of view could not present an adequate substitute. This could be done only by a systematic theology guided by no other purpose than to penetrate to the very nature and meaning of the Christian faith.

[2] Friedrich Schleiermacher, *Brief Outline of the Study of Theology*, trans. William Farrer (Edinburgh: Clark, 1850), p. 161.

It is of course a legitimate theological study to describe the conception of faith accepted by a certain communion, being guided in such work by the existing, authoritative documents of that communion; and also to extend such a study to include the variety of conceptions which may arise within the church. This is a historical and statistical study, which belongs to symbolics or to the study of the church. But this can never be the legitimate function of systematic theology. It cannot, without proving false to its calling, surrender its right to evaluate any confessional documents, to determine whether and to what extent these express that which is genuinely Christian and not simply that which is peculiar to a certain section of Christendom.

Systematic theology can be confessional only in so far as the confessional element is of assistance in understanding and perceiving that which is essentially Christian. It cannot be "Lutheran" in the sense that it rests on statements by Luther *solely* because he made them, but only in so far as Luther proves himself able to help theology to penetrate deeper into the meaning of the Christian faith. The work of systematic theology involves, therefore, with reference to confessionalism a continual self-examination, far removed from all naive confessional self-sufficiency. Theology is not looking for denominational expressions of Christianity but for genuine Christianity itself; and it does not recognize a denominational expression unless it can document itself as genuinely Christian. Its purpose is to present "the *ecumenical* Christian faith." "Ecumenical" is therefore a watchword against every kind of closed and self-sufficient confessionalism. This does not mean that theology should produce a kind of extract of doctrines which would be common to all Christians. Such an endeavor would be of very little value.[3] We are not dealing with a kind of common conception which would represent a Christian faith stripped of all denominational expressions. Such a common Christianity has never existed, just as there has never been a "common religion." The decisive question in relation to these expressions is the

---

[3] Cf. Schleiermacher's statement (*ibid.*, p. 163): "A purely *irenical* composition of this kind will, for the most part, prove so meager and indefinite, that there will be everywhere a want, not only of the *middle terms* which are necessary to effect *proof*, but also of that precision in the definition of notions, which is necessary to procure for the delineation the *confidence* of the reader."

question about their genuinely Christian quality. When Luther and the Reformation are seen from this point of view, their contribution toward the understanding of Christianity can be justly assessed. The Christian universalism of Luther has often been very much obscured because this point of view has been ignored, and Luther has been isolated by being circumscribed within a narrow confessionalism.

That systematic theology which is conscious of its function and also critically oriented must adopt the program comprehended in the term, "the ecumenical Christian faith," which has as its purpose the discovery of what is genuinely Christian. If this is not the case, an "evangelical" theology would have to limit itself to describing a variant of a Christian conception of faith, which would then stand side by side with a number of other equally legitimate variants, as for instance the Roman. Systematic theology cannot be expected to be interested in anything else than the genuinely Christian. This is not something new within evangelical theology; the first evangelical "dogmatics" was called *Loci communes* with good reason, for the Reformation did not aim to present simply a variant of Christianity in addition to that which already existed, but rather to give expression as far as possible to the genuinely Christian. The evangelical principle of Scripture bears witness to this fact.

It is evident that the task of research which according to this interpretation devolves upon systematic theology cannot be successfully and finally accomplished by any single theologian. Every individual student and every period have their own limitations. The goal of such research is an ideal goal toward which theology can approach only through repeated striving for the truth. But this does not mean that we should make this limitation into a principle which would circumscribe the work. Theology cannot under any circumstances deviate from its concentration on that which is essential and genuine in Christianity since this is the whole purpose of its work and dare not be overlooked.

6. *The Scientific Character of Systematic Theology*

It is clear from what we have already said that the function of systematic theology is of a purely scientific nature since its purpose is to investigate a definite object, the Christian faith, and to elucidate .

its meaning in the clearest possible way. This theological discipline which we call systematic theology has often, especially during the nineteenth century, been regarded with suspicion both by those interested in scientific study and by those interested in the spiritual life.

When such suspicion has manifested itself on behalf of scientific interest, the reason has generally been that certain conceptions of the function of "dogmatics" have been accepted as axiomatic. Four such conceptions may be distinguished, among which two or more may at times be conjoined: the exclusively confessional, the metaphysical apologetic, the practical churchly, and the purely subjective. In the first of these the scientific point of view is obscured because the genuinely Christian is identified with a specific confession. This is often combined with an apologetic purpose: the intention is to defend a particular confession contained in the tradition. In the second case the scientific character has disappeared because attempts have been made to present "scientific" proofs of the truth of faith and of the reality of its object. Such attempts cannot be scientifically realized. In the third case the scientific character is corrupted because theology is made to serve the practical ends of the church rather than being a purely scientific investigation. Even Schleiermacher can say that the work of theology is to be done as a "service to the government of the church." [4] Even if this is not taken quite literally, it reveals a misunderstanding of the function of systematic theology which obscures its scientific character. And finally, it is quite clear that the scientific character cannot be maintained if the function of theology is transferred to the sphere of confession. In this way the purely scientific task is confused with a function which belongs to the area of the Christian life. In view of these various conceptions it is not at all strange that this discipline has been suspected of being something less than scientific. On the other hand, it is not surprising that it has also been the object of suspicion by those interested in the religious life. This has been due sometimes to bigotry, but also to the fact that theology has not always aimed, consciously and clearly, at letting faith's own point of view find full expression, but has allowed this purpose to be obscured by subordinate interests and metaphysical speculations.

[4] *Ibid.*, p. 93.

The situation becomes quite different when systematic theology is defined as has been done in this chapter. The problem is then to investigate and with all possible means elucidate that entity, that living reality, which is called the Christian faith, and to examine and analyze its meaning and content. When the task is thus defined and limited, it is evident that this is a definite and necessary task for research, which cannot be challenged from the point of view of either scholarly study or the religious life. All presuppositions which limit the investigation beforehand are then removed. It is not a matter of setting up verifiable goals which cannot be scientifically attained. The study is carried on simply to understand and elucidate, which is the purpose of all scholarly research. Thus, systematic theology is not influenced by secondary aims which lie outside its purview and warp the scientific nature of the work. The lodestar here, as in all scientific reasearch, is the same: objectivity, factualness.

What we have said here must not be interpreted to mean that systematic theology cannot serve Christian life and the Christian church. But it can do this only on condition that its scientific purpose remains unencumbered, and that theology therefore fulfills its one commanding and purely scientific function. When the function is defined in a purely scientific manner as has been done here, those interests which belong properly to the Christian life are always given consideration. The religious life cannot ask anything else of theology than that it try to *understand* faith as it really is. In principle the opposition between faith and theology is removed by this definition. The problem is actually to understand faith; to elucidate it, not from any foreign points of view which misinterpret and pervert it, but from its own purely religious viewpoint. All investigations which do not from beginning to end see the matter from the religious point of view are bound to fail for want of being scientific. In principle the opposition between faith and theology is removed, as has already been pointed out, even though in practice it may still occur. When the antithesis remains, it is due to the fact that the accomplishment of the scientific task is imperfect, or that not everything which goes by the name of Christian faith is the genuine article, or both.

2. Faith as the Expression for the Christian Relationship Between God and Man

1. *Preliminary definition of the concept of faith.* Faith is the comprehensive expression for the Christian relationship between God and man. The Christian faith has a theocentric character. This implies that faith directs itself toward God alone and that in this relationship God is the Sovereign. This relationship, for which Christian faith is the expression, is characterized both by fellowship and remoteness.

2. *Faith and divine revelation.* Faith conceived in terms of *relationship* may be perceived from two points of view. On the one hand, it implies that man is subdued and dominated by God; on the other, that man turns toward and commits himself to God. This paradox means that, on the one hand, faith is grounded in "the divine revelation," and on the other hand, that the divine revelation can be apprehended only by the eye of faith. The divine revelation and faith are therefore, correlative concepts. However, from the religious point of view the divine revelation is primary in relation to faith.

1. Preliminary Definition of the Concept of Faith

According to the definition of the function of systematic theology previously given, its task is the elucidation of the Christian faith. At the very outset, therefore, the word faith appears as the principal word. If now the chief task of systematic theology is the exposition of the Christian faith, then it follows that the complete and definitive presentation of the subject can be given only by an investigation of the entire field. This does not preclude the necessity, however, of endeavoring to give a preliminary definition of the concept of faith at the beginning of our investigation. The following exposition in its entirety will bear witness to the accuracy of such a definition.

Needless to say, there are many difficulties involved in the designation of faith as the principal concept of Christianity. A survey of the history of dogma indicates that through the ages this word has been given various meanings and has ofttimes been employed to becloud rather than to clarify the essential nature of Christianity. Moreover, in popular usage it has often come to mean uncertain knowledge, which is an interpretation as foreign as possible to traditional Christian thought. Whatever else faith may say about itself, it does not say that it is some sort of subordinate knowledge, a kind of uncertain opinion about God and his work. Under these circumstances one might be tempted to search for a substitute for the word "faith." But however desirable it might be that a principal word of Christianity be more unequivocal, we are nevertheless obliged to use it, for there is no other expression which can more adequately serve our purpose. It is not accidental that, from the beginning, the word faith has forced its way to the forefront.

The famous words of Luther in the Large Catechism may well serve as a preliminary definition of the Christian connotation of faith: "These two, God and faith, belong together and must be conjoined." In other words, faith implies a *relationship* between God and man. We are not interested in faith as a psychological or sociological phenomenon, but in faith in a theological sense. That faith is a relationship between God and man implies that every statement of faith is an assertion concerning both God and man at the same time. The affirmations of faith cannot, therefore, be divided into "objective" and "subjective" statements, because they are both.

The relationship of faith is determined by God. Faith is therefore entirely *theocentric*. As has already been indicated in the previous chapter (§ 1, ¶ 2), the theocentric character of faith implies, from one point of view, that God is the sole object of faith. Faith does not concern itself with several objects but is directed toward God alone. Faith may be strong or weak, but whatever may be its quality in this respect, as faith it is entirely a faith in God and in him alone. But the theocentricity of faith has another aspect which must now be delineated. This aspect becomes apparent as God in relation to man appears as the absolute Sovereign. In the realm of faith God is the ruler. His will is supreme. From this viewpoint it is improper to speak of God as the "object" of faith, for as that Power which creates, determines, and controls faith he is rather its subject. This phase of theocentricity has a profound, almost conclusive meaning for the Christian conception of the God-relationship. It certifies that faith is not some sort of anthropocentric approach, more or less subtle, which makes man central and God the obedient servant of human needs, interests, security and self-esteem, and so on. In this relationship God is always Lord and man always the servant.

In connection with what has already been said, it can now be stated, as a fundamental definition of the meaning of faith, that faith gives expression to a relationship of *fellowship* between God and man. Faith does not conceive of God as simply remote, but, above all, as the One who in and through faith unites man with himself. The vital element in faith is the conviction that the God who "dwells in unapproachable light" (I Tim. 6:16) is at the same time the God who is present with us and walks in direct fellowship with us, who, as Augustine declares, "is closer to us than we ourselves." From the viewpoint of faith God is immediately present, living and active. In a variety of expressions Christian faith speaks of God—Christ and the Spirit may be used as parallel expressions—as "dwelling in our hearts," "ruling us," and so on. Thus the significance of faith may be defined as an immediate fellowship with God. "Our fellowship is with the Father and with his Son, Jesus Christ" (I John 1:3).

But if the idea of fellowship is essential to the Christian conception of faith, then in order that its nature might from the outset be clearly delineated, it must be added that this fellowship of faith does not abolish the *distance* between the divine and the human. The Christian faith knows of no hazy commixture of the divine with the human. In the realm of faith God is always God and man is always man. The relationship does not pass over into identity. Instead, the proportion between nearness and remoteness, between fellowship and distance, is this: the closer man comes to God in faith and the more the relation with God is realized, the more clearly man becomes aware of what separates him from God. In the presence of God man's consciousness of sin is intensified. But this peculiar dialectic of the faith-relationship does not nullify man's fellowship with God. The consciousness of remoteness, with which we are concerned here, is itself a manifestation of God's nearness and of the relationship with him, and in no way precludes the idea that the faith-relationship is essentially a fellowship of the most immediate nature. This relationship is therefore the fundamental principle of faith. It cannot be divorced from faith. Wherever it ceases to exist, there faith has also ceased to exist. All other affirmations concerning faith are further clarifications of what is implied in this fellowship with God.

Accordingly, Christian faith is differentiated from all characteristic mysticism as well as from all idealistic theories of the relation between the divine and the human. It is distinctive of both of these that they confuse the divine and the human, and that therefore the idea of fellowship tends to become identity. The difference between Christian faith and mysticism does not lie in the fact that the God-relationship of mysticism represents a higher degree of immediacy, but rather that in mysticism the remoteness is obliterated to the same degree that divine fellowship is realized, while in the case of faith the situation is exactly the opposite. On the other hand, the significance of Christian faith is misinterpreted if, in a legitimate emphasis upon remoteness, the idea of fellowship is weakened or actually dissolved and faith is thereby reduced to merely an eschatologically determined hope. Similar tendencies in contemporary theology can be historically understood as a reaction against the appreciable influence which mysticism and idealism have exerted during a previous theological era. Even in this case, however, the tensional character of Christian faith has been obscured.

It has been pointed out that all definitions of faith are statements of what is implied in the fellowship with God. Among the innumerable definitions which have appeared we would like in this connection to consider two of the most important: trust and assent. Especially during the latter part of the nineteenth century, when Ritschlian theology was dominant, it was customary, citing the Reformation as witness, to consider "trust" [1] as the fundamental element of faith. Actually, there can be no legitimate objection to the characterization of faith as trust as long as it is clearly borne in mind that it is a question of designating an essential aspect of theocentric fellowship with God. The Reformation can be cited as witness only if the matter is understood in this way. But as soon as this viewpoint is obscured, it becomes apparent that the projection of "trust" as the primary definition involves some real dangers, two in particular. The above-mentioned nineteenth century provides sufficient evidence of these two dangers. In the first place, the definition of faith as trust is said to involve a contradiction of faith as assent, with the result that the precise content characteristic of Christian faith is obscured. It would mean that the essential element is trust as such, while actually the all-important consideration for faith is that qualitatively determined will

[1] The Swedish word *Förtröstan* here translated "trust" is to be understood in terms of *fiducia.*—Trans.

of God to which trust and confidence are given. In the second place, there is the danger that the theocentric character will not receive sufficient emphasis. Faith interpreted as trust becomes a means and a guarantee of the "personality development" of man, of man's *Selbstbehauptung* [self-assertion], as the Ritschlian expression has it. We maintain, therefore, that trust expresses an essential element of Christian faith, but that this definition has reference to the theocentric God-relationship. The same is true with respect to the definition of faith as assent. In the measure that fellowship with God is understood as an unqualified assent to that revelation in which faith is rooted, this definition also gives expression to an essential element of faith. But when this definition is no longer considered as expressing simply an element of the theocentric fellowship, but is made primary, then faith becomes prescribed within an intellectual orbit and its meaning thereby obscured.

2. Faith and Divine Revelation

If faith is thus an expression for the relationship between God and man, it must always be considered from two points of view. With reference to what has already been said, faith implies, on the one hand, being subdued and dominated by God. Faith is the result of our being subdued by God, and it continues to exist by reason of our being dominated by him. God's domination prevails unabridged as far as faith extends. The tyranny of egocentricity must yield to God's dominion. Thus, faith is founded in and exists by reason of God's activity. It is entirely a work of God, as faith itself certifies again and again. But faith may also be considered from the human point of view. Here it appears, on our part as *a turning and commitment to God*. It originates through our turning to God and continues as we commit ourselves to him. This aspect of faith has often been obscured within evangelical theology. It has been feared that, with the emphasis upon human activity, faith would no longer be entirely a work of God. Actually, however, this aspect of faith cannot be concealed. All the great witnesses of faith have testified to the fact that faith involves a choice and a decision. It was not simply fortuitous that Luther spoke of faith's audacious "nevertheless," or Kierkegaard of the way faith casts itself upon the deep waters, or Paul of how we must work out our salvation with fear and trembling (Phil. 2:12). In spite of timidity, faith is the soul's audacious *yes* to God. Therefore it makes the greatest demands upon our activity. Here, if ever, it is a matter of being willing to relinquish all else in order to build upon God alone. The parables of the treasure and the pearl (Matt. 13:44 ff) indicate this very clearly.

If God and faith "belong together" so that it is impossible to speak of faith without also speaking of God, it then follows that faith has its basis in what it calls "God's *revelation.*" The God who subdues and dominates us is the God who reveals himself to us. It is this God to whom, in faith, we make our commitment. In and through his revelation he confronts and subdues us. Accordingly, Christian faith has at all times referred to something which it has called God's revelation. Faith indeed speaks also of God as the "hidden" God. It is persuaded that under the conditions of this earthly life we are able to see only "in a mirror dimly" (I Cor. 13:12). God is unfathomable and inscrutable. And this mystery does not disappear by reason of his revelation. On the contrary, faith is confronted with this paradox: the more God reveals himself and the more we understand his will and heart, the more he appears as the unfathomable One. But the essential basis of faith is that the hidden God is at the same time he who has not left himself without witnesses. A God who was entirely hidden could have no connection with us; even less could there exist, under such circumstances, a vital fellowship between him and us. Therefore, just as faith and God belong together, so faith and revelation are conjoined and cannot be separated.

Connected with the twofold aspect of faith we noted earlier is the fact that this revelation can be perceived by *the eye of faith alone.* The divine revelation cannot be indisputably demonstrated; it cannot be substantiated like a mathematical proposition. It cannot be so clearly unveiled and divulged as to be irresistibly seen and acknowledged by everyone. It is impossible, for example, to pick out a certain segment of history and declare: here is an inescapable evidence of God's revelation. It is faith alone which perceives it. We can observe a noble, pure, and spiritual life, but we cannot observe God. We can see religiosity, but not a divine revelation. It is faith that opens the eyes. Through faith we discover something more and something entirely different from what we previously saw. It is as if we looked at a transparency. When it is properly illuminated and the light falls where it should, then we see not only what we previously beheld, but in addition precisely that which the transparency was intended to display. In the same way, the eye of faith discovers not only human religiosity, but first and foremost *the living God and his acts*.

Thus the divine revelation and faith are certified as being two *corresponding concepts*. On the one hand, faith has its origin and nourishment in revelation, and on the other, revelation is discerned and recognized only by the eye of faith. The latter could perhaps be interpreted to mean that faith is conceived as being primary to revelation. Nothing, however, could be more foreign to the viewpoint of faith than such a notion. If here it is a matter of ascertaining the characteristic viewpoint of faith and of permitting this viewpoint to speak without reservation, it must be affirmed that nothing is more essential to the peculiar outlook of faith than its awareness of the fact that the basis of faith is the divine revelation which dominates and subdues. All eudaemonistic thoughts concerning the basis of faith are from the beginning excluded from its characteristic outlook. We "believe," not on account of the advantages which faith is supposed to deliver, but because we have been confronted by the revelation of a God from whom we cannot flee. That choice and that decision, mentioned above, have nothing of subjective discretion about them. The real reason for our *yes* is, from the viewpoint of faith, nothing but that the hand of God has overwhelmed us.

Thus the twofold nature of faith is illuminated. On the one hand, God subdues the human soul, and on the other, man turns and commits himself to God. But when reference is made to man's activity, it does not imply a denial that the origin and existence of faith are altogether God's work. Every attempt to divide the action and to co-ordinate God's "work" and man's "work," or place them in opposition to one another, involves a misleading rationalization. The most profound viewpoint of faith itself concerning that which occurs is that our own seeking is nothing else than what the Bible calls "the Father's drawing" us (John 6:44; 10:16). It implies that our timid but at the same time audacious *yes* is nothing but God subduing us so that we simply are unable to flee. Faith and revelation are corresponding concepts; nevertheless in principle *revelation is primary* in relation to faith.

3. The Divine Revelation

1. *The relation of divine revelation to nature and history.* Christian faith discovers a revelation of God both in the realm of nature and in the realm of history, but it does not identify this revelation with either nature or history in their entirety.

2. *The decisive revelation of God.* The revelation of God which is decisive for Christian faith is that context of revelation in which Christ appears as the One who incarnates God and carries out his redemptive will.

3. *The universalism and exclusiveness of the divine revelation.* Christian faith does not circumscribe the divine revelation; but neither does it recognize any other God than him who has revealed himself in Christ.

4. *The Christian faith and the religion of the Old Testament.* The relation of Christian faith to the Old Testament religion is different from its relation to non-Christian religions, because, on the one hand, God's revelation of himself in Christ implies the fulfilment of the Old Testament religion; but the relation is the same, since, on the other hand, the revelation in Christ involves the fact that "the old covenant" is supplanted by "the new covenant."

5. *The nature of the divine revelation.* The divine revelation is God's self-impartation. Its nature may be defined in the following paradoxical statements: 1) It expresses itself in a struggle against that which opposes the divine will, and is at the same time a revelation of the God who transcends all strife. 2) It is completed in Christ, but is at the same time continually in progress. 3) It utilizes historical means, and is at the same time the form of God's immediate fellowship with men. 4) It is an unveiling of God's "essence," and at the same time confronts faith with the Unfathomable.

1. The Relation of Divine Revelation to
Nature and History

The problem is first of all the locus of the divine revelation. If we start with the fact that man participates in the realms of both nature and history, we may say provisionally that the Christian faith finds traces of a divine revelation in both of these "realms." But it must be added at once that neither nature nor history in its entirety appears in itself to faith as a "revelation" or a reflection of the divine will.

The idea of a divine revelation connected with the world of *nature* is of long standing and finds support even in the Old Testament. "The heavens are telling the glory of God; and the firmament proclaims his handiwork" (Ps. 19:1; cf. also Ps. 104). Such a union of faith in God with the majesty and beauty of nature has time and again appeared also within Christianity. We need only to remind ourselves of St. Francis' celebrated "Hymn to the Sun," or to refer to any of the hymnals of the Christian church.[1] It makes little difference that the world view has changed completely during the last centuries; it might rather be said that the larger conception of the universe makes it easier to connect the idea of the majesty of God with the world of nature.

But this does not mean that the Christian faith conceives of nature as a whole in terms of an explicit and unambiguous revelation of the divine will. It is not a matter of identifying God and nature according to the pattern of Spinoza (*deus sive natura*), or deducing the divine will in a rational fashion from the course of nature, as has sometimes been attempted in the so-called cosmological and teleological arguments for the existence of God. If the cosmological argument concludes on the basis of cause and effect that there must be a first cause, and then calls this cause God, Christian faith must answer, from its point of view, that this pseudonymous "first cause" has nothing in common with the God of faith. Nor can the teleological argument which attempts to find a wise providence on the basis of the purposeful adaptability of the world prepare a way to the God of faith. The "God" who is demonstrated in this way has only the name in common with the God of faith. But it is also true that this purposefulness is not so conspicuous that it can furnish a self-evident starting point. There is in the world of nature an abundance of phenomena which impress upon us the meaninglessness and the cold insensitivity of existence. These imply a testing rather than a support of faith. It is significant that natural catastrophes have often deeply shaken that

---

[1] The author makes reference especially to hymn 174 (stanza 4) in the Swedish Hymnal, by J. O. Wallin: "Thy magnitude, thy majesty, thy mysterious purpose I saw in the path of the sun and in the smallest blade of grass."—Trans.

faith in God which rested on the evidence of purpose in the world of nature. The most conspicuous example is the revolutionary impact of the great earthquake in Lisbon in 1755 on the contemporary world which lived in the naive and optimistic faith that the whole universe was governed in all its details by a consistent and benevolent purpose.

Nature does not under any circumstances give a compelling and unambiguous testimony about the God of faith. Even that revelation of God in nature which Christian faith recognizes is very much incomplete and fragmentary. If faith were dependent on this alone, it would be limited to certain indefinite and uncertain conjectures; it could not appear as a strong, living, and significant faith in God.[2]

History, however, appears to the Christian faith as the bearer of a divine revelation in quite a different way from that discernible in nature. In the sphere of history the Christian faith finds that revelation which is decisive. Faith meets here the divine "heart" of which Wallin spoke in the hymn because here faith is confronted by God's mighty acts of redemption. But it is important to notice that, although history is in a very special sense the locus of the revelation, history as a whole does not appear to faith as a reflection of the divine will. If nature contains much that is mysterious and meaningless, this is true in still greater measure of history. All attempts to find a reflection of the divine will in the course of history as a whole must necessarily fail, because there is so much in the human world that is hostile to this will. These factors do not reveal God, but rather a power separate from and opposed to him. If everything that happens in the sphere of history were to be regarded without further consideration as an expression of God's will, and the judgments of history were thus simply identified with his judgments, faith would become completely uncertain as to the real character of the divine will (cf. § 22 ff.).

2. *The Decisive Revelation of God*

If the Christian faith finds the revelation of God first of all in history, but at the same time does not regard history in its entirety

[2] The author quotes stanza 5 of the hymn by Wallin to illustrate this point. "And yet Thy nature was obscured, I did not find Thy heart; and in the dark and endless space as a speck of dust I disappeared."—Trans.

as the bearer of that revelation, the question arises where in history the divine will is revealed, or what in history is of decisive importance to faith. The answer to this question may be formulated in this way: it is found in that context of revelation in which Christ appears as the one who incarnates God and carries out his redemptive will.

This formulation contains two fundamental points of view in particular. In the first place, faith has its absolute center in Christ. In the second place, Christ is never isolated but stands in a large "context of revelation," which extends from him both back into ancient history and forward into the future. The Christian faith does not conceive of the revelation of God as a point in time, nor as an isolated act of God, but rather as a continuous series of divine acts. God has not only spoken and acted once in the world's history; the record of God's dealings with men is rather a constant and continuous activity, which is characterized by the fact that the divine will is continually realizing itself.

But in this context of divine acts of revelation Christ stands as the decisive and final act. He is the "Lord and King" of this context, to use the expression by which Luther intended to illustrate the relation of Christ to the Scriptures, but which can also be used in reference to the continuity of the revelation. That Christ is the one who incarnates God and carries out his redemptive purpose will be more fully discussed later in this work. In this connection, however, it should be pointed out that the idea of incarnation implies the fulness and expressiveness of the divine revelation: the divine will has entered effectively into human life in this world of sin and death. This character of effectiveness, of realization in action, which is hereby given to the idea of revelation, is further emphasized by the word "victorious." The work of Christ is understood here as the struggle and victory of the divine will; it is that act in which the divine will achieves the decisive and fundamental victory over the opposing powers.

3. The Universalism and Exclusiveness of the Divine Revelation

It is rather surprising, when we examine the way in which Christian faith speaks about the extent of revelation, to find side by side strongly universal and strongly exclusive pronouncements. This has been the case during the whole history of Christianity. Thus Paul declares that God has not let himself be without witnesses among the Gentiles (Rom. 1:14-15; Acts 14:17). But at the same time no one has more strongly emphasized the exclusive character of the divine revelation in Christ which is "a stumbling-block to Jews and folly to Gentiles" (I Cor. 1:23). In almost a similar way the theology of the ancient church, as it made its impact upon the Greek world, on the one hand declared that the rays of the divine *Logos* have appeared outside of the Christian tradition also. But this theology at the same time makes the idea of incarnation a safeguard of the exclusiveness of the Christian revelation. This paradox relative to the extent of the divine revelation which has characterized Christianity since its beginning has repeatedly appeared in various forms. But at the same time it may be noted that this union of presumably opposite perspectives, this both—and, has at times been changed into an either—or. It has happened that the inclusiveness and absolute freedom of the divine revelation have been maintained in such a way as to erase the boundary around that which is characteristically Christian; and it has also happened that some have denied almost every possibility of a revelation outside of that given in Christ.

The problem has naturally become very serious as Christianity has encountered the non-Christian religions on the mission fields. It is possible to find here a vacillation between the two extremes. On the one hand, there has been a tendency to paint everything black or white and to eliminate all intermediary shades. The judgment on non-Christian religions is wholly negative, and all points of contact between them and the gospel are denied. On the other hand, both in ancient and modern times, mission work has been carried on in a spirit of syncretism, and it has been assumed that nothing more is needed than to supplement and correct non-Christian religions with a few Christian additions.

In contrast to this vacillation between two extremes it must be maintained that it is not characteristic of Christian faith to assert either universalism against exclusiveness, or vice versa. On the contrary, *both* the universal and exclusive points of view express the peculiar genius of the Christian faith. On the one hand, it does not establish any limits around divine revelation, but, on the other hand, it *refuses to recognize any other God* than him who reveals himself in Christ. In fact, every attempt to regulate and determine the boundaries within which divine revelation might express itself appears to faith as extreme presumption. In that case man would act as judge in regard to the divine possibilities, which would be both an unreasonable pretension to the ability of penetrating the mystery of the divine government of the world and a claim to divine authority. Rightly understood, the Christian faith has not the slightest interest in limiting and restricting the extent of divine revelation. On the contrary it must be said that faith's encounter with the divine revelation in Christ empowers the eye of faith to discover what men in the ancient church called the broken rays of the divine *Logos*. The clearer the light which the eye of faith beholds, the more it is strengthened to recognize every other light which is a part of God's light.

But on the other hand, this does not in any way imply a tendency in the direction of syncretism, so that the genuinely Christian is blotted out and the exclusiveness of the Christian revelation is weakened. This feature of exclusiveness is expressed in the fact that the Christian faith knows of no other God than him who actively reveals himself in Christ. The words of Luther in the great hymn of the Reformation are here in place: *"und ist kein andrer Gott."* These words are unconditionally valid in reference to that act of God which was decisive for human life, and therefore also in apprehending the real character of the divine will. The expressive words of Luther emphasize an idea which lies strongly embedded in the Christian message and which in various forms meets us in the New Testament. We need only point to the statement in Matt. 11:27: "No one knows the Father except the Son and any one to whom the Son chooses to reveal him."

It is not an accident, therefore, that certain evident tension between the universal and the exclusive points of view appears in the Christian conception of the divine revelation. The Christian faith is broad in so far as it does not set any limits to the possibilities of revelation; but at the same time it does not tolerate the obscuring of the uniqueness of the Christian revelation. This tension belongs in reality to the very nature of the Christian faith. It cannot be eliminated by compromise, as has been tried again and again in scholasticism and in the theology influenced by idealism. The divine revelation acknowledged by the Christian faith must not be conceived of as a complement to something already given or as an addition to a knowledge of God which already existed. What separates the revelation of God comprehended in Christ and in his work from everything which might be called divine revelation is not something quantitative, but something qualitative. It has to do with an absolutely unique action of God. Furthermore, this action of God in a very peculiar way reveals that which in the language of faith is called the "heart" of God. Therefore, this unique action of God has its counterpart in a unique conception of God which does not simply complement and surpass, but actually eliminates all others. In this sense the words *"und ist kein andrer Gott"* are valid.

4. The Christian Faith and the Religion of the Old Testament

In the discussion of the relation of the Christian faith to the other religions the matter of its connection with Judaism must be specifically dealt with, since Christianity stands in a peculiar relation to the Old Testament. A review of the history of dogma indicates that the studies dealing with this subject have often been obscure and uncertain. There is a vacillation between one conception in which the difference in nature between the Christian message and the Old Testament religion is so emphasized that the continuity is obscured, and another in which the continuity is presented in such a way that the unique nature of the Christian message is overshadowed.

Since it is important for our study that both the actual continuity and the actual difference be presented with equal emphasis, the problem may be stated as follows: the relation of the Christian faith to the Old Testament religion is different from its relation to the non-Christian religions, because, on the one hand, God's revelation of himself in Christ implies the fulfilment of the Old Testament religion; and, on the other hand, the relation is the same, since the revelation in Christ involves the fact that "the old covenant" is supplanted by "the new covenant."

This statement has a certain formal resemblance to that made by

Schleiermacher in § 12 of *The Christian Faith*, but it is meant also as a positive correction to his thesis, which is stated in the following words: "Christianity stands to be sure in a special historical relation to Judaism; but in regard to its historical existence and its separation, its relation to Judaism and heathendom is the same."[3] In Schleiermacher's exposition of the relation between "Judaism" and "Christianity" the actual continuity has not been properly expressed. He simply makes a general statement that there exists a certain historical continuity. That Schleiermacher emphasizes the difference at the expense of the continuity is easily explained as a valid reaction to an earlier attempt to place the Old Testament on a par with the classical document of the Christian faith, the New Testament. In accordance with orthodox theology and on the basis of its theory of verbal inspiration, the statements of the Old Testament were regarded, without any further consideration, as having the same validity for Christian faith as those of the New Testament. The suggestion of Schleiermacher was later followed by Harnack, who in his book on Marcion emphatically denied the right of the Old Testament to be included as a part of the canonical documents of Christianity. It is surprising, however, that Harnack's harsh rejection of the Old Testament is not connected with any clear insight into the peculiar nature of the Christian faith. Jesus' conception of God, on which Harnack places the chief emphasis, appears to him simply as a reformation of the earlier prophetic conception, in accordance with a line of thinking popular in nineteenth-century theology. The relation between Christianity and the Old Testament is therefore only partially understood.

In contrast to all tendencies to weaken the continuity between the Old and the New Testaments we insist that this continuity be given due recognition, especially since the Old Testament has been accepted by the church as Holy Scripture. But this emphasis must not be allowed to obscure the radical change which has taken place in the coming of Christ.

The Old Testament is a part of that context of revelation in which Christ appears. The New Testament and its message cannot be understood except in connection with the Old Testament. The New Testament writers link up their proclamation of Jesus as the Christ

[3] Schleiermacher, *Christian Faith*, p. 60.

with sacred Scripture. They maintain that the acts of God recorded in the Old Testament are fulfilled in God's redemptive act in Christ. In the person and work of Christ the promises of God have been fulfilled. Thus the risen Lord tells the two disciples on the way to Emmaus: "Everything written about me in the law of Moses and the prophets and the psalms must be fulfilled" (Luke 24:44). This includes the whole Old Testament.

When the New Testament speaks of the event of Christ as a fulfilment, it maintains at the same time that this "fulfilment" is not only a continuation and a final complement to what had already happened, but also that what has now happened is something radically new. A new situation has been created. God stands now in a relationship to the world different from before. Thus we read in Paul: "Therefore, if any one is in Christ, he is a new creation; the old has passed away, behold, the new has come" (II Cor. 5:17). John writes: "The law was given through Moses; grace and truth came through Jesus Christ" (John 1:17). Jesus himself emphasizes sharply the same distinction. "Truly, I say to you, among those born of women there has risen no one greater than John the Baptist; yet he who is least in the kingdom of heaven is greater than he" (Matt. 11:11).

If, therefore, it is essential to maintain both the continuity and the radical change, then the divine revelation must be allowed to retain the active character which, according to the Christian faith, is its essential characteristic. The revelation is a continuous series of acts of God, beginning in creation, continuing through the election of Israel and its history, and reaching its culmination finally in the decisive and transforming act of God in Christ. If, on the other hand, an attempt is made to explain the relationship between the Old and the New Testaments on the basis of religious conceptions and ideas, justice will not be done either to the continuity or to the radical change. Naturally there are changes of that sort also, but they are secondary in comparison with the creation of a new situation, the establishment of a "new covenant," the beginning of the "new age," which come through the decisive and all-transforming act of God in Christ. The new appears as a gospel, "the good news" about the victory of Christ over the demonic powers that destroy life and about the redemption from bondage under sin and death. Here the radical aspect of the change appears clearly, but at the same time the continuity is preserved. The divine act completes the previous divine activity, and at the same time these previous acts receive their definitive interpretation through the act of God in Christ. The Letter to the Hebrews indicates both the continuity and the new situation in saying that "God spoke of old to our fathers by the prophets; but in these last days he has spoken to us by a Son, whom he appointed the heir of all things" (Heb. 1:1-2).

We have emphasized here that the fundamental difference between the old and the new must not be conceived of in terms of a change in ideas and concepts, but that attention must be focused primarily on the *act* of God in Christ. But having done this we may also add that this primary change has had tremendous consequences for the whole range of the theological concepts of the faith. What these changes involve we can indicate here only in a preliminary way.

The God of the Christian message is none other than the God of the Old Testament. The God of Jesus is "the God of Abraham, and the God of Isaac, and the God of Jacob" (Matt. 22:32). As in the Old Testament he is the Creator and the Judge of the living and the dead. It would indeed be misleading if we were to imply that the Old Testament had said nothing about the love of God, and that in this respect the Christian message stood in direct contradiction to the Old Testament. It is evident that the Old Testament speaks freely about the love, grace, and mercy of God. This theme appears in many variations, especially in connection with the covenant with Israel.

Nevertheless we face here, in regard to the love of God, a decisive change in the conception of God. This appears clearly in the statement: "By this *we know love*, that he laid down his life for us" (I John 3:16). It is only through what has happened in Christ that we behold the depth of God's love. Here we have learned to know a mystery which we previously did not and could not know.

What is involved here becomes clear through the new and revolutionary view of sacrifice which we find in the Christian message. The sacrifice of Christ is definitive, and it makes all other sacrifices obsolete. But the radical aspect of this change appears not only in the fact that a sacrifice is made to God, but that the act of sacrifice is vitally connected with divine love. Man has since ancient times been perfectly familiar with sacrifices offered *to* God, both in Israel and in the religions of the world. But in the New Testament God is not only the One who in exalted majesty receives sacrifices; the divine Majesty himself brings the sacrifice, yea, even sacrifices himself in love. This is something radically new which reveals to us a new aspect of what the love of God involves. "By this we know love," that love which does not recoil from the supreme sacrifice. Here is "the revelation of the mystery which was kept secret for long ages" (Rom. 16:25). Through Christ "the plan of the mystery hidden for ages in God who created all things" has been revealed (Eph. 3:9).

We cannot at this point discuss how the act of God in Christ changes the whole range of the Christian faith. To indicate this is really the object of our whole presentation. God is the same always, but the Christian faith beholds him in a new perspective even as Creator and Judge. This is obvious because the Christian message relates Christ and his redemption directly to creation and the judgment. "In him all things were created, in heaven and on earth, visible and invisible . . .—all things were created through him and for him" (Col. 1:16). The God of creation is also the God of redemption. "When the Son of man comes in his glory, . . . before him will be gathered all the nations, and he will separate them one from another as a shepherd separates the sheep from the goats" (Matt. 25:31-32). Judgment and redemption are joined together, and the judgment is directly connected with the redemptive act of Christ.

We must consider one more very important point—the position of the law. Here again we cannot enter on an extended discussion of law and gospel. This theme will be elucidated from various points of view in the subsequent discussion. But it is obvious that the New Testament message stands in a dialectic relationship to the law. The "law" has been both fulfilled and set aside in Christ. In the Sermon on the Mount we read: "Think not that I have come to abolish the law and the prophets; I have come not to abolish them but to fulfil them" (Matt. 5:17). The "fulfilment" consists not only in Jesus' interpretation of the law, but primarily in the fact that he has fulfilled God's will and realized "the righteousness from God." But the law has also been abolished through the act of Christ. The old covenant was based on law. The relationship to God was determined primarily by the law. The new covenant rests on the foundation of self-giving love. In it the relationship to God is determined primarily on the basis of God's redemptive act in Christ. From this point of view the law represents a stage in this history of redemption which has been superseded by Christ. Thus "Christ is the end of the law" (Rom. 10:4). "The law was given through Moses; grace and truth came through Jesus Christ" (John 1:17). In the new covenant the relationship to God does not rest on law. The law has nothing to do with "justification," which is given with the forgiveness of sins. The law stands revealed here as a false way of salvation. It has lost its right and power to judge *in loco justificationis*, i.e., in that new relationship to God created through the redemptive act of God in Christ. "There is therefore now no condemnation for those who are in Christ Jesus" (Rom. 8:1). In this sense the law is abolished. But this fact does not mean that the Christian life is characterized by "antinomianism." The legal, moralistic aspect of the relationship to God has disappeared, but the commandments of God have unbroken and unconditional validity, and appear in reality more clearly and sharply in that relationship to God where his love reigns supreme.

5. The Nature of the Divine Revelation

The divine revelation is a divine *self-impartation*. It is, as stated in the old confession about Christ, "life of life, light of light." That God reveals himself means not only that he gives certain gifts to men, but, as the Reformers used to say, that he gives nothing less than *himself*. Any definition of revelation which ignores this fact minimizes and misinterprets the significance of the Christian revelation either by intellectualizing or psychologizing the concept. Christian faith sees in revelation first and foremost the self-impartation of God. We shall elucidate this view further by four paradoxical statements.

a. The divine revelation expresses itself in *a struggle against that which opposes the divine will;* but it is at the same time a revelation of that God *who transcends all strife.*

That God reveals himself means that the divine will actualizes itself. The divine will realizes itself as a contending will, engaged in conflict against that which is hostile to it. The divine will overcomes all obstacles, and reveals and establishes its dominion. Revelation is alto-gether *active*, it is divine activity. Whether it manifests itself in word or deed, the divine will realizes itself in its triumph over that which is hostile. The divine revelation appears to Christian faith against the background of enmity to God. From this point of view the perspec-tive may be called "dualistic." The divine will, as it reveals itself, is continually subduing and overpowering opposition. In this con-flict both the law and the gospel are used as means. The purpose of the law is to restrain and suppress the hostile powers. But, as already indicated, the decisive victory in this struggle belongs not to the law but to the gospel. The victory has been won through the crucified and risen Christ.

The divine revelation is therefore *a tense drama*. The biblical mes-sage appears as one large and continuous drama, beginning on the first page of the Bible and continuing until the last. In this drama the victory of Christ is the central act. Through him the new age has come into the world; as yet in the guise of humility, but finally in power and great glory.

This view of the divine revelation as drama excludes any view of it as an inevitable or automatic process. It cannot be incorporated into a pantheistic, monistic, and evolutionary world view. Such ideas are quite foreign to Christian faith, even though they appeared frequently in nineteenth-century theology from Schleiermacher onward. In whatever form these ideas appear, they tend to obscure both the evil against which the divine will contends and the active and striving character of the divine revelation. In contrast to these evolutionary misinterpretations of revelation, the Christian faith perceives it as *dramatic-eschatological*.

But Christian faith finds it just as vital and important that the divine will reveals itself as the *sovereign* will, which, because it is sovereign, transcends all strife which belongs to life on earth. It can therefore not be numbered among the many contending wills as one competing with others. To this we shall return later. But here it must be made clear that this tension which characterizes the Christian conception of revelation cannot be removed by minimizing either the sovereignty or the struggle of the divine will within history.

b. Revelation is *completed* in Christ, but at the same time is continually *in progress*.

Christian faith conceives of the divine revelation as something given once and for all, but at the same time as a continuous, active, and living revelation. Neither of these viewpoints must be minimized at the expense of the other. Faith accepts unconditionally the word, "It is finished." It is not looking for a new divine revelation which should render obsolete the one given once and for all in Christ. The act of reconciliation and victory through which the new fellowship with God has been established cannot be superseded. Nor can the conception of God, given in and with this new fellowship, be improved. Christian faith has expressed this in the words of the confession of the ancient church, that Christ is "of the same substance [*väsen*] as the Father." It is God's "nature" [*väsen*], the real and divine essence, which meets us in Christ. Christian faith cannot conceive of anything beyond this divine essence.

But at the same time the divine revelation is not confined to any certain period of time. Christian faith sees clearly that the divine revelation is constantly in progress in the sense that God is always active in the world. The divine act in Christ is finished, but at the same time continually going on as the divine victory is realized anew in every generation. Christian faith sees Christ as one who does not simply belong to the past, but who as the living Lord is present with his own until the end (Matt. 28:20). The fact that the Christian faith in God is also a faith in the Spirit preserves this dynamic character of revelation. It cannot be localized, but appears rather as a continuity extending to the end of time. Revelation always has the character of something present; it meets man in the present as a living and overwhelming power.

This conception of divine revelation is the opposite of that which is static and which limits it to certain isolated events, or localizes it in a portion of past history. Faith does not use such conceptions. Nothing is more essential to faith than that God continually manifests and reveals himself. Faith cannot tolerate the idea that God has withdrawn and ceased to be active. The living and continuing revelation is inseparably connected with the living God. When revelation is understood as finished at a certain point in time, a deistic conception is introduced which is foreign to faith. Not that God is conceived of in a purely deistic manner as the *primus motor*, the one who has set everything in motion, but God is held to have withdrawn from his work, after the revelation in Christ was finished, and to remain aloof from what is happening in the world. But in that case God would really cease to be the living God. This line of thought obscures both the conception of God and the meaning of faith. If revelation were localized in some past history, faith would mean simply an intellectual assent to a past event and an acceptance of that which once happened. It would not be manifested that faith consists in the fact that God in the present overwhelms and dominates man.

c. Since the divine revelation is a revelation in history, it makes use of historical means, persons, words, acts, and the like. But the divine revelation implies also God's *immediate* fellowship with the soul. Wherever faith speaks of revelation it implies that God directly confronts and addresses man. "The Word" does not become a divine revelation to man unless God, as Luther says, "speaks it in the heart." God's revelation is therefore a manifestation of his active and powerful *presence*.

There are good reasons for emphasizing that revelation is the direct word of God to man. There may otherwise be a temptation to regard revelation as a mediating agency between God and man. In discussing revelation and "mysticism," theology has tended to put the problem thus: Does God work immediately *or* through means? It has been argued that "mysticism" denotes an immediate God-fellowship, while revelation would mean that God works through mediators whose presence detracts from the immediacy of the fellowship. This conception rests on a complete misinterpretation of the nature of revelation. It is conceived as static and historical, and therefore mechanical. The "revelation" then becomes something independent of God, something that enters in between God and the soul. But this alternative disappears when faith's own view is maintained. The question is not whether God works immediately *or* through means; but rather whether he works or does not work. If God works at all, he always works immediately, no matter what "means" he may employ.

d. The divine revelation involves a disclosure of God's "essence," but at the same time it confronts faith with the Unfathomable.

The revelation is a revelation of the divine will. "By this we know love, that he laid down his life for us" (I John 3:16). "For it is the God who said, 'Let light shine out of darkness,' who has shone in our hearts to give the light of the knowledge of the glory of God in the face of Jesus Christ" (II Cor. 4:6). Revelation means, therefore, that God is not simply the great Unknown, or that about which nothing can be stated, because faith has some very definite things to say about him. The Christian conception of God is clearly and qualitatively defined. What faith says about him is not something unessential, but rather, according to its own conviction, the most essential affirmation which can be made. It concerns nothing less than the "disposition of his heart." God is exactly such as he is manifested in the act of Christ. There is no other God. All other "conceptions" of God are eliminated. As far as the Christian faith is concerned they are nothing but caricatures.

What has now been said would be highly misleading unless it be added that faith at the same time beholds God as the Unfathomable. In the presence of the revelation of the divine will faith is compelled to confess: "How unsearchable are his judgments, and how inscrutable his ways" (Rom. 11:33). The God who "reveals himself" is at the same time "the hidden God," who dwells "in unapproachable light, whom no man has ever seen or can see" (I Tim. 6:16). *Deus revelatus* is also *Deus absconditus*. What faith says about God is therefore radically differentiated from any rational metaphysics.

It is important to note in what manner God appears as the Unfathomable. It does not mean simply that there are certain limits to revelation, and that beyond these limits there exists a hidden territory which would grow less and less in the measure that revelation increases. Nor does it mean merely that under these earthly circumstances there always will remain questions which cannot be answered and riddles which cannot be solved; or that the Christian faith cannot become a rational world view to which the divine government of the world would be transparently clear. It means rather that the nature of divine revelation appears to faith as an impenetrable mystery; a "mystery disclosed" (Rom. 16:25-26), which yet remains a mystery. Since the very center of this revelation is divine love which gives itself in order to establish fellowship with sinners, that love itself

41

appears inscrutable and impenetrable. Faith beholds the revealed God as the Unfathomable, the "hidden" God. In fact, we may even agree to this proposition: the more God reveals himself and the deeper faith looks into the mystery of his divine heart, the more he appears as the Unfathomable. Thus the apostle writes: "This is how one should regard us . . . as stewards of the mysteries of God" (I Cor 4:1).

4. Divine Revelation and History

1. *Divine revelation cannot be detached from history.* The relation of faith to history is characterized by two antitheses. In the first place faith opposes every endeavor to separate divine revelation from history. This holds true whether it be by a speculative replacing of divine revelation with rational ideas, or by mystically dissolving the historical revelation, or finally by substituting "the spiritual Christ" for the Christ of history.

2. *Divine revelation cannot be identified with something historical.* In the second place faith opposes every endeavor to identify divine revelation with something historical and human. This is true whether the identification is built upon a general theory of immanence or has reference to the "historical Jesus" as such.

3. *The dialectic of faith.* Thus, for Christian faith divine revelation is indissolubly connected with history, but without being confused with the human element of history.

4. *Note on faith in Christ and historical criticism.* Although recent criticism has dispelled the theory of contradictions in the New Testament and emphasizes instead the unity in diversity, a natural tension remains between its historical investigations and faith in Christ. Despite this tension, faith stands unafraid.

1. Divine Revelation Cannot Be Detached from History

The problem of the relation of divine revelation to history now demands a more exact analysis. In principle, this relation is established in two negative propositions. Faith opposes alike all efforts to detach divine revelation from history and to identify it with something historical and human. When Christian faith speaks of a divine revelation *in* history, it has reference to *God's* revelation of himself. Christian faith discovers in history the God who acts and speaks

But faith is not directed toward anything historical as such. That which is historical has meaning only in the measure that it is a transparent medium of the *divine* revelation. Faith is concerned solely with a God-relationship, and in such a relationship man is exalted beyond all merely earthly and historical connections.

Through the ages various attempts have been made to separate divine revelation from history. Three such attempts are typical: the *speculative* endeavor to replace divine revelation in history with rational ideas; the effort of *mysticism* to make divine revelation in history ultimately superfluous; and the theological attempt to eliminate the historical Christ by directing attention to the *"spiritual"* Christ. An examination of these types reveals the attitude of each toward that which is central to Christian faith, namely, the incarnation of the divine will in Christ.

The *speculative* and *rationalistic* line of thought has been given classic expression in the famous words of Lessing, "Eternal truths cannot be based upon incidental historical facts." Two things are characteristic here; in the first place, the attempt to effect a liberation from history, and in the second, the endeavor to interpret the content of "revelation" as "inescapable rational truth." The fortuitous "facts" of history cannot constitute a firm foundation for the "eternal truths." These do not depend upon that which occurs in the realm of history. If Christian faith pretends to give expression to these eternal truths, it must cease to seek support in history.

When this approach is applied to the problem of *the meaning of Christ*, it often results in an effort to separate the historically transient from the eternal verities. It is not the historical figure of Jesus but those eternal verities of reason to which he was able to give expression that are meaningful for faith. The essential element is the teaching which he gave concerning "God, virtue, and immortality." The significance of Jesus depends, therefore, upon the value of his teaching, and the value of his teaching depends entirely upon its agreement with that which human reason conceives to be eternal truth. Christianity is "the true religion" just because it does not need to depend upon the historical and in so far as it can be separated from the "incidental" and transient in human affairs which has accompanied the "teaching."

If the older rationalism of the later stages of the Enlightenment was inclined to separate itself as much as possible from history, later speculative theology, especially that which is based on Hegel's philosophy, makes an even greater effort to unite revelation and history. It maintains that the basic and central "principle" of religion—the principle of a Divine Humanity—is realized in history. It is well known that from this starting point Christology became the center of theology and thus, ostensibly, the divine revelation in Christ was strongly emphasized. This approach is differentiated from the rationalism of the Enlightenment in that history is no longer considered simply "incidental"; the Idea is realized in history. There is nevertheless an obvious affinity inasmuch as the historical person of Jesus is separated from the eternal principle of a Divine Humanity of which he is the bearer and which is realized in him. This type of thought is also characterized by a tendency to dismiss entirely every thought of a supernatural revelation, because the metaphysical-cosmological viewpoint becomes anthropological, and humanity as such is understood as "the incarnation of God" (Strauss).

It is obvious that the speculative approach has been unable to express the conception of the relation of revelation to history which is characteristic of faith. From the viewpoint of faith it is decisive that whenever history has been ignored the *dynamic* revelation has been lost. Speculation confuses the divine revelation of faith with rationalistic metaphysics. Faith is not concerned with eternal truths of reason or an eternal idea, but only with the living God who speaks and acts in history. But instead of this living God there now appears only an abstract idea conceived by the older rationalism deistically and by speculative idealism pantheistically. In the measure that the idea of God is in this way weakened, faith no longer implies being subdued and dominated by God, but involves rather an acceptance of certain "religious" ideas. When history ceases to be the bearer of revelation, the danger is that the meaningful and definite concept of God fades, and faith itself withers away.

In many respects *mysticism* is very unlike the tendencies of rationalistic speculation which we have noted. Nevertheless there does exist a certain obvious affinity between mysticism and rational metaphysics. A review of the history of Christian thought shows that the two

have often been drawn together and have in certain respects complemented each other. There has been a manifest agreement between
them especially with reference to the question with which we are concerned here, the relation of the religious life to history. Both mysticism and rational metaphysics tend to separate the religious life from
any connection with history.

This is of course the case wherever mysticism appears in its purest
and most characteristic form as "the mysticism of infinity," as Söderblom expressed it.[1] In all such mysticism history plays no part. When
it affirms an "immediacy" in the God-relationship apart from any
connection with history, it of course ignores history altogether. That
"infinity" which absorbs personality has nothing to do with history.
The consequence of this approach is first of all that the content and
quality of the idea of God are lost. The deity can only be described
in static terms; God is the great Infinity, the Absolute, the Exalted
One, and so forth. Secondly, the relationship with God is lost. In
the final analysis there can be no real relationship with a God who
lacks quality. In other words, the mysticism of infinity, in spite of
its talk about the extinction of the ego, never really gets beyond the
magic sphere of egocentricity. It never reaches the living God who
dominates and subdues. The dissolution of the idea of God involves
the dissolution of the very relationship with God. Thus, the mysticism of infinity which separates itself from history demonstrates, no
less than does speculative rationalism, how important it is for Christian faith to direct attention to a divine revelation in history. What
may be observed from the foregoing is how the very content and
dynamic character of the idea of God are indissolubly connected with
the divine revelation located in history.

It must now be added that such a pure mysticism of infinity does
not belong to the history of Christian thought. Within this area such
mysticism as may be mentioned has been leavened by that conception
of revelation peculiar to Christian faith. Thus here mysticism is
oriented to history and particularly to the figure of Christ. A characteristic example of this type of mysticism is that of the Middle
Ages. Here the influence of the Christian conception of revelation

[1] Translated by Samuel McComb as "personality-denying mysticism" in
Freidrich Heiler, *Prayer* (New York: Oxford, 1932), p. 135.—Trans.

was at times feeble, as with Eckhart, and at other times more pronounced, as with the Passion mysticism of Bernard of Clairvaux. But
even in this latter case where the Passion of Christ and commitment
to his path of suffering are central ideas, the characteristic approach
of pure mysticism is apparent. The mystic's relation to Christ and
his Passion is regarded as a stage upon the upward way toward the
realization of the vision of and absorption in God. It is regarded as
an aid which becomes unnecessary once its task is accomplished. This
means, furthermore, that the concept of God is not delineated and determined by Christ and his work. This approach passes from a definite
conception of God to a mystically indefinite concept which eventuates
finally in negative statements. With this transformation of the concept of God, the approach of medieval mysticism to the God-relationship presents a singular vacillation between the most emphatic denial
of the self and a vast self-assurance of being received into the divine.[2]

A third type of endeavor seeking to separate divine revelation from
history has emerged in the recent theological attempts to *detach the
exalted "spiritual" Christ* from the historical Jesus. Thus Paul's assertion that he no longer knew Christ "after the flesh" (II Cor. 5:16)
has received an interpretation never contemplated by the apostle. It
has been vitally important ever since the days of the primitive church
for Christian faith to direct attention to Christ as Lord. It has been
equally essential for Christian faith to insist that the exalted Christ is
identical with him who was crucified outside the walls of Jerusalem.
If tendencies to isolate the spiritual Christ have emerged in recent
theologies, this may be explained by a number of conspiring circumstances. It is partly due to a legitimate reaction against previous one-
sided and mistaken theological emphases upon the "historical Jesus."

[2] When reference is sometimes made to a "Christ-mysticism," for example in
the writings of Paul, such terminology is apt to confuse rather than clarify, inasmuch as this so-called mysticism is devoid of all the elements which characterize
a genuine mysticism. In recent times the term mysticism has been so generally
misused that it can be employed only with the greatest care. It would be well
if the term were reserved to designate only the so-called mysticism of infinity.
To speak of a mysticism of faith serves only to obscure the issue. The desire
to "complement" faith with a so-called mysticism is simply an evidence of the
fact that the nature of Christian faith has not been rightly understood. A "faith"
which would require such a "complement" is beforehand in one way or another
an ethically, or intellectually, or otherwise impoverished faith.

And doubtless the exegetical uncertainty concerning that which can definitely be traced back to the historical Jesus has also been partially responsible for the emergence of these tendencies. Meanwhile, it is evident that the interpretation of revelation given by faith becomes a metaphysically oriented viewpoint when the isolation of the spiritual Christ is carried to its logical conclusions. In this situation there emerges the same phenomenon which we exposed in the previous paragraphs, namely that the concept of God tends to lose that distinctive quality given to it by the work of Christ. As a matter of fact, in whatever form it may appear, every effort to separate divine revelation from history has the same result, namely, the obscuring of both the God-relationship and the God-concept which are characteristically Christian.

2. Divine Revelation Cannot be Identified with Something Historical

Just as Christian faith will not permit divine revelation to be separated from history, so neither can it be comprehended in or be identified with anything historical as such. The identification of revelation with history was especially prevalent in the theology of the nineteenth century. Two principal types may be discerned: that which is based on the theory of divine immanence in humanity and that which possesses the structure of "historicism."

The first type emerge in the idealism of the nineteenth century and the theology it influenced. Inasmuch as there is no clear distinction here between "humanity at its highest" and the divine, the result is a confusion of revelation with history. As a consequence humanity at its best is regarded as identical with the divine.

From this point of view Christ is regarded as the incarnation of the religious ideal. He is the religious "archetype" (Schleiermacher) or the "ideal man." This latter designation enjoyed a wide popularity during the nineteenth century. The underlying thought is that here humanity at its best becomes and reflects the divine. This point of view gives to the figure of Christ an abstract quality. The "ideal man" is actually a hybrid being, partly divine and partly human, a fantasy to which various "ideals" may be imputed by various people. Critically, the most important consideration, however, is that this line of thought involves a dissolution of the concept of *divine* revelation. What is "revealed" is something which claims to be ideally human. As far as revelation is concerned, it is not a question of God's approach to man but rather the exaltation of the human to the divine sphere. Thus under the influence of idealism there occurs a dissolution of Christianity's basic fact, namely the act of God in Christ.

The Ritschlian theology, which was dominant during the latter decades of the nineteenth century, endeavored chiefly to concentrate divine revelation around the "historical Jesus." The purpose was to oppose both the supposedly metaphysical formulas of ancient Christology and the idealistic and speculative Christology of the first half of the nineteenth century. It implied a return to the "purely historical" figure of Jesus, to his teaching according to the Gospels.

A closer examination of this line of thought makes it clear, however, that this supposedly historical picture is in reality an invention. When, for example, Ritschl makes the teaching of Jesus concerning the kingdom of God central, the conception of the kingdom he defines is certainly not a mere return to Jesus' strongly eschatological teaching according to the Gospel. On the contrary, Ritschl's concept of the kingdom with its decidedly this-worldly, ethico-cultural orientation is obviously dependent upon idealistic theories and especially the thought forms of Kant. The same is true of Harnack's presentation of "the essence of Christianity." In his famous book[3] which appeared at the turn of the century, he locates "the essence of Christianity" in Jesus' teaching of the fatherhood of God, the brotherhood of man, and the eternal value of the human soul. It is clear that the definition of the content of revelation given here is strangely similar to the old theology of the Enlightenment; its "God, virtue, and immortality" reappear in modern dress. The decisive element does not lie in the historical as such, nor in the purely historical fact, if it can be shown to be a fact, that the propositions in question were once uttered by Jesus. Both Ritschl and Harnack reinterpret the history to which they refer. There is a certain standard by which the historical is judged, even though it is not made clear just what this standard is. When finally Herrmann refers to Jesus' "inner life"

[3] Adolph Harnack, *What Is Christianity?* trans. Thomas B. Saunders (New York: Putnam, 1901).

rather than to certain aspects of his teaching, it does not mean that he is concerned either with the "historical Jesus" as such. An investigation of Herrmann's line of thought reveals a return to the Christology typical of idealism. Jesus represents for both Herrmann and idealism a certain "ideal." Herrmann's chief concern is the "moral" ideal, as if the idea of moral goodness became incarnate in Jesus' "inner life."

From the viewpoint of Christian faith there are essentially two defects in the thought of historicism. In the first place, revelation is understood as dated and static. When revelation is located at an isolated point in the past, an imaginary chasm is created between faith and revelation. Because of its one-sided emphasis upon the "historical Jesus," the interpretation which historicism gives to revelation overlooks the fact that revelation for Christian faith emerges in a continuing context which is distinguished by the fact that the Crucified is also the Exalted One, and that Christian faith in God is also faith in the Spirit. Historicism thus separates faith from revelation. From the point of view of faith, such a construction is unrealistic. In the second place, and of greater importance from the religious point of view, the fundamental defect of historicism lies in the fact that, like the idealistic theory of immanence, the character of revelation as being a revelation of *God* is obscured. It directs the attention of faith to a human life of the highest moral and religious quality and to high and pure human thoughts about God and his kingdom. But that which is essential for faith does not have reference to human thoughts, however high and noble, nor to the life of any human personality, however completely "religious." Faith does not practice a hero cult. It does not confuse humanity even at its best with the divine. Faith is related to nothing but God alone. When it speaks of revelation it has reference only and entirely to *God's* revelation to God's way down to mankind from above; to this and nothing else.

3. The Dialectic of Faith

The conception Christian faith has of the relation of divine revelation to history may be said to be dialectic. The conclusions of the foregoing critical reflections may be summarized in the following formula: for Christian faith divine revelation is inseparably connected with history but without being confused with what is human. This is a formula well known to the ancient church. The merit of this formula is precisely that which has often been considered its shortcoming, namely, its negatively delimiting character. The concept faith has of the relation between divine revelation and history can actually be described and defined only in the measure that it can be differentiated from two opposing misinterpretations.

Divine revelation cannot, on the one hand, be separated from history. Every attempt in this direction invariably eventuates, as we have seen, in a dissolution of both the relation to God and the concept of God characteristic of Christian faith. That God is present in the historical process and that he is active in history is the chief viewpoint of faith. Divine revelation is therefore something wholly other than general, abstract, and unhistorical ideas. Revelation is the activity of the divine will in history. But at the same time divine revelation cannot be identified or confused with anything historical and human. Divine revelation is not identical with some unique aspect of man's inner life, even though it be of the very highest religious quality. Such thoughts, by idealizing the human, destroy that distance between the divine and the human which is fundamental for faith. Divine revelation does not imply that something human has been exalted to the divine realm, but that the divine will from above condescends to and is active in the human. Luther has given this situation a meaningful expression when he says that God is "hidden in the despised man, Christ." In this connection one may employ the ancient Lutheran and Reformed watchwords, *finitum capax infiniti, finitum non capax infiniti*. It can be said that the Lutheran formula certainly seeks to express the factual character of divine revelation but in doing so lays itself open to certain misinterpretations. The Reformed formula emphasizes, to be sure, the distance between the divine and the human, but in such a way as to endanger the factual character of divine revelation. Sooner than abiding by any of these formulas, one would prefer to transcend both of them with the formula *infinitum capax finiti*, which would affirm that *God* through his revelation in history creates fellowship with man.

4. Note on Faith in Christ and Historical Criticism

It has been stated in the previous discussion that Christian faith in

God regards Christ as the center of divine revelation. Since our
knowledge of Jesus Christ comes to us through the New Testament,
and this historical document is an object of investigation by historical
criticism, the problem of the relation between faith and this historical
criticism becomes very real and important.

This problem was hardly known as long as the theory of verbal
inspiration held sway and the content of the Bible was therefore assumed to be a homogeneous and uniform word of God. This situation changed when the classical documents of Christianity were subjected to the same examination by historical criticism as any other
historical documents. The problem assumed a twofold aspect. On
the one hand, historical criticism by its very nature must take into
account probabilities and relative judgments. It was difficult, for
instance, and sometimes impossible, to state with certainty what parts
in the Gospels came from Jesus himself and what may have originated with his disciples and others. On the other hand, it often
seemed that the older conception of the Bible as a unity without
diversity would be changed into a conception of it as a diversity
without unity.

It was, of course, of greatest importance that the multiplicity and
diversity to be found not only within the Bible as a whole but also
within the New Testament should be realistically appraised. But it
seemed at times as if the result would be, not only diversity, but also
acute contradictions. The most obvious was the contradiction believed to exist between Jesus' own "teaching" and the apostolic
preaching, a contradiction which divided the Christian message and
rendered it uncertain. Although in this way the situation became
critical, it has by now been practically overcome through a continued and more decisive application of historical criticism. The
theory of contradictions within the New Testament has been shown
to be an invention which arose because the critics read their own
"modern" ideas into the Gospel accounts of Jesus' preaching. The
picture which historical criticism now gives us is not one of diversity
without unity, but of unity in diversity. The diversity is obvious.
The Synoptic Gospels, John, Paul, Hebrews, and so on, represent
complementary types of New Testament teaching. But in the midst
of this diversity the fundamental unity stands secure. The New

Testament message is an indivisible unity and has a definite content throughout (cf. § 7). Its center is Christ as *Kyrios* and the new age, the new aeon, which has come through him and his work. There is no contradiction here between Jesus and his disciples, but rather a clear and indisputable continuity. The apostles did not invent a new religion with Christ as the center. As far as we can go back to Jesus' own preaching, we find that his message is inseparable from his own person.

Even though it is extremely important that the mutual suspicions of faith and criticism have been removed, it is quite natural that there remains a tension between Christian faith and the investigations carried on by historical criticism. It is obvious that when historical criticism tries to determine what in a purely historical sense was Jesus' own contribution, it has to be satisfied with a lesser or greater degree of probability. It is likewise obvious that these investigations of areas which to faith are holy ground must vitally affect the interests of faith itself. But in spite of this tension faith preserves its complete fearlessness. The changes in our conception of the primitive history of Christianity which may be occasioned through this research cannot prevent faith from drawing fully and freely on the accumulated riches of the whole New Testament. This research cannot take away from faith anything which it regards as the revelation of God. It cannot challenge, and least of all destroy, that fundamental conception of faith which perceives and interprets the work of Christ in the light of the continuous context of revelation, and which in his life and work beholds the self-realization of the divine love in human life and the new age which comes in *Christus-Kyrios*.

5. Faith in God and Faith in Christ

1. *The problem.* All Christian faith is faith in God. All typically Christian faith is at the same time centered in Christ. This raises the problem of the relation between the theocentricity and the Christocentricity of faith.

2. *The meaning of Christocentricity.* The Christian faith in God is characterized by faith in Christ. It is not a faith in something besides God, but a faith in the God who was incarnate in Christ, and who

thus realizes his will and reveals his "nature." The event of Christ therefore defines the Christian relationship to God and the Christian conception of God. The antithesis between theocentricity and Christocentricity is thereby removed. Christian faith is Christocentric precisely because it is thoroughly theocentric.

3. *Misleading interpretations of the relation between faith in God and faith in Christ.* A misleading conception of the relation between theocentricity and Christocentricity arises in three instances: 1) when Christ is separated from God and conceived of as an intermediary being between men and God; 2) when Christ is identified with God and takes his place; 3) when the divine Being is, so to speak, split up and divided between God and Christ.

1. The Problem

When we take up the problem here of the relation between faith in God and faith in Christ, we do not intend to anticipate the discussion of the Christological problem which has its own place in this exposition (§§ 25-29). We simply intend through some preliminary qualifications to guard against misunderstandings and accusations of obscuring the monotheistic character of faith, which might be occasioned by the assertion that Christian faith is at the same time faith in God and faith in Christ. In § 2, it was stated emphatically that Christian faith has only one object, that it has reference to God and to him alone. At the same time it is a well-known fact that Christian faith began as faith in Christ, and that this is its distinctive feature. It could be argued that this Christocentricity is opposed to, or at least obscures, the theocentricity of faith. It cannot be denied that this has often been the case in the history of Christian thought. Under these circumstances a preliminary explanation of the relation between faith in God and faith in Christ cannot be omitted.

2. The Meaning of Christocentricity

The meaning of faith in Christ is entirely misunderstood if it is assumed that because of its concern for Christ the Christian faith finds a center other than God. The attitude of faith in this matter can be illustrated by the words of Jesus in John 12:44: "He that believes in me, believes *not* in me but in him who sent me." The Christian faith in Christ is a faith in God, who appears actively in the event of Christ, realizes his will, removes that which conceals his face, and triumphs over that

which separates us from him. A complete analysis of this event of
Christ and of how God is active in it can be given only as an exposition
of the whole content of Christian faith. At this stage we can only suggest in a preliminary way the fundamental idea of this faith in Christ,
and elucidate its relation to faith in God. It will then become clear that
Christocentricity is not opposed to, but rather serves to emphasize,
theocentricity. The confession of faith in Christ is really nothing else
than a statement about *God*, his "essence," his presence, and his power
to triumph over that which is opposed to him. Its real point of view
is simply this: where Christ is, there is God; and where Christ works,
there God effectively realizes his will. The work of Christ is not
something separated from God; it is God's own work. Faith in Christ
does not draw attention away from God; rather it permits his image
to appear as clearly as it is possible under the conditions to which
human life is subject.

Faith in Christ is therefore the secure safeguard of Christian faith
in God. Faith is certain that in Christ it has found God's "essence,"
will, and inner "disposition of the heart." Once faith has found God
in Christ, it does not seek him elsewhere. The real purpose of
Christology is, therefore, to guard the purity and completeness of the
Christian faith in God. If the chief statement of the confession of the
ancient church, "of the same substance [*väsen*] as the Father," has
any meaning at all, it must be that we learn to know the essence
[*väsen*] of "the Father" in "the Son." If the confession of faith in
Christ is not permitted effectively to perform this function, it loses its
real significance and becomes merely empty words.

If this analysis is correct, the Christological problem must not
be stated in such a way as to imply that the "divinity" of Christ can
be measured by a previously determined conception of God. Faith
regards such a proposition as unreal and incompatible with its situation and nature. It is true that revelation is by no means limited to
Christ. But this does not mean that revelation apart from Christ can
serve as a standard whereby the degree of revelation found in him
can be measured. We cannot, for instance, measure the revelation
in Christ according to the standard of the Old Testament; we must
rather measure the nature of revelation in the Old Testament according to the standard of the Christ event. From the point of view of

faith the endeavor to measure the "divinity" of Christ under the tacit assumption that it is possible to achieve a clear and authentic knowledge of God apart from the event of Christ is inevitably misleading. This supposed possibility does not exist. God is not a previously definable essence with which we can start and proceed without further reference. In reality these attempts to measure the "divinity" of Christ imply a denial of him as the revealer of God. It is not God who is the known, and Christ, the riddle; it is rather the opposite. The first and foremost question is: What is the nature of the hidden God? What is the nature of his will, and how does he act? The event of Christ supplies the answer to these questions.

Faith in Christ, therefore, does not obscure the consistent faith in God, but rather provides it with power, purity, and decisive content. Exactly because Christian faith is altogether theocentric, it must at the same time be Christocentric. The whole history of Christianity illustrates and confirms this intimate connection between faith in God and faith in Christ. This history shows conclusively that faith in God has been strong, living, and dynamic in the measure in which Christ has been its focus and center. All great revivals have been intimately connected with a Christocentric emphasis. On the contrary, when the bond between faith in God and faith in Christ has been dissolved or weakened, faith in God has languished and the concept of God has become vague. The conception of God has lost its living features, God has been removed into the distance, and has been conceived in terms of an abstract idea rather than as the living and active God. The rationalism of the Enlightenment constitutes a classic example.

3. Misleading Interpretations of the Relation Between Faith in God and Faith in Christ

Misleading interpretations of the relation of faith in Christ to faith in God have often appeared in the history of Christian thought. The fear that Christocentricity should prove to be a danger to theocentricity, and to the purity and unity of faith in God, arises from such misinterpretations. A study of them, therefore, will throw further light on the real significance of Christocentricity. These misinterpretations are of three main types.

In the first place a misinterpretation of the meaning of faith in Christ emerges when Christ himself is thought of as an intermediary being between men and God. This type of Christology appeared in various forms within the ancient church and found its most characteristic expression in Arianism. This line of thought both obscured the position of Christ as the revealer of God and threatened to destroy the unity and theocentric character of faith. The ancient church opposed this antithesis between theocentricity and Christocentricity with its formula, "of the same substance as the Father." The church thereby affirmed that when its faith was directed toward Christ, it was directed toward none other than God. Certain related conceptions have also appeared in later times, especially when Christ is spoken of as the religious "prototype" of humanity, or "the ideal man," and so on. This unrealistic Christology, influenced by idealistic philosophy, also makes of Christ an intermediary being. It obscures the most vital center of Christian faith, namely, that it is God himself who is incarnate in Christ and acts through him. It tends to deny that God's approach to man is through Christ and his work.

In the second place, the meaning of Christocentricity is misinterpreted when God and Christ are identified, as occurred in Modalism. (See § 25.) This has often been done more or less naively in much popular preaching, in which the preaching of Christ practically supersedes the preaching of God. It is undeniable that in this case Christocentricity tends to hide and impair the theocentricity of faith. Christ replaces God. What is legitimate in this line of thought is its understanding that in the realm of faith nothing else matters but God alone. However, it fails to see that the real question is about a *revelation* of God in the real meaning of the word, and that this revelation take place *in* history, in "the despised man, Christ," as Luther expressed it. As soon as this is realized, it becomes impossible to identify Christ with God, or to conceive of the divine "essence" as synonymous with the man Christ.

In the third place, this relation is misinterpreted if an attempt is made to divide the Supreme Being and to apportion certain aspects to God and others to Christ. Certain divine "attributes" are then given to Christ which do not in the same degree belong to God. Such ideas lie behind the theory of the atonement developed in Latin scholasticism, which has greatly influenced the history of Christian doctrine. In this line of thought Christ represents pre-eminently the divine love, while the idea of retributive justice dominates the conception of God as such. The result has been that Christ is placed, so to speak, over against God. This line of thought may be explained partly by the legitimate interest in maintaining the reality of divine judgment on all wickedness, and partly by the fact that the fulness of divine love meets us in the person and work of Christ. Nevertheless, this conception of the relation between God and Christ is diametrically opposed to the meaning of the confession of Christ. It is misleading because the act of Christ is not in this case understood as God's own act. But when the work of Christ is conceived of as the work of God, it becomes impossible to ascribe a greater degree of divine love to Christ than to God, or to introduce a division into the Divine Being. The act of Christ is altogether an act of God's own love, and an act through which this love realizes itself.

6. The Content of Faith

1. *Faith and the content of faith.* The divine revelation from which faith derives its existence gives it a definite quality and a fixed content. This content is in principle given in and with the God-relationship as such. The content of faith is therefore neither primary in relation to faith (intellectualism) nor secondary (subjectivism, psychologism).

2. *The Christian message and its interpretation.* Since the content of the Christian faith is defined by the act of God in Christ and the message about this event, it is something unalterably given once and for all. If theology is to explicate the content of this message to the present age, however, it cannot be satisfied merely to reproduce the conceptions and formulas of another age.

3. *Motifs and forms of expression.* That which is decisive for the content of faith does not lie in the forms of presentation as such. It is to be found rather in the underlying religious motifs for which the forms are expressions.

1. Faith and the Content of Faith

The content of Christian faith is, in principle, something fixed and definite. It is not a question of just any vague and indefinite "faith" whatever, for God is not the great Unknown about whom nothing really positive can be affirmed. God is not only hidden, but is at the same time the God who has disclosed himself in the past and continues to make himself known. It is the divine will given in revelation and qualitatively determined by the work of Christ which faith embraces, or rather which embraces and subdues man and thereby creates faith and establishes the relationship to God. Faith is thus from man's viewpoint a *yes* to the self-disclosure of the divine will, and is determined by the divine revelation which both creates it and gives it a unique content. Faith cannot be isolated from this revelation so that it would have its own existence apart from divine revelation. Faith is nothing in itself. It is what it is by reason of that divine revelation which subdues man. To "understand faith" is to understand the revelation of God given in Christ.

From what has been said it follows that the content of faith is in principle given in and by the relationship to God. The implication of this statement becomes clear if we observe how this conception of the content of faith differentiates itself from two mutually opposing interpretations, the intellectual and the subjective or psychological. The first type belongs chiefly to the older period of scholasticism and rationalism. The second has repeatedly asserted itself especially during the last century. However, these two types can hardly be consigned to different periods. To a certain extent there has been a continual struggle between these two rival interpretations.

The *intellectual* interpretation considers the content of faith to be primary in relationship to faith. It attempts to demonstrate rationally those ideas about God which are supposed to be the objects of "faith." This line of thought has from the beginning characterized scholastic theology, which attempts to "complement" rational demonstration by "revelation." Within fully developed rationalism, however, the rational demonstration becomes entirely dominant. Relative to all such demonstrations it is enough to say that as long as one is limited to this sphere there has been no real contact with the realm of faith. But the intellectual tendency within scholastic theology is not limited to such attempts to co-ordinate faith with rational metaphysics. It appears also in connection with the very concept of faith by making "assent" primary in relation to the other aspects of faith. In such a manner medieval theology distinguished between faith as

"thinking with approbation" (*cum assensione cogitare*) and faith as
fides caritates formata (Thomas). The post-Reformation scholastics
of the seventeenth century distinguished similarly between faith as
assensus and faith as *fiducia*. Under such circumstances "faith" was
interpreted in the first place as man's submissive acceptance of certain
authoritative and doctrinal theological propositions. This was a presupposition for faith's subsequently becoming *fides caritate formata* or
fiducia. It is self-evident that this intellectual approach exercised a
severe constraint upon the Christian life. In the measure that the
acceptance of a certain given system of doctrine became the chief
concern, the Christian life was confronted by fictitious difficulties,
while the real difficulties, which the Gospel describes as it points to
life's pathway through "the narrow gate," were obscured. It gradually became necessary for theology to try in some way to ease the
constraint originating in the intellectual conception of faith. This
occurred within medieval scholasticism through the doctrine of *fides
implicita*, that is to say, through the assertion that it was sufficient to
possess a rather simple faith, so long as one lived in the certain conviction that the teachings of the church were true. Within the post-
Reformation scholasticism there developed gradually an attempt to
differentiate between "fundamental articles," which demanded acceptance, and teachings of lesser importance. It is clear that such
adjustments while bringing a certain amount of relief to the circumstances at hand, could not, however, produce any real clarity
or give any promise of overcoming intellectualism.

The weakness in the intellectual approach to faith is not that the
content of Christian faith is presented as something definite and determined. This is rather its strength. The weakness is due partly to
the confusion of divine revelation with some given, authoritative theological system of doctrine, and partly, to use the terminology of post-
Reformation scholasticism, to the fact that *assensus* was considered
primary in relation to *fiducia*. If one is, therefore, to be emancipated
from the intellectual approach without losing the truth which is
affirmed there, it is necessary to maintain that, as far as faith is concerned, it is a question of only one thing, namely, the *will of God*
revealed in the event of Christ, and further that *assensus* is at the same
time *fiducia*. In this way Luther can speak of faith as implying noth-

ing else than an *assensus*, a *yes* to "God's work and promise," but this *yes* is at the same time an expression of the very highest trust, which is to say, an expression of man's having been subdued by the will of God.

The *subjective* or *psychological* conception of faith has often appeared as a reaction against intellectualism. This viewpoint is characterized by the notion that the content of faith is something secondary in relation to faith "itself." "Faith" is understood as identical with certain religious feelings or with a "pious state of mind." It is thought of as something given in the spiritual life of man, as a self-contained, independent entity. The pious feelings or state of mind are primary. The content of faith, however, is secondary and originates through reflection upon these pious feelings or state of mind. It is natural that from this point of view the significance of the content of faith will be sharply reduced. A distinction was made between *fides qua creditur* and *fides quae creditur*, and the latter was made subordinate to the former. This approach to the relation between faith and its content has received classic expression in the pregnant words of Schleiermacher in the fifteenth section of *The Christian Faith:* "Christian affirmations of faith are accounts of the Christian religious affections set forth in speech." Fundamentally, the question here is not about the affirmations of faith in God, but about the affirmations concerning the religious subject. This approach which has its roots in pietism and romanticism exerted a great influence throughout the nineteenth century. It was responsible for the emergence of the so-called "experiential theology" for which the "religious experience," whether individual or collective, appears as the subject for theological analysis (cf. § 1, ¶ 4). It was claimed that this theory could be projected so that, beginning with the subjective experience and working from effect to cause, one could be led back to the "objective realities of revelation." But the illusory element in this line of thought could not be long concealed.

The weakness in the psychological approach to the relation between faith and its content does not lie in its refusal to construct a supposedly objective doctrine of God. On the contrary, this is the very strength of this viewpoint in contradistinction to all rational metaphysics. But the weakness lies in the fact that faith is no longer clearly understood *as faith*, but as a "pious, spiritual state" independent of divine revelation. In intellectualism faith tended to lose its character of a direct relationship between God and man by becoming chiefly a matter of adhering to a system of doctrine about God. Similarly the psychological interpretation obscures the character of faith as being a God-relationship. It does not become clear that faith is what it is only in and through the divine revelation, that the affirmations of faith are by their very nature affirmations about the God who reveals himself, and that therefore the content of faith is not secondary but essential to faith and its unique character. The content of faith is in reality nothing else than the God who reveals himself.

2. *The Christian Message and its Interpretation*

The church of Christ and Christian faith have their origin and existence in the event of Christ and in the apostolic message concerning it. The message is given. If it should be changed and transformed, the Christian faith would cease to be what it is. No matter what changes take place in time, the message remains unchanged. The theological task of elucidating the meaning of faith can be done only through an elucidation of the meaning of the Christian message.

But although the message itself is something given once for all, the theological analysis of the message is not of that nature. The theological interpretation never becomes definitive. The theological task becomes relevant again in every new generation. The theological interpretation, therefore, cannot be limited to a reproduction of the conceptions and formulas found in the original message of the ancient church, and still less in those which belong to later times. In reality none of the interpretations which have appeared in the history of the church have been mere reproductions. Luther and the Reformation, for example, were not simply a reproduction of the apostle Paul. Luther's proclamation was a rediscovery of something essential in the Christian message, and Paul was his chief guide. But Luther was no imitator.

Theology cannot neglect or cut itself off from the age in which it performs its work. It has to interpret the content of the changeless, Christian message, but this must be done in such a way that people will understand the interpretation. The theological task is not done in a vacuum or in a timeless order, but rather under the conditions and in the circumstances which obtain in a given period of the life of the church. The people of the twentieth century do not speak the same language as those of the first or the sixteenth. Even this fact makes a mere reproduction impossible. What is necessary is an interpretation that expresses everything essential in the Christian faith in the contemporary idiom.

One difficulty in such an interpretation lies in the fact that we approach the ancient Christian message with presuppositions differing from those inherent in the message itself; presuppositions which appear to us self-evident, but which nevertheless easily prevent us from grasping the essential import of the message. The history of theology presents many frightening examples of a procedure through which the essential content of the message has been changed in the attempt to make it "modern." Through accommodation, elimination, and selection the Christian message has become incorporated into a system of thought foreign to it. The objection is not against the attempt to bring the message into contact with contemporary life. On the contrary, that must be done. The danger is rather that in pursuing this legitimate objective the presuppositions and the unique character of the message may be misunderstood.

3. Motifs and Forms of Expression

As theology investigates the content of Christian faith, it is important to make a distinction between the fundamental motifs and the forms of expression. The word "motif" has reference primarily to those religious forces which so to speak produce the respective forms of expression. In our presentation "motif" means the religious intention, content, and reality which is contained and appears in a certain form of expression. If it is a matter of explicating the meaning of Christian faith, then theology must not stop with a consideration of the various forms of expression which we meet at the first appearance of Christianity and which during the ages since that time have appeared in various new forms. It is necessary to push beyond these forms and formulas, and to reach the dynamic religious ideas, the religious motifs, which are active here. The essential element is not the forms as such, but what underlies the whole, the religious content which these forms seek to express.

The distinction proposed here may be substituted for the usual nineteenth-century differentiation between "life" and "teaching." The intention which lay behind this latter distinction was indeed noteworthy, inasmuch as it recognized that theology could not, without becoming intellectualistic and doctrinaire, stop simply with the "teaching" and its forms of expressions. But this differentiation exposes its subjective and psychological background when it places the "teaching" in contrast to "life," "experience," and the like. If the starting point is taken from this distinction, the consequence may be that the content of faith is regarded as something secondary or of minor importance in comparison with the so-called *fides qua creditur;* at best, the result will be a lack of clarity due to the ambiguity of the word "life." However, when a distinction is made between the religious motif and the form of expression, the purpose is both to escape the restraint imposed by the various forms and to assert freely the primary meaning of the content of Christian faith.

A theological investigation which is not impelled by the efforts to push beyond forms and formulas to the underlying driving powers, to the decisive religious motifs, will inevitably stop at the periphery in its effort to interpret the content of Christian faith. The inner quality of questions relating to faith would then be concealed. This has been exemplified by numerous theological debaters through the ages, who, just because they have become entangled in forms and formulas, have never pushed on to the essential core of the matter. Such an approach to fundamental motifs is necessary because it may easily happen that the forms change while the religious intention remains the same, or that the same forms and expressions may have a completely different meaning, depending upon whether they express one religious motif or another. The former alternative may be exemplified in the "dualistic" approach, the struggle between the will of God and the demonic forces. This motif has often been presented in an extreme form, but it is not inevitably connected with such an expression. The motif *can* be separated from that form and nevertheless continue to exist with uncurtailed power. It may be added that when a theology becomes entangled in the "primitive" forms of expression, it is apt to lose sight of the significance of the conflict motif for Christian faith. It may be natural to consider the emphasis on "pure" forms as a sure sign of a clearer and deeper conception of Christianity. Such a point of view has very often obtained in theology during the past several centuries and has given rise to very superficial conceptions. Sufficient consideration has not been given to the fact that this emphasis may result in a fundamental weakening of the central Christian motifs.

Rudolph Bultmann has sought to solve these problems by his well-known thesis of "demythologizing" faith. With the help of the philosophy of existentialism he has attempt to free the Christian faith from the "mythological" concepts which characterize the New Testament proclamation. According to Bultmann the theological task is to describe human existence as it understands itself in faith. An analysis of the merits and weaknesses of this thesis lies beyond the scope of this work. But it must be pointed out that the theological intention behind "demythologizing" is of a different nature than the one presupposed in our discussion. To be sure, what we have said about the relationship between motifs and forms of expression is designed to secure the necessary freedom in regard to those conceptions connected with a view of the universe different from our own. But Bultmann's theory involves in reality making the content of the faith conform to those modern conceptions which Bultmann considers self-evident. Such an attempt at conformity is foreign to a theology which distinguishes between motif and form of expression in order to define the religious intention and meaning. If the task of theology were to describe how faith understands human existence, the content of faith would become secondary in relation to faith. Theology would then become concerned with psychology rather than with the divine revelation which creates faith.

7. The Biblical Validation of the Content of Faith

1. *The message of the Bible*. Since the act of God in Christ defines the content of faith, and since the Bible is not only the fundamental but also the decisively authoritative message concerning this act, and

therefore also itself a message of God, all Christian doctrines must be subjected to a biblical validation.

2. *The nature and possibility of validation.* Biblical validation is possible because of the unity which, in spite of all diversity, characterizes the biblical message. This unity rests on the dominant position which Christ has in the biblical context of revelation. Thus the validation refers to the Bible as a whole. At the same time the variety of the biblical message excludes all formal and legalistic validation.

1. The Message of the Bible

When theology attempts to present the meaning of the Christian faith, it encounters the whole multiplicity of testimonies within Christianity. Its work must therefore assume a critical character. It is obvious that not all statements of faith which have ever appeared can be accepted as genuinely Christian. Thus the question of the validation of Christian concepts of faith is raised. It must be possible in some way to investigate and verify the Christian character of the affirmations of faith.

When such verification is attempted, the decisive factor must be found in that which makes faith to be faith, in that which constitutes the Christian relationship to God. As we have stated, this is the act of God in Christ. Theology, therefore, has to concern itself with the Scriptures which contain the message of this act of God. Theology must do so even on purely historical grounds. Anyone who wants to understand a certain event must as far as possible study the sources in order to find the fundamental causes which produce the event. No one can deny that the Bible contains the fundamental testimony concerning that event which gave rise to and constituted the Christian faith. It is pre-eminently in the Bible that we find the ancient message of *Christus-Kyrios,* the apostolic kerygma.

But systematic theology is not a historical discipline. Its task is not to describe the origin of a historical event, but to explicate the meaning of the faith. If it were to regard Scripture simply as an original and genuine witness concerning the faith of the ancient church, or as a priceless human document describing a historical event, theology would be totally unable to understand faith and the relationship of faith to the Scriptures. Faith insists that the message contained in Scripture, which on the one hand is a message proclaimed by men, is at the same time a divine message directed to us with all the authority inherent in a word of God. When we here speak of the Bible as a message and as a word of God, it is not a question only of an impartation of knowledge or ideas about God. Even in its character as message and Word of God, the message concerning the act of God in Christ is itself an act of God through which the once-completed work of Christ continues in the present.

All doctrines and ideas which claim a place in the Christian context of faith must be examined and tested in reference to this authority of the biblical message. As we have already indicated in other connections, this does not mean that a theological presentation of the content of the Christian faith should consist in a repetition of biblical statements. But it does mean that all affirmations of faith are of a biblical nature and stand in an organic connection to the divine message of the Bible. If a statement of faith lacks such a connection, it is not a Christian affirmation no matter how many people may have accepted it as such.

2. The Nature and Possibility of Validation

It is undeniable that the Bible contains a great variety of elements. This character of the Bible has been effectively demonstrated by historical criticism. In reality there are not only variety and differences but also contradictions. It is not difficult to discover discrepancies between various statements within the Old Testament, nor between the Old Testament and the New. Even the New Testament contains many differences, not only between the various authors but also between various statements by the same author. C. H. Dodd, for example, has called attention to a change in Paul's eschatological conceptions in his later letters as compared with those addressed to the Thessalonians. If we could say nothing else about the biblical documents than that they present an abundant and almost immeasurable variety, there would be no possibility of arriving at a biblical validation of the content of the Christian faith.

But in the midst of the multiplicity in the Bible there is also a continuous context of revelation which has its center in Christ. When Christ is spoken of in various hymns as "the Sun of righteousness," "Sun of my soul," "the Sun of life," these terms are expressive of his central position in the context of God's revelatory activity. The light from the revelation in Christ illuminates both the past and the future. Seen from this vantage point, the biblical history of revelation appears as a continuous series of acts of God, beginning with creation, continuing through the election and nurture of Israel, coming to a climax in the incarnation of Christ, and then continuing age after age until the eschatological consummation. Thus faith apprehends the unity of the biblical message through the central position which Christ occupies in it. Apart from this the biblical content would be a truncated message, a series of unfulfilled promises. But in and through Christ the fulfilment of the promises appear in clear light. The "humiliation" and "exaltation" of Christ, his sacrifice and victory, are intimately connected with the Old Testament message about the suffering Servant of the Lord and the messianic kingdom. "All the promises of God find their Yes in him" (II Cor. 1:20). The promises of God have been fulfilled in Christ, although in a way different from what was expected. But this fulfilment is not the end. From one point of view the work of Christ is finished. It is completed in so far as the work which he was sent to perform in the days of his flesh has been finished. But from another point of view his activity continues in and through his church until the Parousia and "the life of the world to come." Hence the biblical history of revelation is one continuous eschatological drama which has its center in the act of God in Christ.

It is evident, therefore, that the biblical validation of the content of the Christian faith is concerned with the whole Bible, not only with the New Testament. The authoritative position of the Old Testament depends on its intimate religious connection with the New Testament. The light emanating from the event of Christ illumines the Old Testament record. Here is the criterion which must be the guide in all biblical verification. The reference to the Bible as a whole does not mean that every biblical statement is of equal value for the verification of the Christian affirmations of faith. Nor is it possible to secure a biblical verification by selecting certain portions of the Bible and regarding them as infallible "doctrinal authority." These attempts are doomed to failure, because such external and mechanical rules do not furnish any sure guidance. Verification is concerned with the Bible as a whole, because it is in the Bible as a whole that we find that context of revelation in which Christ is the Lord. This content and message of the Bible is the decisive factor. Every affirmation of faith, if it claims to be Christian, must be in conformity with this message.

If biblical verification is thus determined by the biblical message, the validating arguments cannot be presented in a formal and legalistic manner. The theory of verbal inspiration at one time sought to provide this. The consequence of this theory would be that everything within the Bible had the same obligatory, divine authority. But this theory is impossible in view of the multiplicity and the differences which appear in the biblical documents. The decisive objection against this viewpoint, however, is that it degrades the act of God in Christ. The event of Christ loses its dominant position; it is no longer the standard by which everything is measured, or the divining rod which guides us to the springs of living water.

8. Scripture and Tradition

1. *The living testimony of the church.* Since theology is to explicate the meaning of faith for the present generation, it must take into account not only Scripture but also the continuing, living testimony of faith within the Christian church, or, in other words, the "tradition."

2. *The legitimacy of the tradition.* The tradition must be considered in so far as it explicates ideas of faith which are in line with and latent in the biblical message. A denial of this claim indicates an inadequate understanding of the richness of the biblical message.

3. *Tradition as a guard in biblical interpretation.* The significance of the tradition, however, does not consist only in liberating and explicating the biblical motifs. It is significant also because in the confessions of the church it defines ideas of faith which are essential for the interpretation of the biblical message, and thus guards against irresponsible interpretation of the Bible.

4. *The primacy of Scripture.* Scripture remains primary in reference to the tradition. A tradition that is contrary to or not in line with the biblical message cannot be verified as Christian. The primacy of Scripture is not impaired by the fact that the New Testament may be regarded as a part of the tradition, i.e., the primary, *apostolic* tradition.

5. *Tradition must not be interpreted in a legalistic or evolutionary way.* The interpretation of tradition given here rejects both a legalistic and an evolutionary conception of the tradition.

6. *"Pure doctrine."* The purpose of the critical examination made by theology is the delineation of "pure doctrine." From one point of view this pure doctrine is something given in principle once and for all; but from another point of view it is an ideal goal toward which theology is constantly striving in its pursuit of truth.

1. *The Living Testimony of the Church*

The work of systematic theology to explicate the meaning of the Christian faith in the contemporary world is a task which cannot be completed once and for all. What is involved is not merely a reproduction of the biblical message. None of the innumerable interpretations produced within Christendom have been simply a reproduction. Each one belongs to its own age and bears the marks of the situation in which it appeared. This connection with contemporary life obviously involves the possibility of a distortion and corruption of the original, biblical message; theology must be clearly aware of this risk. But this connection is necessary if the result of the work is to be significant and meaningful.

The theological task is thus set in a large context, continuing through the centuries down to our own day. Theology must find contact with and listen to the living testimony of the church through the centuries. It cannot act as if nothing had happened since the close of the canon, or as if there were a vacuum between Scripture and our own day. The idea that the Spirit of God ceased his activity when the last page of the Bible had been written stands in obvious contradiction to the biblical message. Theology must consider especially that living testimony of faith which appears in the church through its worship, proclamation, the sacraments, confession, prayer, and hymnody. As theology seeks to elucidate the meaning of the faith for the present generation, it must take into account not only Scripture but also the living testimony of the church which has generally been referred to as the "tradition" of the church.

The problem of Scripture and tradition has become acute because of the divisions in the church and the different attitudes taken by the various confessions. The Orthodox churches, if we listen to their contemporary theologians, would seem to deny that this relationship constitutes any problem. We note here the differences between the Eastern and the Western churches. The Orthodox church rejects the attempts of the Western churches to invest the authority of the church in some person, or institution, or in some churchly documents. Its conception is somewhat more elastic. Even if the Orthodox church regards the decisions of the councils of the undivided church as extremely important, it does not say that authority has ceased to function in the church since that time. G. Florovsky writes: "The tradition is the testimony of the Holy Spirit, and his continuous revelation and proclamation of the gospel. For the living members of the church this is not a historical authority, but God's eternal and continuous voice; not the voice of ancient times but of eternity." [1] The authority of the tradition becomes therefore inseparably connected with the authority which speaks in Scripture. The situation is quite different in the Roman church. Here the "infallible" authority which determines what is churchly tradition and true teaching in the church is incorporated in the person of the pope. Among the evangelical churches it has sometimes appeared as if the emphasis on the authority of Scripture had resulted in a negative attitude to the tradition, and sometimes as if the confessions of the church possessed the decisive authority. This negative attitude, however, is both historically and in principle foreign to the Reformation and its intentions. Historically the connection with the earlier tradition, especially that of the ancient church, is obvious. In principle it has generally been maintained that the tradition expressed in the confessions is of secondary authority. The confessions are *normae normatae*, Scripture is *norma normans*.

2. *The Legitimacy of the Tradition*

It is obvious that the question about Scripture and tradition has become a central problem in the theological discussions held within the ecumenical movement. The living tradition of the church speaks with many voices but not in unison. We find many conceptions in conflict with one another. In this situation would it be best to eliminate all tradition and confine ourselves exclusively to the expressions

[1] G. Florovsky, *The Church of God*, p. 64.

and formulas found in Scripture? Are we compelled to draw this conclusion because Scripture provides us with the decisive and infallible message about the event of Christ? The answer must be No. Such a negative attitude toward the living tradition in the church would amount to a denial of the activity of the Holy Spirit in the church. The decisive question is if and to what extent the living testimony of the church, the "tradition," actually expresses the continuing activity of the Spirit. Two passages in the sixteenth chapter of the Gospel of John do suggest some guidance. "When the Spirit of truth comes, he will guide you into all the truth" (vs. 13). "He will take what is mine and declare it to you" (vs. 14). The first points forward to a continuing witness; it opens new possibilities. The second connects this continuing testimony securely to the person and work of Christ; the Spirit who bears witness is the Spirit of Jesus Christ. On this basis the relationship between Scripture and tradition is definitely settled. The living testimony of the tradition has its proper place, and to deny this would be to impoverish the church, but not because Scripture is not sufficiently rich by itself. On the contrary, it is rather because the rich variety contained in the Scriptures finds expression in the living tradition of the church. The tradition has a legitimate place in so far as it expresses and interprets anew what is manifest or latent in the biblical message. Scripture and tradition do not compete with one another. Tradition does not imply a lack in the biblical message; it emphasizes rather its inexhaustible richness. The living tradition of the church bears witness to the regenerative power of the biblical message, because every real renewal of the Christian life stems from this source. But the renewal itself lives and expresses itself in the church's testimony of faith. To this tradition we might apply the words of the psalmist: "There is a river whose streams make glad the city of God." But the source of this stream is the inexhaustible spring of the biblical message. It is a false viewpoint to put Scripture and tradition in opposition and then try to solve the problem by balancing one against the other. The tradition which is not in line with the Bible, or does not develop biblical conceptions, is not a Christian tradition. But Scripture itself does not deny the tradition. It opens its doors wide and bids us trust in the guidance of the Spirit.

3. Tradition as a Guard in Biblical Interpretation

The primary significance of the tradition lies in the fact that the church's living testimony through the ages develops the riches of the biblical message. But the tradition has another function. When it appears in the form of fixed confessions of faith, it stands guard against irresponsible interpretations of the Bible. The history of the church indicates clearly the necessity of such control. The message of the Bible is indeed clear and homogeneous. But this does not mean that exegesis has always been aware of the homogeneity present in the great variety. The diversity may obscure the unity. When the Bible's own perspective is lost, interpretation may go completely astray. From the very earliest times in the history of the church there has always been much irresponsible interpretation, and this continues even today. A recent example is to be seen in the strange interpretations found in the teachings of Jehovah's Witnesses.

The ancient church expressed the central content of the Christian message in such brief confessions as the Apostles' and the Nicene Creeds. There were good reasons for this action. These ancient confessions have a thoroughly positive character. The purpose was to define and express the essential content of the New Testament message. But these statements had also a delimiting effect. They stand guard against various aberrations, a fact clearly seen in the Christological formula of Chalcedon.

When we consider the relationship between the ancient confession and the New Testament, we may properly regard the New Testament also from a confessional point of view as the primary confession of the church. Because of the message it proclaims, the New Testament is primarily a confession of Jesus Christ as Lord. Because he is the risen Christ, he is *Kyrios*, Lord. The resurrection is the presupposition on which the whole New Testament rests. Paul could even say: "If Christ has not been raised, your faith is futile" (I Cor. 15:17). The New Testament is, therefore, a confession of that victory which God has secured in and through Christ, and therefore also a confession of his transforming and re-creating act of redemption.

If the resurrection is the heart of the New Testament confession, the incarnation is the center of the confession of the ancient church. What this ancient confession declares is that the victory Christ won is *God's* own victory secured in the life of a historical *person*. What the Formula of Chalcedon rejects is, on the one hand, that Christ was some kind of half-God, or, in other words, that it was not God himself who appeared and worked in Christ; and, on the other hand, that his appearance was some kind of a theophany, and therefore he was not a real human being and our brother. The significance of the formula is not to be sought in the terminology used, such as the ancient conception of substance, etc., but rather in the rejection of the two extremes. The terms of the formula itself are not the decisive element, but the conception safeguarded by the rejection of these two extremes is definitive for faith.

Besides the New Testament confession of the resurrection of Christ and the ancient church's confession of the incarnation, Christianity possesses a third primary confession: the *Iustificatio sola fide—sola gratia* of the Reformation. Here, too, we find a delimitation, a rejection of the conception that man's salvation rests on any kind of human "merit." This third confession has not received such world-wide acceptance as the other two. It may nevertheless be regarded as a primary Christian confession, because it stands in a clear and unmistakable connection with the two earlier statements. If the foundation of our salvation is the act of God in Christ, then salvation is the work of God's grace alone. The formula, "through faith alone," has no other purpose than to stand guard over the other formula, "by grace alone." The Christian nature of this statement can be questioned only after it has become misinterpreted; which has frequently happened both within Roman and evangelical theology. It has not been accepted by the whole church, but it is unmistakably making progress. One indication of this is the fact that the Orthodox and evangelical communions represented at the Conference in Edinburgh, 1937, agreed on a statement concerning the meaning of the grace of God. "Our salvation is the gift of God and the fruit of his grace. It is not based on the merit of man, but has its root and foundation in the forgiveness which God in his grace grants to the sinner whom he receives to sanctify him." Another indication is the change that has appeared in the attitude of some Roman theologians toward the Reformation. They are beginning to appreciate in a new way what the fundamental religious forces at work in the Reformation were.

If we thus may speak of the three primary Christian confessions, we must recognize that fundamentally they are one. All three represent the same Christian confession, seen from three different points of view.

4. The Primacy of Scripture

Before we finish the discussion of the relationship between Scripture and tradition, we must consider two additional problems. The first is concerned with what we have said above about the confession as a guardian. It might appear as if the tradition would become superior to the Scriptures. This is not so, however, because the confession exercises no control over Scripture, only over the irresponsible interpretations of it. The confessions serve Scripture and stand under its control. The confessional statements must be subject to verification by Scripture. The guidance the confessions provide depends entirely on the fact that their content proves itself as something essential to the Christian message, and that the rejected conceptions are shown to be contrary to this biblical message.

The other problem concerns the distinction between Scripture and tradition. In modern times it has been emphatically asserted that the accepted distinction between Scripture and tradition is to some extent artificial since, from one point of view, Scripture is nothing but a record of the primitive tradition of the church. Historically this is no doubt a correct interpretation. The situation is not that the church is founded on Scripture, i.e., the New Testament, but rather that the collection and canonization of these documents was the work of the church itself.

Even though the New Testament may be regarded as primary tradition, its authority is not thereby diminished. We must point first of all to the immense and boundless importance of the development of the canon. Several modern scholars, especially Oscar Cullmann, have shown that the New Testament canon originated at a time when the danger of aberrations was especially acute in the early church. Only the formation of the canon provided the stability necessary for preventing a corruption and dissolution of the Christian message. The fundamental principle in the formation of the canon was that the documents to be included possessed apostolic character.

Apostolicity and canonicity were almost synonymous concepts. The apostles had been called to become the witnesses of Christ. The apostolicity of the New Testament made it for all time the fundamental and decisive witness to the act of God in Christ. The message appears here in original, pure, and uncorrupted form. Under these circumstances it becomes merely a question of terminology whether we are to speak of the New Testament canon as "primitive tradition." That it *may* be so designated does not in any way invalidate the primacy of Scripture in reference to later tradition within the church.

5. Tradition Must Not Be Interpreted in a Legalistic or Evolutionary Manner

The legitimacy of the tradition rests on the fact that the Holy Spirit is at work in the church. But the Spirit must not be identified with a certain ecclesiastical authority, nor with a continuous process of development. Both a legalistic and an evolutionary conception of tradition must be rejected.

A legalistic traditionalism implies that some ecclesiastical ruler is invested with divine authority. This development has taken place in the Roman church through the doctrine of the infallibility of the Pope in matters of teaching. The Pope has power "of himself without the consent of the church" (*ex sese sine consensu ecclesiae*) to determine what is to be the teaching of the church. A recent example of what the result of this great power might be is found in the new dogma of the Assumption of Mary. From the point of view of the biblical message this doctrine is nothing but sheer fantasy. What happened was only that the Pope sanctioned a concept which originated in the unbridled imagination of folk piety.

A legalistic view of the tradition has appeared also both in the Orthodox and the evangelical communions. This happens when the authority of councils and confessions is formally accepted; i.e., when the appeal is made to the external authority with which these documents have been invested rather than to their inherent quality and biblical derivation.

An evolutionary conception of the tradition has appeared both in Roman and evangelical theology. In both instances it has been connected with so-called modernistic movements. Roman theology, as for example in Cardinal Newman and in Loisy's book, *L'évangile et l'église*, conceives of the "development" in the figure of a seed that has gradually grown into a large tree. The implication is that growth itself sanctions what has appeared. The most prominent exponent of the evolutionary conception within evangelical theology was Schleiermacher, who fits the interpretation of the Christian faith into the framework of a monistic-evolutionary world view. This conception received classic expression in his formula: "*immer vollständiger durchdringt der heilige Geist das Ganze*" [more and more fully the Holy Spirit permeates the whole], a formula which applies to the Christian life as well as to the content of the Christian faith. "The whole" appears as a continuous progress, an incessant crescendo. Because the "development" is identified with the activity of the Holy Spirit, both Roman and evangelical "progress" becomes an uncritical and unrealistic optimism. The fact that the Christian message must in every age guard its purity against the heresies which in one way or another corrupt its biblical character is simply ignored.

6. "Pure Doctrine"

The expression "pure doctrine" has sometimes been used in a disparaging sense. The reason for this has been twofold. On the one hand, the theology which most energetically emphasized the concept of pure doctrine revealed in itself many shortcomings in regard to purity of teaching. On the other hand, the obscure and misleading distinction between *fides qua creditur* and *fides quae creditur*, common in the theology of a later period, created the impression that the content of faith was something relatively unimportant. It was not without good reason that our fathers placed such great emphasis on "pure doctrine." The content of faith cannot be separated from "faith itself." From one point of view faith depends entirely on what it believes about that God who is the object of faith. It is not unimportant for faith that the content of faith be "clearly and purely" conceived.

Christian history testifies to the fact that clarity in this matter is of immense importance for the life of faith. All the great revivals in the history of Christianity have been connected with a clearer insight into the meaning of the Christian message. It soon becomes apparent that the neglect or contempt of the efforts to secure clarity in regard to the meaning and content of faith leads to a weakening of faith itself. It can be stated that the uncertainty which has recently characterized the religious situation has been intimately connected with uncertainty in regard to the most central problems of Christian faith.

When it is stated that the purpose of theological work is to produce "pure doctrine," the function is exactly that which was stated in the first chapter. The function of theology is to state what Christian faith really is and what is genuinely Christian. This is something given once and for all in the biblical message concerning the deed of God in Christ. In this sense "pure doctrine" is something *in principle* given once and for all. But it is at the same time an ideal goal toward which theology must always strive. The "teaching" of any one period in the history of the church cannot lay claim to have spoken the last word and therefore to be regarded as "pure" for all time. The theological task is never finished. This is due to the fact that the object of theological study is so enormously rich that every new generation finds new treasures in it. It is true, however, that it is not a question of taking over certain concepts and formulas, but rather of fundamental motifs which must be expressed in terms of the new situation if they are to be understood at all. Each generation is confronted with the problem of interpreting the content of the Christian faith anew. The continuity lies in the fact that the fundamental event is the same in all ages. The Bible expresses this in the words: "Jesus Christ is the same yesterday and today and for ever" (Heb. 13:8). The changing aspects appear because the expressions change, and also because the Christian message is engaged in a continuous struggle with rival powers. This struggle at times threatens to obscure the meaning of faith, but it may also serve to reveal new aspects of its rich treasures. For both reasons theology must take it into serious consideration.

If theology therefore must continually work toward its ultimate and ideal goal, its attention must also at the same time be fixed on that biblical message which has been given once and for all, and likewise on that work which has been accomplished over the course of time in the interest of interpreting the content of faith. The ongoing theological research must be in intimate contact with this work. The history of Christian thought is not only a history of apostasy from an originally pure and genuine Christian faith. There is much in this history which appears both temporary and imperfect, but there are also gains which cannot, indeed, *must* not, be ignored. Theology may also gain a certain negative insight even from that which is imperfect. Neither does the history of Christian thought present simply a blurred confusion. There is in reality a deep, inner coherence, which is such that the vital viewpoints of faith itself break through wherever they have been suppressed. Each such experience brings new gains. But if theology consequently has something to learn from the whole history of Christian thought, it must be understood that it does not stop with the external formulas but penetrates to the motifs and purposes which these formulas are intended to express.

9. The Nature of the Affirmations of Faith

1. *The affirmations of faith are not metaphysical statements.* The affirmations of faith are *faith's* affirmations about God. They are therefore radically different from all rational metaphysics and cannot be confused or connected with metaphysical propositions.

2. *The symbolic character of the affirmations of faith.* The affirmations of faith are, without exception, of a symbolic character.

3. *The comprehensible and the incomprehensible.* The affirmations of faith are characterized by the fact that God is for faith both *Deus revelatus* and *Deus absconditus*. The consequence of this is not only that faith understands in part, but even that which faith grasps has an unfathomable character.

4. *The tension in the affirmations of faith.* The affirmations of faith are characterized throughout by a certain tension. As soon as this tension is changed into a logical or metaphysical paradox, the result is an irrationalism which is foreign to faith.

5. *The tension-filled unity of the content of faith.* If theology really wants to understand faith, it must forsake both the attempts of scholasticism to create a rationally consistent system and all endeavors to remove the cause of the tension. The collection of affirmations of faith which theology presents appear as a tension-filled unity.

1. *The Affirmations of Faith Are Not Metaphysical Statements*

When the nature of the affirmations of faith is to be determined, it must first of all be stated that these affirmations are affirmations of *faith*. This statement is tautological and may seem quite unnecessary. But in the history of theology it has frequently happened that this simple fact has been ignored. It is of utmost importance that a clear distinction be made between the affirmations of faith and rational metaphysics. Faith and its affirmation are one thing; metaphysics is something entirely different.

Since Christian faith is a faith in God who has revealed himself in Christ, it has something very definite to say about this God. The affirmations of faith, therefore, have their foundation in the divine revelation and in nothing else. They do not rest on a rational demonstration, nor on a theoretical and logical argumentation. They are not in the nature of conclusions drawn from that which can be theoretically demonstrated about the world and humanity. Faith does not become certain on the basis of logical proofs. In contrast to theoretical knowledge the position taken by faith is "existential," to use Kierkegaard's terminology. From the point of view of man's activity, faith appears always as an audacious and daring decision. Faith's affirmations about God, therefore, do not represent a segment of theoretical knowledge which might complement and correct the rest of our knowledge. It is not a question about some metaphysical knowledge of "God and the supernatural" which might complete and perfect the empirical knowledge of "the sensual world."

In the pure rationalism of the last period of the Enlightenment the affirmations of faith were simply identified with rational metaphysics. Apart from such identification the history of theology shows two ways in which the affirmations of faith have been united with metaphysics. One of these received its classic formulation in scholasticism, in which the affirmations of faith were regarded as complements to a knowledge of God received in a purely rational manner. A distinction was made between *articuli mixti* and *articuli puri* (cf. § 1, ¶ 3). Among the "mixed articles" derived partly from *ratio* and partly from *revelatio* were especially the theses about God. Metaphysics therefore found a place in the very center of the conception of faith. The result was that faith was confused with a supposed theoretical knowledge, and that the nature of the Christian conception of God was seriously obscured. The other way is that of the more recent idealistically influenced theology which places the Christian faith into an already given rational conception of the world. Schleiermacher may stand as the best example of this tendency. When the Christian faith is incorporated into a monistic and evolutionary world view, the natural result is that the pressure of this view is felt at all points and that it produces a perversion of the central content of faith. If the purpose of theology is to understand faith, it has every reason to be careful lest the affirmations of faith be mixed with metaphysics.

2. The Symbolic Character of the Affirmations of Faith

Since God is the whole content of Christian faith, and since the expressions which must be used in faith's affirmations about this God belong to this finite world, the affirmations necessarily are of a figurative or symbolic character. God is to faith the Eternal who cannot be contained within the limits of time and space. But all the categories which may be used belong within these limits. Under such circumstances no words can be found adequate to the subject. If theology pretends to speak of God in adequate terms, it is a sure sign that the interpretation of faith has become metaphysical and that the God of faith has been changed into an "object" among other objects. A theology which adheres to its function of understanding and interpreting faith must realize fully that all its expressions are of symbolic nature.

All the words used by faith to designate the attributes of God are figures taken from personal life. God's "love," God's "wrath," God as "Father" or as "Judge," are all human figures of speech. Faith itself is quite conscious that these words are imperfect tools, that it can speak only in a groping way about that which belongs to God, and that the reality is something much more than the words suggest. But this does not imply that faith should regard these symbolic expressions as unnecessary, or less essential, or not serviceable, or that they do not reveal that which is essential to faith. Quite the contrary. The symbols express a religious reality and are filled with the richest content. When faith speaks of God's love, forgiveness, wrath, and judgment, these expressions are concerned with that which is most real and essential to faith.

This fact that the affirmations of faith are of a symbolic character presents a twofold temptation. On the one hand, theology is tempted to seek to become independent of the figures and to remove from its exposition of the content of faith everything of anthropomorphic character. This tendency appears in scholastic theology and especially in that theology which has been influenced by idealistic philosophy. The desire is to elevate faith into a more rarefied and intellectual atmosphere. The actual result, however, is that faith is reinterpreted along metaphysical lines, faith's conception of God loses its vital content, and theology finally becomes nothing but unrealistic abstractions. The attempt to remove these allegedly offensive anthropomorphisms does not serve the best interest of theology.

On the other hand, it is important that theology be conscious of the limitations and dangers presented by the symbolic character of the affirmations of faith. Theology must not succumb to the temptation to regard the symbolic expressions as adequate definitions. There is always a danger that these human figures of speech may bring the conception of God down into the temporal sphere of human measurements and judgments. This is absolutely contrary to the intention of Christian faith, since the idea of the distance between the divine and the human is its most fundamental axiom. It may be added that the history of theology records many a discussion which has been more confusing than clarifying just because the symbolic character of faith's affirmations has not been adequately recognized. Thus, for example, it has been frequently debated whether it is legitimate to speak of God's "wrath," and the debate has been conducted on the assumption that this is a really adequate expression. When it has been concluded that the use of this term is not proper, the result has been that an essential feature of the Christian conception of God, his radical opposition to evil, is in danger of being lost. The inescapable conclusion is, therefore, that these figures of speech are necessary, but they must not be accepted as adequate concepts.

3. The Comprehensible and the Incomprehensible

The affirmations of faith are statements about the meaning of God's revelation or self-disclosure. Faith declares what it has comprehended of this revelation. But God is to faith not only *Deus revelatus* but also *Deus absconditus* (cf. § 3, ¶ 5). God does not cease to be *absconditus* because he appears as *revelatus*. The problem is to find what this means and what the consequences are in regard to the nature of the affirmations of faith.

It is obvious that the idea of the hidden God tends to limit the scope of the affirmations. This means, in the first place, that faith does not perceive the whole, it does not look at it with the eyes of God. When speculative theology used to say that man with the help of divine revelation thinks God's own thoughts, such an assertion is understandable from the point of view of rational metaphysics, but it is completely foreign to faith (Isa. 55:8 ff). Faith does not, like the philosophy of immanence, remove the boundary between the divine and the human. Faith understands, but it understands *in part*. The claim cannot be made that faith is able to perceive the whole world development from the point of view of divine government, or that it can survey the whole from God's point of view, or claim to be informed about the significance and purpose of everything that occurs. Faith does not have a ready answer to all the questions of the human spirit, nor can it solve all the riddles of human existence. The revelation of God means a revelation of God's inmost character, which provides a sure foundation for life; but it does not mean that all the obscurity which surrounds human life and history is removed. The desire to remove this obscurity would be a transgression of the limits which have been established as the conditions of the life of faith. Faith cannot be transformed into a rational world view. It is pertinent to mention the constant warnings of Luther against rationalistic speculations about "the hidden divine Majesty." Such speculations would be arrogance. This is the Tempter's voice: "You will be like God." To fall for this temptation is to commit *crimen laesae majestatis*, and implies that man brings the divine activity before the judgment seat of human reason and judicial concepts. *Deus absconditus* stands guard lest the limits of faith be transgressed, and emphasizes that under the conditions of this life faith only "understands in part."

But the idea of "the hidden God" does not mean *merely* that the understanding of faith has its insurmountable limitations. As has already been indicated (cf. § 3, ¶ 5), this idea is significant also in regard to the nature of these affirmations of faith. That which faith comprehends is likewise unfathomable, and the revelation itself is inscrutable. The New Testament often declares that the revelation is a revelation of a mystery (cf. Matt. 13:11; I Cor. 4:1; Eph. 1:9). But the decisive element is that revelation does not remove the mysteriousness.

Two things must be emphasized in this connection. In the first place, *every* pregnant affirmation of faith bears the mark of incomprehensibility. When faith declares that God is love, it is an expression of something that faith "comprehends." But at the same time it is perfectly clear that *precisely here* divine love appears as incomprehensible. Divine love is not of a rational character, and cannot be demonstrated in a rational fashion. It comes as a miracle. It cannot be measured according to human standards. It is perfectly obvious to faith that the love of God exceeds all human measurements, that human "love" can be so called only if it is an overflow of divine love, and that even then it is only a weak reflection of this divine love. When divine love "reveals itself" and meets man in action, it "surpasses knowledge" (Eph. 3:19), and the peace it gives "passes all understanding" (Phil. 4:7).

In the second place we must note the relation which exists in the realm of faith between the comprehensible and the incomprehensible. On the basis of what has already been said it is clear that this relation cannot mean that the incomprehensible grows less and disappears in the measure that faith perceives the revelation. In reality the very opposite is true. The more faith penetrates into the realm of divine revelation, the more it is confronted with the unsearchable. When Otto in his book, *The Idea of the Holy,* seems to understand the "rational" and the "irrational" in faith as two entities which counterbalance each other, the characteristic viewpoint of faith is not thereby very clearly expressed. The unfathomable is not something which lies by the side of the comprehensible, but that which faith perceives is by its nature incomprehensible even to faith. The deeper Luther penetrated into God's act of forgiveness whereby he enters into communion with sinful man, and the more this divine activity appeared as something *contra rationem et legem,* the more clearly he perceived that here he confronted an inscrutable mystery, a miracle which defied all description. The "miracle" in a religious sense is not identical with that which one does not understand, but with that which faith perceives. The miraculous is inseparably connected with the perception of something of God's activity. Consequently it is not something to be abolished as soon as theology has accomplished its work of clarification, but rather something which appears more clearly in the measure that the viewpoint of faith becomes clearer.

4. Tension in the Affirmations of Faith

The Christian affirmations of faith are characterized by a certain tension which cannot be eliminated. The reason for this tension is that all these affirmations, directly or indirectly, are affirmations about God. This element of tension has appeared already in the very idea of revelation in so far as "revelation" retains its active character, in so far as it is a question of that God who works in history. Faith perceives God as the Eternal, exalted above all temporal change; but also as the One who is active in the changing phases of history and present in contemporary life. The resultant tension cannot be removed by an application of the philosophical concepts of transcendence and immanence without at the same time removing the living God of faith. A very important aspect of this tension appears in the fact that the God of faith is the Sovereign who at the same time is engaged in a struggle against hostile forces in history. A solution cannot be found by taking the edge off either point of view. The peculiar viewpoint of faith would be obscured, whether the attempt is made to incorporate the "dualistic" element into a monistic system, or to find a rational world view on the basis of a thoroughgoing "dualism." The same tension is apparent in regard to the central content of the conception of God, divine love. It may be illustrated by faith's understanding of divine forgiveness. God stands as judge in a radical opposition to sin, but at the same time he enters into communion with sinful man, who then, as Luther says, becomes at the same time justified and a sinner (*simul iustus et peccator*). On the basis of this inner tension in the conception of God all the affirmations of faith might be examined. The same conditions would prevail everywhere. Two examples may be added. Sin is something given in the very condition of human life, and at the same time something completely voluntary. Faith is altogether a work of God, but it is at the same time man's choice and decision. Every attempt to harmonize these leads to a "synergism" which is foreign to faith.

It is obvious that this inner tension of faith places the most drastic demands on the theological analysis of the content of Christian faith. A review of the history of Christian thought indicates that two dangers lie particularly near. On the one hand theology is tempted to adjust or eliminate the tension in one way or another. On the other hand the danger is that the tensions are misinterpreted, so that paradoxes are constructed for their own sake. This is just as foreign to faith as rationalistic reinterpretations.

The tensional character of the affirmations of faith is purely *religious*. It is misinterpreted and perverted when it becomes logical or metaphysical. The paradoxes then become an end in themselves, and the result is an irrationalism that is foreign to faith. It becomes necessary to hold together contradictory theoretical and metaphysical propositions. *Credo quia absurdum* becomes the watchword. The background of these ideas has generally been a scholasticism or idealism which has attempted to adjust or to eliminate the tensions in Christian affirmations of faith. But this "irrational" reaction is dependent on the methodology of the opposition. This was the case with the nominalistic theology of the late Middle Ages and the same is true in regard to certain later theological schools which have been associated rightly or wrongly with the influence of Kierkegaard. A metaphysically oriented rationalism is opposed by a metaphysically oriented irrationalism. But this is something entirely different from the tensional character of the affirmations of faith. It is not a question here of holding fast to contradictory propositions of a logical and metaphysical nature. When, for example, God in forgiveness receives the sinner into communion with himself, this is a miracle, but it is not at all a *logically* contradictory proposition (cf. § 33, ¶ 2). Here the tension is not found in theories but in the active revelation and in the tension-filled event itself. It is this event which is reflected in the conceptions of faith. There is nothing of absurdity in this tension. It is rather a question of a content which cannot be rationally motivated and which is so abundant that it cannot be contained within rational categories.

5. The Tension-filled Unity of the Content of Faith

It was stated in the previous paragraph that theology is tempted to remove the inner tension which characterizes the Christian affirmations of faith. In the history of theology the principal attempts have been made by scholasticism and the theology influenced by idealism.

The essential mark of all scholastic theology is that it seeks to polish off those motifs of faith which stand in a relation of mutual tension in order to arrive at a rational adjustment. The most obvious examples of this process are found in Thomas Aquinas and in the scholasticism of the seventeenth century. In both of these the atonement is conceived of as an adjustment between God's love and his severe justice. The compensation given to God through Christ is the logical middle way between the exaction and remission of punishment (cf. § 26, ¶ 4). This means that both divine love and divine justice have been so adjusted that they can be logically held together. The divine love has lost its unmediated and spontaneous character, and has lost that ineffable depth which transcends the judicial system as it enters into communion with the sinner. But divine justice has also lost its full power. If its demand is satisfied by a compensation, its barb has been removed and its radicalism broken. Scholasticism treats all the other affirmations of faith in the same way. The process of rational adjustment is in evidence everywhere. As an additional example its understanding of the idea of faith is a case in point. In one way or another the offensive tension between faith as altogether God's work and faith as man's choice and decision is lessened. The result is invariably a "synergism" in which neither point of view is properly recognized.

Idealistic theology has attempted to remove this tension by suppressing its causative factors. The tension between divine love and divine justice or wrath is removed by suppressing the latter. The idea of God is "humanized." Everything is concentrated around the divine "Fatherhood," and divine love is given a rational character, even though it is still derived from the "revelation."

It is obvious that the viewpoint characteristic of faith cannot be expressed either in scholasticism's adjustments or in idealism's removal of the cause of the tension. If theology is to understand and explicate the content of faith, it must obviously pay strict attention to this element of tension which belongs to the life of faith and expresses itself in the affirmations of faith. Otherwise the interpretation of theology becomes a reinterpretation. But the presence of this tension does not at all mean that the content of faith lacks unity. Unity exists in spite of tension. Even if this unity cannot be expressed in a harmonious system of thought, faith nevertheless has a unified point of view which includes all tensions. The reason for this is that it is not concerned with metaphysical propositions which are logically contradictory and mutually incompatible. Faith's conception of God is in the last analysis not broken (cf. § 13), and the divine activity is not divided but unified. The unity is the tension-filled unity of the active revelation. Faith is not rationalistic. Its nature is not metaphysical irrationalism. But its affirmations have a tensional character, since the wealth of the divine activity of revelation is so vast that it cannot be comprehended within the categories of human thought.

10. The Certainty of Faith

1. *Theology and the problem of certainty of faith.* The certainty of faith is a certainty about that revelation of God whereby faith lives. The problem of the certainty of faith can be dealt with by theology only in so far as it analyzes and defines the nature of this certainty.

2. *The certainty of faith is not demonstrable.* The certainty of faith does not possess a *demonstrable* character. The idea that it can be based on rational proofs is contrary to the nature of both science and faith.

3. *The certainty of faith is not pragmatic.* Neither does the certainty of faith possess a *pragmatic* character. It cannot be certified by citing the significance of faith for other areas of life, or by showing that faith satisfies a human "need." A pragmatism of this kind is contrary to the theocentric character of faith and is more apt to destroy than to establish certainty.

4. *The certainty of faith—a certainty by experience?* Nor is the certainty of faith *experiential* in the sense that the certainty of the God-relationship should be based on an inference drawn from past

"experiences" and events. Individual "experiences" do not undergird faith; it is rather faith that undergirds and makes possible these "experiences."

5. *The nature of Christian certainty*. In the analysis of the nature of the certainty of faith it must be noted that from one point of view faith is audacious; but, on the other hand, it must be emphasized that its audacious *yes* is an inescapable necessity, the subjugation of man by the revelation of God through which he "is led away from himself." In this sense the *testimonium spiritus sancti internum* determines the nature of this certainty.

1. Theology and the Problem of Certainty of Faith

The problem of Christian certainty must receive notice in this part which deals with faith and theology. There are few problems that have received a more questionable treatment from the point of view of both faith itself and scientific study. The history of theology is full of so-called apologetic attempts which display as much ignorance of the nature and conditions of faith as they are questionable from a theological and scientific point of view. Under these circumstances we must at the outset define the manner in which this problem can be treated by theology.

The same principle must govern here as in all theological research, which is that the only purpose is to understand and interpret the nature of Christian faith. The problem of Christian certainty must be treated from the same point of view. The intention must not be to present some kind of "apology" for faith or in a general way to demonstrate its "truth." The problem is rather to analyze and eluci-date the nature of that certainty which is found in faith itself.

It has already been shown that faith and divine revelation are cor-relative concepts (cf. § 2, ¶ 2). The certainty of faith cannot have reference to anything other than that revelation of God which mani-fests itself to faith and by which faith lives. An investigation into the problem of the certainty of faith must under the circumstances have no other purpose than to define the nature of the relationship of faith to this revelation and to indicate how this relation appears to faith itself. The theological investigation cannot go beyond this point. To do so would be at the same time to transgress the boundaries of theology.

2. The Certainty of Faith Is Not Demonstrable

The certainty of Christian faith is not dependent upon the demonstrable character of divine revelation. The idea that scientific studies and investigations should provide a solid foundation for faith and give it certainty is contrary to the nature of both science and faith. If this were indeed possible, it would mean that science, within the empirical reality which is the object of its study, could discover something of that revelation of which faith speaks. The discoveries of science would in that case verify faith. But this would obviously be to ask something of science which it cannot give without ceasing to be scientific. Whether it be a question of a scientific investigation of nature or of history, such a study cannot penetrate to that which is decisive for faith—the revelation of God. What has been said (§ 4) about historical research is just as true in regard to the study of nature. God is not found by telescopes and chemical experiments any more than through a methodical analysis of humanity's historical documents. It is quite a different matter when the great scientists even of our own day stand humbly before the mystery of existence and let their surmises range beyond the boundaries of research.

Faith on its part is not conscious of having originated in or of resting upon any argumentation of a theoretic and demonstrative character. It is, however, fully conscious of its character as an audacious personal decision and a bold *yes*. Every attempt to demonstrate theoretically the reality and universality of revelation is absolutely foreign to faith and contrary to its fundamental point of view. Even if some results could be obtained in this way, these could produce only a metaphysically defined idea of God, which is something entirely different from that living and active revelation of which faith speaks.

3. The Certainty of Faith Is Not Pragmatic

If then scientific study cannot give a decisive testimony for the certainty of faith, it might easily be suggested that the defense of the Christian faith must be made on the basis of the significance which this faith has in the various areas of life. Such pragmatic arguments have been widely used in Christian apologetics. It can hardly be denied that Christian faith has demonstrated its "value" both in general cultural life and especially in the sphere of ethics. As a matter of fact it is also important that these "values" be studied and clarified. But it is quite a different matter to base Christian certainty on the consideration of the significance of faith for the various areas of life. It is impossible to complete such a demonstration, for two reasons in particular. On the one hand, it is obvious that by this method one arrives only at a postulated certainty. The achievements of faith are noted and the conclusion is drawn that the power which has produced these must be inviolate. It goes without saying, however, that such a reference to human achievements of faith hardly affords the desired security; on the contrary, the continuous search for external results must lead finally to a constant insecurity. On the other hand, it must be said that the evidence adduced here is not congruous with faith itself. It implies that the Christian faith should be evaluated and verified according to other criteria than those which are essential to faith itself. The dominant principle of faith is communion with God, and faith must unconditionally decline to be judged in a court in which this principle is not recognized as supreme. It does not recognize "culture" or any other human values as the court of last appeal. Through its communion with God it is lifted up above everything that belongs to the "world," and in it there is always something otherworldly and supramundane. Under such conditions it would be impossible to accept the judgment of the court of culture and human values as decisive. A judgment from this court would be decisive only if faith were nothing more than a world-affirming optimism. It generally becomes apparent that the attempt to maintain Christian faith by emphasizing its general cultural significance is easily combined with a reinterpretation of faith along this line. But then it happens, strangely and characteristically enough, that this reinterpretation of faith undermines and finally destroys even that significance which faith actually has in reference to human "values." This significance is inseparably connected with the fact that faith is *not* a world-affirming optimism, and that it does *not* establish in the world a new immanent goal in addition to others. The real significance of faith depends entirely on the fact that it lives in "a kingdom which is not of this world."

In this connection the attempts to verify the certainty of faith through its ethical effects must be noted. It is especially important to note this "ethical proof," because in the recent period of theological study it has been frequently regarded as being in the last analysis decisive. The claim is thus made that the Christian faith is the necessary condition for the realization of the moral task. The moral ideal which is contained in the Christian idea of the kingdom of God is the *absolute* moral ideal, and Christian faith appears as that power which actualizes this idea and guarantees its realization within ourselves and others. This is supposed to be the validation of the Christian faith. It cannot, of course, be said that a reference to the moral power of Christian faith is unwarranted or unessential. It must rather be acknowledged that the Christian message contains a heightening of the moral demand, and that it has proved to be the mightiest ethical power.

But the question is whether this constitutes a decisive argument in regard to the certainty of faith. It must rather be maintained that this argumentation, if it claims to be decisive, does not lead to certainty, but to continuous uncertainty. The certainty of faith cannot be based on the ethical effects of faith. What would this ultimately imply? Evidently that our certainty of faith would be entirely dependent upon our ability to fulfill the ethical demand which Christianity presents. A real certainty of faith would then be possible only when it has been definitely established that the ethical demand for perfection has been fully met. It is clear that this can lead to nothing else than a constant uncertainty. It is just as evident that this argumentation does not agree with the testimony of faith itself, and that it leads straight to a moralism against which the deeper testimony of faith reacts most vigorously. Even in this case faith has been judged and evaluated from without, not according to the points of view which are determinative for faith itself. The ethical "proof" could, after all, claim to give the decisive verdict only if Christianity becomes pure ethics. It is consequently typical that this "proof" has been regarded as so important in the most recent period of theological study. This indicates how real the danger has been that Christianity may be completely transformed and become purely ethical.

Faith itself must reject all attempts to "save" faith by transforming it into something other than what it really is. It might be in the interest of faith to see and ponder its significance for the various areas of life, and especially for the moral life. But faith cannot buy its right to exist by selling its birthright for a mess of pottage. It is such a transaction which faith perceives in the attempt to make its significance for the various areas of life central, in utter disregard of that what faith itself conceives of as the beginning and the end, the Alpha and Omega, namely, communion with God.

4. The Certainty of Faith—A Certainty by Experience?

When in the interest of apologetics enthusiastic references have been made to "experience," the idea has generally been that these experiences should become a surety for faith and a guarantee of its security. In this sense the expression, "experiential proof" of faith has been used. It is obvious that in so far as certainty belongs to the Christian life, it must be connected with "experience." It is after all a part of human life. It is, however, indubitable that the nature of Christian certainty is completely misinterpreted if it is made to find its support and basis in religious experiences and in religious feelings as such. This would obscure the fact that faith knows no other basis than divine revelation. If the strength and intensity of religious feelings were made the basis of certainty, it would rest on something human, just as much as is the case when certainty is predicated on man's moral transformation and his ethical qualifications. In reference to certainty Luther has spoken a classic word: *haec est ratio, cur nostra theologia certa sit: quia rapit nos a nobis et ponit nos extra nos, ut non nitamur viribus, conscientia, sensu, persona, operibus nostris . . .* ["This is the reason why our theology is certain: because it snatches us away from ourselves and places us outside of ourselves, lest we rest upon human strength, conscience, feelings, character, our own works . . ."].[1] The certainty of faith does not depend upon anything; rather, faith "snatches us away from ourselves and places us outside of ourselves." It is just as impossible to depend on "experiences" (*sensu, persona*) as it is to build on our own works, on "work-righteousness." In contrast to any such argumentation Luther points to the divine revelation, to "the word and promise of God."

The testimony of experience cannot therefore be accepted in such a way that experience is separated from divine revelation as some-

[1] *WA*, 40¹, p. 589.

thing given in and by itself. The certainty of faith about the revelation is not founded on personal experiences, nor is it a conclusion based on these experiences. Faith does not find God at the end of a logical syllogism. All experiences have their foundation in the divine revelation as far as faith is concerned. Faith is a faith in the divine revelation, not in personal experiences. This is fully attested by an analysis of the testimony of Christian life. Such an analysis indicates that the certainty of faith does not simply come and go, depending upon changing religious experiences, and that faith does not rely on these changing experiences, but only on God. Consequently faith *can* persist in the midst of tribulation and distress—yes, even when the experiences of life seem to speak a language directly opposite to that of faith. Faith is not "confuted" by this. Even under those circumstances faith finds expression in a "nevertheless." Living and striving faith finds that even these experiences which endanger its existence serve as an incentive to hold fast still more securely to that God from whom no temporal distress can separate the believer. Thus Christian certainty finds classic expression in the Johannine word: "Did I not tell you that if you would believe you would see the glory of God?" (John 11:40). There is a faith that does "not see," and yet believes. Because faith is not a faith in experiences, but altogether a faith in God alone, it can live even under those circumstances when God seems most remote, and can carry on to new experiences and a new vision of "the glory of God."

5. The Nature of Christian Certainty

The examination of the various attempts to prove and substantiate faith which has been made in the previous paragraphs may appear as a process of undressing, until faith stands naked and in want of all protective covering. In reality it is self-evident that faith cannot in the last analysis rely on any such line of argumentation. Faith is communion with God. When faith is true to its own nature, it is clear that no certainty of faith can arise and continue except as an inner conviction of being overwhelmed by God, or as an encounter with something which validates itself as a "revelation" of God. All other argumentation is merely a substitute. If this foundation is wanting, all other supports are in vain; if it is there, all other supports are superfluous. The foundation of faith is the divine revelation; and the certainty of faith is characterized by an inner conviction that this "revelation" really is a *divine* revelation, or, in other words, by what faith calls "the testimony of the Holy Spirit" (*testimonium spiritus sancti internum*). Christian faith has from the beginning again and again pointed to this testimony of the Spirit. The decisive element, according to Paul, is that "it is the Spirit himself bearing witness with our spirit" (Rom. 8:16), because "no one comprehends the thoughts of God except the Spirit of God. Now we have received not the spirit of the world, but the Spirit which is from God" (I Cor. 2:11-12). In a similar way the Johannine writings speak at length of that testimony which "the Spirit of truth" gives (cf. I John 4:13; 5:10). "Consequently," says Luther, "God must tell you in your heart: this is God's word." It is true that sometimes in the history of Christian thought this testimony has been co-ordinated with other foundations of certainty by reference to a multitude of reasons supporting the divine authority of the Scriptures, but this cannot be justified. The proof of which we are speaking here cannot be either replaced or complemented by attempts to verify divine revelation in any other way.

The nature of Christian certainty can be defined only by delineating those features of faith which are relevant and important in this connection. We have already called attention to the twofold aspect of faith. On the one hand it is a daring decision, and on the other hand it is man's subjection by God.

Faith, as decision, as a daring and audacious *yes,* stands guard against all attempts to make the certainty of faith secure by means of external proofs. The decision in question lies beyond all such argumentation. The revelation of God cannot be certified by any rational arguments. It is, as stated before, a revelation in secret, a revelation which appears in the guise of history. The revealed God is also the hidden God. This is true of everything that is called a revelation of God, and consequently also of the revelation in Christ. In him, too, the revelation of God appears in a humble form and in the guise of history. This character of the revelation cannot be reasoned away by constructing a humanly idealized Christ. This would lead only to a fatal confusion between the divine and "the highest

human." There is always something of audacity and bold discovery
when faith perceives in the guise of history the direct voice of God.

But the interpretation of the nature of faith could not be more
thoroughly perverted than if, on the basis of what has just been said,
it is concluded that faith's *yes* to the voice of God should have a
subjective and arbitrary character. This is completely contrary to the
testimony of faith about itself. We must listen very carefully to this
testimony if we are to be able to understand and define the nature of
Christian certainty. It is not within the realm of possibility to suggest
that man should place the alleged voice of God before his own bar
of judgment and decide whether or not it is a real voice of God. This
voice meets man rather with an authority which he cannot escape
and from which there is no appeal. It overwhelms and subdues him
with an inner compulsion he cannot escape. That which is decisive
for faith is that man is *vanquished* and, in Luther's words, snatched
out from himself. In this inner, inescapable compulsion the certainty
of faith is hidden. This is *testimonium spiritus sancti internum.*

The Content
of the
Christian Faith

11. The Plan of the Book

The following exposition of the content of Christian faith will be divided into three chief parts: The Living God, The Act of God in Christ, and The Church of God.

In the previous chapters we maintained that the Christian faith is founded upon and determined by that context of revelation, or drama of revelation, whose center is the act of God in Christ. Faith receives its content from the message about this context of revelation and this divine act. We must now explicate in greater detail this content of faith which is given therewith. We must present what faith has to say about that God who is the sovereign ruler in the realm of faith; the act of God in Christ; the realization of the God-relationship, and its position within the church—that communion in which faith lives and is nourished. Part I begins with a presentation of the essential features of the Christian conception of God centered in divine love, and then proceeds to define faith's conception of the divine activity in its three parts: salvation, creation, and judgment. On the basis of this exposition Part II considers in more detail how divine love establishes the God-relationship. The subject of the first division of this part is divine love's act of reconciliation in Christ; of the second, the divine act of forgiveness which establishes the Christian relationship to God. Finally, Part III presents the continuing activity of God as a work of the Spirit which creates the communion of saints, and then proceeds to examine the constitutive factors of the church and the relation of the individual Christian to it.

It may be necessary to indicate briefly why this particular order has been adopted, and especially why the Christian conception of God has been placed first. Since we have already declared in previous chapters that the foundation of Christian faith has been laid in the context of revelation dominated by the event of Christ, it might be assumed that this event of Christ which is definitive for the conception of God ought to be placed first. But from a systematic point of view this is not necessary. It is necessary only that the conception of God presented here—whatever its place—really receive its decisive character from the revelation in Christ.

From another point of view it might be suggested that the presentation ought to begin with the communion created by God. This order could be justified on the basis of the fact that all Christian life is a life in and through the church of Christ. The theological task might then be defined as the obligation to explain and interpret what is taking place within the church. From this starting point the whole content of the Christian faith could easily be described. That we have decided to begin our presentation with a discussion of "the living God" is not due simply to the influence of the traditional order of the articles of the Creed. By the very order of the subjects we have intended to indicate that God is sovereign in the realm of faith, that Christian faith is thoroughly theocentric, and that all its affirmations are affirmations about God. The character of the conception of God is decisive for the whole content of Christian faith.

In other respects the outline of the book speaks for itself. The main purpose has been that the method of presentation might to some extent indicate the inner, organic connection between the various phases of Christian faith.

A remark may be added relative to the treatment of the eschatological problems. It was formerly common to treat these questions in a final chapter. This method could be interpreted to mean that eschatology constitutes the highest and final point in the content of faith. But in reality the result was that the subject came to be regarded as an appendix to the main discussion. In recent expositions of the Christian faith the eschatological point of view has, as a rule, been sadly neglected. Even though these problems are not directly discussed in any special section of this work, the intention is not to obscure their significance for Christian faith. Since they are treated here in various places in all parts of this work, it becomes clear that eschatological viewpoints must not be regarded as an appendage, but rather as representing an essential aspect which belongs to the whole content of Christian faith, and that Christian faith and life as a whole are eschatologically determined.

From one point of view eschatology is, as C. H. Dodd expresses it, "realized eschatology." The new age has come in Christ. But the eschatological perspective points at the same time to that which shall come: "the life of the world to come." The drama of revelation is an eschatological drama of redemption.

Part 1

THE LIVING GOD

The Christian Concept of God

12. Holiness as the Background of the Concept of God

1. *The background of the concept of God.* The expression, the Holy One, is synonymous with the term God. Holiness does not express the content of the Christian concept of God, but it is that background without which the idea of God cannot be projected. *Everything* which belongs to God and his realm bears the imprint of holiness, and appears, therefore, in relation to everything human as exalted and sovereign.

2. *Holiness as a sentinel.* As such a background, holiness has a four-fold significance. It asserts the purely religious character of the idea of God (in contrast to moralism and ethicism), the majesty of God (in contrast to eudaemonism), and his unfathomableness (in contrast to rationalism); and it repudiates all attempts to identify the divine and the human (in contrast to mysticism).

1. *The Background of the Concept of God*

The word "holy" is such a fundamental word in religion that "the Holy One" is accepted as synonymous with God. To say that God is holy is in reality the same as saying that God is God. "Holy" is a word which belongs exclusively within the sphere of religion. In religious language "holy" signifies something that is "other" and "different" from what is worldly and relative. That God is the Holy One means, therefore, that in relationship to the world he is exalted and sovereign. God's "holiness" establishes therefore a definite line of demarcation between the divine and the merely human. God is God and man is man. The holiness of God stands as a guardian against all attempts to weaken and obliterate this line. The divine is something other than the human, and must not be confused with "humanity at its highest."

When the word "holy" is used in connection with God, it is important that it retain its original religious significance. It is well known that the idea of the holy has often been reinterpreted in the direction of ethics, in an attempt to identify it with moral perfection. It is indeed unquestionable that the idea of the holy in reference to the concept of God strongly emphasizes also moral perfection. But as holiness is reinterpreted in the direction of morality, sin is likewise interpreted moralistically and loses its religious orientation. It is therefore, as has been stated, very important that holiness retain its original and purely religious meaning. Only when the separation between the divine and the human implied in holiness is given due consideration, and the divine is allowed to appear as unconditioned majesty in relation to the human, can holiness be of fundamental significance for the Christian conception of God.

Even if the Holy One is accepted as synonymous with God, it does not mean that we have thereby obtained a living and significant conception of the God of faith. We may not even say that this holiness constitutes a divine "attribute" which could be compared with other divine attributes. It is not accidental that holiness is more easily defined in negative than in positive terms. If holiness were understood as a divine "attribute" among others, as has often been done, this definition would be both too ample and too limited. Too ample, inasmuch as the significance of holiness is intended to give a certain concrete content to the conception of God; and too limited, for holiness is not confined to any one phase or feature, but belongs to the idea of God as a whole.

Holiness is the background and the atmosphere of the conception of God. This word "background" may seem to minimize its significance, but this is certainly not the case, for this background is first of all absolutely necessary. Without it there would in reality be no conception of *God*. The perspective would lack the depth which is absolutely necessary if the idea of God is to be properly projected. Holiness is the foundation on which the whole conception of God rests. In addition it gives a specific tone to each of the various elements in the idea of God and makes them parts of a fuller conception of *God*. Every statement about God, whether in reference to his love, power, righteousness, and so on, ceases to be an affirmation about God when it is not projected against the background of his holiness.

Only when holiness colors the concept of love do we understand that
we are dealing with divine love (cf. § 14).

The God of Christian faith is, therefore, not less "holy" than the
God of the Old Testament, even though the word itself may not
appear as frequently in the New Testament. The relation between
the Old and the New Testaments could hardly be more grossly misinterpreted than by setting the fatherhood of God in opposition to
the idea of God as the Holy One. Holiness is the obvious presupposition of the testimony of primitive Christianity concerning God.
It is significant that the first petition of the Lord's Prayer reads: "Hal-
lowed be thy name." It is also significant that the word holy, or its
cognates, almost automatically enters the Christian vocabulary when
we talk about something which *belongs to the sphere of God:* Christ
—the Holy One of God; the Holy Spirit; the Holy Christian Church;
Holy Writ; holy sacraments, and so on. Neither is it an accident that
the Swedish Mass begins with the *Trisagion,* which constitutes an
important background for the whole subsequent worship service.

2. Holiness as a Sentinel

When holiness constitutes the background of the idea of God, it
guarantees that every affirmation about God retains its *purely religious*
character. It has been customary to divide the attributes of God into
metaphysical and ethical categories, but this division, although it may
be serviceable for a rationally constructed idea, is entirely inappro-
priate to a Christian conception of God. Metaphysical scholastic
theology, both before and after the Reformation, had no inner contact with faith itself, and consequently lost itself in abstract and unrealistic speculations about the essence of God. It can readily be
understood that as a reaction to this approach "the ethical attributes"
should be made central, as in the theology of the nineteenth century,
but the result was a moralism which left out of religion much that
was essential. When A. Ritschl found that holiness could not be contained within the ethical categories and consequently eliminated it from
his conception of religion, it indicates how strong this moralistic
tendency really was. This moralistic limitation of religion cannot be
overcome by adding the "metaphysical attributes" to the ethical. This
is not a guarantee that the religious character of the conception of

God will be adequately expressed. The only method whereby this can be accomplished is really to allow holiness to appear as the background of *every* statement that is made about God. Then, and only then, is there a guarantee that abstract and irrelevant speculations will be eliminated, and that religion will not be transformed into ethics.

Holiness stands as a sentinel against all eudaemonistic and anthropocentric interpretations of religion. Holiness meets us as unconditional majesty. Every attempt to transform Christian faith into a religion of saisfaction and enjoyment is thereby doomed to failure. Egocentricity masquerading in the robes of religion is excluded. Faith in God cannot be measured and evaluated from the point of view of human happiness and needs, even if these concepts be ever so refined and "spiritualized." God is not someone faith employs with an eye to the higher or lower advantages which he may be able to furnish; nor is he someone we can call upon in order that our needs and desires may be met. Even if anthropocentricity should disguise itself in the most clever costume, it will inevitably be unmasked by the Holy One. Every tendency to make God serve human interests is irrevocably doomed. When Ritschl found the "value" of religion in its ability to give man "dominion over the world" and spiritual *Selbstbehauptung* [self-assertion], he misinterpreted Christian faith in an anthropocentric direction. To meet God as the Holy One is to be placed under a supreme compulsion, and to be confronted by a power advancing in sovereign majesty. If God is the Holy One, he is also the One on whom we are "absolutely dependent." We are in his power, not he in ours. He is the undisputed ruler in the realm of faith.

Finally, the idea of holiness emphasizes the separation between the divine and the human in opposition to both rationalistic and mystical interpretations of religion. Rationalistic speculation and mysticism are, to be sure, very different. They have, however, more in common than is at first apparent, and it is not accidental that mysticism very often runs parallel to rationalistic speculation. Each in its own way tends to eliminate the distinction between the divine and the human. When rationalistic speculation with profane familiarity attempts to capture the divine in human thought forms and to make the spirit of man think the thoughts of God, the idea of holiness resists such

presumption, because it will not let us forget that the revealed God
is at the same time the hidden God (cf. § 9, ¶ 3). But it is likewise
opposed to the elimination of the separation between the divine and
the human by that mysticism whose goal is identity and the absorption of the human into the divine. To stand before the Holy One
is something entirely different from being absorbed into the infinite
where all differences are obliterated and disappear.[1]

13. Tension and Unity in the Concept of God

1. *The tension in the concept of God.* The tension between different aspects which characterize the conception of God cannot be
resolved by a rational compromise, nor can it be eliminated by
humanizing the idea of God.

2. *The unity in the concept of God.* If the Christian idea of God
nevertheless appears as a unity, it is a unity in tension. Only in and
through such a tension-filled synthesis can Love appear as the last
word of faith about God, and consequently as the governing center
of the Christian conception of God.

1. Tension in the Concept of God

When, by way of introduction to our discussion of the content of
faith, the subject of tension and unity in the concept of God is
introduced here, we may be permitted to refer to what has already
been stated in principle about the tension and unity of the affirmations of faith (cf. § 9, ¶ 4 and 5). The fundamental principles enunciated there must now be applied as we sketch the Christian conception
of God. The word in First John, "God is love," tells us what is the
center and focus of this conception. This is the most essential and
important statement that can be made about God. But it is one thing
that love is maintained as the center of the Christian conception of
God, it is quite a different thing *how* it is maintained. It can never
be sufficiently emphasized that this latter, *how divine love is treated,*

---

[1] The idea of holiness is well expressed in the hymn by Reginald Heber:
    Holy, Holy, Holy! though the darkness hide Thee,
    Though the eye of sinful man Thy glory may not see,
    Only Thou art holy: there is none beside Thee
    Perfect in power, in love, and purity.

is the most important question of all. That Christian faith centers in divine love as the essential element in the Christian conception of God is of utmost and decisive importance. The history of theology makes it very evident that this divine love has easily been interpreted in such a way that its depth has been lost and its distinctive features obscured. This is ineviably the case when, on the basis of love, the attempt is made to construct a uniform, homogeneous, and rational idea of God; or, in other words, as soon as the inner tension which characterizes the Christian conception of God is resolved or eliminated. The peculiar viewpoint of the Christian faith cannot be consistently maintained unless this tension is seriously taken into consideration. Then it becomes impossible to arrive at a rationally constructed concept of God. But in its stead appears a living figure whose features change and clash one with the other, but whose character nevertheless, as far as faith is concerned, bears the mark of unity, the living God.

In regard to the Christian affirmations about God three thematic ideas may be distinguished: the idea of *power*, to which a number of expressions belong, such as omnipotence, sovereignty, eternity, omnipresence, omniscience, etc.; the idea of *judgment*, which deals with God's avenging and condemning justice, his wrath, etc.; the idea of *love*, which contains a number of varying expressions such as goodness, mercy, grace, etc. The relation between these three ideas has always been a source of difficulty to theology, because, humanly speaking, there seems to be a tension between them. This tension can be illustrated most readily by asking the following questions. How can God's "love" for men co-exist with his radical condemnation of sin? How can God be Power and Love at the same time? If all power belongs to him, then this power does not seem to possess the character of love. But if God is love, then this love does not seem to be the sovereign power in the world. When theology has had to take account of this tension within the relationship between God and man, it has (cf. § 9) sometimes adopted an irrationalism which is satisfied to place contradictory, theoretical propositions side by side ("metaphysical irrationalism"), and at other times has tried to readjust or to eliminate the tension by a process of rationalization.

We stated in previous chapters that all scholastic theology is char-

acterized by the attempt to adjust the tension rationally, and that the
theology influenced by idealistic philosophy has always tried to eliminate it. These attempts must now be more closely analyzed. The
attempt of *scholastic* theology to effect a rational adjustment has
always been characterized by *compromise*. The scholasticism of both
the Middle Ages and the post-Reformation era abounds in such compromises. One example of this has already been given (§ 9, ¶ 5),
namely, the rational adjustment of the tension between divine love
and "retributive justice" in the Latin theory of the atonement. The
result is that love is weakened and justice loses its radical opposition
to evil. But it may also be added that although the sharp point of
"justice" is broken, it nevertheless appears as primary in relation to
love. Divine love is incorporated into a system of retributive justice;
it is governed by *iustitia*. Love is not free until justice has been given
due compensation. In the same way scholastic theology attempts by
compromise to adjust the tension between power and love. Thomistic
theology furnishes abundant illustrations. In his interpretation of
divine power Thomas makes use of the category of cause. The
"omnipotence" of God means that God is *causa prima*, and consequently he is the cause of everything that occurs. When divine love
is incorporated into this scheme of cause and effect, it becomes, so
to speak, naturalistic. From this point of view it is not strange that
divine "grace" is obscurely defined as substantial "powers," and that
love is thus demoted. But it may also happen that the theology of
compromise leads to an infringement on divine power. Thus man's
salvation and "justification" are not completely the work of divine
love. Human "merits" must also be given a place. Then, no matter
how closely these merits are circumscribed, the divine sovereignty
is limited. Post-Reformation scholasticism, which at least *desired* to
maintain the *sola gratia* of the Reformation, was naturally strongly
opposed to the medieval idea of merits. But its very scholasticism
forced it into making compromises. This can be seen in the idea,
popular in "orthodox" circles, that God justifies man *ex praevisa fide*.
Finally, it is characteristic of all scholasticism that it attempts to give
an explanation of how the evil in the world can co-exist with the
divine will. This is connected with the desire to "extend" faith into
a rational explanation of the universe. It is self-evident that this must

lead to a minimizing of the radical opposition of the divine will to evil.

The theology which began with the Enlightenment and flourished during the eighteenth and nineteenth centuries attempted to remove the tension by *humanizing* the idea of God. In contrast to scholasticism it accepted divine love as the central content of "the Christian conception of God." The program of this whole theological approach was expressed in the title of a book published in the eighteenth century: *Dass die Lehre von Gottes Vaterliebe die Grundlehre der christlichen Religion sie* [*The Doctrine of God's Fatherly Love is the Fundamental Doctrine of the Christian Religion*]. Thus Schleiermacher also summed up his theory of the reflection of the divine "attributes" in "the pious state of the soul" in this statement: *Gott ist die Liebe* [God is love]. From a purely formal point of view there can be no objection to this. Schleiermacher's statement is formally identical with the Johannine word: God is love, which includes everything that is essential to the New Testament as a whole. But here we must use the criterion that the most important question in relation to the conception of God is *how* the divine love is brought in. It cannot be denied that the dominant theology during the eighteenth and nineteenth centuries often described divine love in such a way that its sovereign majesty, its radical opposition to evil, and its unfathomable depth were obscured. The idea of God became superficial by being humanized. There has been an abundant proclamation of the love of God which has lacked power and firmness. There have been two reasons for this superficiality. In the first place, the radical opposition of divine love to evil has been obscured and broken —which, from another point of view, means that the concept of sin has been weakened or lost. In the second place, the attempt has been made, on the basis of idealistic philosophy, to incorporate Christian faith into a monistic and evolutionistic world view. If it is assumed, on the basis of such a monistic metaphysic, that divine love is reflected everywhere, the danger is that it loses its character, and also that the supposed everywhere becomes nowhere. Under these circumstances men were unable to comprehend the difficult conditions under which divine love operates in human life, and became insensible to the deepest perceptions of Christian faith, which sees divine love as a cross-bearing love engaged in a bitter struggle and winning its victory by a self-giving sacrifice. We may summarize, therefore, the result of our investigation in this statement: In the measure that the tension is removed, divine love loses its most significant character and content.

2. Unity in the Concept of God

If theology really desires to understand and interpret faith, it cannot either adjust or eliminate rationally the tension between the various motifs in the conception of God. Such an "interpretation" would be falsification. But neither can theology be satisfied with presenting discordant metaphysical propositions. This would not express the peculiar nature of faith, and its active point of view would be transformed into a foreign metaphysic. The idea of God revealed through the activity of revelation contains an inevitable tension, but this does not destroy its unity. Faith's conception of God is not divided or disparate—it has a center, or, as faith itself expresses it, a "heart." Its final and most exalted affirmation about that God who is active in Christ is the word of God's love. The "nature" of God is, as Luther says, *eitel Liebe* [pure Love]. But theology cannot properly analyze the significance of this love without taking seriously into account the tension in which this love appears to faith. Divine love cannot be incorporated into either a legalistic or a monistic and rationalistic system. It acts *contra legem*. But this does not mean that the radical opposition of the divine will toward evil disappears; it is rather expressed more emphatically. Divine love disrupts the system of monistic rationalism: God's love is a love which under historical conditions, strives against opposing forces. And yet divine sovereignty does not disappear; it stands forth in unconditional majesty. In the last analysis all the affirmations of Christian faith about God are concentrated around the central idea of God's love. This love destroys all legalistic and rational systems. But at the same time the condemning God who judges is the God of love, and the sovereign power is the power of love. Faith cannot penetrate deeper than to this divine love. The more clearly faith perceives its activity, the more it sees itself confronted by the unfathomable and the ineffable. Every theology which dissolves the tension of this divine love obscures its unfathomableness and misinterprets faith. But the same is true also of the theology which replaces the religious tension with a metaphysical paradox and irrationalism.

14. God is Love

1. *Love is the center of the concept of God.* The inmost character of the Christian conception of God is determined by Christ and his work. This implies that here faith finds the God who seeks and enters into communion with sinful man; or, in other words, a love which destroys the system into which legalism and rationalism would incorporate the relationship between God and man.

2. *The nature of divine love.* When love therefore appears as the dominant center of the Christian conception of God, the peculiar nature of this love is revealed in its spontaneity and its self-giving. Divine love is not called forth by anything outside itself. Its character is defined by the cross.

3. *The unfathomableness of love.* Although divine love is most easily perceived in the cross, it appears there at the same time as most inscrutable.

1. Love is the Center of the Concept of God

The Christian idea of God is not a vague and undefined conception. On the contrary, Christian faith has something very definite to say about God's relation to men, and therefore also about the character of the divine will and the divine person. The character of God is decisively defined by Christ and his work. When faith looks at Christ, it beholds in him the God who imparts himself to men. When faith speaks about Christ as the One in whom the divine will is incarnate and that he is "of the same substance" with the Father, the "substance" or nature of God must then be defined by what faith finds in Christ. Otherwise all "Christology" consists merely in empty formulas (cf. § 3, ¶ 3; § 5, ¶ 1).

The essential element in the fellowship created by the event of Christ is that here God seeks sinful man and enters into communion with him. This is the most important characteristic of the Christian fellowship between God and man. If that were removed, the fellowship would lose its character and would cease to exist. Consequently it must be accepted as the definitive content of the Christian message.

This implies that the inmost character of the conception of God is love. Consequently, every affirmation about God becomes an affirmation about his love. Nothing can be said about God, his power, his opposition to evil, or anything else, which is not in the last analysis a statement about his love. The Johannine statement, "God is love," summarizes not only what is essential for the New Testament, but also everything that can be said about the character of the Christian idea of God. No other divine "attributes" can be co-ordinated with love, nor can these express something that would cancel love. Nothing more decisive can be stated about the Christian conception of God than the affirmation: "God is love." Paul agrees with John. His whole Christian faith is expressed in this word: "Nothing shall separate us from the love of God in Christ Jesus." In the same way the great evangelicals in Christianity have been able to proclaim in a fresh and living way that God is love. "The law," says Luther, is God's "alien work" (*opus alienum*), "the gospel" is his "proper work" (*opus proprium*). Even though Luther spoke emphatically and realistically about the "wrath" of God, love was nevertheless to him the very "nature" of God. "In God's great hall and castle dwells only love." "Christ is the mirror of God's fatherly heart." "*Und ist kein andrer Gott.*"

But the most important element in this connection is not the mere statement that God is love, but the *manner* in which this love appears as characteristic for the Christian faith. Divine love active in Christ is that love which seeks sinful man and enters into communion with him. The distinctive mark of this love is that it creates a fellowship between God and man different from that based on reason and law. Divine love is not a rationally motivated idea obtained by reflection on the nature of the world and human life, and it is not a goal which human thought reaches by sublimating the highest human qualities. A divine love which descends to and enters into communion with sinful man is something foreign to reason. But in the same way that it is foolishness to the Greeks it is also a stumbling block to the Jews. It cannot be contained within an order of legal justice. It is not legalism, not the law, that has the final word about God's relation to men. Fellowship with God cannot be attained on the basis of law. It can be attained only when divine love breaks the legal ordinances and, in a way that is offensive to all exclusive legalism, receives sinful man into communion with itself. The fellowship with God thus created rests exclusively on the foundation of divine love.

When we seek to define the character of divine love according to Christian faith, it is important to note the antithesis in which this fellowship with God, created by divine love, stands—both to rationalism and to legalism. This antithesis is a fundamental Christian factor since it is a question of something constitutive for the Christian relationship between God and man, not something which may be removed without impairing this relationship itself. The whole history of Christian thought from one essential point of view is the history of this motif, the history of its struggle against rationalism and legalism, and the history of its triumphant emergence with new and irresistible power in spite of all opposition.

2. The Nature of Divine Love

The nature of divine love, which we have touched upon in previous chapters, must now be more fully investigated. But it is possible to deal only with the main features of this subject. The whole exposition of the content of Christian faith is in reality the only adequate presentation of this fundamental theme. Christian faith cannot make a statement which does not in one way or another throw light on the nature of divine love. In this preliminary presentation there are two features especially which must be emphasized: the spontaneity and the self-giving of divine love.

In the first place, divine love is *spontaneous*. This implies that its cause is contained within itself, not in anything else. It is not called forth by external causes, but breaks forth by itself. Another expression for the same idea is the old formula: "the prevenient grace of God." God's love is *always* prevenient. Its cause is not something outside of God, but in God himself and in his nature. "To the question, Why does God love? there is only one right answer: *Because it is His nature to love.*" [1]

It is important to emphasize this point of view, especially since it has often been obscured by attempts to supply a motivation for divine

[1] Anders Nygren, *Agape and Eros*, trans. A. G. Hebert (London: Macmillan, 1932), p. 75.

love. But the very fact that the love of God in Christ appears as a love which seeks sinners and enters into fellowship with them proves conclusively that the cause of the divine work of love is not to be found in anything human, nor in a certain value which the object of this love possesses and which should make it desirable, nor in the fact that man has in some way made himself worthy of the divine love. "In this is love, not that we love God but that he loved us" (I John 4:10). Every attempt to demonstrate something in man, some "incorruptible essence" or some quality pleasing to God, which would explain rationally why God meets man in love, is in principle foreign to Christian faith. Such attempts prove only that divine love is again being incarcerated within the walls of rationalism and legalism. "When fellowship with God is conceived of as a legal relationship, Divine love must in the last resort be dependent upon the worth of its object. But in Christ there is revealed a Divine love which breaks all bounds, refusing to be controlled by the value of its object, and being determined only by its own intrinsic nature. According to Christianity, 'motivated' love is human; spontaneous and 'unmotivated' love is Divine." [2]

Spontaneous, divine love appears to faith as *self-giving*. Different aspects of this characteristic may be noted according as the emphasis falls on the first or the second part of this word. Divine love means that God gives *himself*. The Reformers used to say that God not only gives certain gifts to men, but first and foremost he gives himself. The same idea may be expressed by saying that divine love opens the way to fellowship with God. A fellowship between God and men can be established only if God descends and gives himself to men. There is for man no way to God except the way of God's *self-giving* love. Then if we try to analyze how this divine way to man is constituted, the emphasis is shifted to the second part of the word. This tells us that divine love "seeketh not its own," and does not spare itself, but rather empties and sacrifices itself. Faith perceives that the way of divine love is the way of the cross. The nature of this love is determined by the fact that it is marked by the cross. It is not an accident that the eye of faith has always been attracted to the cross.

[2] *Ibid.*, p. 76.

There is nothing that reveals more clearly the nature, depth, and sovereignty of divine love. When the Christian conception of God is characterized and defined by the act of Christ, the spontaneous self-giving of divine love appears most clearly, both in the fact that this love has descended into the human world and accepted its conditions, and also in that it has thus given the supreme sacrifice. The conception faith has of the divine Majesty is not that of a God who in exalted eminence receives sacrifices from below, which are meant to coerce him; it is rather the picture of a love which sacrifices of its own and in extreme humility sacrifices itself. This is the way the majesty of love appears to the eye of faith. In this experience faith learns to know what divine love is. "God shows his love for us in that while we were yet sinners Christ died for us" (Rom. 5:8). "By this we know love, that he laid down his life for us" (I John 3:16).

3. The Unfathomableness of Love

The essential content of the revelation of God is given in the self-giving of divine love. Through this self-giving, faith "learns to know" God. But this highest and most unmistakable revelation of love is at the same time entirely inscrutable. Here faith can speak only with groping and tentative words. Even the word "love" comes from the area of human experience. But this does not imply that faith conceives of the love of God in terms of human love, nor that it measures his love by the standard of human love. The very opposite is true. "Love . . . that you may be sons of your Father who is in heaven" (Matt. 5:44-45); "You therefore must be perfect, as your heavenly Father is perfect" (Matt. 5:48). We can speak of human love in the Christian sense of the word only if divine love has become active in human life and has created this love, which even then becomes nothing more than a pale reflection of God's love. If divine love is conceived of as a sublimation of human "love," the result would be something radically different; it would be the very opposite of divine love, it would be "eros" instead of "agape."

What has been said about love applies also to the word "Father" when it is used about God. The "fatherhood" of God cannot be measured by the standard of human fatherhood. When faith speaks of God as Father and thereby intends to express something of fundamental importance in regard to the idea of God, it is very conscious that this "Father" is "the Father from whom every family in heaven and on earth is named" (Eph. 3:15).[3] God is "The Father in heaven." This expression serves to bring out the unfathomableness of divine "fatherly love." To share in this love means to be filled with that peace "which passes all understanding" (Phil. 4:7). In pure mysticism God is simply the inscrutable, and in rationalism he is contained within human reason. But in Christian faith, precisely as "love," he is both the revealed and hidden God (cf. § 3, ¶ 5; § 9). The hidden and unfathomable element in God's being is not a surplus remaining after we have understood a part of his essence. Nor, as in mysticism, is the unfathomable the undifferentiated and undefinable, but rather that which is definite and definable. The mystery of divine love increases in the measure that faith perceives more of its essence.

By way of transition to the next section we may add that the intimate fellowship with the man of faith which divine love creates is at the same time a relation of remoteness. The distance between the divine and the human is not obliterated by this fellowship; rather it is brought more sharply into focus. The position of Christian faith is therefore quite different from the relation of identity common in mysticism. The reason for this remoteness lies in the fact that divine love is characterized by a continuous and implacable opposition to evil.

15. The Opposition of Love to Evil

1. *The purity of love.* God's will stands in radical opposition to evil. The reason why the tension between divine love and divine wrath against sin does not destroy the unity of the conception of God is that "divine wrath" appears to faith as merged with love. Consequently God's opposition to evil is in reality the opposition of love whereby love maintains its purity.

2. *The wrath of love.* From a negative point of view God's opposition to evil is expressed in a number of figures of speech, such as severity, hate, wrath, condemning and retributive justice, and so on. All such figures are legitimate and inseparably connected with the

[3] Swedish trans., "From whom everything that is called Father derives its name."

Christian conception of God, since and in so far as they express love's radical opposition to evil.

3. *The struggle of love.* But faith finds the deepest expression of the opposition of divine love to evil in the fact that in its struggle against evil this love does everything to overcome it, even going so far as to carry its burden and to sacrifice itself. The cross stands, therefore, as the synthesis of love's radical opposition to evil and of its sovereignty over it.

1. The Purity of Love

The will of God stands in unbroken opposition to everything which is not in harmony with it, or hostile and indifferent to it. Nothing could be more false than to assume that, because the New Testament speaks differently and in a more powerful manner about the love of God than the Old Testament, therefore God's opposition to evil was weakened. In reality the very opposite is true. This appears clearly in the fact that the demand placed upon man is infinitely greater ("perfect, even as your heavenly Father is perfect") (Matt. 5:48). The New Testament picture of God as Father is not a humanized and enfeebled idea of God. The "Father" is at the same time the uncompromising Judge. Christian faith has from the very beginning expressed this opposition of God to evil in the strongest terms. It has well understood that, if this feature is missing or even slightly obscured, love loses its essence and is reduced to a caricature of real divine love. The idea that divine love is complacent and indulgent, that God overlooks sin and does not "take it seriously," and that he will "obviously" forgive since it is his "business" to do so, as Voltaire asserted, is foreign to Christian faith.

A review of the history of the Christian conception of God indicates that theology has encountered two temptations in its endeavor to define the nature of the opposition of the divine will to evil. One of these is the tendency to discount this opposition and thereby present an enfeebled idea of divine love. Examples of this can be found, not only in that "humanized" theology which has flourished during the later centuries since the Enlightenment, but also in ancient times. It appears in Marcion, who refused to combine the idea of active judgment with the God of love. It is present also in the hyperevangelical wing of pietism, since here also the idea of judgment is not

given its proper place in the conception of God. The other danger
has been that theology has isolated God's opposition to evil from his
love, and then has sought to solve the problem of their relation by a
rational adjustment (§ 13). The tension which is unquestionably
present has been changed into a dualism within God's own nature, and
the unity of the conception of God has thus become divided. For the
Christian faith the existing tension does not result in a dualism, nor
does it destroy the unity of the conception of God, because the divine
activity in judgment does not appear as something separated from
divine love, but rather as something inseparably connected with it.
No one in the history of Christianity has more seriously struggled
with this problem than Luther. It was far from his intention to
weaken the idea of divine "wrath." He boasts, and not without justification, that he has spoken more powerfully about this than had
been done under the papacy. The judgment of wrath, says Luther,
is not only something in the future; sinful man stands *here and now*
under the wrath of God. But the eye of faith discovers that in the
last analysis love and wrath stand in intimate relation. Wrath, says
Luther, is God's *opus alienum*, love is his *opus proprium*. Wrath is
the mask behind which God hides himself, the means he uses to attain
his purpose. Without this connection with wrath, love would no
longer be love, it would lose its purity. Love shines behind the dark
cloud of wrath; yea, even more, it is active even in wrath. Luther
speaks of *die zornige Liebe* ["the angry love"], and declares that it
does not destroy anything, as hate and envy do, but simply wants to
separate the evil from the good, in order that love and the good
may remain. It is not only wrath which is defined and purified by
its dependence upon love, but love itself is affected by its relation to
wrath. When wrath is, as it were, merged with love, every possibility
of enfeebling its meaning is removed; love remains strong and firm,
and retains its purity under all circumstances. The radical opposition
of the divine will to evil becomes then in the last analysis the opposition of divine love itself. This is the reason the opposition is radical
and unconditional. No opposition to evil can be more decisive and
critical than the opposition of love. It lies in the very nature of love
that it must react against that which is incompatible with itself. If it
is not to lose its own character, it *must* preserve its purity.

2. *The Wrath of Love*

Within the Christian testimony of faith there occur a number of more or less anthropomorphic expressions which are intended to set forth plainly the incongruity between the divine will and that which is is opposed to it. Thus sin is spoken of as an abomination in the sight of God, and mention is made of God's hate, enmity, wrath, and the like. In regard to these and other similar expressions it is important to remember that they are symbolic and that in the last analysis they tell us something about divine love. Only in so far as these two points of view are strictly maintained can such qualifications of God's relation to evil be validated as Christian. When such a word as God's "wrath" was rejected sometimes in the history of Christian thought, or relegated to "the final judgment" (Ritschl), the reason was either that the figurative nature of the word was considered, or that the radical opposition of the divine will to evil was weakened. Many a time, when theology has prided itself on having secured "a philosophically purified conception of God," it has become evident that this process of refining was only an expression of the lack of religious depth and the inability to comprehend the characteristic viewpoint of faith. Christian vocabulary cannot dispense with those figures of speech which belong to the sphere of human experience. These strongly volitional words serve to set forth in a picturesque, concrete, and active manner the constant, radical, and spontaneous opposition of the divine will to everything that is opposed to it. There is no reason to limit God's "wrath" to a "final judgment." God is always and under all circumstances hostile to sin. His wrath expresses the intensity and radical character of his repudiation of sin. The God of faith is a God who wills, and his will in reference to evil is a radical indignation and unmitigated severity. The Christian church has a legitimate reason to sing, "Turn now away thy wrath." But "wrath" brings an element of strong-willed and healthy firmness into divine love. Love does not hesitate to wound and break down. God's love does not appear at all to Christian faith as sentimental and effeminate. It was an expression of the deepest insight of faith when Luther was able to see the activity of God's love in the tempest of divine wrath.

When it has sometimes been said that God hates sin but loves the sinner, we might approve the intention of such a distinction, provided it is meant to maintain the divine love in the midst of "wrath." But the distinction is of questionable value. It presupposes that sin can be distinguished from the sinner in a way that really obscures the nature of sin as a perversion of the will. It is very easy on this basis to relegate sin to some external part of man (§ 30). The very thing which this symbolic figure of speech is intended to express is thereby obscured, namely, the continuous and unconditional opposition of God to sin and therefore also to man as sinner. It is more correct to insist that God both hates and loves the sinner, and that his wrath is connected with and depends on his love.

As a comprehensive expression of God's opposition to evil, theology has frequently used the term God's "righteousness." This word can unquestionably be used for this purpose. *If* righteousness is understood as a comprehensive expression of God's opposition to evil, this reaction also must be understood as the reaction of love, which then implies nothing else than the judgment and separation which occur of necessity when divine love appears in its purity. It is not, therefore, a question of a dualism between God's love and his righteousness. The theories of atonement which have been built on such a dualism obscure the nature of the Christian conception of God because they incorporate the atonement into a legalistic system. God's righteousness is not a righteousness which stands over against his love, but rather, it is, to use an expressive phrase by Nietzsche, "love with its eyes open." Righteousness watches over the purity of love and guards it against sentimental misinterpretations. But love also watches over the peculiar nature of righteousness. A righteousness without love is only hardness and a perversion of divine righteousness. It is significant that in biblical language, in both the Old and New Testaments, the "righteousness" of God expresses not *only* his opposition to evil from a negative point of view, but is very often synonymous with his "grace," "help," "salvation," and "kindness." This indicates, on the one hand, that Christian faith can never under any circumstances separate righteousness from love as something co-ordinate with it, but must always regard righteousness as an element defining love; and, on the other hand, that God's opposition to evil is never purely negative, but in reality always intends to conquer what stands in opposition to his love.

3. *The Struggle of Love*

The highest form of the self-assertion of divine love is its self-giving whereby it overcomes evil. Consequently the negative terms used to describe God's antagonism to evil are not adequate to express this relationship. It is understood in a much deeper and more conclusive sense through those affirmations about God which present the self-giving of divine love. When the "negative" terms are separated from these "positive" affirmations, they become really misleading. The nature of the antagonism of divine love is characterized as far as faith is concerned by the fact that the cross stands in the center of the history of God's dealings with men. An interpretation of divine love that ignores this cannot claim to be Christian in the fullest sense. From this point of view the purpose of God's antagonism to evil is to overcome it; and even the negative aspects of the antithesis contribute toward this end. But the deepest expressions of the reaction of God's love are those indicating how much it really costs God to overcome evil, how he entered into this struggle rather than stand indifferently at a distance, how he takes the burden upon himself and pours himself out in the sacrifice of love. This activity of God will be discussed more fully in following chapters (§§ 18, 25, 26). Here we are concerned simply to emphasize that divine love from this point of view is a self-giving and self-sacrificing love. Consequently, the nature of this love cannot be understood simply as passive, but rather as the most intense activity and as the basis of that activity which reveals God as a "saving," "forgiving," "merciful," and "gracious" God, who in giving himself triumphs over that which is antagonistic to love. This very fact, which so unmistakably reveals God's antagonism to evil, manifests at the same time the sovereignty of divine love. This cannot be more clearly revealed than in his triumph and transformation of what is opposed to his love. It is quite appropriate that we read in one of our collects: God declares his "almighty power chiefly in showing mercy and pity." [1]

16. The Sovereignty of Love

1. *God's sovereignty is the sovereignty of love.* The tension between God's love and his sovereignty, which has sometimes threatened to

[1] Collect for the Tenth Sunday after Trinity.

destroy the unity of the conception of God, cannot be rationally adjusted or resolved. But Christian faith finds the solution in the fact that divine love itself is the sovereign power in creation. Every approach which separates power from love, and understands the former as a more or less undefinable, capricious, and despotic power, leads to a conception of God which is foreign to faith and below the Christian level. The same is true of every approach which limits the sovereignty of divine love.

2. *The various aspects of God's sovereignty.* From this point of view God's "omnipotence" is not the causality of the divine will in relation to everything that happens, but the sovereignty of love in relation to everything that happens. The "eternity" of God is not an abstract timelessness, but the sovereignty of love in relation to time. God's "unchangeableness" is not an abstract inertia, but an expression of love's sovereign steadfastness. God's "omnipresence" is not deistic transcendence or pantheistic immanence, but the sovereignty of love in relation to space. God's "omniscience" is not abstract foreknowledge, but love's sovereign and penetrating eye to which everything is crystal clear.

3. *Love and sovereignty.* Just as God's sovereignty is characterized by love, so also divine love is characterized by sovereignty. Thus all competition between God's love and his sovereignty is eliminated.

1. *God's Sovereignty is the Sovereignty of Love*

We have already touch upon the tension, which undeniably reveals itself in Christian faith, between divine power and divine love (§ 13). The reason for this is that to Christian faith God appears both as the sovereign God exalted above all strife and change, and as the loving and divine will which in history is engaged in a struggle against opposing forces. The reality of this tension is abundantly evidenced in the history of Christian thought. Here we find again and again how these two principal motifs struggle against each other, and how men have repeatedly attempted to remove this clash by rational adjustments. History also indicates that this tension may eventuate in a division in which one of the motifs is maintained in opposition to the other. A typical example of how the motif of power suppresses the motif of love is seen in the nominalistic theology of the late Middle Ages. The suppression of divine love which had appeared even during early scholasticism had proceeded so far that God's *potentia absoluta* [absolute power] had now become a pure, capricious, and indefinable will to power. The Christian conception of God had thereby lost its characteristic nature. An example of the opposite type we find in Marcion. Here the motif of sovereignty is in reality suppressed by the motif of love. Marcion wanted to maintain that the highest and "unknown" God is a God of love, and of nothing but love. But this is accomplished in such a way that the "God of creation" becomes another and lower god than the God of love. The significance of this is that the God of love is not sovereign with respect to "creation." Such ideas have been advanced also in more recent times, when it has been suggested that God is a "finite" God, or a "growing" God who emerges in history.[1]

In contradistinction to such a division between power and love, Christian faith maintains that divine power is nothing else than the power of love. The power of God is not some obscure and inert *fatum* [fate or destiny] or a capricious and indefinable will to power, but only and exclusively the power of love. The Christian faith, therefore, in spite of all appearances to the contrary, makes the affirmation that the sovereign power in the universe possesses the character of divine love. The tension in this affirmation cannot be removed by rationalization, since it is obvious to faith both that the divine power *is* sovereign, and that it is engaged in a continuous struggle under historical conditions against that which is opposed to it. What prevents a rational solution of the tension is, therefore, the reality of that evil which struggles against the sovereign will of God.

The viewpoint of faith cannot under such circumstances be transformed into a rational world view, either monistic or dualistic. A monistic world view can be constructed only by weakening or destroying the radical hostility of evil to the divine will. Only in that case can everything that happens be referred to the divine will and accepted as an expression of the same. This line of thought is completely at variance with that which is axiomatic and clear to faith, namely, that what faith calls sin cannot be the result of the divine will, but stands rather in open antagonism to this will. If in some way it could be shown that sin has its matrix in and is an expression

[1] Cf. H. G. Wells, "God the Invisible King," and H. R. Mackintosh, "The Conception of a Finite God," in *Some Aspects of Christian Belief* (New York: 1924).

of the divine will, then this will would no longer bear the marks of love and it would cease to be a divine will. Neither can the viewpoint of faith be transformed into a dualistic world view. Such a view would presuppose that the opposing evil is considered from a metaphysical point of view. When Marcion attributed the origin of this world, where the evil powers are active, to "a lower creator-god," his theory in reality represented a rational explanation of evil and of the universe along metaphysical and dualistic lines. Christian faith had good reasons to repudiate this dissolution of the divine sovereignty.

As far as faith is concerned it cannot accept *either* a monistic *or* a dualistic world view. The affirmation of faith that the divine love which struggles against evil is at the same time the sovereign power contains a tension which cannot be dismissed.

When faith nevertheless maintains that divine sovereignty bears the mark of love, and that there is no *other* divine power except love, it does so because the divine love which reveals itself in the act of Christ appears to faith as unconditionally supreme and as the only sovereign power. Every attempt to maintain God's sovereignty by discounting divine love implies not only a weakening of love but in reality also an impairment of divine sovereignty. If God's power were despotic, coercive, and violent, it would not be for faith the power beyond all power. Whatever the might of pure, external power may be able to accomplish, it cannot subdue human wills and set them free from the tyranny of egocentricity. Love cannot be induced by force. The hearts of men can be won only by the power of love. If the might of God were simply an external power, it would be ineffective against evil; God would not be able to win that which, according to the certainty of faith, he has demonstrated himself able to win. Consequently, the point of view that regards God's power as despotic and capricious does not exalt but rather depreciates the divine power, and accords less to God than the Christian faith must give. Despotic power is a caricature of divine sovereignty. It is significant that Luther's emphasis on love as the "nature" of God is connected with a new and powerful view of the meaning of God's "omnipotence." In medieval theology there had been room for a division between God's "grace" and human merit. But this division disappeared when Luther discovered that God's power is the power of his love. Then all mention of human "merit" must cease. Then it must be said: *"Wir handeln nicht, sondern wir werden gehandelt"* [We do not act; we are acted upon].

As soon as God's sovereignty is separated from his love and is understood as something independent alongside of it, the conception of God becomes unrealistic, i.e., it does not correspond to what faith beholds when the conception derives its essential content from the event of Christ. Then when the conception of God is made the object of thoughtful analysis, it becomes inert. When the primitive, despotic feature is removed, there emerges a deistic or pantheistic reinterpretation of God's sovereignty. But in this way the conception of God becomes not only unrealistic but lifeless. The god of pantheism who penetrates all things is just as inactive as the god of deism who is exalted and removed from the world (§ 17). We cannot speak of a living God except in so far as his sovereignty is understood as identical with the sovereignty of divine love.

2. The Various Aspects of God's Sovereignty

We touch here the whole array of conceptions of faith which in the history of theology have been brought together under such captions as God's "formal" or "metaphysical" or "absolute" attributes. It is not too much to say that here theology has used speculative concepts which are foreign to faith and has assumed that these belong among the so-called *articuli mixti*. There is hardly any indication that these belong to the study of *faith*. If we are to remain within the area of faith, it is necessary to maintain firmly the idea that God's sovereignty is entirely the sovereignty of love.

If God's sovereignty has this character, then what is implied in the *omnipotence* of God? It is clear at once that we need not be concerned with a number of meaningless questions about God's omnipotence which have appeared even within theology. Can God do everything? Can he transform a stone into an animal? All such questions are beside the point and completely meaningless. They have nothing to do with faith. They are based on a conception of the will of God as entirely capricious, which fails to understand that here it is a question about the power of love and nothing else. The question of God's possibilities is a question of the possibilities of divine love. God does and wills nothing else than that wherein divine love realizes itself.

In regard to the relation of divine sovereignty to the course of history, two things are absolutely certain as far as faith is concerned. In the first place it is clear that not everything that happens is an expression of the divine will in the sense that everything that happens reflects the will of God. Such a point of view could be maintained only by identifying sin with the divine will. Faith cannot, therefore, incorporate the divine will under the aspect of a universal cause. It is completely misleading when Schleiermacher says that "the religious self-consciousness, by means of which we place all that affects or influences us in absolute dependence on God, coincides entirely with the view that all things are conditioned and determined by the interdependence of nature."[2] This thought is completely foreign to faith. The God of faith is not identified with "the interdependence of nature," which is nothing else than the attempt to trace the relation between the individual events. Such an identification is impossible and completely opposed to the viewpoint of faith. The reason for this is not simply that the God of faith is not an abstract idea, but a living and continually active God. The reason is rather that this point of view leads to the result that every event must be accepted as an expression of God's will. But this is obviously contrary to faith's viewpoint. Faith knows that in this universe there is much that stands in direct opposition to the will of God.

In the second place, it is evident to faith that the activity of divine love cannot be judged or verified according to human standards. It is not man who from the point of view of his own power decides what is and what is not the work of divine love. Faith knows very well that divine love can hide itself in wrath, which seems the very opposite of love. It does not presume to interpret the ways of divine love on the basis of historical development. It does not forget that God is not only the revealed God, but also the God who under the conditions of this earthly life is hidden from us. The tenacity of faith in holding fast to divine love in spite of the testimony of earthly events always has the character of a "nevertheless."

[2] Schleiermacher, *Christian Faith*, p. 170.

126

Faith's view of the sovereignty of divine love implies that everything is unconditionally dependent upon the will and love of God. Nothing is outside the sphere of God's power; no situation can arise in which his power would not be able to assert itself. In relation to evil, therefore, divine power appears under a double aspect: *as grace and as judgment.* In grace evil is overcome and compelled to serve the purpose of the divine will. In the judgment of condemnation the unconquered evil encounters divine sovereignty. Understood in this way the divine will is not simply a power superior to all other powers, but, in the real sense of the word, it is the sovereign power of the universe (cf. § 22). Everything else that is called power, or has a semblance of power, contains the seeds of its own dissolution, desolation, and destruction. It is subject to judgment. The power of divine love is the only power of life. To be separated from this power is destruction, to be united with it is "life eternal."

In accordance with the point of view here presented, the *eternity* of God does not imply any speculation about his being outside of time, or that time has no significance for God. It is, on the contrary, essential to faith to conceive of God as being present *in* time and effectively active in whatever happens here; although he nevertheless is "above" time. Eternal rest and blessedness belong to the Christian conception of God, but at the same time it can be said of him, in the words of Luther, that he "never rests" (*nimmer ruhet*). The "eternal" does not suggest something "before" time, or something that is to come "after" time. Eternity is not quantitatively different from time. As soon as we follow out the consequences of such a thought, we come to the conception of an unending extent of time; but even such a time is not eternity. The eternity of God is the *sovereignty of divine love in relation to time.* God's love is not transient and changing as is everything which belongs to time. The apostolic word is perfectly applicable here: "Love never fails." God cannot be contained within any limits, spatial or temporal. Faith expresses this by saying that God is "he who was, and who is, and who is to come." He is "Alpha and Omega, the beginning and the end," and "a thousand years are to him as one day." Eternal life, whether we think of the present or of the future, partakes of this sovereign love. Eternal life is to faith *not only* an object of hope.

"This is eternal life, that they know thee the only true God" (John 17:3). Eternal life is a qualitative expression for a life lived in communion with the living God.

This independence of all temporal limits which characterizes the divine life expresses itself also with reference to divine revelation. There is a continuous reciprocal action between what has been done and what is being done. What has happened in history is not only something which is past: it is at the same time present and active. Christ's work of reconciliation has been done once for all, but it is at the same time a reality which is active in the present. The victory of Christ was won once for all, but it is continually realized and "won" anew in the present.

In connection with what we have said about eternity we may add that God's *unchangeableness*, from the point of view of the sovereignty of divine love, cannot be understood as stereotyped inertia. This word has often been interpreted along that line under the influence of Greek philosophy, which tended to emphasize the so-called *apatheia* of God. In that case God is placed outside of history in a way that does not at all correspond to the viewpoint of Christian faith. Faith understands the unchangeableness of God as an expression of the unswerving direction of God's will and an affirmation that this will under all circumstances and in all its activity is characterized by love.

God's *omnipresence* must also be understood from the point of view of the sovereignty of divine love. It is not a question here of some abstract and deistic space-beyond-space, which in reality becomes simply another space, nor of a pantheistic conception of the presence of God in all that exists. All questions as to whether God is in the flower or in the stone, and the like, are immaterial to faith. The "omnipresence" Christian faith affirms is entirely different. It implies nothing less than the ability of divine love to maintain itself everywhere unhindered by limitations of space. There is no place closed to the sovereign power of divine love. God can reach us wherever we are, and it is useless for a man to attempt to flee from his power. "If I ascend to heaven, thou art there! If I make my bed in Sheol, thou art there!" (Ps. 139:8.) But God *is present* only where his love realizes itself in grace and judgment. Wherever the love of

God is active, there is God, even if human lips do not dare to speak the name of the Highest. But where his love is not active, there he is not, even though his praises may be sung in the most beautiful hymns. God's omnipresence is entirely the active presence of divine love.

Finally, God's *omniscience* becomes from this point of view something entirely different from the abstract idea of his "foreknowledge." This latter term is connected with a deistically conceived idea of God which is not compatible with faith's conception of the living God who is active in history. This idea of God's abstract foreknowledge has given rise to a number of speculations which are foreign to faith; as for instance, the question whether God saves man because he foreknows his faith. In reality God's "omniscience" expresses the unerring certainty of God's judgment, and denotes the all-seeing eye of love which sees everything in a crystal clear light. He knows what is in man (John 2:25). This omniscience is verified by faith again and again. It knows that nothing is hidden from God; yea, even "darkness itself is not dark in his presence," as the psalmist pointedly and aptly expresses it. Every attempt to hide something from this all-seeing eye is doomed to failure. In this connection the word is entirely appropriate that there is nothing hidden which shall not be revealed.

3. Love and Sovereignty

God's sovereignty is entirely a sovereignty of love. There is no divine power which is not the power of love. Sovereignty is a necessary qualification of divine love. Love is always a sovereign, almighty, eternal, active, and all-seeing love. This sovereignty characterizes divine love and reveals its majesty. Divine love is not a power alongside of others; it is the sovereign power of all the universe.

It is not, however, always clear and unmistakable to faith that God's sovereignty is the sovereignty of love. Love can be hidden under the aspect of wrath. God's sovereign love cannot be measured and evaluated according to human standards. Luther's words in regard to God's righteousness apply equally well to love. "If the righteousness of God were such that human reason could declare it to be righteousness, it would not be divine and would not be different from human righteousness. Since, however, he is the only true God, who is unfathomable and inscrutable for human reason, it is proper, no, really necessary, that his righteousness also is inscrutable, as Paul says. . . . His ways would not be past tracing out if we could at all times perceive why they are righteous."[3] But even when God's love is hidden and his actions do not seem to bear the marks of love, faith holds fast its inmost and unshakable conviction that the sovereignty of God is nothing else than the sovereignty of love.

If God's sovereignty therefore implies a qualification of his love, the rivalry between love and power is in principle excluded. The question whether power or love shall be emphasized is meaningless. This question rests on the false assumption that these are two coordinate "attributes" of God, and that power should be understood as pure and unqualified might. The difference between the older Lutheran and Reformed theologies was sometimes expressed in this manner: The Reformed emphasized power, the Lutheran love, as the primary attribute of God. The danger in such an analysis, from the point of view of faith, was that the former failed to perceive the character of power as the power of *love,* and the latter obscured the *sovereignty* of love. In both cases there is introduced a separation between power and love in the nature of God which is contrary to faith's perception of divine love as the sovereign power in the universe. The inner tension which results from this point of view has been clearly indicated in previous chapters. We have not tried to hide the fact that divine love cannot be measured by human standards, nor that the attitude of faith always tends to have the character of a "nevertheless." But against this tension as a background Christian faith projects its unified conception of God, concentrated and comprehended in the idea of *sovereign love.*

17. The Living God

1. *The God of faith is the living God.* The God of the Christian faith is the living and active God. Every affirmation of faith is therefore at the same time a statement of his nearness and his remoteness.

[3] Martin Luther, *The Bondage of the Will,* trans. J. I. Packer and O. R. Johnston (London: Clarke, 1957), pp. 314-15.

2. *Deistic and pantheistic ideas of God.* The conception of God in Christian faith is distinguished both from a transcendental-deistic and from an immanent-pantheistic approach. At first sight it might appear that the former accentuates God's remoteness and the latter his nearness. In reality the remoteness is transformed into unapproachableness and impassivity, and the nearness into an identity between the divine and the human. At the same time the twofold aspect of nearness and remoteness which characterizes the Christian conception of God is disrupted. This twofold aspect depends on the fact that this conception is clearly and qualitatively defined.

3. *God's personality.* When Christian faith speaks of God as a "person," it maintains both the activity of God as an expression of his will and the personal and spiritual nature of the Christian relationship between God and men. The term "person," which naturally is a figure of speech, stands guard against the transformation of the conception of God into an abstract idea, and against its being understood as a force of nature.

1. The God of Faith is the Living God

In the previous chapters the essential characteristics of the Christian conception of God were delineated. The next section will deal more in detail with the divine activity as faith perceives it. As a transition to this section we insert here a chapter on "the living God." The purpose is also to mark the essential difference between the Christian conception and deistic and pantheistic ideas of God.

That the God of the Christian faith is the living and active God has already become evident in our earlier discussion of the nature of divine love and in the definition of the concept of revelation. The revelation of God is divine self-impartation in the form of activity. There is nothing more essential to faith than the living character of this idea of God. God's revelation is from one point of view finished in the event of Christ, which to faith means the entrance of divine love into human life and the finished work of salvation and reconciliation on the basis of divine self-giving. This is the highest possible form of the divine presence. But the revelation of God is at the same time something which is continually going on, something that happens *quotidie spiritualiter in quolibet christiano* [daily, spiritually, in every Christian]. This phase of a continuing and immediate activity is expressed in the fact that Christian faith is a faith in the Holy

Spirit." Fellowship with God rests completely on divine activity. There is no other way to God than God's way to man.

Christian faith, therefore, speaks about God's nearness, an effective divine presence in the human world. But this does not imply that the divine can be contained within or confused with the human. It is perfectly clear to faith that the divine presence at the same time accentuates the separation between the divine and the human. The more faith perceives the presence of God and experiences fellowship, the more definitely appears also the distance between God and man. The divine act of love which establishes the fellowship between God and man at the same time makes more vividly known to the man of faith his separation and unworthiness in the presence of divine love. The twofold aspect of nearness and remoteness, fellowship and separation, which is inseparably connected with the Christian conception of God, depends on the clearly defined character of this conception. Its quality of sovereign love demands both distance and fellowship.

The living, clearly defined conception of God held by Christian faith is sharply differentiated from all conceptions of God which are "philosophically" or metaphysically oriented. Such speculations have always influenced theology in the direction of weakening the living content of the Christian conception of God.

2. Deistic and Pantheistic Ideas of God

The metaphysical conceptions of God which have appeared in history may be divided into two representative groups: the deistic, which emphasizes the "transcendental," and the pantheistic, which emphasizes the "immanent" conception of God. Even though these two types seem to be very different, history indicates that the one has often without difficulty passed over into the other. It must be emphasized, however, that from a religious point of view both are in conflict with the Christian faith. There is no overwhelming difference between conceiving of God as "the first cause," as deism does, or as pantheism's principle of order in the universe. In either case man is simply confronted with the idea of causality, and faith's living conception of God is lost.

Since we have stated that the twofold aspect of distance and nearness is inseparably connected with the Christian conception of God, it might seem quite natural to assume that these two metaphysical types represent these two aspects: the transcendental representing distance; and the immanent, nearness. In reality, however, the idea of nearness and distance is here quite different from that which is characteristic of Christian faith. In the transcendental type "distance" becomes unapproachableness, isolation, and impassivity. God is an "extra-mundane" being who is enthroned in abstract space, too highly "exalted" to have any concern for what happens in the human world. In the theology of the ancient church there was a constant conflict with this conception of God derived from Greek philosophy. The Christology of the ancient church represents from one point of view the attempt of theology to preserve the living and active revelation of God against the encroachments of transcendentalism. In the measure that this latter tendency influenced Christology, the Logos-Christ became an intermediary being between the distant God and the world. Arianism is a typical example of this. When the ancient confession of faith in Christ asserts that "the Son is of the same substance with the Father," this is in reality a decisive victory over the influence of metaphysical transcendentalism. In spite of this fact it has exercised considerable influence in theology, especially in scholasticism. The nature of this influence may be indicated in the following examples. Divine love was interpreted in medieval scholasticism primarily as self-love, and therefore became Eros rather than Agape. In regard to the work of Christ it was difficult, in spite of Christology, to take this seriously as the work of God. This is evident in the Latin theory of the atonement. Finally, the "grace" of God was not identical with God's love, but was understood as more or less mysterious powers emanating from the distant God. It is clear, therefore, that the metaphysical transcendental idea which was fully developed in eighteenth-century deism had deep roots in scholastic theology. Deism combined the idea of exclusive transcendentalism with the idea of order in the universe which the new world view had placed in the foreground. The ideal of the pure deist was a God who had constructed the machine so accurately that he did not need to pay any attention to the controls. But there was nothing in this conception of God as the ultimate cause of the universe that would hinder the divine Being from exercising a certain amount of control, or at least that the whole would proceed toward a final assize when judgment would be pronounced over the whole course of events with a dispensing of rewards and punishments. But the more exclusively transcendent the conception of God becomes, the more abstract, unrealistic, and insignificant the idea appears. What religious significance can there be in an idea of God as the first cause? Suppose this so-called first cause is removed. What then? The only result would be a slight revision in the theory of the origin of the universe.[1] This proves conclusively that the deistic conception of God has no religious significance. Only that idea of God has religious significance in which God is understood as the living, present, and active God.

The immanent-pantheistic idea of God's nearness is also different from that of Christian faith. In this view it is not a question of God's entrance into and activity in history, but of a certain divine indwelling in the world. The idea of immanence blurs the distinction between the divine and the human, and results finally in an apotheosis of the human. The metaphysic of immanence has exercised a great influence on theology from the time of the ancient church down to the present. A characteristic example is found in mysticism's attempt to find God in the "depth" of the soul, and in its talk about "the divine spark" in man, etc. When this line of thought became influential in the nineteenth-century idealistic theology, it did not come as something completely new, even though it did not play as prominent a part in the theology of the ancient church as transcendentalism. The more this idea of immanence penetrated theology, the clearer became the difference between its conception of God and the living God of faith. In the measure that the conception of God, on the basis of speculative idealism, especially in Hegel, became metaphysically immanent and pantheistic, it was transformed into an abstract idea and lost its religious character. The God of speculative idealism was no more living and active than the God of transcendentalism, and did not permit a personal relationship such as Christian faith demands. The religious character of the conception of God was lost because the fully developed pantheistic idea

---

[1] Cf. Sorley, *Moral Values and the Idea of God* (New York: 1930), "Surely a God who does not interfere will hardly be missed," p. 146.

removed the distance, the qualitative difference between the divine and the human, and made God into a comprehensive symbol of all existence. It is not an accident that the speculative theology was followed by Strauss, who, on the basis of the conception that the divine spirit realizes himself in the human through the process of divine immanence, declared that humanity as such is the incarnate God.

If, therefore, the conception of God in Christian faith differs from the idea of both transcendence and immanence, we cannot arrive at a substitute by a combination of the two. That such attempts do not come very close to the Christian conception derives from the fact that the concepts of nearness and distance are entirely different. A combination of transcendence and immanence would result only in a metaphysical irrationalism (§ 9). But in this way one does not arrive at that tension-filled synthesis in which Christian faith combines God's nearness and distance. The clearly defined quality of faith's conception of God prevents the unity from being destroyed by this tension and at the same time differentiates this conception from all metaphysical concepts of God. It is this quality which is the basis of the fellowship between God and man, but it also delineates more sharply the distance between the human and God's sovereign love.

3. God's "Personality"

The designation "person" is not applied to God in the New Testament. God is spoken of rather as "spirit" (John 4:24). Nevertheless, many personal terms, such as "Father," "Lord," and so on, indicate that the conception of God was "personal." The ancient confessional formulas do not speak of God as a person, but about three "persons" in the Godhead. But the word person did not then have the sharply defined meaning that it has today. The use of the word person as applied to God did not come into theology until relatively late. To begin with, it seems that certain unitarian interests were served by the use of the word. That is true in the case of Socinus. Gradually, however, it appeared self-evident that the word should be used about God. In later theology, however, the question about God's personality was the object of discussion. Schleiermacher regarded the word as a "one-sidedness": a *Bewusstseinsvergötterung* [deification of consciousness] which represented one extreme, while *Naturver-götterung* [deification of nature] represented another. The Hegelian theologian Biedermann refused to use the concept of personality with reference to "the absolute spirit," since the word belongs to the temporal sphere: "personality is the definition of a temporal spirit." Hesitation to use the concept of personality rests on the suspicion that the idea of God would thereby become too thoroughly human. Those defending its use have usually answered that the concept of personality does not imply any such restriction, and affirmed that in the personality is found "positively and intensively the power of a being over himself." [2]

Before we make a decision in this matter, we must note carefully, whether we attack or defend its use, that the term "person," with reference to God, is a figure of speech. If personality is not an adequate expression for the conception of God, it is certainly not difficult to find points of attack. But even if the use of the word is connected with certain dangers, this does not necessarily destroy its usefulness. The question about the "personality" of God is not a question whether God *is* a person or not, but how and to what extent this word is able to express something that is essential to faith. *If* faith were compelled to understand God's "personality" as identical with human personality, it could certainly not use the word. One might then seek for a substitute, such as "superpersonality," but this concept would be void of content and unsuitable for the purpose. As a figure of speech "personality" serves to guard the conception of God in important respects. It brings out vividly the voluntary and active character of the idea of God, and thus guards it from two tendencies: the transformation of the conception of God into an abstract idea, and the identification of God with some force of nature, thus obscuring the fact that God's power is nothing else than the power of love. In addition the conception of personality guards the spiritual and personal character of fellowship with God, and repudiates both the idea of the dissolution of personality into the "infinite" as conceived in the "mysticism of infinity," and all tendencies to understand God's "grace" in a more or less material sense;

[2] O. Kirn, *Grundriss der evangelischen Dogmatik*, II, 6.

an example is the designation of grace as "medicine," to use the terminology of Melanchthon, rather than as the love of God which saves and restores man. A negative proof of the importance of the concept of personality is the fact that attacks on God's "personality" frequently are associated with the obscuring both of the active volitional character of the conception of God and of the spiritual and personal character of the relationship between God and man.

CHAPTER TWO

The God Who Acts

18. God as Saviour

1. *Various aspects of the divine activity.* The living God realizes his loving will in continuous activity. Christian faith beholds this divine activity from three points of view: as an act of salvation, an act of judgment, and an act of creation.

2. *The divine activity as an act of salvation.* When God's activity is seen as an act of salvation which establishes communion and fellowship with man, it implies the assertion both of the radical opposition of sin to the will of God and the power of this divine will to overcome the evil of sin. The possibility of salvation rests entirely in the will of God and cannot be rationally explained. When evil which opposes the divine will is attributed to the finite as such, there emerge two different doctrines of salvation which are fundamentally at variance with the Christian conception. *Either* salvation is rationally motivated, as in idealism which suggests that human nature as such encompasses something divine, *or* when man is wholly consigned to the finite world, the religious miracle of salvation is replaced by a metaphysical irrationalism which attempts to combine the metaphysical antitheses, finite and infinite.

3. *The twofold perspective of Christian faith.* From the viewpoint of Christian faith history appears as the arena where the divine will struggles against the power of opposing evil. Here, indeed, as far as faith is concerned, the decisive victory is won. Nevertheless, though the struggle is indissolubly connected with the circumstances of history, the perfect dominion of God—the kingdom of God—does not lie within the realm of history.

1. *Various Aspects of the Divine Activity of God*

It was the purpose of the previous chapter to sketch the main outlines of that conception of God which is decisive for Christian faith. That sketch concluded with a paragraph about the living God. The purpose of this chapter will be to attempt to see this conception of God from the viewpoint of activity. Christian faith perceives in divine revelation a continuing activity on God's part. "My Father is working still, and I am working" (John 5:17). This "still" has no limits. When, therefore, the attempt is made to apprehend the idea of God from the viewpoint of activity, it does not imply that the idea of God previously indicated is to be supplemented with any new features, but instead that the conception of God we have indicated may be more directly seen in action. It should be emphasized that only in this way do we obtain that perspective of the idea of God which is decisive for Christian faith, inasmuch as the relation of faith to God is entirely a relation to the active divine will.

Just as the content of the Christian conception of God is focused in divine love, so to the eye of faith all of God's activity is concentrated upon the realization of his purpose. Faith knows of no divine activity which can be separated from God's love, and which is not in some way or other an expression of his will. Every act of God signifies in the final analysis a realization of his love, even if the act at first sight would seem to have an entirely different meaning. The activity of God has no other "goal" than that of realizing his loving will. Furthermore, it has no other basis than divine love itself. All attempts to advance other bases will eventuate in a conflict with the character of divine love as spontaneous love (cf. § 14, ¶ 2).

Just as we have spoken of a threefold conflux of fundamental motifs in regard to the conception of God, so with reference to the divine activity we may distinguish three cardinal points of view, and designate the work of God as an act of salvation, an act of judgment, and an act of creation. If the act of salvation is an immediate result of the spontaneous love of God, then the act of judgment accentuates especially the radical opposition of this divine will to evil, while the act of creation emphasizes the sovereignty of divine love. It must be expressly stated that this does not imply an isolation of the various principal motifs; all three are apprehensible in the three divine acts. Thus, for example, the act of salvation is indeed an act in which both the radical opposition of the divine will to evil and its creative sovereignty find expression. In conclusion it may be remarked that this section dealing with the activity of God intends to present simply an outline and that both of the following sections, dealing with the act of God in Christ and the church of God, will seek to develop further the meaning of the whole activity of God's loving will, and to make clear the ways in which this will is realized. When in the following exposition the act of creation is placed after the acts of salvation and judgment it must not be interpreted as a subordination of creation and its significance, which in reality is basic for Christian faith. The purpose is rather to guard the purely religious character of the idea of creation and to exclude every possibility of transforming the concept of creation into a rational explanation of the universe.

2. The Divine Activity as an Act of Salvation

To conceive of divine activity as an act of salvation is to emphasize what faith primarily has to say about the action of divine love. In this context the word "salvation" has been chosen as the most comprehensive among the many expressions which are relevant to this subject and which include the ideas of reconciliation, forgiveness, sanctification, etc. The salvation is a salvation from the bondage of sin and death. In the act of salvation God establishes communion and fellowship between himself and a humanity which is sinful and lost. In the word salvation there is this twofold implication: on the one hand that man is, by reason of sin, separated from God; and on the other that God overcomes that which separates him from man. If the relation of fellowship between God and man cannot be established by any other means than by an act of salvation on God's part, then both the character of sin as a radical and devastating evil and the continuous opposition of divine love to this evil become inescapably apparent. Sin is then revealed not merely as something imperfect, nor does it imply simply that divine love has not yet attained complete dominion. Sin is seen rather as a militant power diametrically opposed to the divine will and its purposes. Christian faith is uncompromisingly realistic and radically unreserved in its criticism of the evil in life. It considers as naive optimism the notion that evil is only the necessary shadows in the picture, or that there is a "growth toward perfection" which is a part of an inner necessarily progressive development in the direction of ultimate perfection. According to the realistic viewpoint of faith there is no basis in fact for such dreams; it tears them unmercifully apart like cobwebs. On the contrary, the divine will realizes itself only in bitter struggle against

everything that opposes it. The victories of this divine will in the
sphere of the human soul, as indicated by the word "salvation," are
in the nature of a rescue, a radical transformation, a giving of new
life, all of which is at the same time the infliction of death. It is
definitely not a matter of the development of something given or of
a salvation of self by self, but salvation actually implies, from one
point of view, as Luther trenchantly expresses it, that we are "snatched
away from ourselves and are placed outside ourselves," or, in other
words, that the domination of egocentricity is broken and replaced
by the dominion of God.

As far as Christian faith is concerned, the possibility of salvation
lies entirely in the divine will and not in any human quality. Therefore, from the viewpoint of faith, it is idle to attempt to explain by
rational means how salvation occurs. For faith there is no other
explanation than that which refers to God's spontaneously active,
unfathomable, and loving will. Salvation cannot be explained by
asserting that man possesses such intrinsic worth as thereby to evoke
the divine act of love. On the contrary, when man is confronted
with the divine act of salvation, it becomes apparent to him that he
does not possess such an intrinsic worth, that he is not gifted with
any quality which would, in itself, move the divine will to activity.
If for this reason the conclusion is drawn that the possibility of salvation must be excluded, inasmuch as there is apparently nothing in
man which can motivate and thereby make salvation possible, then
it must be emphasized that from the viewpoint of faith the possibility
of salvation is clearly evident in and with its actual existence. In
general, faith can say nothing more about the possibility of salvation
than is given in the Bible passage, "With men this is impossible, but
with God all things are possible" (Matt. 19:26). The divine will to
save appears to faith as absolutely unmerited love, and salvation by
faith as entirely a work of God. When it was asserted in a previous
section that faith also, as seen from one point of view, has the character of a decision, an audacious choice on man's part, it does not
mean in any sense whatsoever that the character of faith as entirely
a work of God is encroached upon in any way. Every "synergistic"
approach is excluded. Even when man assumes an affirmative position

relative to God, this is nothing else to the eye of faith than the work of God, his conquest of man (cf. § 35).

The Christian conception of salvation is distinguished from both the idealistic and the metaphysical-dualistic doctrines. Both of these otherwise mutually hostile doctrines emanate from a metaphysical tension between the infinite and the finite, and both regard evil as synonymous with the finite as such. The difference between the two is that while metaphysical dualism regards man as entirely a finite creature, the idealistic type considers him as a citizen of both the finite and infinite worlds. Behind idealistic thought lie the ancient conceptions emanating from Greek mystery religion and philosophy which divide man into two parts, a higher, spiritual self issuing from the world of divine infinity, and a lower, sensual, and finite self. Man's present misfortune is that his higher, spiritual ego has been confined in the prison of finite and material existence. Salvation consists in the release of the higher self from this prison. These ideas have through the ages exercised an influence upon Christianity in many ways. This influence has been primarily characterized by two tendencies; in the first place, with idealism as a starting point, there has been an inclination to regard salvation as an ascending movement of the soul. In the second place, by reference to the divine element existing in many, the attempt has been made to bring about a rational motivation for the possibility of salvation by claiming that man possesses an "untainted core" or something similar, in any event a value, which God must take into consideration and which is calculated to move him to an appreciation of man. Both of these tendencies stand in sharp contrast to the Christian conception of salvation. The former substitutes man's ascension to God for God's condescension to man, while the latter abolishes the religious miracle in salvation by permitting salvation to be at least partially rooted in something other than in God's unsearchable, spontaneous love.

When a metaphysical-dualistic approach has pushed its way into theology and influenced the interpretation of Christianity, it has, as a rule, been in the form of a reaction against the idealistically oriented doctrine of salvation. But even such a reaction has actually been negatively dependent upon the very idealistic viewpoint it opposed. A similar phenomenon has at times been apparent in "dialectic theology." Against the blurring of the demarcation line between the divine and the human by the idealistic theory, metaphysical dualism seeks to guard this boundary line with utmost energy by conceiving the contrast between the divine and human to be a contrast between the infinite and the finite. The purpose is to give the strongest possible expression to the contrast between God and that which is separated from him. Actually, however, the contrast is not clearly apprehended, for it is undefined and does not possess, as does Christian faith, a clear and qualitatively determined character. The consequence of the metaphysical-dualistic line of thought is that the religious miracle of the Christian conception of salvation is replaced by a metaphysical paradox: Salvation is found in the inconceivable union of the infinite and the finite. Since such a union is out of the question in the circumstances of life on earth, salvation must be conceived of in terms of a metaphysical eschatology. Here also the opposition to the idealistic metaphysical doctrine of salvation appears. When this approach argues its case from the viewpoint of immanence and is inclined to permit the human to become absorbed in the divine, the emphasis is shifted from the eschatological to the present. The dominion of God becomes essentially something which by a process of evolution actualizes itself in life here on earth.

3. The Twofold Perspective of Christian Faith

From the viewpoint of idealism, salvation is essentially a process of evolution belonging to life here on earth which, because of the inner necessity of its own nature, gradually advances toward perfection. For metaphysical dualism, salvation is located beyond this life, that is to say, it is eschatologically conceived. In contrast to these viewpoints, Christian faith regards salvation as something which both occurs in the present and is at the same time a part of the "good things to come" (Heb. 9:11).

To Christian faith history appears as an arena where the conflict between the will of God and that which is inimical to it takes place. Two things are therefore essential for faith. In the first place, the decisive encounter between the mutually hostile forces has taken place, and the work of Christ has resulted in a victory of God's will over that of the demonic powers (cf. § 26). In the second place, this

does not mean that the battle between these forces has been concluded; it continues unabated, but because of the victorious work of
Christ it is a battle under changed circumstances.

With reference to salvation, this implies on the one hand that in
the circumstances of life on earth salvation already exists as a divine
act of reconciliation and forgiveness through which fellowship between God and man has been established; on the other hand, this
fellowship as existing under circumstances of this life is found to be
a perpetually ongoing struggle. Therefore Christian faith conceives
of salvation as something present as well as something in the future.
In both cases an eschatological perspective is involved. A new age
has come in Christ, but its fulfilment belongs in the realm of "*the
world to come.*" And the proportion between these two viewpoints
is by no means such that an emphasis upon fellowship with God here
and now leads to a suppression of the "final eschatological" perspective or vice versa. The situation is rather this—that the more clearly
salvation is seen to be a fellowship with God here and now, the more
clearly does it receive the character of a hope of good things to
come (cf. § 36). The reason Christian faith is characterized by such
a two-sidedness is that for faith the fellowship with God *eo ipso* implies a keener appreciation of the distance between man and the divine
will. The nearer God's saving love comes to man, the more clearly
he comprehends what separates him from God. The Christian conception of salvation is radically different from all perfectionist doctrines. Indeed, it is the "justified" person, the one who has been
incorporated into the divine fellowship, who understands with in-
creasing clarity that he is still a sinner (*simul iustus et peccator*).

Therefore, as far as Christian faith is concerned, the *perfect*
dominion of God, the "kingdom of God," lies entirely outside the
bounds of history. The idea that the kingdom of God is realized
through an evolutionary and inner world-process is entirely foreign
to Christian faith. The kingdom of God does not belong to this
world (John 18:36), nor does it have anything to do with earthly
ideals of blessedness. From this point of view the eschatological character of the kingdom of God *cannot* be emphasized strongly enough.
But this does not imply, however, that the kingdom of God has nothing to do with the world of history. On the contrary, history is the

arena where the kingdom of God struggles and wins its victories. If
the evil spirits are driven out by the finger of God (Luke 11:20),
then the kingdom of God is indeed not perfected (this is not the
meaning of the gospel), but it is in action. It has not become, but
is becoming. When new victories are won, it does not mean that in
the circumstances of history the kingdom of God ascends in a rising
crescendo toward perfection. It implies only that the kingdom is in
constant activity; that after every new victory there comes a new
struggle, though perhaps on another front. The battle lines may
change, but fundamentally it is always the same battle. The kingdom
of God is just as near and just as remote for every new generation.
The chief thing about the kingdom of God in its relation to history
is its active character. Luther speaks clearly of this when, in the
explanation of the third petition, he answers the question, "When is
the will of God done?" by saying,

"When God frustrates and brings to naught every evil counsel and purpose, which would hinder us from hallowing the name of God, and prevent
His kingdom from coming to us, such as the will of the devil, of the
world, and of our own flesh. . . ."

This is the extremely realistic approach of Christian faith; no evolutionary idealism, but no resignation either. In spite of everything,
the voice of victory sounds forth: "And though this world, with
devils filled, should threaten to undo us; we will not fear. . . ."

19. God as Judge

1. *The active judgment of God.* The viewpoint which conceives of
the work of God as an act of judgment expresses the radical opposition of divine love to sin. The judgment of God either restores or
rejects. It becomes a rejection and condemnation when the opposition
to the divine will continues unconquered. Judgment may therefore
be understood as being in part a judgment in the present and in part
a "final judgment." The significance of the judgment of rejection
consists in separation from God.

2. *Judgment and punishment.* When the divine and loving will is not
dominant, the consequent desolation and suffering may be characterized as divine judgment, with the qualification that: a) this viewpoint

must not be used to establish a rational explanation of the universe, and b) the punitive activity of God is distinguished, as his *opus alienum*, from his *opus proprium*.

3. *Note on the boundary line of faith.* The result of God's final judgment cannot be made the object of any definite statement of faith. On this subject the thoughts of faith must emanate from and be determined by the following fundamental rules: the possibilities of God's love must not be restricted and his radical opposition to sin must not be obscured. Under such circumstances faith will reject both a rationally motivated and unconditionally maintained universal restoration (*apokatastasis*) and a rationally motivated and unconditionally maintained so-called twofold destiny.

1. The Active Judgment of God

The God of salvation is also the God of judgment. The interpretation of the divine act of judgment is exposed to two mutually opposed fundamental dangers: first, the possibility of separating God's act of judgment from his loving will; and second, the possibility of weakening the significance of the idea of judgment. The first possibility is characteristic of scholastic theology, and the second is typical of the humanized theology influenced by idealistic metaphysics. If the characteristic viewpoint of faith is to receive due consideration it is necessary to preserve both the connection between the loving will and the judgment of God, and the unbroken radicalism of divine judgment against sin. Between these two points of view there ensues a relationship full of tension. But actually the latter viewpoint can be effectively maintained only under the assumption that the judgment of God is understood in the final analysis as an expression of his love. For the only really radical judgment of sin is that of pure love. Christian faith has frequently spoken of Christ as the one who exercises God's power of judgment, as judge of "the quick and the dead." This in itself is the strongest possible expression of the fact that Christian faith cannot conceive of God's judgment in any other terms than as a judgment of love itself, and that no assertion about God's judgment can be identified as Christian which cannot also be ascribed to and affirmed of Christ and the Holy Spirit.

It can hardly be denied that various notions have crept into the thought of the divine act of judgment which cannot in the least be reconciled with the idea that the work of God, from whatever viewpoint it may be considered, is always an act of love. Thus it has been possible for primitive ideas to appear which have attributed something capricious, unreliable, and envious to the nature of God. When such ideas were connected especially with thoughts about God as "the avenger," it was due to the fact that the anthropomorphic and symbolical character of this expression has not been sufficiently considered. The attempt thus was made to find in "vengeance" a divine characteristic opposed to love, instead of understanding it simply as an imperfect figure of speech which may be used to illustrate the spontaneous power in God's opposition to evil. The act of judgment has, however, most often been given a judaizing interpretation according to the principle of pure retribution: like for like, an eye for an eye, a tooth for a tooth. Indeed, the idea of retribution has a relative legitimacy, inasmuch as it gives elementary expression to punitive justice, to that fundamental principle which says that evil must be condemned and punished in conformity with that law of life which requires that of necessity evil begets evil. Thus the idea of retribution may be said to be related to God's act of judgment, since his judgment occurs because of an inner necessity and on account of sin. However, the idea of retribution is dangerous whenever retributive justice is separated from divine love and is made the highest principle in the relationship between God and man. The consequence of such an isolation of the idea of retribution is that God's relationship to man is again imprisoned within the confines of the legal system which was burst asunder through the divine revelation in Christ. Furthermore, the idea of reward and punishment becomes, in the final analysis, decisive, and thus the purely religious conception of Christian faith concerning man's relation to God is replaced by a eudaemonistic moralism. Consequently, Christian faith accepts as relatively legitimate the idea of retribution, but this idea forfeits its rights when it is made the decisive principle between God and man.

If, therefore, the judgment of God cannot be separated from his will to love, but is, in the last analysis, simply an expression of it, then it is of fundamental importance for Christian faith that the seriousness and severity of this judgment not be obscured or suppressed. It should be emphasized that, as far as Christian faith is concerned, the judgment of God has an active, and not only a passive, character. Judgment does not merely imply, as Marcion declared, that man separates himself from divine love. To be sure, that is indeed an aspect of judgment, as indicated in the words of the Gospel of John: "And this is the judgment, that the light has come into the world, and men loved darkness rather than light" (John 3:19). Nevertheless, judgment is at the same time a positive act toward men in such circumstances. When Marcion was unwilling to acknowledge such an active judgment of God, it was not because he was overemphasizing divine love, but rather because he has misinterpreted it.

To be confronted by divine love involves always and everywhere a judgment. To stand before God is to be judged. But this judgment may be of various kinds; it is inevitably a judgment either of restoration or of rejection. In the presence of divine love there are, fundamentally, only two possibilities: either it subdues man, or it does not. In the former case the judgment of God restores and saves; in the latter case it rejects and separates. In this connection we are primarily concerned with the latter alternative, inasmuch as the restoring judgment coincides exactly with God's act of salvation. With reference to this act it is sufficient to emphasize that God's act of salvation *must* be understood also as an act of judgment; it is a "justifying" judgment, which, while it restores and unites man with God, at the same time reveals man's estrangement from pure love and his unworthiness before God.

But since God's judgment of rejection or separation must also be understood as a judgment of love, it follows that this judgment is fundamentally nothing less than a *separation from God*. This occurs by reason both of the inner necessity occasioned by the purity of love itself and by man's unconquered hostility to God. The sole purpose of God's loving will is to realize the dominion of love. This is also the sole purpose of divine revelation, as the words of John so well express it, "God sent his Son into the world, not to condemn the world, but that the world might be saved through him" (John 3:17). The purpose was entirely other than that of simply passing judgment upon the world. Nevertheless, all revelation of divine love implies a judgment; indeed, the purer and clearer the revelation, the higher must be the degree of judgment. Although love has nothing to do with external coercion, the very nature of love is such as to produce either attraction or repulsion, either liberation or condemnation.[1]

Therefore it may be rightfully said of the Lord of revelation, "This child is set for the fall and rising of many" (Luke 2:34). In the same vein we sing of the Holy Spirit, "With him who unbelieving spurns Thy love, Thou canst ne'er abide" (Swedish Hymnal, No. 136, vs. 6). Such an expression reveals what is fundamental in God's judgment: love cannot "abide" with that individual who in unbelief has refused to be subdued by it. From another point of view, the same principle is apparent in the well-known scene before the judgment seat (Matt. 25:31-46). Here the revelation of divine love (the "Son of Man") makes known those who have and those who have not permitted themselves to be subdued and ruled by divine love. That the judgment of God is a judgment of love means that no one will be rejected and separated except those who have refused to tolerate the presence of love. According to Christian faith, the judgment of God in history is a preliminary judgment. In addition to this constantly ongoing act of judgment, but at the same time in connection with it, faith speaks of a definitive judgment, which it identifies with the expression "final judgment."

2. Judgment and Punishment

The idea of judgment is closely connected with the thought of punishment. Judgment implies punishment. As we have previously noted, the punishment of the judgment of rejection consists primarily in separation from God. But the conception of divine punishment has also at the same time been made to refer to "temporal" punishments of various kinds. It is, of course, indubitable that sin, that is, the absence of the dominion of divine love, is connected with and leads to the most extensive desolation and the deepest suffering. This is verified again and again in every new generation. To Christian faith the inner connection between sin and desolation appears as a divine law. Then it may be asked in what measure this desolation and suf-

[1] The expression "Whom he will he hardeneth" may also be interpreted from this viewpoint (cf. Paul in Romans and Luther in De Servo Arbitrio). The significance of the expression cannot be that of God's *desire* to "harden" man in sin. "Hardening" consists rather in the hardening reaction of sin itself when it is confronted by that which is good, by the revelation of pure love.

fering shall be considered as a divine "*punishment*" and what is meant by the punishment of God. If we are to use this symbolic expression as a legitimate Christian designation of God's relation to what opposes him, and at the same time do justice to the divine nature as "pure love," our usage must be limited by certain definite considerations, namely the two following: this concept cannot be used to establish a rational explanation of the universe; and the punitive act of God must be distinguished, as his "alien activity" (*opus alienum*), from his "proper activity" (*opus proprium*).

In the first place, the conception of divine punishment cannot be employed as a rational explanation of the world's desolation and suffering. This tribulation cannot be thought of as a proportionate punishment in relation to the sin which has been committed. Such reasoning, which gives evidence of a relapse into the doctrine of pure retribution, stands most emphatically opposed to the fundamental viewpoint of the Gospels. Thus Jesus, according to Luke 13, dismissed the suggestion that those Galileans whose blood Pilate had mingled with their sacrifices were sinners above all others because they had suffered such things (Luke 13:1 ff; cf. John 9:2 f). And this Gospel viewpoint is abundantly verified by the mysterious contaminating and infectious nature of sin: the consequences of sin do not fall only upon the guilty; the innocent must suffer with the guilty, indeed, often in greater measure. Thus the idea which Jesus, according to the Gospel, repudiated is clearly connected with a Pharisaic self-righteousness which judges without love and therefore unrighteously. Such judgments, which are in harmony with the predilections of "natural" man, are more concerned with establishing the degrees of guilt than conquering evil (cf. § 23).

In the second place, since faith includes a certain type of suffering in its conception of divine judgment, it must be assumed that such punishment is, as Luther termed it, an "alien work" of God, which ultimately serves his "proper work," that is, the work of divine love. There can be no question therefore of God's desire to "punish" simply to bring upon the sinner a certain amount of suffering. As far as faith is concerned, it is meaningless to speak, under historical circumstances of divine punishment which does not in some way serve the divine purpose, namely, the establishment of the dominion

150

of God's love. It is evident to faith, however, that desolation and suffering actually *can* serve this purpose. It is true in a negative sense, for these tribulations reveal the consequences of being separated from that power which is supreme in the life and growth of all creation. But it is true in even greater measure because divine love, as faith clearly testifies, is able to use desolation and suffering as a means to accomplish its positive purposes. From the viewpoint of faith, therefore, the concept of divine punishment is indissolubly connected with the idea of warning, discipline, testing, cleansing, quickening, deepening, and so on, or, in other words, with positive purposes. However, when the thought of divine punishment is separated from these purposes, it loses its meaning.

A marginal note must be inserted at this point to the effect that faith cannot conceive of any suffering emanating from sin, as a result of the divine will. Faith, indeed, refers to *this* type of suffering as being related to God and points out that the inner connection between sin and desolation is an expression of divine law, and that God can even employ it as a means to accomplish his purpose. But this does not mean that this evil can be traced to the divine will and that therefore it is a direct realization of the will of God. Whenever these viewpoints are blurred the result is disastrous; the conception of God characteristic of Christian faith is entirely obscured. When that evil which has its roots in sin is said to be an expression of God's will, it implies that sin, or in other words, that which opposes the will of God, is synonymous with that will (cf. § 22). Under no circumstances can Christian faith ascribe to God anything which stands in opposition to that which the event of Christ has revealed as divine, and which faith is unable to ascribe to God the Holy Spirit. The God of Christian faith desires no evil; his sole concern is to overcome it.

3. Note on the Boundary Line of Faith

The judgment of God continues constantly. Divine love unceasingly carries on its activity of restoration and separation. But according to the Christian message faith must simultaneously consider the divine act of judgment from an eschatological viewpoint, as a "final," definitive judgment. The judgment of God is not fully completed within a certain specified time. It cannot be assigned to some "final period" within history. From the viewpoint of faith, the identification of world history with world judgment is only a half-truth. Any attempt to discern the judgment of God in the course of history in accord with the pure laws of retribution would result in something less than a "half-truth" (cf. § 19, ¶ 2).

The idea of final judgment is an essential, inalienable, and fundamental aspect of the outlook of faith. But this does not mean that faith is able to answer all the questions that can be asked in this connection. Here we find ourselves at the boundary line of faith. Faith is unable to express itself relative to these matters in the same way that it can witness to the divine act of revelation in the present. It must relinquish all supposedly certain knowledge about that which lies beyond its grasp. In this connection it is well to recall Luther's reference to the three kingdoms in his *De Servo Arbitrio*, namely, the kingdoms of nature, grace, and glory. In the kingdom of grace, says Luther, much is revealed of that which is hidden in the kingdom of nature. Likewise, in the kingdom of glory much will be revealed which is now hidden in the kingdom of grace. Therefore faith, which exists in the kingdom of grace, would be presumptuous if it endeavored to express itself about the kingdom of glory, as if all its secrets had already been revealed.

But if faith, in spite of everything, attempts, in groping thoughts, to feel its way across the boundary, it does so only on the condition that these thoughts must harmonize with that which faith has already seen of God's loving will and its activity in judgment. This is doubly important, for in these matters a number of viewpoints foreign to Christian faith have appeared from many directions. The ideas of faith concerning the final judgment and its consequences can contain no element opposing those verities which have reference to the Christian concept of the nature of God and the relationship between God and man. If faith is convinced that the divine will never operates through external coercion but through the power of an inner compulsion, then this fundamental point of view cannot be set aside when it is a question of God's "final judgment." Divine love does not change its approach; it is "unchangeable." If faith has been confronted by God's love as the supreme power in all creation and knows something of the limitless possibilities at its disposal, it is not tempted to ignore or diminish these possibilities when the question of God's final judgment is being considered. If faith has also seen that to be united with this power involves "eternal" and indestructible life, but to be separated therefrom results in desolation and defeat, then this fundamental idea must also be applied to the question of the "final goal" set by the will of God. And finally, if faith has become aware of God's inexorable, unmitigated opposition to evil, it cannot readily succumb to notions which attempt to blunt this unbroken opposition when it is a question of the consummation of the act of judgment. This discussion may be summarized in two principles, namely: the possibilities of the sovereign love of God cannot be curtailed or diminished; and his radical, condemning opposition to sin must not be obscured.

With its starting point rooted in these principles, Christian faith overrules the theories of both scholastic and idealistic theologians. The characteristic viewpoint of scholasticism is a rationally motivated and unconditionally maintained twofold destiny; idealism is characterized by a rationally motivated and unconditionally maintained *apokatastasis*. As far as the scholastic type is concerned, we can ignore the question it presents relative to the "eternal torment" of the damned. It is clear, however, that this divine retributive justice triumphs both over evil and over divine love when it is asserted, for example, that in the torments of the damned, the redeemed hosts behold and admire the justice of God. The chief objection of Christian faith to scholasticism is the assumption of this theory that its conclusions alone are acceptable, and that it can therefore arrogantly limit the possibilities of divine love. In contrast, Christian faith must reckon with the unlimited possibilities of divine love. But at the same time faith is unable to assert, as does the idealistic and evolutionary theory, that everything is progressing toward a so-called *apokatastasis* because of an inner, positive urge. When this theory refers to the sovereignty of divine love as proof of its assertion, it forgets that this divine love never operates as a coercive force. It would be possible to construct an *apokatastasis* as a self-evident final goal only if divine love were found to operate as an irresistible force of coercion. When Christian faith gives due consideration to the manner in which divine love accomplishes its work—by means of an inner compulsion, without which it would not be love—and also takes into account the actual fact of opposition to this love, it must also *reckon with the possibility* of a hardening of the heart which definitely separates itself from fellowship with divine love.

Christian faith must therefore reject both a rationally conceived dualistic starting point and a rationally constructed doctrine of an *apokatastasis*. In general, it cannot establish any definite propositions in this matter. Instead, faith must reckon with the twofold possibility based upon the Christian conception of God's relation to man and the character of the Christian idea of God. Faith's view of what lies beyond the boundary is therefore characterized by a tension-filled dialectic. Least of all can the idea of the continuing possibilities of divine love be used in the interests of a lax quietism without thereby losing its Christian legitimacy. Everyone who has been confronted by the divine love must thenceforth live as if the present possibilities were the only ones, under the constraint that "the acceptable time" is *now* and that every day is the "last day." The idea of a continued possibility of decision beyond death is accessible *to faith*, and then only as a thought inspired by love and hope for the benefit of others. It emerges in the presence of the sovereignty of divine love and implies that this love can no more be halted by death than can our own.

It should be added that a presentation of "the last things" must take into account not only the two possibilities already mentioned, but also a third, namely, the so-called theory of annihilation. A closer examination of this idea reveals, however, that this is but a variation of the theory of the twofold destiny.

When the argument relating to condemnation and annihilation is examined, it is evident at the outset that the discussion all too often rests upon postulates foreign to Christian faith, especially the theory maintaining that the "immortality of the soul" is something axiomatically given. This line of thought, which has emanated from a philosophical and idealistic matrix, stands in sharp contrast to the characteristic viewpoint of Christian faith. For Christian faith "eternal life" is not a self-evident prerogative of man, but is rather a gift given in and with man's fellowship with God and realized in and through the "resurrection." When the conflux of ideas that have emerged in connection with the concept of eternal condemnation is further investigated, it becomes clear that a host of unworthy notions have made their appearance, since it has been possible to regard "torment" as an end in itself, or in any event as having the purpose of celebrating the *iustitia distributiva et vindicativa* which is separated from divine love. When these unworthy notions are eliminated, the legitimately Christian element in the conception of condemnation appears, namely, the idea that the judgment of God confronts sinful man as an unconditional judgment of rejection. If the results of both of these investigations are now finally applied to the debatable question of eternal punishment and annihilation, the consequence is a certain obvious dissolution of their mutual opposition. What remains is the twofold idea that the judgment of God reaches sinful man as an unconditional judgment of rejection, and that this final judgment involves separation from God. When Christian faith employs the contradictory expression "the eternal death" to designate this separation from God, the very expression itself makes it plain that it is outside the realm of possibility for faith to affirm anything about the result of the judgment of rejection except that it involves a separation from God.

20. God as Creator

1. *The scope and significance of the doctrine of creation.* The scope of the Christian doctrine of creation is expressed in the words of Paul: "For from him and through him and to him are all things." God's creative activity includes beginning, continuation, and goal. The full significance of this all-comprehending activity is interpreted from the point of view that creation as a whole is inseparably connected with Christ.

2. *The distinctive character of the doctrine of creation.* Christian faith as faith in the Creator differentiates itself, on the one hand, from metaphysical idealism which blurs the distinction between the divine and "the highest human"; and, on the other hand, from metaphysical dualism which regards this finite life as evil. Faith in God as Creator affirms on the contrary, that all existence is entirely dependent on God, that this life is good since it is given by him who is the giver of all good gifts, and that this gift therefore imposes an unconditional obligation on the creature.

155

3. *Creation and history.* If creation, therefore, is primarily the life-giving work of sovereign divine love, it implies that its origin as well as its perdurance depends on this loving will, which also gives it its meaning. The ultimate goal of creation does not lie within the course of this world. It is attained through the continuous creation, but it leads forward to "new heavens and a new earth."

1. The Scope and Significance of the Doctrine of Creation

Strictly speaking it *ought* to be superfluous to emphasize the religious character of faith in God as Creator. But in reality nothing is more imperative, since it is at this point in particular that foreign metaphysical points of view have appeared. It has been very common to confuse the affirmations of faith about creation with cosmological theories, or to interpret these affirmations as a theory of the origin of the universe coincident with or perhaps in conflict with other more or less scientific theories of its origin and development. The old scholastic theology with its predilection for rational argumentation explained creation by reference to God as "the first cause." Even after this kind of argumentation had lost favor, metaphysical points of view stubbornly remained. Faith in God as Creator was accepted as a theoretical proposition about what had happened "in the beginning of time." Even if such a theory of origins could be theoretically demonstrated, which is impossible, this whole conception is completely meaningless to faith, since it has no religious character. The various theories about the origin and development of the universe which might be suggested by natural science cannot encroach upon or exercise any influence on the convictions of faith regarding creation. The fact that the old geocentric world view was long ago abandoned, and that we now reckon with incomprehensible space, serves simply to accentuate that which has always been a commonplace to faith: human lowliness in the presence of the divine majesty. But this cannot in any way change Christian faith in God as Creator, nor affect its religious character.

The Christian doctrine of creation as found in the New Testament has been expressed in a clear and pregnant word of Paul: "From him and through him and to him are all things" (Rom. 11:36). The perspective comprises the whole eschatological drama of revelation. Its starting point is found in the first words of the Bible: "In the begin-

ning God created the heavens and the earth" (Gen. 1:1). Creation
has a beginning, but it has also a continuation and a goal. It is not
only an act at a certain moment which God has done and finished
at a certain point of time, "in the beginning." Creation continues.
The content of its significance and goal derives from the fact that
the *whole* act of creation is connected with Christ. This is true not
only of the continuation and the goal, but also of "the beginning."
"For in him all things were created, in heaven and on earth, visible
and invisible, whether thrones or dominions or principalities or authorities—all things were created through him and for him" (Col.
1:16. Cf. Heb. 1:2). When the act of creation is thus "from the
beginning" connected with Christ, the assertion is made that the God
of creation is none other than the God of redemption, and likewise,
that the redemptive act is a continuous creation. It creates anew. God
creates when in Christ he struggles with and subdues the hostile and
destructive powers in the universe. Creation continues until its goal
is reached. The Christian message speaks not simply of a completed
act of creation, but also of "the new creation." This new creation has
come through the victory of Christ and is continually being realized
in the present. "If anyone is in Christ, he is a new creation" (II Cor.
5:17). But this new creation cannot be confined within the limits of
history. Faith knows it continues in the present. But at the same
time it looks forward to the completion of this new creation in the
eschatological consummation. This future is the final goal of creation (I Cor. 15:20-28).

When Christ is connected in this way with creation as a whole,
and his act of redemption illumines it, the meaning and purpose of
God's creative will becomes clear and unequivocal. It is therefore
highly important to view creation as a whole under this perspective.
But it would nevertheless be wrong and contrary to the Christian
message if we insisted that the creative will could be perceived only
through this perspective, and that apart from this God's creative will
would be completely hidden. The Christian faith does not deny that
creation and existence as such bear witness to the Creator. What the
Old Testament has said again and again, "The heavens are telling the
glory of God; and the firmament proclaims his handiwork" (Ps.
19:1), is verified also in the testimony of the New Testament: "Ever

since the creation of the world his invisible nature, namely, his eternal power and deity, has been clearly perceived in the things that have been made" (Rom. 1:20).[1] It must not be forgotten that the will of the Creator makes itself known in that demand, that "law," which is inherent in creation precisely because it is the work of God. (Cf. § 21). Both of these points of view belong in the context of the Christian faith, but they must be subordinated to and defined by the redemptive act of God in Christ through which God's creative will is realized.

We must emphasize, finally, that from this point of view the work of creation as a whole is an expression of God's sovereign love. When we speak of creation we must understand it as the life-giving activity of divine love. The love of God must be understood as a creative love. The nature of love is to impart itself, to give itself; and this self-impartation implies creation. The creative activity of God is not something incidental, or something that could be separated from him. If God is love, then by inner necessity he is the creating God. If God really is love, faith cannot think of him except as creating. As Luther says, God is "a gushing spring constantly overflowing with goodness. *By his very nature,* not only occasionally as the scholastics claimed, he makes man the object of his love."

2. *The Distinctive Character of the Doctrine of Creation*

The religious meaning of faith in God as Creator is illuminated to a certain extent when we note how this faith is differentiated from two opposing and foreign theories of creation.

In the first place, faith in God as Creator stands in opposition to metaphysical idealism. The theories of metaphysical idealism may be expressed in various ways, but in one way or another they always manage to find the divine and infinite in the human and finite. The "spiritual" part of man belongs to the divine life. Under such circumstances what is human passes over into the divine. No definite line of demarcation is drawn between the spiritual aspect of man, which is

---

[1] This and other similar statements in the New Testament do not intend to prove the existence of God, as the Stoic *theologia naturalis,* or to claim that man can find God by the powers of his own intellect. Cf. B. Gaertner, *The Areopagus Speech and Natural Revelation* (Lund: 1955).

"the highest human" and is in itself indestructible and eternal, and the divine. This conception is in principle differentiated from faith in God as Creator, not only because it is a metaphysical speculation, but also because the relationship between God and man in this case is not characterized and defined by the sovereignty of the divine. As far as faith is concerned all creation is finite, and therefore of a different nature from that of the eternal God. This is true also of man. He possesses nothing incorruptible and eternal which belongs automatically to him; he has no divine, spiritual nature. God is God, and man is *qua homo* finite, corruptible, *creatura*. There is a sharp line of demarcation between Christian faith and idealism, no matter how frequently they have been confused and commingled. As far as faith is concerned, the divine cannot be included in the finite, but instead, the eternal God meets man, speaks to him, and has fellowship with him in the finite world of his existence. The attempt of idealism to escape the finite appears to faith as a failure to realize the seriousness of the situation in which man actually stands, as visionary optimism, and as a false apotheosis of the human.

But Christian faith in God as Creator is also differentiated from a metaphysical dualism which regards this finite life as evil and separates it from the sovereign and divine love. It is well known that the ancient church in its struggle to preserve faith in God as Creator faced just such a situation in its conflict with Gnosticism and Marcion, who attributed the creation of the world to a lower god. It should be pointed out that it is not at all impossible for a metaphysical dualism to pass over into a metaphysical idealism. This is made possible by the idea that man belongs to a higher sphere but has become imprisoned in the finite world. Under all circumstances metaphysical dualism regards life in this world as evil. To this idea the Christian doctrine of creation is opposed. Evil is not to be found in the finite as such. To Christian faith evil does not make its appearances in an undefined, metaphysical opposition between the finite and the infinite, but in the definite opposition between the divine will and that which is inimical to it. It does not perceive life itself as evil. The God of creation is none other than the God of salvation.

When the Christian doctrine of creation is viewed against the background of these two foreign conceptions, two fundamental features become evident. In the first place, the relationship between God and man, characterized by faith in creation, is one of complete dependence upon God. The relationship to God is, in the famous phrase of Schleiermacher, "a relationship of absolute dependence." The content of this fundamental idea is obscured when this relationship of dependence is confused with a relationship of cause and effect, as Schleiermacher confused it. The religious significance of this dependence is that in relation to existence and to man God is sovereign, that in every circumstance man is completely subordinate to the power of God, and that he can trust only in God, not in something divine within himself. It is this status of unconditional dependence, which, as an element of faith in God as Creator, characterizes the Christian relationship between God and man.

But in the second place, faith in God as Creator perceives this life as something good, a gift from him who is the giver of all good gifts (Jas. 1:17). To regard life in this finite world as evil results in an ascetic view which is foreign to faith. *The finite world in which man lives is God's world.* It cannot be divided into spiritual and profane parts. Not only "the spiritual life," but also that part of existence which we call the secular is subject to the government of God. Just because life is a gift and this world is God's world, the strongest obligation and the most unconditional responsibility are involved in life.

3. Creation and History

According to our previous exposition, creation is that work of divine love through which this love appears as the sovereign power in relation to existence. Faith perceives the divine love as that power which gives life to, and in the fullest meaning of the word sustains, all things; it is that power which by its continuous creative activity establishes its kingdom out of chaos. The proposition that creation is founded upon and is sustained by the divine will expresses the thesis that the creation is completely dependent on God. Nothing perdures which is not sustained by this divine love. If divine love is the sovereign and life-giving power of existence, then everything not connected with or sustained by this love is marked for corruption and destruction (cf. § 16, ¶ 2). When theology designates this part of

God's activity as "providence," it should be noted that this is not some new activity over and above creation, but precisely his creative activity seen from the standpoint of its continuity as a *creatio continua*. We could speak of it as a different work only if creation had been finished at a certain point of time. Since this is not the case, the idea of providence is inseparably connected with God's creative activity as a *creatio continua*.[2] God's providence is his continuous creative activity. There is, of course, a different connotation in providence from that in creation. Providence suggests the maintenance of what already exists. Nevertheless, providence must be connected with the fundamental idea of creation. When we pray God to preserve his Christian church, this preservation is in reality nothing else than the continuous, life-giving activity of divine love.

From the point of view of faith in God as Creator divine love gives meaning to all existence. Since existence and history are not in themselves a complete whole, this meaning is not to be found in history as such. As long as history is viewed without connection with the will of God, the meaning is hidden; but it is revealed through the continuous struggle of the divine will against the opposing forces. The Christian doctrine of creation is opposed, therefore, both to that pessimistic world view which regards existence as a meaningless repetition, and to that evolutionistic and optimistic view which attempts to find meaning in a continuous progress toward a goal of perfection attainable in this world. Christian faith finds the meaning of existence in the fact that every moment has eternal significance, since it involves a decision for or against the will of God. The divine will is not indifference to history when history is understood as the arena in which the divine will struggles against inimical forces. The attitude of the divine will toward history is not merely that of a negative condemnation, but is rather a positive desire to save and thereby to re-create. But the ultimate goal does not lie in a certain "end period"

[2] Schleiermacher, *Christian Faith*, pp. 142-49. The trouble with Schleiermacher's analysis is not that he combines the idea of providence with creation; this is in reality its merit. Since, however, the consciousness of absolute dependence upon God is combined with the insight that all things are conditioned and determined by the interdependence of nature, the idea of God's providence as *creatio continua* tends to become lifeless. Cf. § 16, ¶ 2.

of world history. It must rather be understood as a new creation, "new heavens and a new earth" (Rev. 21:1; II Pet. 3:13).

Faith perceives clearly that such ultimate goals within history are figments of the imagination, since every historical period must be subject to divine creative activity, which is at the same time salvation and judgment. The perfection faith contemplates implies, therefore, a radical transformation of the present order. This is symbolically expressed in the words about new heavens and a new earth (cf. § 52, ¶ 1). From this point of view the perfection cannot be referred to certain "last times" within time, but is just as near to every time and generation. Every period must in reality be regarded as "the last times."

21. The Law of Creation

1. *Lex creationis.* If God's loving and sovereign will is the matrix of creation, this creative will acts as a law of creation when it struggles against chaos and condemns that which threatens creation with disaster and destruction. Since it is a function of the divine will, this law of creation is universal.

2. *Lex creationis and lex revelationis.* Since God's purpose for man and the world is changeless, the commandments and laws appearing in the biblical message must not be understood as new laws in relation to the law of creation. They are rather intended to elucidate the content of the universal law of creation; or, in other words, to give expression to the divine will acting as "law."

1. Lex creationis

In the previous chapter we discussed the relation of creation to redemption, and redemption as God's continuing act of creation. We also stated that creation stands in a relationship to God's law. Since the questions relating to redemption will be discussed fully later, we call attention here only to that continuing, creative work of God in which he uses "the law" as an instrument in realizing his will in conflict with the powers of chaos.

The doctrine of creation implies that God's loving and sovereign will is the matrix of creation. The purpose of creation is that God's will should rule and control all things. In other words, God's loving will is the law of creation. God's will is that earthly society shall be characterized and defined by the will of love which is the matrix of creation.

When Christian faith speaks of the law of creation, or rather the law of the Creator, it does not refer to any collection of laws, fixed commandments, or statutes. The reference is to that divine will which maintains creation and preserves it from disaster and destruction. What we call "law" is really nothing else than the divine will itself in operation. The Creator has not set a certain law or a penal code to rule over his creation. The law of creation cannot be thus separated from the Creator as somehow independent of his will. Here everything depends on the conception that the God of creation is the continually active, working, and creative God who makes his will known and effective anew in the various contexts and situations in the world.

When the divine will acts as law, this law has a twofold purpose. In the first place, it must check and suppress everything that threatens creation with calamity and ruin. This is the primary function of the divine law in a negative sense. But in a positive sense God's will as law urges and even compels men to actions which advance and further the purposes of God. In this sense God makes men his partners in the continuing work of creation, which is intended to create in human society order instead of chaos, fellowship instead of dissension and dissolution, and mutual service instead of injury. His constant purpose is to create a human society characterized by concern for the neighbor in whatever forms and combinations mutual relations may appear: family, people, state, and humanity as a whole. Wherever this concern is found, it implies obedience to the divine will.

In the second place, God's will as law has another function very closely related to the first. In its struggle against the powers that destroy life the law of creation acts as accuser and judge. The idea is contained in the very struggle itself. The conflict involves a rejection of and a judgment upon everything that opposes the divine will of love, even though men may not always apprehend and understand these judgments.

Since the law of creation is a function of and inseparable from the creative will, it is also universal. It exists "from the beginning" and functions from the beginning, quite apart from the enactment and interpretation of the law appearing in the biblical message. The law of God functions not only where God has "revealed" his will in a special manner, but also in the entire creation. Man as a created being is subject to the reign of God. If existence is God's creation, it stands in a relationship to God, even though man may not be consciously aware of the relationship.

The universality of the law of creation is clearly expressed in the words of Paul, which have been often misinterpreted: "When Gentiles who have not the law do by nature what the law requires, they are a law to themselves, even though they do not have the law. They show that what the law requires is written on their hearts" (Rom. 2:14-15). It has been suggested that Paul here reveals the influence of stoicism, and that the background of his words is the conception of a *lex naturae* in the sense that there is found in "nature" certain principles guiding human behavior. This conception is foreign to Paul. He says twice that the Gentiles "do not have the law." They have neither the biblical law nor a *lex naturae*. Nevertheless, they can do works which are congruent with God's will. "What the law requires is written on their hearts." The background of this statement is not a rationally deduced *lex naturae*, but the conviction that the God of creation can communicate his will in various concrete situations, and can guide men so that they conform to his will. When the Gentiles thus do God's will, it becomes clear that his law is functioning and setting up a barrier against the depredations of the destructive powers.

What we have said indicates the difference between *lex creationis* and *lex naturae*. The latter may be regarded as a secularized variety of the former. The law of creation is a thoroughly religious conception. It is inseparably connected with faith in the living, active, and creating God. The idea of *lex naturae* or natural law rests on the false assumption that in a purely rational way a reasonable system of law and justice could be deduced which would be both universally applicable and definite in content. Wherever such a theory has been connected with a conception of God, it has been under the influence of deistic ideas. God may then be regarded as the originator of the universe, who, after he had finished his work and laid down certain ethical principles in human nature, has now withdrawn from his work. But when the Christian faith speaks of a law of creation or of the Creator, it maintains that God is the living and constantly active God who continually makes known his will in *concrete situations of life*.[1]

2. Lex creationis and lex revelationis

God's creative will is changeless, removed above all flux. In his relationship to men and the world his will is constant. There is not a variety of divine laws, but only one, the will of sovereign love. The statutes and commandments of God which appear in the biblical message are not a new law in contrast to the law of creation. They originate from the same source; the Creator's sovereign will of love; and, whether they appear as commands or prohibitions, they express his struggle against the destructive powers in existence. What is "revealed" is therefore nothing else than that law of creation which appears as operating in secret. What is contained in the biblical message is, from this point of view, rather an "interpretation of the law" which in various ways explains what the meaning of the law of creation is, and how it operates in secret. The direct message discloses the significance and the twofold purpose of the law of creation: to restrain and arrest that which destroys creation, and to expose and condemn that which is contrary to the will of the Creator. That which opposes is thus revealed as sin and guilt (cf. §§ 30-32). God's commandments and statutes "enlighten" the conscience so that it functions according to the demands of the divine will. The Christian conception of conscience has two aspects. On the one hand we have an appeal to conscience as a witness to the divine will in creation. The function of conscience, as Paul says, is "to accuse or excuse" (Rom. 2:15). But on the other hand it cannot be maintained that conscience is able to give under all circumstances an absolutely certain testimony, or that it constitutes an infallible basis for action in accordance with the divine will. Conscience may be obscured, "darkened," and even the worst criminals have been able to appeal to the "dictates of con-

[1] Cf. Gustaf Aulén, *Church, Law and Society* (New York: Scribner, 1948), Chap. 4, "The Place of the Law in Christian Thinking."

science." Conscience must be "enlightened" if it is to function as a reliable compass in accord with the divine will.

The *lex revelationis* implies, therefore, that the *lex creationis* is interpreted by God's various messengers as they proclaim the demands of God and interpret their meaning. This "law of revelation" is perfected in Christ, who, from one point of view, is also "the fulfilment of the law." "Think not that I have come to abolish the law and the prophets; I have come not to abolish them but to fulfil them" (Matt. 5:17).

This law of revelation, perfected in Christ, in its essence is the law of love. There can be no doubt about this. The demand of love is the fundamental and comprehensive demand. According to the word of Jesus "the whole law depends" on the commandment of love (Matt. 22:40). Paul writes: "love is the fulfilling of the law" (Rom. 13:10). And also: "For the whole law is fulfilled in one word, 'You shall love your neighbor as yourself'" (Gal. 5:14). The Johannine writings, which emphasize the same point of view in regard to the significance of law, present the commandment of love as the "new" commandment. It is "new" in that the meaning of love has been revealed and realized in and through Christ. But it is also significant that this "new" commandment is described as "an old commandment which you had from the beginning" (I John 2:7).

It must be strongly emphasized again that this law of love which Christ has revealed and fulfilled is in principle nothing else than the law of creation. There is no contrast between these two laws. No other will than God's will of love is the basis of the conflict in which the law of creation is engaged on behalf of order as over against chaos. Christian faith has always emphatically maintained that creation rests on God's love. There are at the present time special reasons for a strong emphasis on these points of view. In certain theological circles the idea of "orders of creation" has caused considerable mischief, not the least when the state has been identified as one of these "orders." It has even been suggested that these "orders" of the state are sacrosanct, even when their appearance and activity militate against the most elementary demands of the divine will of love. It seems to have been forgotten, both that their function is to serve this will of love and that they exist under the conditions imposed by sin.

Man's own ordinances, "laws" that enhance his own position, may be substituted for the divine will. Everything depends upon the fact that the law of God must really rule in the orders of human society. If this is not the case, the agencies which were intended to serve God by controlling and defeating the destructive powers enter into the service of these diabolical forces. The theological aberrations which we have seen in our time remind us how important it is to hold fast the conviction that God's will in creation is nothing else than that will whose essence had been revealed in Christ, and that *lex creatonis* is nothing else than *lex revelationis* (cf. § 49).

22. God and the World

1. *Two kinds of evil.* The problem of God and the course of this world becomes particularly acute in relation to evil. Evil is of two main kinds: physical evil and religious evil or sin. The latter kind of evil stands under all circumstances in radical antithesis to the will of God.

2. *The will of God and the course of events.* Christian faith does not conceive of everything that happens as a direct expression of the divine will. If this is done, it obscures the reality of evil and destroys the character of the Christian conception of God. Since existence also contains elements that are hostile to the divine will, a certain "dualism" is inseparably connected with the viewpoint of faith. In relation to this hostile element the divine will is sovereign in grace and judgment (cf. § 16, ¶ 2).

3. *God's care (faith in providence).* To be included in God's care ("faith in providence") means neither a fatalistic submission to the inevitable course of events nor a eudaemonistic attitude which attempts to make God a servant of man; but unconditional trust in that God who is sovereign in relation to evil. "Faith in providence" means, in other words, not that we "accept everything from God's hand" in the sense that God is the cause of everything that happens; but a conviction that God cares for all things, that his purpose is present in all events, and that therefore we may confidently place everything in God's hand.

1. Two Kinds of Evil

The existence of evil creates the most acute problem of the relation of the divine will to the course of this world. Evil is, however, of two main kinds: physical evil, and religious evil, which in the Chris-

167

tian vocabulary is called sin (cf. §§ 30-32). The German language has two words to denote these two kinds: *das Ubel* and *das Böse*. Evil in the first sense includes everything connected with the fact that human life is subject to finiteness and corruption. Here we think especially of physical suffering and death. In so far as this evil is inseparably connected with the conditions of the present life, Christian faith finds herein nothing that *in itself* is contrary to God's will, but rather accepts it as a part of the order of creation. In so far as this physical evil is inseparably connected with the fact that human life is subject to finiteness and corruption, it cannot be separated from the divine will without dethroning God as the Lord also over death and corruption, and without removing creation from its complete dependence upon God. On the other hand, Christian faith maintains emphatically that evil as sin under all circumstances stands in a radical antithesis to the will of God.

The distinction made here does not imply, however, that everything we call physical evil can without further consideration be referred to as the will of God. Christian faith refuses to be satisfied with such a simplified solution of the problem, not just because the evil in the world of nature presents continually insoluble riddles, but primarily because there is an evident connection between physical evil and sin. This latter situation is revealed in part by the fact that sin gives a sting to physical evil which it does not possess in itself. In this connection we are reminded of the words of Paul: "The sting of death is sin" (I Cor. 15:56). It is also evident that in specific instances no clear distinction can be made between physical evil which has its origin in finiteness, and that which is the result of the corrupting and destructive power of sin. It is perfectly evident that physical evil in general has its origin in sin, and therefore in a factor which stands in direct conflict with the will of God.

2. The Will of God and the Course of Events

It is indubitable that the treatment of the problem of God and the course of this world has often been vague and obscure. The reason for this has been not only that faith here as everywhere else perceives "in part," but also because the most vital, inescapable, and fundamental ideas of faith have been obscured. The confusion arises because, on the one hand, it is necessary to speak of sin and its consequences, and consequently about that which is in conflict with God's will; but, on the other hand, it has been maintained, in the interest of a monistic world view, that the course of events is to be understood as a reflection of the divine will. It is self-evident that such a combination of disparate views must present a great temptation to confuse black and white. We need not take the trouble here to analyze the various attempts at rational adjustments. But it is extremely important to fix clearly in mind that faith has no interest whatever in such adjustments, simply because the attempt to find a reflection of the will of God in the general course of events results either in concealing evil, or in obscuring God's constant opposition to it, or in a denial of that God who is "pure love." All these are consequences which stand in direct and violent conflict with the fundamental viewpoint of Christian faith.

If we are to hold fast to Christian faith's conception of God and at the same time accept everything that happens as an expression of God's will, it is necessary to minimize and, as far as possible, conceal the terrible reality of sin and God's antagonism to it. We may then speak about evil as the dark shadows of existence, or as that which is incomplete, etc. This means that the conception of God has been naturalized and humanized. It is also possible by rational adjustments to obscure God's continuous opposition to evil by such vague and ambiguous expressions as God's "sufferance" or "permission" of evil. But such expressions in reality indicate a certain resignation or indulgence on God's part, and fail utterly to affirm that the divine will stands in a radical and condemning opposition to evil and is always intent on its subjugation.

If, on the contrary, evil is conceived of as really evil while God nevertheless is made responsible for everything that happens, the inevitable result is the negation of God as a God of love. This relationship is only slightly hidden when in the presence of the devastation of sin we resort to arguments about God's inscrutable will and suggest that, if we knew the whole situation, even that which most obviously is in conflict with love could somehow be made compatible with divine love. To hide behind the phrase that "God's ways are not our ways" is only a covert way of repudiating God as a God of love.

Love is given lip service, but in reality it is made responsible for that which according to God's own revelation is obviously evil. God's will becomes indefinable, and God himself becomes nothing but blind and inscrutable fate. It is true that God is unfathomable to faith, but this means that God's love meets us as an unfathomable miracle, and that the closer it comes to us the more marvelous and boundless it appears. It certainly does not mean that its unfathomableness is a covering for that which is the opposite of love. Faith holds, indeed, that divine love cannot be measured by human standards, that this love may hide itself behind the mask of wrath, and that to attain its purpose it may use even the harshest means. But this does not imply that sin and the resultant evil are an expression of the divine will. We cannot attribute to the divine will that which is contrary to the revelation and action of this will in the work of Christ. When evil is surreptitiously attributed to the divine will, it is common to confuse two things which must be kept strictly separated: God can indeed turn evil into good and "compel even injury to profit us," but the conclusion must not therefore be drawn that evil is sent by God and is an expression of his will (§ 19, ¶ 2).

Islam proclaims the fatalistic doctrine that everything that occurs is the inscrutable will of Allah, but this is not the language of Christian faith. Christian faith is not blind to the fact that actual existence is not in every respect a reflection of the divine will, but on the contrary contains much that is antagonistic to this will, whether it appears as indifference or hostility. Faith refuses to attribute to God that which the Gospel attributes to Satan. It says also that the desolation and nameless suffering which follow sin are as far from God's will as the blackest darkness is from the brightest sunshine. Faith does not perceive the course of events in its entirety as a realization of the divine will, nor does it identify God's will with the course of nature. It looks upon existence as a *dramatic struggle* and sees the inner meaning of existence emerging out of this struggle where the divine will stands in conflict with hostile forces. That which faith designates as divine revelation consists precisely in this victorious struggle of the divine will. If God's will were comprehended in everything that happens, there would be no need of a "revelation." The very fact that faith points to a divine revelation indicates that it does not accept everything that happens as a reflection of God's will. The background against which faith beholds the active revelation of God is not simply that certain events do not clearly reveal God's will, but that existence is filled with elements which, far from revealing God, are rather opposed to his will.

The reason that Christian faith refuses to be incorporated into a completely monistic system is not that it is afraid to consider what from the human standpoint seem the harsh means and difficult ways of divine love. The purpose is not to preserve some poor human conceptions of happiness which could not endure the misfortunes and unhappiness caused by divine love. If monism had no stronger foe than such a eudaemonistic world view, it could feel quite secure. The purpose is only to guard the purity of the Christian conception of God. Faith cannot attribute human sin and its consequences to the divine will without practicing sleight of hand and transforming black into white. Faith therefore stands before an inescapable decision. Either God discloses himself in Christ and in that spiritual life which he dominates, in which event he is divine love but his will is not reflected in every occurrence; or everything that happens is actually an expression of the divine will, in which event the characteristic feature of love in the Christian idea of God is enveloped in obscurity, and nothing remains except mysterious and impenetrable Fate.

God does not will everything that happens, but with everything that happens he does will something. Nothing is indifferent to him. There is nothing that lies outside his sphere of interest. There is no situation in which God does not desire to realize his purpose. According to the conviction of Christian faith God does realize his will even in relation to that which opposes him. Even in relation to evil the love of God is sovereign love. This means, from one point of view, that every situation, even though it is called forth by hostile "powers," has a divine meaning, and that divine love is capable of making itself effective in every situation. No situation can arise which would overpower God, or would be able, as it were, to wrest the power from his hands and thus bring the absolute sovereignty of divine love to nought. Divine love always appears to the eye of faith as the irresistible power, sovereign *in grace and in judgment*. Everything else that is called power, no matter how much it may have the semblance of power, is doomed to dissolution, desolation, and defeat. In vain does this "power" assault the divine power. Only of divine love and whatever belongs thereto can it be said that it "never ends," and its goal is the only goal that is ultimately realized.

3. God's Care ("Faith in Providence")

When Christian faith places God's love in relation to the course of this world, faith appears as trust in God's care, or "faith in providence." If we are to define this faith more definitely, we must differentiate it from two misinterpretations. On the one hand, faith in God's providence is something entirely different from a simple submission to the actual course of events. If every occurrence could without further consideration be regarded as a reflection of the divine will, the attitude of faith to the suffering and tribulation of the world would be abject resignation, and the only possible course of action would be to submit as gracefully as possible to the "inscrutable" will of God. The attitude of faith does contain an element of patience and steadfastness, but this does not imply that faith retires within itself with a fatalistic statement: God wills it. If faith has become aware that existence contains infinitely much that is contrary to and in conflict with God's will, it must, since it sees only "in part," again and again suspend judgment in regard to God's ways and activity. But under no circumstances can resignation be the last word of faith or the expression of its attitude. As far as faith is concerned any reference to abject resignation leads ultimately to a paralysis of courage and spiritual vigor.

On the other hand, faith in God's providence is far removed from that eudaemonistic attitude which desires to make God a servant of man. Such conceptions have sometimes appeared in Christian thought. A line of thought which makes God the servant of man reverses the relation which, according to faith, exists between God and man. The theocentric character of faith means that all eudaemonism must be radically removed from the relationship between God and man. Under these circumstances faith in God's providence cannot mean that man is thereby immune from all suffering and pain. In the presence of actual facts such an interpretation appears unrealistic and cannot be verified by faith itself. The prayer of faith for God's protection is not a prayer to be delivered from suffering and grief, but a prayer that God will preserve us *in* all danger and harm, and above all that God's dominion may be realized.

The meaning of Christian faith in God's care is an unconditional trust in that God who is sovereign even in relation to evil. Paul has expressed this trust in a classic word: *Nothing* whatever *"will be able to separate* us from the love of God in Christ Jesus" (Rom. 8:38-39). There is nothing that can force itself between God's love and the man of faith; no evil is able to do so. Even if we were thrust into utter darkness, there is no situation in which we can be placed outside the sphere of divine love and care. God is near even when he seems farthest removed. We are continually in his care and under his protection. The Christian "faith in providence" appears therefore as confidence in relation to everything that happens. "If God is for us, who is against us?" (Rom. 8:31). This is vastly different from mere resignation before the vicissitudes of life.

But the words that nothing can separate us from the love of God must not be given a wholly negative interpretation. Confidence in God's care is a trust in the God who is *able to overcome* evil and compel even suffering and harm to serve the purpose of his divine love. Faith does not deny that suffering and want are in themselves evil. Jesus' struggle was also directed against this very evil. If God is not permitted to take suffering and make it serve his purpose, it is not a purifying but a ravaging power, not improving but embittering. Suffering and want are not in themselves an expression of the divine will. But the sovereignty of divine love is revealed in that God's care appears as both condemning and redeeming love. Suffering in which God's love is present and active is changed from a dull and meaningless pain into a purifying and saving power. Thus it becomes a means whereby God adds new areas to his dominion, and through this act of God it receives a significance which it did not possess in itself. Although faith cannot certify God's care as immunity against all suffering, it verifies again and again the power of God to make sufferings serve as the birth pangs of a new and richer life. Faith flees to God, its helper in all need. As far as faith is concerned there is no time when it does not flee to him for help, no difficulties which he cannot solve, and no situation in which faith is not completely dependent upon his aid. But faith in God's providence does not mean that the course of events is mapped out beforehand by God. This would be a deistic and inert conception of God's care and providence, dependent on the idea of God as an extramundane being. Faith in providence affirms on the contrary that God is living and active in what happens, that God has resources sufficient for all emergencies, and that the sovereignty of his care is revealed by his ability to turn evil into good. When faith stands before this expression of God's power it is able to confess in spite of suffering and buffeting: "This has happened that the works of God might be made manifest" (John 9:3). Faith is certain that "In everything God works for good with those who love him" (Rom. 8:28), i.e., with those who are subdued by and trust in divine love. It is here that the nature of faith in God's providence is differentiated from mere resignation. Faith is not resignation, but a conquering conviction. The prayer of prayers, "thy will be done," is not, as it has sometimes been interpreted, an expression of resignation, but of conquering faith in the power of God (cf. ¶ 46).

The statement that faith in God's providence means that man receives everything as from the hand of God may be subject to misinterpretation. It can easily be understood to mean that the divine will is the cause of everything that happens. But this attempt to explain what is hostile to God is, as we have seen, contrary to the characteristic viewpoint of Christian faith. Furthermore, such a theory would have no power to help anyone who is suffering under the oppression of evil. Nothing is gained by a theoretical argument about its origin, and certainly not if that argument derives what is hostile to God from the divine will. Such an elucidation simply makes matters worse. Christian faith in providence does not attempt to give a theoretical explanation of evil. The essential element in this faith is that God *cares for all things,* that his love wills something in everything that happens and that the man of faith may therefore confidently place everything in his hands.

23. The Legitimacy and Limitation of Dualism

1. *No metaphysical dualism.* When Christian faith combines God's will and the course of this world, a tension is created which proves to be a part of that situation within which faith exists. This tension arises because faith opposes every attempt to eliminate or obscure the evil which is hostile to God's will (the legitimacy of dualism), and at the same time opposes all encroachments upon the sovereignty of the divine will in relation to existence (the limitation of dualism).

2. *No rational explanation of evil.* All endeavors to overcome this tension through a supposedly rational explanation of evil must necessarily fail. For Christian faith the problem of evil is concentrated in the question of its being overcome. The answer is given in faith's reference to God who in his struggle against evil gains the victory. Through the victory of divine love even vanquished evil receives finally a significance which it did not have in itself.

1. No Metaphysical Dualism

In the previous exposition of the conception of God and his activity we have constantly found that a certain antagonistic element is inseparably connected with faith's view of existence and its relation to the divine will. Existence contains elements that are foreign to the divine will and in conflict with it. Existence as such is not an adequate expression of this divine will. Faith would be tempted to find the will of God reflected in everything that happens only if it could ignore sin and its consequences, which represent a will in conflict with the divine (§ 30). But faith opposes every attempt to eliminate or in any way to hide and obscure the terrible reality of evil. All such attempts to explain away evil appear to faith as unrealistic arguments which are constantly refuted by the actual conditions in existence. Faith is also opposed to every attempt to blunt and minimize God's continuous antagonism to this evil. Precisely because the God of Christian faith is love, all compromises with evil on God's part are completely excluded. The God of faith is that God whose only purpose is to vanquish evil and thus realize the dominion of his love.

But this viewpoint of faith implies that it is placed in a tension which proves to be a part of the conditions of its existence. Just as faith is opposed to hiding the dualistic element, so it is also opposed to an absolute dualism. As far as faith is concerned God is not a power coincident with other powers and stronger than these, but the power upon which all existence is absolutely dependent. In relation to evil he is *unconditionally sovereign* whether this sovereignty reveals itself *in grace or in judgment*.

The conflict motif has a central place within primitive Christianity. Every attempt to understand primitive Christianity without giving sufficient attention to this fact is doomed to failure. Nothing could be more misleading than the attempts made in the eighteenth century to dismiss the talk about hostile, demonic powers in primitive Christianity by saying that Jesus "accommodated" himself to his contemporaries, or, as in the nineteenth century, by assigning a secondary significance to it by showing its connection with Parseeism. For the Gospels it is fundamental that there is a struggle between the divine will and the power of evil, however this power may be described. It is perfectly evident that Jesus' struggle for the kingdom of God is a struggle against the power of "Satan." "But if it is by the finger of God that I cast out demons, then the kingdom of God has come upon you" (Luke 11:20). "The reason the Son of God appeared was to destroy the works of the devil" (I John 3:8).

A review of the history of theology from this point of view indicates clearly that theology has often attempted to suppress this conflict motif of primitive Christianity, and that this tendency has been connected with the endeavor to incorporate Christian faith into a monistic world view. But we may also note that sometimes this early Christian "dualism" was given a metaphysical character foreign to it. This was Marcion's point of view, and the same misunderstanding has always occurred when a metaphysical antithesis between the infinite and the finite has been set over against idealistic monism.

The conflict motif which is characteristic of Christian faith appears, therefore, as a double antithesis. On the one hand it stands in contrast to an idealistic monism which in one way or another tries to minimize evil that it may be fitted into a monistic scheme, and which at the same time blots out the boundary between the divine and the human. But on the other hand it stands in an equally sharp contrast to a metaphysical dualism which conceives the contrast between the divine and the human as an absolute antithesis between the finite and the infinite. The intention is to make this antithesis as sharp as possible:

the finite and the infinite cannot be joined together. But in this view the antithesis between "good" and "evil" is not as radically conceived as in Christian faith. The antithesis of metaphysical dualism is undefined. But in Christian faith the antithesis is between the divine will, defined as love, and the hostile forces which oppose this will.

2. No Rational Explanation of Evil

The tension to which we have referred cannot be resolved, since this would imply either a toning down of evil or an abridgment of the sovereignty of divine love. All attempts to explain evil rationally are therefore foreign to faith. It does not feel competent to incorporate evil into the divine government of the world in a rational manner, any more than it attempts to present a rational explanation of the origin of evil in general. It is not interested in "theodicies." Neither the idea of punishment nor the insight that God is able to make evil serve his purpose can be used in trying to find a rational place for evil in God's government of the world. The idea of punishment is to some extent legitimate, but it is not sufficient as a rational explanation, since it would imply a proportional relation between sin and punishment (cf. § 19, ¶ 2). Faith has, however, no deeper insight into God's relation to evil than the conviction that he is able to make evil serve the purposes of his love. But neither can this idea be used as a rational explanation of the existence of evil. Such an idea would be acceptable only if it could be demonstrated that the gain under all circumstances exceeds the loss. But this would mean that *all* evil in reality is turned into good, because every loss would be an argument against this rational explanation. To use this deepest conviction of faith as a rational explanation would lead to an easy judgment of evil, which would be incompatible with faith. But the idea of punishment as a rational explanation would, on the contrary, obscure the Christian conception of God as love.

Just as faith cannot rationally incorporate evil into God's government of the world, so neither can it give a rational explanation of the origin of evil. The problem of the origin of evil is for faith a question of the origin of sin. The attitude of faith to this problem will be discussed more in detail in a later chapter (§ 31). Here we need only state that all proffered explanations, in so far as they do simply explain the problem away, are nothing else, and can be nothing else, than expressions of something inexplicable. There is no answer which does not present a new question, whether the reference be to "the freedom of the will," to human nature, to a pre-existent fall, or to a supernatural evil power. In reality faith perceives that a rational explanation of the origin of sin cannot be given. In so far as the meaning of existence is to faith inseparably connected with the divine will, it cannot conceive of sin in any other sense than as something meaningless and irrational. But an attempt to give a rational explanation of the irrational is obviously impossible. In addition, every such explanation would inevitably take the form of an excuse, and the idea of excusing sin is altogether foreign to faith (cf § 32).

Christianity is not a religion which has an easy explanation at hand for everything that happens. On the contrary, it refuses to attempt to provide a rational world view or, in other words, to incorporate faith into a monistic system of thought which is capable of solving all riddles. When classical idealism made this attempt, it succeeded only in cutting the central nerve of Christian faith. Christian faith would rather leave these problems unsolved than adopt explanations and harmonizations which can result in nothing else than explaining away that which is to faith Alpha and Omega: the divine and loving will.

To faith, the problem of evil is the problem of conquering it. This is the essential point. Faith is indifferent to all questions which do not touch on this main problem. Consequently, all the meta-physical speculations about the origin and ultimate cause of evil have no interest for faith. Even if a satisfactory explanation of the origin of evil could be given, the problem of overcoming it would not be any nearer to a solution. Faith has, however, a tremendous interest in the methods and character of evil, because these questions are inseparably connected with the problem of conquering it. It is important to have a clear view of what is to be conquered and the way in which evil works in the world. In the last analysis, there-fore, the problem is the possibility and reality of the victory over evil. The fundamental religious question in view of the actual nature of existence is whether there really exists a power able to conquer evil at its deepest level. The answer of faith, given on the basis of what it perceives of God's active, redeeming, and re-creating revelation, is this: Nothing is impossible for God. If evil is unconquerable, faith in God is dead. It would then be meaningless to talk about a God. But the eye of faith sees not only evil in all its ugliness, but also and above all the God who is victorious.

The question about the way in which God wins the victory and the meaning of this victory will be discussed in the next part. We add here only a concluding word about the light which this victory of God sheds over the darkness of existence. Victory over evil gives a meaning even to that which is in itself meaningless. Using a graphic expression of William Temple's we might say that "evil is justified when it is conquered."[1] Love realizes its inner riches when it breaks down indifference and hostility and captures the opposition by sacrificing itself. This is the meaning of the message that there is more joy in heaven over one sinner who repents than over ninety-nine righteous persons who need no repentance (Luke 15:7). The victory of divine love removes the meaninglessness of existence. But this light in the darkness is something entirely different from a rational explanation of evil.

[1] William Temple, *Mens Createx* (London: Macmillan, 1917), p. 287.

Part II

THE ACT OF GOD IN CHRIST

CHAPTER THREE

The Victorious Act of Reconciliation

24. The Completed and Continuing Work of Christ

1. *The way to fellowship with God.* When we speak in the following pages of God's way to men, the work of God is to be primarily
understood as a work of redemption.

2. *Two aspects of the act of God in Christ.* The work of divine
love is, from one point of view, once and for all accomplished in
Christ and finished through the cross. But from another point of
view, it is a constantly continuing work, the work of *Christus-Kyrios,*
and of the Spirit, the Life-giver, who "proceeds from the Father and
the Son."

1. The Way to Fellowship with God

In the previous pages we encountered again and again the problem
of the relation of the divine will to evil. We have established the
fact that there is a radical antithesis between these two wills. Under
the conditions of history there is a constant conflict between the
divine will and the forces opposed to it. We have seen that the
problem which faith perceives as central is the question of the subjugation of evil, or, in other words, the establishment of the rule
of God and fellowship with God. This question, which we have
merely touched upon in previous pages (cf. § 18) must now be discussed in greater detail. This part of our exposition of the content
of Christian faith is therefore entitled: The Act of God in Christ.
Even this title in itself indicates that freedom from the destructive
powers of evil and the establishment of fellowship with God depend
entirely and completely on an act of God. This point of view has
in reality a decisive significance for everything that follows. According to the viewpoint of Christian faith there is no way from
man to God, no way in which man could gradually strive upward
toward the divine. The way to fellowship with God is God's way
to man.

182

Part III is divided into two general sections, A and B. The purpose of the first is to clarify the way in which divine love itself makes possible the redemption of man. The central point here is the act of reconciliation and victory of self-sacrificing, divine love. When the act of Christ is thus placed in the center, it cannot be too strongly emphasized that this act, in accordance with the fundamental proposition just stated, must be understood as the act of divine love itself. The purpose of the second section is to discover how divine love re-establishes the broken fellowship between God and man through the act of forgiveness that creates faith. The background of this discussion is an analysis of the nature of sin, or of that evil which opposes the realization of fellowship between God and man.

It is clear, therefore, that the chief content of this part implies a more detailed explication of that divine act of redemption to which we alluded in previous sections. We must add, however, that this act of redemption is at the same time an act of judgment and creation.

2. *Two Aspects of the Act of God in Christ*

In our discussion of the idea of revelation (§ 3, ¶ 5) we stated that Christian faith perceives this revelation to be both completed and continuing. The full significance of this twofold aspect becomes clear, however, only as we analyze more fully the act of God in Christ. The revelation of God's redemptive work is from one point of view completed. That which has taken place is decisive and definite. Christian faith expresses this fact in various ways. It speaks of the incarnation of the divine "essence," divine love, in Christ. This means that Christian faith does not expect another revelation of God to supplement and correct the one already given. The Christian relationship between God and man is once and for all defined by the revelation of God in Christ. Faith can also view this matter from the point of view of activity and say: That work of God which has been done in and through Christ has been done once and for all. It is finished and it is of decisive significance. Here the reconciliation between God and man is once and for all established. "God was in Christ, reconciling the world to himself" (II Cor. 5:19).

The victory over the powers hostile to God has been won once and for all.

But Christian faith perceives this redemptive act of God as at the same time continually in progress. It is not a question merely about something that has happened and now belongs to the past, but about something that happens continuously, *quotidie spiritualiter in quolibet christiano* [daily, spiritually, in every Christian] (Luther). Christ is continually engaged in his work of revelation and reconciliation in the world. The victory over the forces hostile to God is won anew in a renewed struggle. Christian faith expresses this contemporaneous aspect of the work of Christ both by confessing him as Kyrios, the risen, living and active Victor; and by its proclamation of the work of the Holy Spirit who is also the Spirit of Christ. The relation between these two affirmations about *Christus-Kyrios* and about the Spirit will be discussed further in the following chapters. Here we desire merely to emphasize that faith in Christ as Kyrios and faith in the Spirit are analogous in so far as both express the character of the revelation of God as a living and active revelation in the present. It may be added that Christian faith does not view the continuing activity of God as different in nature from the finished work. It is precisely this finished act which in the present is continually realized anew.

25. The Incarnation

1. *The religious meaning of the confession of faith in Christ.* The Christian confession of faith in Christ is essentially a confession that God was incarnate in the man Jesus Christ. In this sense Christ is "of the same substance with the Father," and the Father is of the same substance as Christ. The confession of the divine incarnation in Christ is thereby a statement relative to the essential nature of the Christian conception of God.

2. *The distinctive character of the confession of faith in Christ.* The confession of faith in Christ stands in a double antithesis. On the one hand it repudiates the conception of Christ as an intermediary being (separation Christology), whether this is stated in such a way that Christ becomes some kind of half-god, or, on the basis of an idealistic line of thought, he is conceived as "the ideal man," "humanity's prototype," etc. On the other hand it rejects all attempts to identify

Christ with God and thus view him as a divinity walking around on the earth (theophany). What is essential to faith is to see God "in the despised man Christ" (Luther).

3. *The theology of incarnation and the theology of atonement.* The incarnation in Christ is something given in and with the advent of Christ, but also something which is perfected in and with his completed work. The confession of Christ is based, therefore, on the finished work of Christ.

4. *Note on the boundary line of faith.* Since it is contrary to the genius of faith to attempt an explanation of the unfathomable, theology must not attempt to give a rational explanation of the possibility of the incarnation. Faith cannot do more than refer the person and work of Christ to God's eternal and sovereign love.

1. The Religious Meaning of the Confession of Faith in Christ

The confession of faith in Christ is not something that appeared gradually; it was from the beginning identified with Christian faith itself and has continued to be so through the ages. According to the Gospel narratives it even appeared sporadically during Jesus' earthly ministry (Matt. 16:16; John 6:68f). Later it was proclaimed in the message of the resurrection as a confession of *Christus-Kyrios.*

The confession of faith in Christ was from the beginning the focal point, the symbol which identified Christian faith. The ancient church gradually worked it out into definite, theological formulations, among which those of Nicaea and Chalcedon are of greatest importance. The work on Christology was of the greatest importance during this period, and the results along this line can be said to represent the essential contribution of the theology of the ancient church. They fought in the interest of these Christological formulas, convinced that here something essential to Christian faith was at stake, and that the issue was in reality the very existence of Christianity. The focal point was the idea of the incarnation. Christ is "of one substance with the Father;" it is the "substance" of the Father which is "incarnate" in Christ.

If we are to understand the issue, we must follow the principle that our task is to elucidate the religious motifs expressed in the development of the Christological dogmas and their formulations. The reason so many discussions of the Christological problem have brought such meager results has been that they were concerned with the external forms and failed to penetrate to the heart of the matter. This is true of the attempts to defend as well as of the attempts to attack Christology.

The Christian confession of faith in Christ is essentially a confession of faith in the incarnation of divine love, thus the incarnation of God himself, in the man Jesus Christ. It is by deliberate choice that we accept here the principal word of the ancient church: incarnation. Even if this word may be misinterpreted and has therefore resulted in some conceptions of the nature of revelation which are foreign to faith, there is no other Christological concept which has so faithfully preserved the deepest intentions of the Christian faith. This expression affirms first and last that the revelation in Christ has reference to God's approach to man and that here divine love itself enters the hostile and finite world. It affirms that the "essence" of God, or in other words the divine and loving will, is "incarnate" in Christ (John 1:14). It is not an accident that the idea of incarnation served as a bulwark against all external attacks and all attempts to reinterpret the faith which occurred in the ancient church. It is not an accident that Augustine, who had been strongly influenced by Neo-Platonism, perceived in the "incarnation" the point at which the specifically Christian differentiated itself from Neo-Platonism. He never tires of repeating that the failure of Neo-Platonism lies in its inability to understand the incarnation. The concept of incarnation preserved the fundamental motif of Christianity during the early centuries when all kinds of moralistic and speculative influences threatened to destroy the Christian conception of God. The incarnation proclaims the gospel of divine self-giving, and has thus guarded the fulness of the Christian revelation of God. It declares that no one but God, or divine love itself, is incarnate in Christ and performs the work of redemption. To say, therefore, that the Christology of the ancient church was a "Hellenization" of Christianity is to turn the actual historical situation upside down. It was the Christological idea of the incarnation that more than anything else served as a bulwark against the process of Hellenization at work in the church. It was "foolishness to the Greeks," to be sure, but it was also an expression of the fundamental content of Christian faith.

It is important to emphasize that for faith the incarnation means the incarnation of *divine love*. When the idea of incarnation led to ambiguous interpretations of the nature of divine revelation, the reason was that the "essence" of God was understood in a more or less "physical" sense. Even though we may note tendencies toward such an interpretation both within the ancient church and in later times, the fathers of the ancient church did not use such "naturalistic" concepts as their eighteenth-century interpreters supposed. Even if the Christological formulas of the ancient church employed expressions that sound to us "naturalistic," it is beyond doubt that their chief purpose was to maintain that in Christ we meet that which is *essentially* divine. The decisive element in the Christian confession of faith in Christ is stated in the simple and expressive words of Luther: "We find the heart and will of the Father in Christ." Therein lies his "unity of substance with the Father." The event of Christ removes the veil and reveals the heart of God. Christ "reflects the glory of God and bears the very stamp of his nature" (Heb. 1:3). He is not identical with God, but he and the Father are "one" (John 10:30); one in will, in heart, in purpose, and in work. This reflection of God's heart does not mean merely that faith should find here a certain likeness to God and that the love of Christ should be like God's love. "The substance of the Son" is not only *like* the Father's, it is the *same* as his; and the love of Christ is to faith the love of God himself. Where Christ is, there is God; and where Christ is active, there God is active also. The self-sacrificing and self-giving love of Christ is the love of God himself, its struggle against evil is God's own struggle, and its victory is God's own victory. In the event of Christ God realizes his own loving will.

This view of the "unity of substance" does not imply a depreciation of it, but rather an emphasis on its religious meaning. The religious intention in the confession of faith in Christ is obscured as soon as something other than God's "disposition of heart" becomes essential and as soon as the idea of a more or less "physical" unity of substance appears. Just as we do not know the "essence" of a man unless we know the disposition of his heart, will, personality, and character, so faith cannot adopt any other point of view in regard to the essence of God. It can speak of the essence of God only in tentative figures, but the import of the question cannot be of anything less than the heart of God. God's essence is his loving will, not some obscure "substance" behind this will. It is meaningless to attempt to draw a distinction between God's will and his nature or his "substance." If God is "spirit" (John 4:24), then there is nothing more "substantial," or better, more *essential,* than precisely his will, his disposition of heart. If we should speak of a substantial unity which would mean something other than this unity of disposition, we would thereby assert something less rather than something more. We would not thereby lift the question of the unity of Christ with the Father to a higher plane, but rather we would bring it down to a lower—a plane on which the real meaning of the question is lost.

While the terminology in these propositions differs somewhat from that of the ancient church because of their use of the concept of substance, this does not really signify any basic difference. The basic interest of the theologians of the ancient church was in that which is essential in the revelation of God in Christ; it is this essential revelation which creates the redemptive fellowship between God and man. When the Christology of the ancient church, with its concept of substance, rejected the expression of an identity of will between God and Christ, it did so because to the fathers this expression contained something else and something less than is contained in the theses which we have just stated, and consequently it could not be used by them to express the essential meaning of the revelation of God. The theology of the ancient church was guided by the same basic interest which has been definitive for the presentation given here. From a basic point of view that which is essential to Christology is and remains this one matter: if love is the expression for what is the inner being of God, for *die Natur Gottes* (Luther), then Christ's unity of substance with the Father means nothing else, i.e., *nothing less* than the incarnation in Christ of the divine and loving will.

But if, therefore, "the Son is of the same substance with the Father," then this proposition must also be reversible. It must then also be true that the Father is of the same substance with the Son. Such a transposition of the principal statement of the Christology of the ancient church reveals its real religious meaning. The question about the "divinity" of Christ cannot, as we have already stated (§ 5, ¶ 2), be put in such a way as to imply that God is the known being, and that with this given concept of God we can measure the divinity of Christ. The question to which the confession of faith in Christ gives an answer is the question as to *what kind* of being God is, what his will is, and how he acts. The confession of faith in Christ is, therefore, not a statement about Christ; it is first and last an affirmation about that God who has revealed himself. If Christian faith affirms that Christ is of the same substance with the Father, it thereby makes a statement about the character of the Father's being. Then the real function of the confession of faith in Christ is to guard the content and purity of the Christian conception of God. To a certain extent the formulas of the ancient church have really served this purpose and have stood as a bulwark against the processes of Hellenization and moralization. But it is quite evident that the theology of the ancient church was not able to follow consistently this principal point of view which it had adopted in Christology, but allowed the conception of God to be determined also by other factors. This became even more the case within the later scholasticism of the Latin church. The ancient confession of faith in Christ was accepted as a revered heritage, but its influence was greatly reduced. From this point of view the Reformation meant a reversal. The whole of Luther's work as a reformer could be explained from the point of view that he accepted and followed the full consequence of the ancient confession of Christ. No approach can be more misleading than to suppose that the Reformation meant a dissolution of ancient Christology. The very opposite is the truth. It was Luther who more than anyone before him took the ancient confession seriously and saw the "nature" of God reflected in the event of Christ. This is the foundation of his deeper conception of the Christian relationship between God and man.

2. The Distinctive Character of the Confession of Faith in Christ

If we are to understand fully the real purpose of the confession of Christ, it is instructive to note how it is differentiated from two opposite lines of thought. Its struggle on these two fronts began in the early days of Christianity and has continued ever since. The two Christological types which confronted the ancient church may be designated *the separation type* and *the theophany type*. On the one hand the church opposed all tendencies to separate Christ from God that would make Christ a kind of intermediary being, a half-god, or a lower god; and, on the other hand, it opposed all attempts to identify Christ with God, that would make of the appearance of Christ a theophany, or a divinity wandering around in disguise on the earth.

The first type appears to some extent even in the Apologists, who talk about Christ as an "other" (lower) God. It appears later in the so-called Dynamic Monarchianism, and above all in Arianism, which later returned in more subtle forms. This rejected separation-Christology was strongly influenced by the god and Logos concepts of Greek philosophy. Wherever this philosophy has had a serious influence on Christology, it has led to a conception of Christ as an intermediary being. The presupposition is the conception of God as a being enthroned in isolated majesty, and the philosophical idea of the Logos is well adapted to serve this metaphysical conception of God. The ancient church doctrine of the incarnation stands in definite opposition to this line of thought. The Son is of the *same* substance with the Father, it is the divine nature itself which is incarnate in Christ, not an intermediary being. It may be pointed out that what has been said of the influence of Greek philosophy in general is true also in regard to Neo-Platonism. It might be assumed that the situation was different, since the idea of emanation has a certain affinity to the idea of incarnation. But the antithesis is really the same. The fundamental idea in Neo-Platonism's conception of God is the exalted tranquillity and isolation of the Deity. Emanation is from this point of view a cosmic process in which the divine is attenuated and weakened as the emanation progresses. The idea of the incarnation of the divine is entirely foreign to Neo-Platonism, inasmuch as the Deity remains in his isolated exaltation and the process of emanation is in reality conceived of as a fall into sin.[1] It is clear, therefore, that the influence of Neo-Platonism on Christology, and

[1] Cf. Nygren, *Agape and Eros*, pp. 144 ff.

that of Greek philosophy in general, tends to interpret Christ as an intermediary being.

The theophany type includes all endeavors to identify Christ with God in such a way that the historical is removed and concrete human features disappear from the person of Christ. Among these are such Christological types as Docetism and Modalism, which reappeared after Nicaea in somewhat milder form in Monophysitism, Monotheletism, and other related forms. If separation-Christology has been influenced by Greek philosophy, the decisive influence in theophany-Christology came from the Hellenistic mystery cults. This is the natural habitat of the ideas of theophany. It is extremely significant that the confession of Christ in the ancient church turns as decisively against this doctrine of identity as against the separation-Christology. It continues the sharp polemic which occurs already in the Johannine writings against the contemporary "Gnostics" who denied that "Jesus Christ has come in the flesh" (I John 4:2 ff). The formula of Chalcedon settled the irrelevancy of theophany-Christology. It declares that Christ is not a divinity wandering around in disguise on the earth, but that he is our brother and a man like us. The real purpose of the doctrine of the "two natures," which are inseparably and indivisibly united without change and confusion, was to maintain both his "unity of substance" with the Father and his "true humanity." The church declares that it is the divine being himself who meets us in the lowliness of the historical, human person. It should be emphasized that its purpose is not to explain rationally how such a "union" is possible. In this respect it differs from the subsequent scholastic theology.

This review of the struggle on two fronts in the ancient church confirms the statement previously made that the Christology of the ancient church cannot be understood as a "Hellenization" of Christianity. When we note the fundamental motifs behind the formulations of the dogmas of the ancient church, they do not appear as a Hellenization, but rather imply the most determined opposition against *both* forms of that process of Hellenization which endeavored to gain a foothold within the church. The real meaning of the struggle of the ancient church is that the fundamental motifs of Christianity are maintained, both against that Hellenization which had its roots in

Greek philosophy and tended toward a separation of Christ from God, and against that which had its roots in the mystery cults and resulted in an identification of Christ with God analogous to divine theophanies.

It is not our intention to write a history of Christology. But we must present an example from the Christological discussions of a later time to illustrate the importance of this twofold opposition for the Christian confession of faith in Christ. Scholastic theology, both older and more recent, has never been satisfied to stop with the negative attitude of the formula of Chalcedon toward all rational explanations. On the contrary, scholasticism has always endeavored to elucidate and explain how the divine nature in Christ is connected with the human. In reality these explanations tended to favor the theophany type of Christology, or in other words to obscure the "true humanity." The human element was conceived of as a kind of abstract humanity, a cloak which the divine subject had assumed. There was no appreciation of that true humanity to which both the Gospels and the New Testament writings in general give unimpeachable testimony (cf. for example, Heb. 2:18; 5:8).

Against this scholastic theology there appeared during the eighteenth and nineteenth centuries a humanized Christology based on idealistic philosophy. The purpose was to emphasize the "true humanity," which had been neglected by scholasticism. But the result was simply a change from the theophany type to the separation type. Christ became a kind of intermediary being. The starting point was the human person, but this was idealized in various ways. Christ was regarded as "the religious prototype of humanity," "the ideal man," the incarnation of the religious or moral ideal, and so on. This meant that, contrary to the intention, Christ's human individuality was not properly expressed, and the result was the creation of an unrealistic and fantastic being who, as an intermediary being, was in reality neither god nor man. Such a concept as "the ideal man" is nothing but a fantasy. In this process the religious meaning of the fundamental motif of Christology, the idea of incarnation, was lost, and it became impossible to express clearly the idea that the divine enters and dwells in the world of humanity, and that Christ is God's way to man. The Christology of the ideal man represents, on the contrary, an apotheosis of the human. The theology of the nineteenth century is filled with unprofitable discussions between the scholastic and the idealistic, humanized type of Christology.

Against this background the real meaning of the confession of faith in Christ is sharply depicted. From the point of view of Christian faith the failure of scholastic theology did not consists in its desire to take the idea of incarnation seriously, but in its inability to comprehend clearly the lowliness of the historical and human elements. The defect of idealistic Christology did not lie in its attempt to emphasize the true humanity of Christ, but partially in its inability to accomplish this intention effectively, and, even more important, in the fact that Christian faith is not concerned with an idealized humanity, but with the divine, with God. The confusion of these two is in principle foreign to faith. The characteristic viewpoint of faith is well expressed in Luther's words that it is most vital to perceive that God who is "hidden in the despised man Christ." These words contain the whole inner tension of the confession of Christ—God in the humble circumstances of man. Here no attempt is made to escape the tension by means of a Christology of separation or theophany. The revelation of God is a revelation "in secret." The eye beholds a human figure who lived under historical conditions and was crucified on Golgotha, but in this lowliness faith sees nothing less than the incarnation of divine love. Christian faith thus preserves its twofold front. It will not be induced to remove the tension by adopting the idea of an idealized humanity. Faith is not interested in a hero cult. But neither will it accept any "modern" versions of the theophany type of approach, which are designed to remove the historical difficulties, the *skandalon* of history, by substituting "the exalted Christ" for the historical person of Jesus. Faith cannot forget what happened outside the gates of Jerusalem. Certainly it turns its eyes toward the exalted Christ. But he is none other than the Crucified.

3. The Theology of Incarnation and the Theology of Atonement

In Christian theology there has appeared at times a certain tendency to pit the doctrine of the incarnation and that of the atonement against each other. In Anglican theology a certain polemic emphasis has sometimes been placed on the doctrine of incarnation, and support for this has been sought in the tradition of the ancient church. In more pietistic circles, however, the idea of incarnation has often been overshadowed by an emphasis on the redemptive work of Christ. Historically it is easy to show how such a conflict has arisen. But in principle such a conflict is not legitimate as far as Christian faith is concerned. Faith perceives the incarnation of the divine and loving will and the redemptive work of this divine will as an indivisible whole. Any isolation of the doctrine of incarnation would in reality only obscure the active character of the revelation of God and would fail to indicate that the divine revelation appears only in the form of a redemptive and condemning creative act. If the incarnation is emphasized at the expense of the work of Christ, the result would be a more or less "naturalistic" interpretation of Christianity. But the isolation of the doctrine of atonement would, on the contrary, obscure the fact that the work of reconciliation and redemption is altogether the work of divine love. This has often happened in theology (cf. § 26, ¶ 4). In reality the theology of the ancient church does not lend support to a one-sided theology of incarnation. The incarnation is regarded as the prerequisite, the only possible prerequisite, of the work of redemption. No other power than the divine could accomplish this. Traces can also be found of the genuinely Christian idea that the incarnation itself is completed in the accomplishment of the work of redemption. The divine and loving will becomes fully "incarnate" when the work is finished. The important thing is that there is an intimate connection between faith's affirmations about the "person" and the "work" of Christ. Theology has often severed this connection. But in so doing it has only obscured the viewpoint characteristic of faith. As far as Christian faith is concerned, everything depends on the actualization of divine love in the work of atonement and salvation. Or, in other words, Christ has brought divine love into the world through his life, suffering and sacrifice, struggle and victory. Through him the divine and loving will has entered the world. Luther has expressed this in a classic passage. "To blot out sin, destroy death, and remove the curse through himself; to impart righteousness, to bring life to light, and to bestow blessings; to bring the former to nought and to bring the

194

latter into being—this is *the work of divine omnipotence alone.*" [2] The confession of faith in Christ is based on his finished work. The incarnation is perfected on the cross. Here divine love appears in its unfathomableness and inexhaustible power. This becomes evident when the light from the resurrection illuminates the completed work of his ministry.

4. Note on the Boundary Line of Faith

In the event of Christ faith encounters the inscrutable miracle of divine love. Since faith meets Christ as the incarnation of divine love, it comprehends the mystery of his person in the eternal and divine will and in nothing else. He is, in other words, "begotten of the Father from eternity." In this matter, as in everything else, faith is unable to give a "rational explanation" of the miracle. When faith says that Jesus came "in the fulness of time," it points to a divine plan for the life of humanity, but it does not imply that his ministry can be explained on the basis of a conjunction of favorable contemporary conditions. Faith perceives, on the contrary, that both his work and the mystery of his person rest on the nature of God himself, or in other words, on the incarnation. "And the Word became flesh and dwelt among us, full of grace and truth; we have beheld his glory, glory as of the only Son from the Father" (John 1:14). "For in him the whole fulness of deity dwells bodily" (Col. 2:9). The church expressed the truth and the mystery of this incarnation in the words of the Nicene Creed: "Who for us men, and for our salvation, came down from heaven, And was incarnate by the Holy Ghost of the Virgin Mary, And was made man." The church, therefore, traces the mystery of his person to his divine origin, to his being "in the bosom of the Father" (John 1:18). In this sense the words of Nathan Söderblom are true: "the miracle of his being was present already in the bosom of Mary." This is also the religious import of the statement that Jesus became man without a human father, which we find in the Gospel narratives, especially in Matthew. Though in later theology the attempt has been made to use this idea *as a rational explanation* of the mystery of the person of Christ, it appears at once that it is impotent. Theology has attempted to find in the birth of Christ

[2] *WA,* 40[I], p. 441.

without the will of man an explanation of his "sinlessness," or at least of his "freedom from original sin." It is perfectly evident that this "explanation" explains nothing. *If* one wants to gain an explanation this way, one must be consistent and remove "inherited sin" also from Mary. The Roman doctrine of the immaculate conception of Mary is at least consistent. It must be added, however, that this rationalistic explanation has a *semblance* of legitimacy only as long as one, disregarding the fact that "God is Spirit" (John 4:24), conceives "the Son's unity of substance with the Father" in a physical sense; but that it loses even this semblance of legitimacy as soon as it becomes evident that the unity of substance, about which faith never ceases to speak, does not consist in some special physiological nature, which would jeopardize Christ's true humanity, but in nothing less than this: that we possess "the heart and will of the Father in Christ." Under such circumstances Christian faith must reject these rationalistic explanations of theology, as well as all others. The function of theology is not to explain the possibility of the person and the work of Christ. In the presence of the unfathomable love of God, which is and remains the one great miracle, all attempts toward a rational explanation remain useless.

26. Christus Crucifixus—Christus Victor

1. *The finished work.* The work of Christ finished on the cross is that act of divine love through which God establishes the reconciliation between himself and the world. Here is the center of the eschatological drama of redemption.

2. *Victory and reconciliation.* This finished work appears to faith as a victory over those demonic powers which have enslaved humanity, and is, therefore, the victorious breakthrough of the divine will and the establishment of "the new covenant." Since, however, these destructive powers are in part an expression of the divine judgment, the victory implies not only an altered situation for humanity, but also an act whereby God is reconciled in and through his reconciliation.

3. *Propter Christum.* The way of reconciliation is the way of the self-giving, self-sacrificing, suffering, and vicarious divine love. In and through this uninterrupted activity of God the order of justice as the pattern of the relationship between God and man has been breached,

but in such a way that at the same time the radical and condemning opposition of divine love to evil has been perfectly expressed.

4. *The distinctive character of the Christian doctrine of atonement.* The Christian conception of atonement is obscured if it is interpreted *in part* as a divine act and *in part* as a compensation to divine righteousness rendered by Christ as Man; when it is no longer understood as a divine act it is entirely destroyed. The traditional distinction between objective and subjective atonement is calculated to confuse rather than clarify the issue, and these two can in no case be proposed as the alternatives.

1. The Finished Work

Christian faith perceives the work of Christ finished on the cross as an act of reconciliation, as a deed accomplished by divine love through which God effects reconciliation between himself and the world. The expression, "the work finished on the cross," has been chosen for a twofold reason. It is intended to indicate the central place the cross has in Christian faith, and also to emphasize that the cross must be seen in *connection with the whole life* of Christ. The cross summarizes the totality of his ministry.

This formulation, therefore, accentuates a twofold antithesis. It takes issue with any theology which isolates the cross from the rest of his life and thereby assumes that the work of reconciliation has reference only to the cross. This approach is characteristic of some tendencies in medieval scholasticism. But it also takes issue with those tendencies which assign a secondary significance to the cross, as was done in the idealistic-humanistic theology of the last centuries. The teachings of primitive Christianity testify that the eyes of faith are irresistibly drawn to the cross. "For I decided to know nothing among you except Jesus Christ and him crucified" (I Cor. 2:2). The reason for this is that the cross gathers up and summarizes the totality of his life. The conflict to which his life had been dedicated was epitomized in his struggle and victory on the cross, and therefore this deed is the consummation of the incarnation.

Faith perceives the work finished on the cross as a *divine deed,* an act of divine love. This point of view is of vital significance for the Christian faith. It cannot be compromised or curtailed. The moment other points of view are permitted to intrude, it is no longer apparent that fellowship with God is based entirely on divine love and is established entirely through its activity. It is also clear that every approach which does not perceive the finished work of Christ as an act of God is at complete variance with the central content of the confession of Christ as expressed in the doctrine of the incarnation.

In the previous part we spoke of God as Saviour (§ 18). When we now say that the finished work of Christ is that divine act whereby God establishes *reconciliation* between himself and the world, this term is intended to indicate the nature of the salvation we are discussing. The essential character of salvation is a reconciliation, the re-establishment of a broken fellowship between God and the world. Since the fellowship has been broken by the hostile power of evil, reconciliation implies the destruction and subjugation of that power which separates God and the world. Faith perceives the divine act in Christ primarily as an act of liberation and redemption, as Luther expresses it in his explanation of the second article: "who has redeemed me, a lost and condemned creature, bought and freed me from all sins, from death, and from the power of the devil." But this very act of redemption is at the same time an act of reconciliation. The victory over the powers hostile to God is at the same time essentially an act of reconciliation, the establishment of a fellowship between God and man (cf. also ¶ 2).

A reconciliation between two partners can be effected in various ways. It can be accomplished by negotiations between the two parties, or by mediation by a third party, or by the action of one of the parties. All three of these approaches have been used by theology in its effort to set forth the nature of reconciliation. But this is a mistake. From the point of view of Christian faith the first two are excluded. Faith cannot accept the idea that man should negotiate with God as with an equal, or that the reconciliation should be based, even in part, on some accomplishments on the part of man. Nor can the idea of a third party as mediator be accepted. To be sure, theology has often argued along this line and used the idea of Christ as "the Mediator," which occurs a few times in the New Testament. But faith cannot speak about Christ as Mediator in any other sense than as the means through which divine love realizes its purpose. This is the decisive viewpoint in the New Testament. As far as faith is concerned it is imperative that this work be understood as an act of which the divine and loving will itself is the subject. Reconciliation between the two hostile parties is based entirely on the activity of one party, the God of love.

2. Victory and Reconciliation

If we are to investigate how Christian faith understands the meaning of the work of Christ finished on the cross, we must first of all note the motif of *struggle and victory* revealed here. The divine will carries out its purpose through a bitter struggle with hostile forces. Christ carries on the struggle of the divine will against the evil powers, those demonic powers which have enslaved man. The cross is the victory over these powers. The cross is the chief Christian symbol because it is a symbol of victory. It is a crucifix of triumph. Those images of the Crucified which have reveled in picturing the sufferings of martyrdom in the most gruesome manner have missed what is essential to the Christian faith—the victory motif—and have obscured the fact that suffering love is at the same time victorious and sovereign love.

The motif of struggle and victory meets us in the New Testament in a variety of figures. The Gospels present the work of Jesus as a struggle against unclean spirits, concentrated and incorporated in the figure of Satan. The kingdom of God is established by the defeat of those powers which are inimical to God. In this connection it is said that the Son of Man came to give his life a ransom for many (Mark 10:45). The same fundamental theme is found in the New Testament as a whole. Paul regards sin, death, and the demonic powers as the enemies whom Christ has defeated (cf. especially Rom. 4:25; 6:3 ff; 8:38 f; I Cor. 15:3; 15:24 ff; 15:54; II Cor. 5:18 ff; Gal. 1:4; Phil. 2:6 ff; Col. 2:15). It is especially characteristic of Paul that he also includes "the law" among those destructive powers which Christ has conquered. According to Paul the law is, from one point of view, indeed holy and divine, but from another point of view it is a tyrannical power of destruction (cf. Rom. 7:9; I Cor. 15:56; Gal. 3:13). As the destructive power it is, the law, too, has been overcome by Christ (cf. Rom. 7:4; I Cor. 15:57; Gal. 3:13; Col. 2:14). Christ is "the end of the law" (Rom. 10:4). The other New Testament writings present this same theme of a redemptive act which has occurred in and through the victory of Christ over the destructive powers (cf. Acts 20:28; Eph. 1:17; I Tim. 2:6; II Tim. 1:10; Tit. 2:14; Heb. 2:14; 9:12; I Pet. 1:18; Rev. 1:5; 5:5, 12). In the Johannine writings the dualistic feature appears exceptionally strong and serves as a background to Christ's act of conflict and victory. Cosmos stands as an obscure power hostile to God; and the purpose of the revelation and work of Christ is to vanquish this power and dethrone the devil (cf. John 12:31). The way to death is at the same time the way to glorification (John 12:23). In I John 3:8 the purpose of Christ's coming is summarized thus: "The reason the Son of God appeared was to destroy the works of the devil."

This fundamental theme dominates the viewpoint of the ancient church in regard to the meaning of the work of Christ. The thought of Christ's struggle with and victory over the destructive powers occurs in constantly new variations. These powers are almost always defined as the powers of sin, death, and the devil, and the relation of Christ especially to the last of these is pictured in lurid colors. During the Middle Ages this ancient Christian theme was more or less pushed aside. There were two reasons for this: the Latin theory of the atonement finally formulated by Anselm, and medieval passion mysticism. Yet this fundamental theme of Christianity persisted in various ways, in preaching, in hymns, especially in the Easter hymns, and in art. It returned with new power in the Reformation. As Luther has given new life to the ancient confession of Christ and its doctrine of incarnation, so he has also restored to its central position the ancient motif of conflict and victory. Luther never tires of picturing Christ's "wonderful struggle," *mirabile duellum*. It is significant that Luther not only regards the ancient triad, sin, death, and the devil, as destructive powers, but includes also the law (as Paul did) and wrath, the divine wrath. Through this insight of Luther, Christian faith is able to view the work of Christ in the most profound perspective. This will be discussed more fully later.

We must define in a few words the meaning of this fundamental theme of Christianity. During later centuries it was sometimes looked upon with suspicion, principally because it has been expressed in drastic and even grotesque forms. But if we look at the fundamental religious motif it represents, this classic Christian theme appears in

200

monumental simplicity. The background is the divine will and the forces opposed to it. Christ stands as the warrior and victor of the divine will in the struggle against the evil powers in every form. The antagonism between the divine will and evil comes to a focus in a decisive conflict. The evil powers appear to have won the victory. But Christ wins the victory in apparent defeat and triumphs in his death. Divine love is victorious in self-giving and sacrifice. This decisive victory creates a new situation and changes the estate of both man and the world. A new age has begun. The finished work signifies the victorious breakthrough of divine love. Christian faith is born with a paean of victory in its heart: "In all these things we are more than conquerors," no power whatsoever "will be able to separate us from the love of God in Christ Jesus our Lord" (Rom. 8:37-39; cf. also "Thanks be to God, who gives us the victory through our Lord Jesus Christ," I Cor. 15:57). We need hardly underscore further that this motif of conflict and victory is inseparably connected with the central content of the confession of Christ: the victorious power is none other than God's own power.

Up to this point we have not been directly concerned with the idea of reconciliation. Now the analysis must show how this victory of Christ over the destructive powers appears to faith as an act of reconciliation. As a matter of fact, the triumph of Christ is at once a victorious and reconciling act which involves a transformation of man's estate and a new situation for "the world," and implies a reconciliation between God and world. Since the divine will is radically antagonistic to evil, and since God cannot therefore be reconciled to evil, this reconciliation entails the destruction of the power of evil and its dominion. This reconciliation implies furthermore that the finished work of Christ has a positive significance for the divine will as such and thereby accomplishes reconciliation. In order that this statement may not be misunderstood, we hasten to add that Christian faith always perceives God as the acting subject in reconciliation. Here the classic words of Paul must be accepted without qualification: "God was in Christ reconciling the world to himself" (II Cor. 5:19). But Christian faith can at the same time speak of God as being reconciled; it can say that his wrath is "stayed," "is turned away," and so on. Such expressions are legitimate so long as they do not encroach upon, but are rather incorporated into, the fundamental Christian point of view, namely, that reconciliation is throughout a work of God. To Christian faith the matter appears thus: that God is reconciled in and through his reconciliation of the world unto himself.

In order to see how this line of thought is connected with the victory of divine love in Christ, it is necessary to note that these destructive powers which are vanquished stand partly in an inner relation to and are an expression of divine judgment. This is certainly not true of sin. This hostile power cannot serve the divine will except in so far as the divine will overcomes it and turns it into good. But all the other "destructive powers" of which faith speaks can be seen from two points of view. They are, on the one hand, tyrannical powers which enslave humanity, and on the other hand the instruments of divine judgment. This is the case with those two powers, death and the devil, which the ancient church placed side by side with sin. Death in this case is not simply physical death. The ancient church combined death with sin, and even regarded these two as different expressions for the same thing. Both denote separation from God. The separation from God caused by sin is *eo ipso* death. But this death may also be regarded as an expression of divine judgment. That sin is death is in accordance with God's will and judgment. Even the devil can similarly be placed in relation to the divine will. He is, of course, from one point of view, the incarnation of that which is hostile to God. But, from another viewpoint, it is in accordance with God's will that, because of sin, men have been placed under the dominion of the devil. If we are to understand the primitive conception of Christ's struggle with and victory over the destructive powers, we must keep clearly in mind this inner relation between death and the devil on the one side and the divine will on the other. It then becomes clear that the victory over the destructive powers is at the same time a reconciliation. The religious point of view hidden behind the drastic figures is that the loving will of God prepares a way for itself through judgment. The victory of Christ through his self-giving is the means whereby God reconciles the world to himself and is at the same time reconciled.

When the law and wrath are included among the destructive

powers the concept of reconciliation becomes even more profound. This is especially the case when divine wrath is considered in this connection. It was for this reason that Luther could speak so profoundly about the atonement. While death and the devil can be used only indirectly as instruments of the divine will, the "law" is very closely connected with this will. The law as such is holy and good, and a direct expression of the divine will. But the demand of the divine will expressed in the law becomes at the same time a destructive power. The law cannot save man from the power of sin; the way the law indicates is nothing but salvation of self by self. The sharp words which Paul and later Luther spoke about the law must be understood from this point of view. The law stands as the condemning power, it is connected with the curse (Gal. 3:10), and it even drives men to sin (I Cor. 15:56), since it leads men into the way of salvation of self by self, which in reality is a way that leads away from salvation into sin. Under these circumstances the "victory over the law" means that divine love in Christ breaks through the legal order of justice and establishes a new order in the relationship between God and man.

The tension in the divine will appears, however, most intensively when divine wrath is regarded as one of the destructive powers vanquished through the self-giving of divine love in the finished work of Christ. Here the question is not simply about an instrument of the divine will, but about an essential element in this will. "Wrath" is God's direct and immediate reaction to sin. But at the same time it is, according to Luther, a destructive power and a tyrant, even the worst of all tyrants. When wrath is separated from love it assumes this character. Thus, the conflict is carried into the divine nature itself. Luther expresses this idea in picturesque language: "The curse, therefore, which is God's wrath resting over the whole world, struggled with the blessing which is God's eternal grace and mercy in Christ. The curse encountered the blessing and wanted to destroy it, but it was not able. The blessing is divine and eternal, and consequently the curse must give way. If the blessing in Christ could be made to retreat, then God himself could be overcome. But this it not possible." [1] The overcoming of wrath means, according to this

[1] *WA*, 40I, pp. 441-42.

analysis, that the inmost nature of God, the divine love, "the blessing," makes a way for itself through wrath, "the curse." This occurs when Christ submits to wrath and bears the burden it imposes, or, in other words, through the self-giving sacrifice of love. Divine wrath is thus "reconciled"; it is, so to speak, fused with love. But this act of atonement through which wrath is reconciled is at the same time a divine act, the act of divine love itself. It is hardly possible to penetrate deeper into the mystery of the atonement. The act of reconciliation appears with crystal clarity as the victory of divine love itself. But it remains nevertheless a mystery, the mystery of divine love. It is not dissolved and rendered superficial as in the Latin theory of the atonement (cf. ¶ 4). God is reconciled in that he reconciles the world to himself through the self-giving sacrifice of love. From this point of view we must now examine further how Christian faith comprehends this sacrificial act of love.

3. Propter Christum

There is an abundance of expressions in the vocabulary of the Christian faith which, if rightly understood, reveal what it cost divine love to effect this reconciliation. If these, however, are not understood from this fundamental point of view, the result is a caricature of the work of Christ and of the relation of the divine will to the act of reconciliation. From the beginning of Christianity and down through the ages Christian faith has recurrently proclaimed the self-giving sacrifice of divine love in the crucified Christ. Paul speaks of this freely and frequently. "He . . . did not spare his own Son, but gave him up for us all" (Rom. 8:32). "God shows his love for us in that while we were yet sinners Christ died for us" (Rom. 5:8). Christ "loved me and gave himself for me" (Gal. 2:20; cf. 1:4). "One has died for all" (II Cor. 5:14). Christ became "a curse for us" (Gal. 3:13). "For our sake [God] made him to be sin who knew no sin, so that in him we might become the righteousness of God" (II Cor. 5:21).

The same fundamental theme, the self-giving of divine love *for us*, recurs in constantly new variations in the other writings of the New Testament. "In this is love, not that we loved God but that he loved us and sent his Son to be the expiation for our sins" (I John 4:10).

204

Christ is "the Lamb of God, who takes away the sins of the world" (John 1:29). It is reiterated again and again that the act of Christ was for us, for our sakes, or on our behalf. But the expression "for us" imperceptibly passes over into and assumes the significance of the expression, "in our stead." It can rightly be said that no idea has had a stronger position within the life of faith or has been dearer to the Christian heart. But it cannot be denied that this fundamental Christian theme has become strange and incomprehensible to many within Christianity in these later times. The reasons for this have been many and need not be elaborated here. We should note, however, that one of the principal reasons has been that this fundamental Christian theme has frequently been subjected to grotesque interpretations which have obscured its Christian character. This Christian character can be revealed only when the self-giving of love "for our sake" is firmly connected with *divine* love, or, in other words, when the sacrifice of Christ is understood as the self-giving of divine love. When this point of view is obscured or lost, the expressions mentioned here become false symbols.

Christian faith has used many and varied figures in its attempt to express as well as possible what is involved in the self-giving action of divine love. We shall consider here three fundamental ideas which have played prominent parts in the history of Christian thought. These three illustrate our fundamental theme from various points of view: the act of love as a sacrifice, as an endurance of punishment, and as a vicarious act.

It is not at all surprising that Christian faith looks upon the finished work of Christ as a *sacrifice*. The idea of sacrifice is common in all religions and not least in the Old Testament. The primitive Christian view connects the sacrifice of Christ directly with the Old Testament sacrifices. The Letter to the Hebrews, which is more interested in this line of thought than any other writing in the New Testament, declares that the offering of Christ signifies both the fulfillment and the abolition of all sacrifice. The idea of sacrifice occurs frequently in the New Testament even when the word itself is not used. It is present in those passages which speak of "the blood of Christ": "The new covenant in my blood" (I Cor. 11:23ff), "a participation in the blood of Christ" (I Cor. 10:16), "justified by his blood" (Rom. 5:9), "Christ, our paschal lamb, has been sacrificed" (I Cor. 5:7), etc.

If we want to understand how the sacrifice motif is connected with the whole of Jesus' life on earth, it is not enough to take note of certain isolated biblical passages. It is much more important to recognize the dominant part which the idea of "the suffering Servant of the Lord" (Isa. 53) plays in the biblical conception of the person and work of Jesus as the Messiah. The conception of "the suffering Servant" accounts for the fact that Jesus from the temptation onward had to struggle against false messianic ideals. Jesus himself conceived of his work from this point of view. As the suffering Servant he elects to go the way of sacrifice. In Paul the perspective widens: the sacrifice begins already in his becoming man. He "did not count equality with God a thing to be grasped, but emptied himself, taking the form of a servant, being born in the likeness of men" (Phil. 2:6-7). The incarnation is the starting point of his sacrificial service of redemption. But although the sacrifice motif is thus connected both with the incarnation and the whole ministry, the significance of his death as a sacrifice is in no way diminished. His sacrifice reaches its culmination in the death on the cross. The cross gathers up and completes the sacrifice. It does not tell us simply that his work is ended, but that it is "fulfilled." What has happened has taken place once for all. The sacrifice is final, and valid for all time.

When Christian faith declares that this sacrifice implies the perfection and abolition of all other sacrifices, the reason is that this sacrifice is directly connected with divine love. The sacrifice is in the last analysis the sacrifice of divine love itself. Divine love does not remain outside and apart from that which takes place here; it is active in this offering, it brings the sacrifice, it offers of its own, yea, even itself (cf. Heb. 9:15ff., § 3, ¶ 4). This sacrifice affirms that there is no limit to the self-giving of divine love; it gives itself without measure or restraint. Since it is in the last analysis the sacrifice of divine love itself, the Christian idea of sacrifice has radically reversed all non-Christian conceptions, in which the purpose always and everywhere is to seek to influence the divine power with human gifts and sacrifices. The sacrifice of Christ signifies, therefore, the abolition of all such sacrifices. There is no longer any justification

206

for their existence. But this abolition occurs because the sacrifice of Christ, being the sacrifice of divine love, is perfect and complete.

But Christian faith can also speak of this sacrifice as a sacrifice *to* God (Heb. 9:14). In obedience to God, "obedient unto death" (Phil. 2:8), and in solidarity with a humanity in bondage under destructive powers he made his sacrifice. The sacrifice is therefore an offering brought to and accepted by God, but this statement is possible only because faith looks at the act of reconciliation from two points of view: God is reconciled in that he reconciles the world unto himself. This means that the sacrifice of divine love in Christ has a reconciling significance also for God himself. But it would lose its Christian character, if, as has often happened, it is separated from this connection and conceived of as a compensation given to God by man (cf. ¶ 4). God receives the sacrifice of Christ. But it is also God himself who makes him a sacrifice. He not only "gave" his Son, but he sent him into death. It was not men or enemies who made him a sacrifice. They committed an outrage against him. He gave himself, and God gave him, as a sacrifice.

When Christian faith has understood the finished work of Christ as a suffering or an *endurance of punishment* on the part of divine love, this approach is closely connected with the struggle of Christ against those demonic powers which hold men captive. When divine love becomes "incarnate" and is subjected to the conditions of sin and death, the result is that it must become a suffering love. It has to live under those harsh conditions and consequences which are the results of sin. Through its radical opposition to the sinful life it reveals the nature of sin as hostility to God and the unconditional character of divine judgment. But most significant for Christian faith is the fact that divine love in complete solidarity with men assumes the burden of all the suffering, *the guilt and the punishment,* which has been occasioned by sin. The divine love reaches the very limits of suffering in the fact that its burden is imposed by divine wrath. The divine wrath which rests on humanity strikes at the very heart of divine love. It must, however, be emphasized that this affirmation of Christ's suffering under divine wrath does not imply that this wrath is directed to Christ and his work. It means rather that divine love in Christ enters into complete solidarity and suffers with

the world toward which divine wrath is directed. When divine love
bears the burden of divine wrath, the wrath is transformed into and
fused with love.[1]

The idea of sacrifice and the bearing of the burden imposed by
sin lead directly to the significance of his finished work as *vicarious*.
The vicarious suffering of divine love is to faith the most evident
and the most inscrutable of all spiritual realities. The older theology
often obscured this reality by grotesque misinterpretations, and later
theology has often rejected it because of its superficial view of the
nature and conditions of divine love. But this vicarious love is dear
to the heart of every Christian. We have deliberately chosen the
most direct and questionable word, vicarious. It is clear, however,
that the affirmations of Christian faith to the effect that the work
of Christ was "for our sake," "on our behalf," ultimately include the
conception "in our stead." The first expressions tend to be superseded
by the latter. This approach to the work of Christ is intimately
connected with the idea of his struggle and victory over the demonic
forces. This struggle and victory have occurred for our sake, for
our salvation and redemption. But since we have been unable to
accomplish this work ourselves, it has manifestly been done in our
stead. But this vicarious victory is seen in its depth and power only
when we note that it is at the same time an act of reconciliation
whereby God reconciles and is reconciled, and thus a new relationship
between God and the world is established. Our situation is what it
is *propter Christum* [on account of Christ]. Divine love in Christ
has done what no human power could accomplish. When God meets
man with reconciling and forgiving love, it is *propter Christum* and
per Christum [through Christ]. In this connection one could use the
old and much misinterpreted expression, *satisfaction*, but in a sense
widely different from that which it has in scholastic theology. For
Christian faith it is clear that Christ has "made satisfaction." The
term *satis*, "sufficient," is, to be sure, entirely too weak to express
the significance of the work of Christ. But ignoring this, it can well

[1] Cf. Reinhold Niebuhr, *The Nature and Destiny of Man* (New York: Scribner, 1943), I, 153. "The good news of the gospel is that God takes the sinfulness
of man into himself, and overcomes in His own heart what cannot be overcome
in human life."

be said that Christ has "made satisfaction," not only in the sense that through his obedience unto death he has "satisfied" that God who, precisely because of his love, must radically judge all that is evil, but also and primarily in the sense that he has "adequately performed" all that *God's love* demanded. In so doing he has also made "satisfaction" for us.

The word vicarious is, however, connected with certain dangers. It has sometimes been interpreted as a mechanical and automatic transfer of our burden to him. This is the interpretation which emerges whenever the organic connection between the work of Christ and divine love is even slightly ignored. When this unspiritual interpretation of vicariousness is avoided, however, we gain a new perspective of the vicarious act of suffering and triumphant love. The vicarious aspect of Christ's victory cannot be interpreted to mean that we are set free from the struggle against sin and from the suffering it entails. Such a viewpoint would be completely unrealistic. The vicarious element in the work of divine love is its creation of a new situation while it simultaneously releases in human life a constantly active and quickening power. The vicarious suffering of divine love does not automatically remove the burden, but it gives new power to bear it; vicarious love does not end the struggle, but it furnishes a new possibility to carry on the struggle. Its act is not only a completed act, but a continuous activity. It must be added, however, that the act of forgiveness which issues from reconciliation is not based upon or motivated by this renewing power which flows from vicarious love. The basis of forgiveness is to be found solely in that divine love which in giving itself reconciles the world to itself (cf. §§ 33, 34).

We need only add to what has already been said about the work of divine love as a sacrificial, suffering, and vicarious act that these motifs must be incorporated into and characterized by the fundamental motif of reconciliation and atonement. There is no conflict between the motif of struggle and victory and that of sacrifice. The victory is secured through vicarious suffering and sacrifice. The subject of our previous discussion throughout has been *suffering* love. But this suffering love is *activity*. It does not just passively endure evil; it vanquishes evil in victorious activity and is revealed as soveregn even in apparent defeat. Every viewpoint which one-sidedly presents only the passive side, or emphasizes this over against the active, creates a wrong conception of the relation of divine love to evil. Nothing is more vital to Christian faith than the fact that the act of reconciliation in Christ is a victory.

In this victorious act of self-giving love the system of legal justice as a pattern of the relationship between God and man is breached. Spontaneous and "unmotivated" love is not confined within a purely legalistic system when in sovereign power it creates the new order. But this interruption of the order of justice takes place in such a way that the radical and condemning opposition of love to evil is most fully expressed. The wrath against sin does not cease, but it is fused with love and in this sense "canceled."

4. The Distinctive Character of the Christian Doctrine of Atonement

The Christian doctrine of atonement as presented here is differentiated both from the scholastic and from the idealistic theories.[2] We may define first the classical idea of the atonement by saying that here *the divine action is uninterrupted and the order of justice interrupted*. Even when it is stated that God is reconciled, the meaning is not that divine love has ceased to be the acting subject of atonement, but rather that God is reconciled in and through his act of reconciliation. This is one continuous and divine act accomplished through Christ. But this divine act breaks through the system of legal justice. The self-giving of love creates a new and higher order.

The fundamental character of the *scholastic* theory of the atonement is: *an uninterrupted order of justice and an interrupted action of God*. It has often been argued that, according to the theory of Anselm and later scholasticism, God is simply the object of reconciliation and nothing more. But this is false. God is also the subject in so far as he takes the initiative and sends the Son into the world. But at the decisive point in the act of reconciliation, the rendering of satisfaction, the emphasis is placed on the service which Christ *qua homo* renders. But the action of God is thereby interrupted. The atonement is no longer, as in the classical theory, that act in

[2] Cf. Gustaf Aulén, *Christus Victor*, trans. A. G. Hebert (New York: Macmillan, 1958).

which God at the same time reconciles and is reconciled, but on the contrary, partly a divine work and partly a compensation which Christ as man offers to God on behalf of man. In this way also the order of justice is preserved uninterrupted. The whole theory indicates that the work of reconciliation is securely placed within the system of legal justice.

In the third type, where the theory of the atonement is based on *idealism*, the idea of the atonement as an act of God is more completely set aside. Even when the significance of the work of Christ is emphasized, it is in terms of Jesus as the religious "archetype" of humanity, "the ideal man," or the incarnation of the religious and moral ideal (cf. § 25, ¶ 2). Here, even more than in the scholastic type, the emphasis is placed on human activity, and consequently this viewpoint represents, even as far as Christ is concerned, a line from below upward, from man to God. The idealistic theory of the atonement is sharply critical of the legalistic aspect of the scholastic theory. But this does not mean a breach in the order of justice along the line of the classical theory, but in reality only that legalism is replaced by a moralistic and ethical point of view, since the emphasis is shifted from the divine act to that which is accomplished by man.

When we regard these three different types from the point of view of the *confession of faith in Christ*, it becomes clear that the classical theory of the atonement stands in intimate relation to the central content of this confession: the incarnation of divine love in Christ. This connection is evidenced by the fact that the atonement is throughout the work of divine love, and that it cannot be accomplished by any other power. This connection is broken in the scholastic theory, since here the emphasis is placed on the fact that compensation is given to God through Christ *qua homo*. The "divine" in Christ is significant only in so far as it gives added value to the work of the "human nature." The idealistic type has to an even greater degree lost the appreciation of the central content of the confession of faith in Christ. We may add that what is questionable about the scholastic theory is *not* that Christ appears before God as man's representative. It appears clearly from our previous discussion that this is a legitimate Christian viewpoint. The real objection is to

the way in which a distinction is made between what Christ does
"as God" and what he does "as man." Such a division is contrary
to the meaning of the Christian confession.

If we look at the three types from the point of view of the *conception of God*, the observations may be summarized in the following
statements. In the conception of God connected with the classical
theory we note a twofold tension. In the first place, God is sovereign, but he is also the God who is engaged in a struggle under
historical conditions. In the second place, God struggles against hostile powers, but among them are also powers which represent and
dispense divine judgment. It is characteristic that these tensions are
not dissolved by rational adjustments. On the contrary, the principal
point of view is that divine love wins the victory through self-giving
and sacrifice (*crux triumphans*). Wrath is overcome by being fused
into divine love. But at the same time the radical opposition to evil
on the part of the divine will appears in much clearer light. The
scholastic type knows of such a tension, although in a weaker form,
but this tension between divine mercy and righteousness is resolved
through a rational process: righteousness is given due compensation
and is thereby satisfied. This line of thought indicates that here
neither "righteousness" nor love is understood in its complete Christian sense. That this is true in regard to love is quite clear. In
regard to the opposition of righteousness to evil, the intention is to
emphasize the seriousness of sin and guilt, but the idea of satisfaction
indicates only too clearly that this intention has not been realized. An
opposition to evil which can be satisfied with a compensation is not
very radical. In the idealistic type, finally, there is in reality no
tension. This type wants to maintain a "pure" and "unified" concept
of God, characterized by unchangeable love. But this unity has been
gained at the price of weakening the radical opposition of the divine
will to evil. The concept of God has become humanized, and love
has become something more or less self-evident and stereotyped.
When this occurs, the theory of the atonement has lost its Christian
character.

The distinction made here between the three theories of the atonement replaces the traditional distinction between an "objective" and
a "subjective" theory. This latter distinction has usually been under-

stood to mean that the scholastic type has been called objective, and the idealistic and humanized type subjective. The idea was that in the objective atonement God is regarded as the object, and in the subjective the reconciliation takes place in man. It is immediately clear that this distinction does not at all agree with the classical idea of atonement. The concepts, objective and subjective, are not germane to the subject, since there can be no theory of the atonement which does not include both an objective and a subjective element. The alternative of an objective or subjective atonement therefore becomes misleading. It should rather be stated that the atonement includes both objective and subjective elements. In regard to the classical theory it is clear that this is to an imminent degree "objective," since the finished work of Christ appears to faith as something objectively given. But it is just as clear that this idea of the atonement contains a subjective element, since the divine act of reconciliation continually realizes itself anew in human life, or, in other words, the finished work is at the same time a continuing activity in the present.

27. Christus-Kyrios

1. *The continuing work of Christ.* The continuing work of Christ receives its content from the finished work, and implies a realization of the latter. In his continuing work Christ appears as the Lord of the Christian life, as *Kyrios.*

2. *Cross and resurrection.* The cross and the resurrection belong inseparably together. The resurrection interprets the cross and reveals the victory won over sin and death. The continuing work of the living Christ receives its content and significance through the atonement accomplished on the cross.

3. *Various aspects of the exaltation.* The various expressions for the exaltation contained in the primitive Christian confession—risen, ascended into heaven, sitting on the right hand of God the Father—reveal the meaning of the exaltation from various points of view: Christ lives, he is set free from the earthly limitations of space and time, and belongs entirely to the divine life. He exercises thereby his dominion (*regnum Christi*).

4. *The fact and the how of the resurrection.* Although the reality of the resurrection is essential to faith, any affirmations concerning the

how of the resurrection which seek to reach beyond the scope of
what has already been said lie outside the boundary line of faith.

1. *The Continuing Work of Christ*

In the previous sections we endeavored to view the work of Christ
finished on the cross in the light of Christian faith; or, in other
words, we have tried to understand the essential meaning of this work
as it appears in the light of that which continually takes place in the
Christian life. When we now turn to that which continually occurs
and view it as the continuing work of Christ, it is necessary to note
how this continuing work is anchored to and inseparably connected
with the work once and for all finished on the cross. When Christian faith is directed toward Christ, this implies that it is directed
toward One who is active in the present; and when it uses the
combination Jesus Christ or Christ Jesus, it implies that this continuing work is inseparably connected with the work accomplished in
history.

Christian faith exists as faith in Christ (§ 5). We are not interested
here in the various factors which determined the *formulation* of this
faith in Christ, nor in the various elements which have become a part
of this faith. We are concerned with the significance of the fact
that Christian faith *exists* as faith in Christ. The very center of this
faith in Christ is the conviction that Christ as the object of faith is
the living Christ who is active in the present, and that he is the
central power in the life of Christian faith. The cohesive and governing force in Christianity is not a certain set of doctrines or statutes
which have once been formulated, nor anything that belongs merely to
past history; it is rather the Lord of the church who is present with
his own "always, to the close of the age" (Matt. 28:20), and who
through his presence rules the souls of men. This effective presence
is to faith the essential element in the Christian life and the factor
which makes it *Christian.* The inner history of this Christian life
appears, therefore, from the most profound point of view as a history
of the works of Christ. Faith in Christ stands inseparably connected
with Christ as the one who is active in the present. It would lose
its meaning if it were a question simply of something belonging to
past history. Faith lives primarily in the present since the inner nature

214

of faith implies being gripped and controlled by something which positively declares itself to be a divine revelation. Without this contemporaneity faith in Christ would be reduced to an intellectual assent to certain events in ancient history, or to certain "religious ideas" formulated and delivered in the past. Faith would then lose its religious character, and it would be quite meaningless to speak of faith in Christ. This character of being continually in the present is not something secondary or accidental; it is essential to Christian faith.

The contemporaneity of faith in Christ characterizes the entire life of Christian faith and worship. Christian faith from the beginning and down through the ages has affirmed the presence of Christ and in a variety of expressive figures has declared: *in ipsa fide Christus adest* ("in faith itself Christ is present": Luther). We need only remind ourselves how strongly this is emphasized in primitive Christianity. Christ is the Head, we are the members (Paul); Christ is the vine, we are the branches (John); our life is a life "in Christ"—"it is no longer I who live, but Christ who lives in me" (Gal. 2:20), we must abide in Christ as he abides in us (John 15:4 ff). This presence of Christ is the foundation on which the whole cultus of the church is based. It is abundantly present also in Christian psalms and hymns.

If, then, it is essential for Christian faith to speak of the continuing work of Christ, it is just as essential that this activity of Christ be anchored to the work finished on the cross, and that its concrete content and character be derived from this vital connection. Through this connection the act of Christ is preserved from becoming simply an abstract principle. It is true that living faith in Christ is based on the whole, continuing work of Christ. It is also true that through the exaltation the historical life of Christ is set free from the merely temporal and historical accidents which may have belonged to it. But this does not alter the fact that the continuing work of Christ receives its decisive and abiding character from the work finished on the cross. This means that the character of the living and continuously active Christ is defined by self-giving, victorious, and sovereign love. The act of Christ retains at all times and under all circumstances this character. In continuing work this victorious act of love is raised above all temporal and local limitations (cf. also ¶ 3). It receives eternal validity. There is a continuous reciprocity between that which has occurred and that which continually occurs. It is significant that in the testimony of faith there is a constant interchange of the present with the perfect, and vice versa. The meaning of this disregard of time is that to faith the past is never simply past, but something continually present in the continuing work. The victory of divine love through self-giving is continually realized in the present. It is realized in a continuing struggle. Luther describes in drastic words how Christ always "beats and chokes" in us those enemies which were the object of the one decisive struggle, and how he thus appears as *Kyrios*, as "my Lord." Everything is dependent on the fact that we have him in our midst who is the victorious Lord. "Did we in our own strength confide our striving would be losing; were not the right Man on our side, the Man of God's own choosing." "When you look at this person," Luther writes, "then you see sin, death, wrath, hell, the devil, and everything evil vanquished and killed. In so far as Christ *rules in the hearts of believers*, there is no sin, no death, no curse." The work of the atonement once finished is continually realized anew "in the hearts of the believers." The victory is an "eternal" victory, and therefore also a victory in the present. The existence of the Christian life, therefore, is both *propter Christum and in Christo*. Any opposition between these two points of view is in principle excluded. Everything depends on the finished work of divine love in Christ; from this point of view the watchword *propter Christum* is unconditionally valid. But everything depends also on the work which is continually being done in the hearts of men; and in this sense the watchword *Christus in nobis* is just as unconditionally valid. But *Christus pro nobis* must nevertheless precede *Christus in nobis*, since God's act of forgiveness does not rest on the work of Christ "in us," but on the contrary is based entirely on the divine act of atonement *propter Christum* (cf. § 26, ¶ 3).

2. Cross and Resurrection

The work finished on the cross becomes through the exaltation a continuing activity. The exaltation is God's answer to Christ's act of sacrifice. Because he "became obedient unto death . . . on a cross . . . God has highly exalted him and bestowed on him the name which is above every name," that "every tongue [should] confess that Jesus

Christ is Lord, to the glory of God the Father" (Phil. 2:8-11; cf. Heb. 2:9 ff). The resurrection is the primary testimony to the exaltation. It reveals the victory won through his obedience unto death. This does not mean that the work finished on the cross must be complemented by something which occurs later, nor that the victory was something subsequent to the sacrifice of self-giving love. It means rather the revelation of that victory which was contained in the sacrifice of love. His work does not first become a victory *through* the exaltation, but the exaltation unveils, reveals, and realizes the victorious act contained in his finished work. In reality the exaltation is included in that which appears to be its exact opposite, in the deepest humiliation. It was when the day of his departure had arrived that he said (John 12:23): "The hour has come for the Son of Man to be glorified."

But having said that we must add that it is only in the light of the resurrection that his ministry perfected in the cross appears as a victory. It cannot be sufficiently emphasized that the message coming to us both in the Gospels and in the Epistles is an Easter message. Easter is the starting point for the apostolic proclamation, and therewith also for the origin and the life of the church. Without the resurrection the historical ministry which ended in the cross would be not only ambiguous but incomprehensible. Without the resurrection the confession of Christ made by the apostles during his earthly ministry would disappear into the darkness around Golgotha and become silent. What is true about the apostles is true also for his disciples in all ages. If Christ were not the risen and living Lord, there would be no Christian faith or confession at all. The Christian message is and remains for all time an Easter message.

The cross and the resurrection are therefore inseparably connected. The cross is as essential for the resurrection as the resurrection is for the cross. The living Lord bears the marks of the cross. But without the resurrection the cross would be simply the cross of martyrdom. In the light of the resurrection it is the sign of victory. For Christians, therefore, *theologia crucis* is at the same time *theologia gloriae Christi*. What we have just said may also be expressed in this way: Good Friday appears in its right perspective only when it is seen in the light of Easter. If the note of triumph is not present in preaching on the passion, this preaching has lost its Christian character. It is no accident that the hymns of Easter have often been able to express more clearly than the passion hymns the Christian view of the cross.

3. Various Aspects of the Exaltation

The fact that the work finished on the cross becomes continuing activity appears to faith as God's act of exaltation, whereby the purpose of this work is revealed. When faith beholds the completed work in the light of that which continually occurs, it is confronted with the fact of the exaltation, or more accurately with the exaltation as an act of God, and is compelled to make the confession which the ancient church formulated thus: "God has made him both Lord and Christ, this Jesus whom you crucified" (Acts 2:36). The conceptions which set forth this act of exaltation are summarized in the threefold affirmation of the Apostles' Creed about the resurrection, the ascent into heaven, and the sitting on the right hand of the Father. The continuing work is carried on by this exalted Christ. If we look closer at these three expressions, we note that none of them can be isolated from the others, but that all three together furnish the background against which the continuing work and the dominion of Christ appear to the eye of faith. Faith in the resurrection, the living Christ, Christ set free from the power of death, is to be sure the starting point and the foundation of the other two conceptions of faith; therefore, from this point of view, the resurrection must be regarded as fundamental. But the idea of the living Christ is by itself not a sufficient background for his continuing work. This background is obtained only when the living Christ is also the One exalted above the temporal and spatial limitations of earthly life, and belongs completely to the divine sphere. This is the meaning of the two affirmations about his ascent into heaven and his sitting on the right hand of the Father. The figurative expression, "the right hand of God," is naturally to be understood in accordance with the ancient formula, *dextra dei ubique est*, the right hand of God is everywhere. The exaltation, therefore, does not imply a *separation* from the life and struggle on earth, but on the contrary *nearness*, presence. It is an affirmation that Christ is continually and everywhere active in and through his Spirit, or, in other words, an affirmation about his continuing work.

Christ enters upon his dominion, his kingdom (*regnum Christi*), in and through the exaltation. The name *Kyrios*, Christ is Lord, signifies that he has such a kingdom. This dominion of Christ continues in the present age, according to the New Testament, until the consummation of God's kingdom, and it extends over the whole of creation. Everything is subject to Christ. "He must reign until he has put all his enemies under his feet" (I Cor. 15:25). The universality of this dominion is asserted in Matthew 28:18: "All authority in heaven and on earth has been given to me." It is significant that these words are an introduction to the great commission: "Go therefore and make disciples of all nations." Even if the dominion of Christ in principle can be said to include the whole visible and invisible world (cf. I Pet. 3:22), it is nevertheless concentrated in the church, "the Body of Christ" (cf. § 37). It is especially here, in and through the church, that the rule of Christ is realized. The church is the earthly locus of *regnum Christi*.[1]

4. The Fact and the How of the Resurrection

If the whole Christian message has the character of an Easter message, it follows that the reality of the resurrection becomes *fundamental* for Christian faith in all ages. The Christian faith rests on the fact that Christ "is risen indeed." What the Gospel narratives tell about this event indeed cannot be demonstrated as an empirical fact by critical and historical research. But the problem posed here is really not different in kind from that which obtains generally with respect to the relationship of man to God in faith. Faith in the reality of the resurrection is inseparably connected with faith in the God who creates and gives life. As far as the problem of faith is concerned there is really no difference in principle between faith in the God who forgives sins and faith in the God who gives life and vanquishes the powers of death.

With regard to *how* the exaltation took place, theology cannot make any statement beyond the assertion that the exaltation was the

[1] Oscar Cullmann, *Königsherrschaft Christi und Kirche im Neuen Testament*, p. 32.

mighty act of the God who creates and gives life. This is true in regard to the resurrection as well as to the other formulas expressing the exaltation: ascended into heaven and sitting on the right hand of the Father. It is entirely outside the sphere of systematic theology to make decisions in regard to those historical and exegetical questions which are connected with the resurrection faith of the first disciples, or with the empty tomb, or with the manner in which Christ made himself known to his own. Theology can state only that, according to the evidence, different conceptions of *how* the resurrection took place were current in primitive Christianity. Sometimes it is asserted that the risen Christ appeared to his own in virtually the same form as in the days of his flesh, and at other times it is said that *one* body is buried in the earth and *another*, a spiritual organism, arises (I Cor. 15). Paul does not conceive of a continued bodily existence of the same nature as the earthly. But in neither case do we find a purely spiritualized conception. It is evident that the primitive Christian resurrection faith is of a different nature from the "philosophical" doctrine which regards the "soul" as immortal in itself, and immortality as the liberation of the "soul" from the prison house of the body. Such a distinction between "soul" and "body" is absolutely foreign to the resurrection faith of the early church. It is evident that in the New Testament we meet various ideas of the manifestation of the risen Christ, but it is also evident that the disciples regarded him as having a certain "corporeality," however spiritualized and "transfigured" this might have been. These ideas emphasize the contrast to the philosophical and idealistic conceptions of immortality. At the same time it is clear that the main concern is to assert the identity between *Christus-Kyrios* and Jesus of Nazareth, and to present the resurrection as God's act of exaltation.

Under all circumstances what is essential to faith is the conviction that the exaltation as a whole is an act of God. The essential matter is that he who was "crucified, dead, and buried," was raised by God and installed in his eternal realm. Precisely because this is the essential thing the approach which would compel us to choose between the "subjectivity" or "objectivity" of these visions is eliminated. Neither of these obscure terms expresses the characteristic viewpoint of faith. If "objectivity" should mean here that the resurrection can be demonstrated like any other empirical fact, it would be contrary both to the primitive Christian testimony of faith according to which the risen Christ manifested himself to his own, but not to a Caiaphas, a Herod, or a Pilate; and also to the present Christian experience which affirms that faith alone has fellowship with the exalted and glorified Christ. In this sense we are dealing with something "subjective," since it is not a question of an empirical verification but of an affirmation of faith. On the other hand, however, the whole sequence of the exaltation possesses the greatest possible objectivity, since faith asserts that this sequence is an act of Almighty God through which the completed work of Christ manifests its power in his continuing activity and his dominion is thus exercised (Rom. 1:4; 4:25).

28. Christ and the Spirit

1. *The work of Christ and the work of the Spirit.* When Christian faith conceives of God's act of salvation as the work of the Holy Spirit, it does not in reality intend to distinguish this work from the continuing activity of Christ. The presence and activity of Christ is a presence and activity in the Spirit. The combination of these two expressions guards the characteristic quality of the Spirit and at the same time protects the presence of Christ from unspiritual misinterpretations.

2. *Faith in God as faith in the Spirit.* It is clear from the foregoing that faith does not conceive of the Spirit as a being distinguished from God. On the contrary the Spirit makes known the immediacy and the continuing activity of the revelation of God. The statement that the Spirit "proceeds" not only from the Father but also from the Son is a legitimate Christian concept, since it affirms that through the victorious act of divine love in Christ the Spirit comes "in fulness" (John 1:16).

1. The Work of Christ and the Work of the Spirit

It is essential that Christian faith in God is a faith in Christ; it is also essential that it is a faith in the Spirit. This statement expresses something decisive in regard to the nature of faith. Christian faith has spoken about the Spirit and his work especially in connection with the origin and development of the church in the world. The Holy Spirit "calls, gathers, enlightens, and sanctifies"; and through "the means of grace" he establishes his communion of saints in which he "begets and fosters" every individual Christian. The work of the Spirit has reference first and foremost to the church, and consists in the fact that he creates, establishes, and maintains the church. The church is the temple of God in which the Spirit dwells. The fellowship with God which he establishes is designated as "being born of the Spirit" (John 3:6, 8) and it continues to exist because the Spirit "dwells in" man (Rom. 8:9; I Cor. 3:16; I Thess. 4:8; II Tim. 1:14). The Spirit "is life" (Rom. 8:6), and "gives life" (John 6:63; II Cor. 3:6). Those who "are led by the Spirit of God are sons of God" (Rom. 8:14). The Spirit opens the eyes and "searches out" the things which belong to God's revelation: "For the Spirit searches everything, even the depths of God. . . . No one comprehends the thoughts of God except the Spirit of God. Now we have received not the spirit of the world, but the Spirit which is from God, that we might understand the gifts bestowed on us by God" (I Cor. 2:10 ff). As the Spirit of truth he bears witness to this revelation of God (Rom. 8:16; I John 5:6; Heb. 10:15).

It is clear from our previous discussion (§ 27) that faith can derive from Christ the church and the fellowship with God and attribute its origin and existence to his work. It can be said of Christ, too, that he is "life," that he "gives life," and that he "dwells in our hearts through faith" (Eph. 3:17). Christian life can be described as a life "in the Spirit," but also as a life "in Christ." Consequently there is no real difference between the work of the Spirit and the continuing work of Christ. We are not dealing with two different acts, but with the same divine act of love described in different terms. This inseparable connection between Christ and the Spirit is evident in the designation, the Spirit of Jesus Christ. The Spirit of God cannot be named with the name of anyone else except Jesus Christ; and he must be given this name, if the essential character of the Spirit of whom faith speaks is to be properly designated. If the Spirit is the Spirit of Jesus Christ, it implies that Christ is active in and through the Spirit. It is not surprising, therefore, that the language of Christian faith speaks interchangeably of Christ and the Spirit, and permits the one expression imperceptibly to pass over into the other. Paul can say "the Lord is the Spirit," and he can also speak of the transformation into "the likeness of the Lord" which takes place when the Lord who himself is the Spirit is active (II Cor. 3:17 f). In regard to the Johannine writings we may remind ourselves that the Gospel of John reports Jesus as speaking in the same context in the so-called farewell discourses about the sending of the "Paraclete," "the Spirit of Truth," and then saying: "I will not leave you desolate; I will come to you" (John 14:16 ff).

When faith uses interchangeably these *two* expressions, *Christus-Kyrios* and the Spirit, the significance of this usage must not be obscured or denied. This variation serves a twofold purpose. On the one hand the characteristic quality of the Spirit is preserved. That the Spirit is the Spirit of Jesus Christ indicates something very definite about the nature of this Spirit and his way of working. All spiritualistic movements, which separate the Spirit from Christ and transform him into something indefinite, obscure the meaning of the Christian faith in God. We cannot appeal to "the Spirit" in behalf of something that is foreign to the work of Christ. On the other hand, when the continuing activity of Christ is viewed as the work of the Spirit, the presence of Christ cannot easily be misinterpreted in a mechanistic and unspiritual manner. It serves to emphasize the reality and effectiveness of the presence of Christ. The presence of Christ is a "real presence." It would be misleading, however, if theology should (as has sometimes been done) present the alternative: real presence *or* spiritual presence. Theology would then obscure the fact that to faith it is the spiritual presence which is in the deepest sense of the word the real presence. The localization of the presence of Christ in "the means of grace" may be defended only on the condition that what is called means of grace is not so defined as to obscure the fact that Christ is effectively present wherever his Spirit in word and deed actualizes the divine, self-giving, and sovereign love.

2. Faith in God as Faith in the Spirit

Since the object of faith is God alone, "the Spirit" cannot be conceived of as separate from God or as a being independent of him. Any tendency to regard the Spirit as a separate being apart from God would mean that faith has as its object partly God and partly something distinct from him, which in that case competes with him.

This would destroy the nature of faith as completely dependent on God. When Christian faith refers to the Holy Spirit, its real purpose is something entirely different. To speak of the Holy Spirit is to see God from a positively defined point of view and to actualize certain essential features in the Christian conception of God. What "the Spirit" actualizes is first and foremost the presence of God as an *immediate* and *active* presence. Where the Spirit of God is, there God himself is effectively present. "The Spirit" assures us that God is not distant and that he is not in reality an extramundane being who sits enthroned in exalted eminence, and who from this eminence possibly sends a few messages down to the world; but, on the contrary, that God is near to us and that he is immediately and actively present in our life. The expression that God "reveals himself" in and through his Spirit is intended to indicate the mode of God's "personal" revelation in contrast both to those tendencies which interpret God's activity as some kind of higher natural process, and to those attempts to mechanize in one way or another his self-disclosure and deprive it of its active and living character, in which he immediately realizes his loving will (cf. § 3, ¶ 5). It is also evident in the history of Christianity that whenever the concept of the Spirit is not given a central place but, in contrast to primitive practice, is set aside, the obscuring of the dynamic features of the idea of God follows as a consequence. Thus God is removed into the abstract distance and divine revelation is apt to be limited to a certain point in the past. The content of the conception, "the Holy Spirit," is the same as the content of the conception of God. The Holy Spirit is as such the Spirit of Love, and consequently also that Spirit who stands in unmitigated opposition to evil and is active with all the sovereignty which belongs to divine love. It is significant that the combination "Spirit and power," or "the Spirit of power," occurs so frequently in the primitive Christian testimony of faith, and likewise that the "Nicene" confession gives the Spirit the characteristic designation: *the Giver of life*. We cannot say anything about the Spirit which we cannot at the same time say about God; and neither can we give a content to God which cannot at the same time be given to his Holy Spirit. The Spirit is the appearance of divine love in the present; he is God as he reveals himself to us in active deeds. Wherever God works, he works in and

THE VICTORIOUS ACT OF RECONCILIATION §29

through the Holy Spirit. When faith conceives of "sanctification" in the sense of the realization of divine fellowship as the work of the Holy Spirit, the intention is to emphasize that sanctification is an act in which God himself is *immediately* and *effectively* active.

The Holy Spirit is therefore the Spirit of God and of Jesus Christ. There is a deep significance in the ancient theological formula which states that the Spirit proceeds also from the Son. That which has occurred in history, the completed work of Christ, is the condition for the coming of the Spirit in purity and "fulness." From the viewpoint of Christian faith the whole content of the work of Christ finished on the cross can be summarized in this one statement: the Spirit comes "in fulness" (John 1:16). The Spirit comes when Christ has been "glorified." The statement that the Spirit proceeds from the Son cannot be interpreted to mean that the Spirit is not altogether a divine Spirit. The Spirit which "proceeds from the Son" proceeds also "from the Father," since the work of salvation accomplished here is throughout the work of the Father. The statement that the Spirit "proceeds from the Son" means not only that the work of Christ is the condition for the coming of the Spirit in fulness, but also that the work of "the Son" is not only a work completed and finished once and for all. On the contrary, it is a continuing work in "the Spirit." In reality it is interpreted through the continuing activity of the Spirit, since the real meaning of the finished work is manifested to faith only throught the inner testimony of the Spirit. Thus Paul says significantly: "No one can say: 'Jesus is Lord' except by the Holy Spirit" (I Cor. 12:3). To this we may add one more witness: Luther's explanation to the third article of the Apostles' Creed in his *Small Catechism*.

29. The Trinitarian Element in Christian Faith

The essential purpose of the ancient church's doctrine of the Trinity is to maintain both the definitive and dynamic content and the unity of Christian faith in God. Although the terminology used, "three persons in one Godhead," has tended to threaten the unity of faith in God, especially as the concept of person has become more definitely fixed, nevertheless the threefold and at the same time unified viewpoint of Christian faith is contained in the meaningful and living revelation of the one true God in the world of men.

Note on the boundary line of faith. This mode of God's revelation has its basis, as far as faith is concerned, in the eternal being of God. All speculations about the "immanent trinity" which go beyond this proposition lie outside the boundary line of faith.

In our consideration of the problem of the trinitarian element in the Christian faith, the purpose is not to add anything to our exposition of the way of divine love already presented, but only to define more accurately certain affirmations about the mode of God's revelation which have already been noted. The theology of the ancient church regarded the doctrine of the Trinity as a summary of the content of the Christian revelation. We are concerned here not with the question of the origin of the trinitarian formula, but with the real intention of this conception and its essential meaning for Christian faith.

The purpose of the Christian doctrine of the Trinity is twofold. On the one hand, it serves to indicate the living content of Christian faith in God, and on the other hand, it serves to maintain the unity of this faith. It affirms that Christian faith receives its characteristic content from the fact that it is a faith in Christ, and its living and immediate character from the fact that it is a faith in the Spirit. Faith in Christ gives to divine revelation its historical anchorage and its inner richness, and faith in the Spirit indicates its character as a continuing, present, and living revelation (cf. § 28). Faith in Christ and faith in the Spirit are, therefore, essential elements of the Christian faith in God, and cannot be eliminated without rendering this faith indefinite and superficial. Faith knows God through the work of Christ as intimately as it is possible to know him under earthly conditions, but it comprehends the essential meaning of this work of Christ only because it is continually realized in and through the continuing activity of the Spirit. At the same time that the ancient doctrine of the Trinity thus elucidates the meaning of the Christian faith by maintaining this threefold viewpoint, it also guards the unity of Christian faith in God, or, in other words, its pure monotheism. It declares that when it speaks of Christ and the Spirit, the reference is always to the revelation of the one true God and to nothing else (cf. §§ 5, 28).[1]

It cannot be denied, however, that this terminology, "three persons in one Godhead," endangers the unity of faith in God, and that this formula, therefore, may point in an entirely different direction from the one intended. We must note carefully that the term person (*persona*) at the time of the formulation of this doctrine did not possess the fixed and definite significance of independent individuality which it has today. The ancient church understood the word person in such an indefinite and vague sense that it could readily be combined with a most thoroughgoing monotheistic conception which was firmly held. If we were to explain to the men of the ancient church what we mean by person and personality, the ancient church fathers would no doubt deny us the right to use their trinitarian formula according to *our* concept of person; they would brand us as tritheistic heretics.

In reality the seed of tritheism lies in the expression "three persons." It is interesting to note how theology has tried to avoid the division of the conception of God which seems to be caused by the doctrine of the Trinity. We find one example of this in the statement that "the external works of God are indivisible" (*opera dei ad extra indivisa sunt*). No divine act can be ascribed to a certain "person" of the Godhead, to the exclusion of the others. The purpose of this affirmation is evidently to refute the suspicion of tritheism. Every divine act is an act of the entire Deity. Luther, who incidentally has spoken many a critical word about the term "trinity" and consents to keep it only "on account of the weak" (*pro captu infirmiorum*), asserts emphatically the unity of God: "*Welche Person der Gottheit man nennet, so hat man den rechten wahren Gott genennet*"—"*in der Gottheit ist die höchste Einigkeit*" ["Whatever person in the Godhead is named, it designates the real and true God—in the Godhead there is the highest unity"]. But in spite of these attempts to maintain the unity of God, the pressure of the concept of person became too strong for theology. Theology was forced to adopt in-

---

[1] "The doctrine of the Trinity is really not a 'doctrine of God,' but a 'doctrine of the revelation.' . . . The doctrine of the Trinity is not to be found in the Scriptures since it is not one teaching among others; it expresses rather the nature of *everything* that is taught anywhere in Scripture." Regin Prenter, *Skabelse og Genloesning* (1955), p. 53 f.

terpretations which were foreign to its original purpose. It was not possible to maintain the proposition of the indivisibility of God's works. The development of the doctrine of the Trinity tended, for example, to ascribe the work of salvation more to the Son than to the Father, or, in other words, the loving will of God was not always given its place as subject of the redemptive act of Christ, which, however, was the intention of the confession of faith in Christ (cf. § 26, ¶ 4). In the same way the work of the Spirit was separated from the work of the Father and the Son. The result was that the idea of God's living and continuing revelation was obscured and the conception of grace became mechanized. The grace of God became something else than divine love directed toward men, and this undefined conception of grace became in Latin scholasticism a substitute for the Spirit. But in this way the living, unified, and organic view of the revelation of God, which the doctrine of the Trinity was meant to preserve, became obscured. In comparison with this danger of dividing the conception of God into a tritheism, the numerous abstract speculations about the "immanent" Trinity and the mutual relation of the three divine persons are relatively harmless. These speculations have a detrimental influence only in so far as they draw the attention away from that which is essential to faith, namely, God's concrete revelation of himself in his work. But the tendencies toward tritheism attack the very foundations of the purity and majesty of Christian faith in God. It is evident that these tendencies become stronger as the concept of personality becomes more definite and elaborate. To repeat verbatim the trinitarian confession of the ancient church, "three persons in one Godhead," is under such circumstances contrary to the original intention of maintaining the unity of faith in God, and leads to conclusions which the trinitarian formula was intended to guard against. Faithfulness to the letter in that case becomes faithlessness toward the spirit and purpose of the ancient confession.

But the intention itself contains something essential and inalienable to the Christian faith. *Both* of the fundamental ideas that produced the doctrine of the Trinity belong to the deepest convictions of the Christian faith. The whole previous presentation of the way of divine love is a proof of this. It is not an accident that Christian faith in God is at the same time faith in Christ and in the Spirit. Neither can be eliminated without destroying Christian faith, since the event of Christ involves the self-realization of God's loving will and the Spirit reveals God's immediate and continuing work. This threefold viewpoint of faith expresses, therefore, the meaningful and living revelation of the one true God, and at the same time prevents faith from being impoverished by deistic and pantheistic influences (cf. § 17). A faith in God which is at the same time faith in Christ can never become pantheistic; and a faith which is at the same time faith in the Spirit cannot become deistic. All so-called unitarian interpretations tend inevitably to become pantheistic or deistic and impoverish the content and vividness of faith in God. But as long as Christian faith in God preserves this threefold viewpoint, it also maintains its unified and organic character. The work of Christ is throughout the work of God, and the Spirit is not an independent being by the side of God, but the expression of God's immediate and continuing activity.

Note on the Boundary Line of Faith

The trinitarian element in Christian faith has reference to the revelation of God. The related affirmations of faith deal with the mode of revelation. Since faith is completely dependent upon the revelation, it cannot make any affirmations which are not based upon this revelation. Faith can, therefore, say nothing else about the revelation in Christ and in the Spirit except that it originates in the eternal being of God. Faith has attempted to express these eternal relationships by the symbolical statements that the Son is "begotten of the Father before all worlds," and that the Spirit "proceeds from the Father and the Son." With these statements faith touches that line of demarcation which it cannot cross without passing beyond the area of revelation and thereby becoming something else than faith. Luther had a clear conception of this fact and also of the line of demarcation between Christian faith and metaphysical speculation. He consequently warned against all speculations about "God as he is in himself." Such speculation about the exalted, divine Majesty is nothing but human presumption.

One point in this subject demands further clarification; the question of the extent and center of revelation. When faith affirms that the revelation of God in the Son and in the Spirit is founded in the eternal being of God, it implies that faith does not dare to prescribe a limit to the scope of divine revelation. When the loving will of God became incarnate in Christ, this did not constitute its first appearance. In this connection the idea of pre-existence has a legitimate place as indicated in the conception of the Word who was eternally with God and has made himself known in various ways. But these ideas of the universality of the divine revelation are legitimate only in so far as they do not encroach upon the idea of the incarnation. The viewpoint of Christian faith in regard to revelation is, as has already been stated (§ 3, ¶ 3), both universal and exclusive. Faith does not set a limit for the revelation, but neither does it recognize any other God than that divine Love which has become incarnate in Christ.

The Broken and Restored Relationship With God

30. The Nature of Sin

1. *Sin as a religious concept.* Sin is a concept which cannot be used except in a religious sense. Knowledge of the meaning of sin can be gained only as divine revelation illuminates the fact of sin.

2. *Sin as unbelief and as egocentricity.* Sin is that which breaks fellowship with God. The essence of sin can therefore be more closely defined as unbelief. If in faith man is ruled by the loving will of God, then the essence of sin consists in the fact that man is not dominated by God, but by something distinct from him. This other power is man's own ego. The essence of sin is, therefore, negatively unbelief and positively egocentricity.

3. *Sin as perversion of the will.* Sin from this point of view is not simply isolated deeds or something imperfect, but a perversion of will, which implies a deviation from man's proper destiny, given to him by God. Sin is, therefore, something qualitative; it cannot be reduced to the unqualitative contrast between the finite and the infinite.

4. *Sin applies to the whole man.* It is clear from the foregoing that Christian faith knows of no division of man into a lower and sensuous part which is the seat of sin, and a higher and spiritual part which would lie outside the area of sin. When man is designated as a sinner, it is a religious judgment which refers to man as a whole.

5. *Note on the rejection of psychological schematizations.* The relation of the consciousness of sin to faith cannot be psychologically schematized, either in the sense that a "mature" faith would be a prerequisite for the consciousness of sin, or that a "mature" consciousness of sin is a prerequisite for faith. The words of Luther are applicable here: *quo sanctior quis est, eo magis sentit illam pugnam* [the holier anyone is, the more sensitive he is to that conflict].

1. Sin as a Religious Concept

It cannot be emphasized too strongly that sin is a concept which belongs entirely to the religious realm. As soon as it is removed from

this sphere, it loses its proper meaning. We do not speak of sin in a
juridical environment or in criminal justice. There it is simply a
question of crime and transgression of law. To inject the concept of
sin in this connection would be to introduce an irrelevant category.
In the same way a non-religious philosophy of morals and ethics
cannot use the word sin, even if, in following Kant, it speaks of evil
as a "radical evil." As long as one is concerned only with ethical
points of view, one does not need the concept of sin, in fact cannot
find any use for it. If it is used, it has lost its proper meaning. In
the ethical field the question is about good and evil, right and wrong,
but not about sin. When the concept of sin is removed from the
religious sphere, it becomes weak and enfeebled, as even the common
usage of the language indicates.

On the contrary, faith cannot avoid speaking about sin. The problem of evil becomes acute in relation to the problem of sin. This
means that sin is a concept that is inseparably connected with relationship to God. There is no sin which is not sin against God. It is
meaningless to talk about sin if it has no relation to God. From this
point of view the words of Psalm 51 are unconditionally valid:
"Against thee, thee only, have I sinned" (Ps: 51:4). From the viewpoint of Christian faith it would be meaningless to divide "sins" into
two classes: sins against God and sins against the neighbor. There is
no sin against the neighbor which is not sin against God. The sin
against the neighbor becomes sin just because it is sin against God.
If we were to talk about sins which are not sins against God, the
concept of sin would have lost its meaning. It would have been
moved outside the religious sphere. To say that the concept of sin
belongs entirely in the religious sphere is the same as saying that all
sin is sin against God.

Under such circumstances it is evident that the meaning of sin is
apparent only against the background of divine revelation. Without
divine revelation there can be no concept of sin. The divine revelation
reveals sin. The clearer the eye of faith perceives the divine revelation, and the more brightly its light illuminates the meaning and significance of sin, the more completely the real nature of sin is disclosed. Consequently, Christian faith perceives sin most clearly in the
light of the revelation of divine love in the event of Christ.

2. Sin as Unbelief and as Egocentricity

If sin is a concept that belongs entirely to the religious sphere, it follows that the meaning of sin is to be found in that which is contrary to the fundamental religious relationship. The concept of sin is therefore dependent upon our understanding of this fundamental relationship. If religion is interpreted in a moralistic sense, as for example in Pharisaism, and the essential element is the keeping of certain statutes and precepts, sin consists in the transgression of these precepts. If, however, religion is intellectually interpreted and the essential element is to hold fast to certain religious formulas, "heresy" becomes the chief sin. Both of these tendencies, as is well known, have frequently appeared in Christianity. It is evident, however, that neither of these approaches reaches the heart of the matter. If the fundamental religious relationship according to Christian faith is fellowship with God, it follows that the essence of sin is everything that breaks and hinders this fellowship and causes a separation between man and God. Therefore, when the Reformers asserted that the essence of sin was unbelief, they gave the concept a pertinent definition (cf. Rom. 14:23).

This interpretation of sin, however, needs to be more closely defined. It is indubitable that the definition of sin as unbelief, which is almost purely negative, appears rather unrealistic, and that it seems to be difficult to gain from this definition a more positive determination of the meaning of sin. We find, therefore, that when theology speaks of unbelief as the mark of sin, it has often complemented this interpretation by adding other definitions and has designated egocentricity and sensuality *together* with godlessness as the three chief forms of sin. But it has been difficult to find any organic connection between these three chief forms of sin. Under these circumstances one is forced to face the question whether it is legitimate to speak of unbelief as a fundamental definition of the essence of sin. If in principle we are to interpret sin as unbelief, we must attempt to prove that there is an inseparable connection between this negative definition and a more positive definition of the essence of sin. The meaning of sin as "unbelief" is therefore the chief problem.

It is clear that the connection we seek cannot be found as long as the concept of faith is given a purely intellectual interpretation. If "faith" consists primarily in an intellectual acceptance of certain statements about God, it is misleading and even meaningless to talk about sin as unbelief. From such unbelief there is no connecting link to the positive content of sin. When the definition of sin as unbelief appeared unrealistic, it was due to the influence of this intellectualistic concept of faith. The relation between faith and sin becomes more profound when faith is conceived of as trust and confidence in God. Then it becomes possible to find a connection with the positive content of sin. It is questionable, however, whether even this definition of faith can demonstrate clearly and unequivocally how and why the positive content of sin is comprehended in sin as unbelief.

But the connection between what we have called the negative and positive aspects of sin becomes abundantly evident as soon as we consider, not a specific aspect of faith, but faith in its entirety, faith as fellowship with God; or, in other words, when faith is interpreted to mean that man is subdued and dominated by divine love (cf. § 2, ¶ 2). As far as faith is concerned God is unquestionably the Lord in this fellowship between himself and man. If faith means to live under the dominion of God, then sin as unbelief means that *God does not have dominion*, and that *something else* than God's loving will exercises this dominion. Thereby sin is both negatively and positively defined. This other power which rules man in sin is nothing else than *his own ego*. Indifference or hostility to the divine will—the former must be emphasized as well as the latter—is *eo ipso* egocentricity. When the divine will does not rule, man is, as Luther says *incurvatus in se*, selfishly directed toward himself. But if the character of sin, therefore, appears from a positive point of view as egocentricity, this is not a new fundamental form of sin coincident with unbelief or "godlessness." Sin as unbelief and sin as egocentricity are one and the same thing seen from different points of view. Egocentricity is opposition to the divine will, and therefore "unbelief." Wherever *this* power rules, fellowship with God is destroyed.

The concept of sin is hereby defined from the point of view of divine love. If it is a characteristic of this love that it "seeketh not its own" (I Cor. 13:5), the exact opposite is true of sin. The essence of sin appears in the fact that man "seeks his own." Sin is always concerned with a *quaerere quae sua sunt*. This egocentric seeking of one's own may appear in various forms. It may appear as ego-centricity in a strict sense when it is a question about one's own ego, but it may also appear in a wider sense. There is a nationalistic ego-centricity, a class egocentricity, and so forth. In the widest sense egocentricity appears as "a seeking after that which belongs to this world," and as an attachment to the things of this world in general. But no matter how much it is expanded, it does not cease to be ego-centricity. It can manifest itself in grosser or more refined forms. It appears in its most refined and sublimated form when "the search after God" is incorporated under its aegis. It might be assumed that seeking after the divine, after God, would be the very opposite of sinful egocentricity. If, however, this seeking after God is in the interest of making God serve one's own ego and to secure something for one's own personal benefit by divine help, this does not imply a turning away from sin, but rather that sin here is present in its most sublimated and deceptive form. Sin reveals itself in that it does not recognize God as sovereign, as Lord, but instead seeks to make him the servant of human desires and purposes.

It has sometimes been suggested that sin be defined as disobedience. From a purely factual point of view this does not imply any deviation from the twofold definition: "unbelief-egocentricity." If sin means that the loving will of God does not rule over man, the relation of man to this will is one of disobedience and rebellion. In contrast to this, faith is *obedience* (Rom. 1:5; 16:26; I Pet. 1:14).

We may add that sin has sometimes been defined as sensuality. If this concept is understood in its strict and narrow sense, it may be regarded as the result of egocentricity, "seeking one's own." If, on the contrary, it is understood in a metaphysical sense as identical with finiteness, two possibilities emerge. It may then be asserted that man's nature consists of two parts, one sensual and finite, and another spiritual and infinite. Sin would then be connected with the finite part of man. But in so doing the fact that sin involves the whole man is obscured (cf. also ¶ 4). If, on the contrary, it is asserted that man as a total being is finite and thereby stands in opposition to the divine as infinite, the qualitative difference between the loving will of God and the sinful will of man has been replaced by an unqualitative contrast which in reality obscures the true nature of sin.

3. Sin as Perversion of the Will

If the nature of sin is both unbelief and egocentricity in a narrower or wider sense, it means that sin is in reality perversion of the will. Sin cannot be understood as consisting simply in individual and isolated thoughts and acts. Such an atomistic conception of sin, characteristic of Pelagianism, is both superficial and unrealistic. Sin *expresses* itself in individual thoughts, words, and deeds, but sin itself is of a more profound nature. The various sins depend on the condition of "the heart," as the Bible expresses it. What comes from the heart "defiles a man. For out of the heart come evil thoughts, murder, adultery, fornication, theft, false witness, slander" (Matt. 15:18-19; cf. Matt. 5:28; 12:34; Luke 16:15, etc.). Sin is not something simply "accidental" which is more or less loosely connected with man and which we might be able to separate from us, but it is, on the contrary, something that involves and characterizes man's inmost being, since after all there is nothing more essential to man than the inclination of his will.

It is, therefore, clear that sin cannot be regarded as something incomplete or as something which has not yet reached perfection. Sin is a perverse will, and therefore the exact opposite of what it ought to be. Whether it appears as indifference or hostility to the loving will of God, sin is the direct opposite of this will. Where sin and egocentricity hold sway, there a power rules which is hostile to divine love, the sovereign power of the universe, and which, therefore, inevitably brings desolation and destruction. Man is the "slave of sin" (John 8:34).

Sin is revealed to the eye of faith, therefore, as a deviation from the proper destiny given to man by God. Faith understands this destiny to be life in which the ego with its many desires no longer is the tyrannical master, but in which the loving will of God rules. Faith discovers that the purpose of God is for man to live a life characterized and defined by his will and love, and that consequently this is a *God-given* destiny. That man has this destiny is the meaning of the idea that he is created in the image of God. The concept of the image of God cannot be demonstrated or established independently of faith; it is an affirmation *of faith* which becomes meaningful in and through the revelation of God and in the measure that man grasps what fellowship with God means. It emerges in and through the encounter with God's condemning and restoring love. It then becomes apparent that man's destiny is to live under God's dominion, that sin is that which separates man from that kind of life God intended him to live. But the concept of the image of God is used in a way that is foreign to faith if theology attempts to define this "image" as some "residue untouched by sin," which would explain the possibility of salvation by supplying a motive for God's saving love, and eventually also explain how man is able to accept the proffered salvation. This use of the conception of the image of God is foreign to faith both because Christian faith knows of no "explanation" of salvation except on the basis of the loving will of God, and also because it does not try to explain the activity of divine love by pointing to some quality in man. From the point of view of sin the concept of the "image of God" sets forth the lost destiny of man, and from the point of view of salvation it reveals the divine purpose in creation.

This definition of sin as a perverted inclination of a will hostile to God emphasizes still further the difference between the conception of sin represented by Christian faith and the metaphysically oriented conception which identifies sin with finiteness. In opposition to idealistic conceptions there has sometimes appeared in the history of Christian thought a tendency to shift from a volitional and qualitative to an unqualitative and metaphysical conception of sin. The intention has been to emphasize as strongly as possible the antithesis created by sin between the divine and the human. It is especially opposed to the disposition of idealistic metaphysics to blot out the distinction between the divine and "the highest human" and its inclination to regard sin simply as imperfection. In contrast, the anti-idealistic metaphysic desires to view man as a totality when it speaks of him as a sinner. But in comparison with the conception of sin in Christian faith this unqualitative metaphysical viewpoint blurs rather than clarifies the concept of sin. The questionable element in this approach is not that it proposes to deal with the whole man—Christian faith does that also (cf. ¶ 4)—but that sin refers to something which is constitutive for human nature as such, namely, its finiteness. In spite of its opposition to idealism this approach blunts the point of sin, because sin consists exactly in the antagonism between the divine will and the human egocentric will. The metaphysical conception of sin both obscures the real meaning of sin and exercises a baneful influence upon the conception of salvation. From this point of view a fellowship with God such as is envisaged in Christian faith is excluded, since the chasm between "the infinite" and "the finite" cannot be bridged. But for Christian faith fellowship with God becomes both possible and actual through the forgiving and saving act of the loving will of God.

4. Sin Applies to the Whole Man

When Christian faith understands sin as unbelief and egocentricity, and consequently sees sin as a perverse will hostile to the divine will, it follows that faith cannot divide man into a lower part which would be the "seat" of sin and a higher part which would remain outside this sphere. Such a division has often been suggested. Such theories may vary, but the main principle is that sin belongs to the "sensual" part of man, while his "spiritual" part has remained untouched by this corruption. This theory has in reality appeared in Christianity even from most ancient times, and has come from the mysteries and Greek idealism. We meet it in its typical form in Gnosticism, with its theory that the material and corporeal is the prison house in which the "divine" part of man is held captive. A similar cleavage of human nature was involved when the medieval mystics talked about "the fundamental essence," *das Funklein*, etc., as that part of man in which the divine resided. Essentially the same idea is found in Schleiermacher, in his distinction between the lower, sensual and the higher, spiritual consciousness, and in his proposition that sin consists in the fact that the lower, sensual consciousness has "out-reached" the higher consciousness or the consciousness of God. Between this highest spiritual element in man and the divine there is no definite boundary.

From faith's point of view this division of man is misleading because sin is attributed to man's lower nature, to something external and peripheral, while his "inmost" being is free from the tyranny of sin. But for Christian faith it is evident that sin is located precisely in this inner recess, in the inclination of the will. The theory of division leads to a false idealization of human life and to a minimizing of the seriousness of the human situation. The conception of sin is weakened and destroyed as soon as it is separated from the inner nature of man. Luther expressed the characteristic Christian conception of sin when he turned so decisively against this theory of division and its attempt to locate sin in an external part of man. There is nothing more evident to faith than that man does not possess an area immune to sin to which he could point as something acceptable to God. The judgment that man is a sinner is a total judgment, it applies to the whole of man, and therefore also to "the inner" and "spiritual" in man. Consequently salvation also applies to the whole of man; it does not mean that a certain part of man is set free, or that the "spiritual" is released from the oppression of the "sensual." When men stands face to face with God, *coram deo*, he stands as such under the judgment of God and this judgment pronounces him a sinner.

In this connection it is important to emphasize the statement with which this chapter began, namely, that sin is a concept which belongs entirely within the religious sphere, or in other words that it is applicable only *coram deo*. If we do not hold fast to this religious context, the viewpoint of Christian faith in regard to man's situation would be misinterpreted. It could then easily be accused of painting the situation in overly dark colors and of being therefore monotonous and unrealistic. It is significant that Luther, who strenuously asserts the total judgment implied in *coram deo*, at the same time speaks of another aspect of human life, namely, *coram hominibus*. On this plane the absolute verdict which is applicable *coram deo* is not valid. *In naturalibus* there is room for a variety of human moral actions. It is only in respect to religion, *coram deo*, that all such relative judgments cease. *Coram deo* all human boasting ceases (I Cor. 1:29), man stands before God naked, unprotected, unable to justify himself.

5. *Note on the Rejection of Psychological Schematizations*

When in this chapter we connected the consciousness of sin with faith, this connection cannot be psychologically schematized, either in the sense that a certain amount of faith would be a prerequisite for the consciousness of sin, or that a certain degree of consciousness of sin would be a prerequisite for faith. The latter has been by far the most common. Both in ancient and modern times (for example W. Herrmann) it has been asserted that the way to faith leads of necessity through that crisis to which the "moral demand" drives man, and that the reception of divine grace depends on having passed through the depth of consciousness of sin. The questionable element in this theory is not simply that "the moral" as such does not by any inner necessity lead to a religious crisis, but principally the idea that a complete and mature consciousness of sin serves as a preliminary step toward faith. Such a scheme is contrary to the nature of the Christian life in faith. Both the theory that regards consciousness of sin as a preliminary stage, and that conception which, like Schleiermacher, asserts that the consciousness of sin disappears in the measure that the "consciousness of God" is realized, are foreign to faith. Faith accepts instead the statement which Luther with his clear insight into the actual human situation formulated thus: *quo sanctior quis est, eo magis sentit illam pugnam* [The holier anyone is the more sensitive he is to that conflict]. The nearer God comes to man and the more completely the "fellowship" between God and man is realized, the more acute becomes the consciousness of sin. On the basis of this fundamental rule all psychological schematizations of the relation between faith and the consciousness of sin becomes impossible.

31. The Solidarity of Sin

1. *The doctrine of original sin.* Individual and specific acts of sin are not isolated and unrelated to each other but are rooted in the inclination of man's will; likewise, the sinful will of each man is not isolated but exists within a context of comprehensive human interrelationships. The idea of original sin, in contrast to atomistic conceptions of sin, is significant because it expresses a total view both of the individual man and of the human race.[1] This significance is obscured if

[1] In our translation of the author's discussion of this subject we have found it necessary to employ terms which are not direct translations of the words used by the author. The following formulation may therefore serve to clarify this procedure:
1. The atomistic conception of sin:
    a. Individual acts of sin are independent and unrelated.
    b. Individual sinners are independent and unrelated.
2. The solidary interrelationship of sin:
    a. Individual acts of sin are interdependent and interrelated.
    b. Individual sinners are interdependent and interrelated.
We have translated the author's expression "*syndens överindividuella sammanhang*" as "the solidary interrelationship of sin," and "*syndens överindividuella makt*" as "the demonic power of sin" (cf. § 31, ¶ 2, 3).—Trans.

the conception of sin is transferred from volitional to physical and finite categories.

2. *The power of evil.* This universality of sin, embracing the will of all mankind, appears in the last analysis as a solidary interrelationship of evil which encircles and as a demonic power enslaves humanity.

3. *Sin as both inevitable and volitional.* This solidary interrelationship of sin does not nullify or minimize the character of sin as a perversion of the individual will. From the point of view of faith sin is both inevitable and volitional.

4. *The solidary interrelationship of sin and the problem of its origin.* The solidary interrelationship of sin cannot be used to explain the origin of sin. The purely speculative question about the origin of sin is foreign to faith. The interest of faith is concentrated on the problem of the nature of sin and its subjugation.

1. The Doctrine of Original Sin

We cannot obtain a real insight into the nature of the Christian conception of sin except by noting how Christian faith perceives sin as a solidary interrelationship. This meets us as the idea of original sin. In regard to the common distinction between original and actual sin it must be stated that this does not imply two different categories of sin. The expression "original sin" refers to all sin. From the point of view of Christian faith all sin is "original sin." "Actual sin," therefore, is an expression which denotes the external manifestation of original sin. Since the term "original sin" can easily be misinterpreted and lead to conceptions foreign to Christian faith, it is necessary first of all to turn our attention on those points of view which theology has endeavored to reject by means of this conception if we are to be able to understand the Christian meaning of the idea of original sin, or, in other words, the fundamental religious motifs expressed herin.

When the doctrine of original sin was formulated in the ancient church in opposition to Pelagianism, the intention was to overcome the casuistic and atomistic Pelagian view of sin. The weakness and unreality of the Pelagian view were its isolation of the individual and sinful decisions of will. It was a twofold isolation. On the one hand, sinful acts of will were understood as independent one of the other, and the will was considered free to decide either for or against sin. There was no feeling for the continuity of volition, nor for the fact that the nature of sin is a corruption of the will. On the other hand, men were regarded as isolated individuals without any consideration of their solidarity with humanity as a whole. In either case this is an abstract conception which does not correspond to the viewpoint of Christian faith relative to the actual situation. Personal decisions are not isolated one from the other, but are closely connected and stem from a certain definite character of the will. Nor are individual human beings isolated from the race, but rather stand in a very close and intimate relationship. The real significance of the doctrine of original sin consists in its opposition to this twofold and unrealistic isolation, and in its emphasis that sin is a perversion of the will and a solidary interrelationship. In both of these respects the intentions of the doctrine of original sin express realistically faith's conception of the character and extent of sin.

In the first place, therefore, the doctrine of original sin is concerned with man as a whole. Sin does not refer to something external and peripheral in man nor to something "accidental"; it has its "seat" in his inner being, in the inclination of the will, and applies, therefore, to man as a whole. Luther has given clear expression to this idea, which is contained but not clearly and fully expressed in the term "original sin," when he translates original sin by "sin of the person." "This original sin, or the sin of nature, or the *sin of the person*, is the principal sin. If it did not exist, neither would there be any actual sin." [2] In reality "sin of the person" expresses much more clearly than "original sin" the idea that the latter phrase is intended to convey.

But, in the second place, the concept of original sin is also intended to view humanity as a whole. Sinfulness does not belong simply to separate individuals; it is characteristic of the whole human race. Individual man as a member of society participates in the sinfulness of the race. This brings to the fore the idea of the inevitability of sin. Man stands by inner necessity under the power of sin. The context of sin surrounds him and determines his life. If, from this

---

[2] *WA* 10I, 1, 508, quoted by Karl Holl in "Was verstant Luther unter Religion," in *Gesammelte Aufsätze zur Kirchengeschichte* (Tübingen: 1928-1932), I, 66. Cf. also *"dass also die Reue gehe nicht stücklich über etliche Werke, die du öffentlich begangen hast wider die zehen Gebot—sondern über die ganze Person mit alle ihrem Leben und Wessen"* (*EA*, 11, 309).

point of view, we use the *expression* "original sin," it must be said that this expression is designed to emphasize this total view of mankind. The word "original sin" tells us that the solidarity of the race is solidarity in sin. There is in humanity a sinful inclination which is reproduced from generation to generation. This context of sin lies as a heavy burden on the life of humanity, and, in relation to the individual man, appears as a demonic power. It must be emphasized, however, that this "inheritance" consists not simply in inherited dispositions and tendencies; in fact the whole inner inheritance is a sinful inheritance, which spins its net around the individual in the most varied manner and through innumerable means. In the final analysis, the view of Christian faith regarding this context of sin is adequately expressed only when the idea of the sinful interrelationships of the race passes over into the concept of a spiritual power of evil, a demonic power which is active in relation to the human will (cf. also ¶ 2).

We have now tried to define the two main motifs which have been expressed in the concept of original sin. If, therefore, it is essential for Christian faith to use the concept of original sin in the sense previously explained, it must at the same time be added that this term involves certain very evident dangers. Ever since the days of Augustine the concept of original sin has tended to relate sin to the purely physical and has thereby obscured the nature of sin as volition and as a corruption of the will. When this occurs, the concept no longer serves to deepen the perception of sin, but rather injects into it an element foreign to faith.

In view of what we have just said about the solidary interrelationship of sin and the inner inheritance of sinfulness, it should be added that Christian faith knows not only about an inheritance of sin, but also knows and reckons with an *inheritance of blessing*, a context of blessedness. As far as faith is concerned, the situation of the race and of the individual is characterized by the continual conflict between these two powers: the blessing and the curse. Man is the arena where this conflict takes place.

2. *The Power of Evil*

We have already suggested that faith did not stop with the idea of an interrelationship of sin in which individuals are united with one another. At the same time that sinfulness in human life is defined as always volitional, it also appears to faith in the form of a demonic spiritual power which commands and subjugates the human will. The solidary interrelationship of sin concretizes itself in inscrutable and obscure powers, a mysterious complex which cannot be accurately delimited and defined, and which slips away and becomes shadowy as soon as one tries to grasp and comprehend it. Nevertheless it shows its power in the most fearful manner and by the most cruel oppression of human life.[3] Evil shows itself to be in possession of a sphere of power which stretches beyond individuals and their direct and definable relationships. In the New Testament we often meet more or less mythologically formulated expressions for this complex of evil powers (cf. Rom. 8:38-39; Gal. 1:4; Col. 2:15; Eph. 6:12). In the last analysis Christian faith perceives this evil as concentrated in the satanic power in conflict with the divine will. Man is placed in a vast conflict between the two powers: the kingdom of God and the kingdom from below. The divine will contends with the hostile spiritual powers which tyrannize man. When the New Testament and the Christian church speak about the devil as the incarnation of this concentrated evil power, it is necessary to distinguish between the motif and its expression. The use of the conception of the devil is not in and by itself the least guarantee of a profound insight into the nature and terrific power of evil. Many examples can be cited to show that the idea of the devil has been used in such a way that the conception of evil has been weakened. It is of greatest importance for Christian faith that the "dualistic" element contained in this conception not be obscured, or, in other words, that the element in creation which is hostile to God be allowed to appear with all the realism and intensity it possesses for faith. It is not a demonic mythology which is important, but an insight into the nature of evil, its power and extent. Thus Luther, with a clear insight into the imperfections and dangers of these conceptions pictures the contrast

---

[3] In recent times we have had a wide experience of demonic "ideological" powers. But the idea which has been advanced at times about a "demonic technology" must be rejected. The demonic does not reside in the technical instruments but in the use man makes of them.

between the divine and the satanic as the contrast between love and hate. *"Denn wie die Liebe ist ein Bild Gottes, und nicht ein tot Bild noch auf Papier gemalet, sondern ein lebendig Wesen in göttlicher Natur, die da brennet voll alles Guten, also ist wiederum Hass und Neid ein recht Bild des Teufels . . . dass man den Teufel nicht besser malen könnte denn wenn man könnte eitel Hass und Neid malen."* [For as love is an image of God, and not just a dead image drawn on paper, but a living essence, divine in nature and full of everything good, so also hate and envy in turn make a true image of the devil . . . so that we cannot more truly picture the devil than by picturing pure hate and envy.][4]

3. Sin as Both Inevitable and Volitional

When reference is made to the solidary interrelationship of sin it may seem to suggest a contrast between sin as a demonic power (original sin) and sin as an individual act (actual sin). It might seem that to regard sin as a demonic power minimizes its character as perversion of the individual will; in other words, if sin is conceived of in terms of a demonic power it cannot be attributed to the individual will. But if this is done and sin is attributed to the individual will only in the measure that it is *not* dependent upon this demonic power, a conception is introduced which is foreign to faith, i.e., it does not correspond to the judgment of the religious self-consciousness (cf. § 32, ¶ 1). But from the point of view of faith and of the judgment of the religious self-consciousness there exists no such contrast. Sin of the person is always a perversion of the will, and all individual sin is a result of the fact that not the loving will of God but the ego separated from God holds sway. No matter how much the sin of person stands in an intimate connection with sin as a demonic power, this sin of the person is nevertheless something which adheres to and determines the personal will as such and is a result of this personal will and a reflection of its character. There is no logical contradiction between these two points of view. That sin is inevitable does not imply that it is some kind of natural defect.

Christian faith perceives sin, therefore, as both inevitable and voli-

‘ *EA*, 19, p. 366.

tional. The solidary interrelationship of evil is a demonic power which man cannot escape. But sin has at the same time the character of volitional activity. As soon as one or the other of these points of view is suppressed, the conception of sin becomes either moralistically superficial or naturalistically obscured.

4. The Solidary Interrelationship of Sin and the Problem of its Origin

In the history of theology the question of the solidary interrelationship of sin has frequently been combined with the problem of the origin of sin. The attempt has been made to use the idea of this interrelationship as an explanation of the origin of sin. But if the solidary interrelationship of sin does not nullify or even minimize the character of sin as corruption of the will, it follows that faith cannot easily find an explanation of its origin in this interrelationship. In reality the confusing ideas which have been connected with the doctrine of original sin have been the result of attempts to use this doctrine for speculative purposes foreign to faith and to explain the ultimate origin of sin. In regard to these attempts it should be said both that they have not been able to give a satisfactory explanation, and that they have come into conflict with certain vital interests of faith. They have not, in other words, reflected the characteristic viewpoint of faith in regard to the relationship between sin as demonic and sin as an individual act.

The doctrine of original sin has usually been employed in the interest of such an explanation by making a distinction between the sin of the first man, which was occasioned by the misuse of his freedom induced by the misleading suggestion of an evil, superhuman power, and all other sin, which is due to the change in the nature of man as the result of this first sin. It is clear, however, that this is not a real explanation, but simply removes the question one step further back.[5] To attribute the cause of sin to free will is in reality nothing but a retreat to something unexplained and inexplicable. This becomes even more inexplicable if it is maintained that the will of the first man was originally a good will given to him by God in creation.

[5] Cf. Schleiermacher, *Christian Faith*, pp. 291 ff.

Nor can we obtain an adequate explanation by going back to a super-human evil power which acts as the tempter. Such an explanation places us simply before a new question, unless we are satisfied with an ultimate dualism. But the most serious defect in this theory is not that it offers an inadequate explanation, which is no explanation at all, but that it obscures the nature of sin as this is understood in the light of faith. According to this theory only the first sin was in reality "a sin of the person," to use Luther's expression. All other sin must then be regarded as a certain physical attribute in man, a sinful "sub-stance," which exists independently of man's nature as a person. This approach is, therefore, in conflict with the purpose which the doctrine of original sin was intended to serve against the Pelagian atomistic and casuistic conception of sin; or, in other words, it conceals the fact that sin is a condition of the will. It should be added that such a conception of the relation between the first sin and all subsequent sin leads to a division of responsibility which does not correspond to the Christian consciousness of sin (cf. § 32, ¶ 1). If, after the first act, sin is separated from the personal will, this implies that there is an excuse for all subsequent sin. This leads inevitably to a contradic-tion between the solidary interrelationship of sin and individual sin.

But if we cannot combine the doctrine of original sin with the idea of an original state and the fall in order to provide a rational explanation of the origin of sin, it does not follow that Christian faith finds the ideas of the original state and the fall useless. "The original state" and "the fall" are not simply myths, but neither are they simply an event belonging to a definite period in human history. As creation is not something finished once and for all, but a continuously ongoing activity of God (cf. § 20), so the original state and the fall are not individual events, but belong to the life of humanity as a whole. When the idea of the original state and the fall is combined with Christian faith, the "original state" reveals to every man the destiny given him by God, and "the fall" declares that the solidary interrela-tionship of sin does not remove the character of sin as an act of will; or, in other words, when sin becomes actual in our lives, we are engaged in destroying the destiny given us by God.

Christian faith, therefore, deliberately rejects all attempts to furnish a rational explanation of the origin of sin in human life, not only because all these explanations fail and every answer places us before a new question, but especially because these explanations obscure what faith perceives to be essential in regard to the nature of sin and the relationship between sin as a demonic power and sin as an individual act. Theology is content to leave the problems of the origin and first appearance of sin in the world to that speculative "philosophy" which is delighted to deal with them. But the interest of faith itself is concentrated on the problems of the nature of sin and its subjugation, for these are to faith the most vital questions.

32. Sin and Guilt

1. *Consciousness of sin and consciousness of guilt.* Sin is *eo ipso* guilt. Guilt means that man is a debtor to God. The consciousness of guilt is the consciousness of deserving to be "cast . . . away from [God's] presence." Every attempt to make guilt dependent on the connection between individual sinfulness and the solidary interrelationship of sin leads to a casuistic and relative conception of sin which is foreign to Christian faith.

2. *Religious consciousness of guilt knows no degrees of guilt.* Since the religious conception of sin refers to man as a whole, and since God's judgment on sin is unconditional, it follows that from a religious point of view there can be no degrees of guilt. The decisive element lies entirely in the different relations of men to the divine and gracious will. From this point of view "hardening" appears as definite rejection of the divine and gracious will characterized by the suspension of the consciousness of guilt.

3. *The relative point of view.* A relative point of view is justified, however, when the mutual relationships of men in this world are made the object of judgments based on empirical and psychological premises. In that case different degrees of "guilt" can be established, and the evaluation does not depend only on the character of individual acts but also on environmental conditions. When we pass over to the religious sphere, this relativistic conception loses its validity.

1. Consciousness of Sin and Consciousness of Guilt

Sin and guilt cannot be separated. Sin is *eo ipso* guilt. When we speak about sin and guilt, we are in reality dealing with the same thing from two different points of view. Sinful man is the one who is guilty before God. Because he is guilty, man is a debtor to God

(Matt. 18:23 ff.) and likewise to his neighbor. To deny one's guilt is to continue unrepentant in sin and to attempt—unsuccessfully—to escape the judgment of God.

Consciousness of guilt is consciousness of being separated from God and, as his debtor, being subject to his judgment. The divine judgment is a judgment on man's life as opposed to the divine will, on that egocentric corruption of will which is the essence of sin. The judgment reveals man's distance from God and his unworthiness to stand in his presence. When we read in the parable of the prodigal son: "Father, I have sinned against heaven and before you; I am *no longer worthy* to be called your son" (Luke 15:18 ff), these words express the characteristically religious consciousness of guilt. This note is sounded wherever the consciousness of guilt manifests itself spontaneously and unreflectively. It is found in the confession of sin in the Swedish church: "We are worthy, therefore, to be cast away from Thy presence, if Thou shouldst judge us according to our sins." The religious consciousness of guilt always says: Because I am what I am, I am unclean, defiled, separated from God, and unworthy to stand in his presence. "Woe is me! For I am lost; for I am a man of unclean lips, and I dwell in the midst of a people of unclean lips; for my eyes have seen the King, the Lord of hosts!" (Isa. 6:5).

It is clear from what we have just said that the religious consciousness of sin, which always expresses a relation to God (cf. § 30), immediately and unavoidably appears as a consciousness of guilt. Religious self-consciousness unites sin and guilt in an inseparable connection. As soon as man stands face to face with God and his judgment is pronounced upon him, every sin becomes also guilt; every sin points to and is a product of that sinfulness which characterizes our will and marks our ego as unworthy and guilty before God. Consciousness of guilt, in the real and purely religious meaning of the word, is consciousness that this ego in its present state is worthy of rejection by God.

It must be especially underscored that consciousness of guilt implies that man knows and submits to *God's* judgment. The idea is not that men set up certain "ideals" which pronounce a more or less severe judgment upon them. It is not human ideals, but God who judges. Nor can man's "conscience" as such be the court of last appeal. It is undeniable that in this connection there has been much obscure and confusing talk about conscience as a judge, as if here man without further consideration had recourse to an infallible standard. That conscience cannot lay claim to such an infallibility is altogether too plain when we consider what judgments have been pronounced in the name of "conscience." A reference to conscience as a judgment seat cannot even be considered, if it means that conscience of and by itself determines what is and is not divine justice, and the power of judgment is thereby transferred to the human. If we are to refer to conscience in this connection at all, it cannot be a question of conscience as a unique and constant factor, but only of that conscience which has been "awakened," "enlightened," and dominated by God. Under all circumstances it is clear to Christian faith that it is the divine will itself which subjects man to its judgment and reveals his unworthiness.

When the consciousness of sin appears directly as a consciousness of guilt, it is already evident that the question of guilt cannot be made dependent upon the relation between individual sinfulness and the solidary interrelationship of sin. If sin is at the same time both inevitable and voluntary, inevitability cannot remove or minimize its character as guilt. No appeal to the solidary interrelationship of sin is able to erase or reduce the guilt. When man stands face to face with God and meets his judgment, he does not analyze whether or not his sins have been committed wilfully and deliberately, nor does he hide behind some theories about the lesser or greater bondage of the will in order thereby to minimize and possibly excuse his sin. He can no more appeal to the solidary interrelationship of sin as the cause or basis for God's forgiveness than he can seek shelter behind this interrelationship as a protection from the accusations and judgment of the voice of God. It is not only a matter of man's *inability* to seek such a shelter, he does not *want* to do so. Religious consciousness does not seek excuses for sin. Nothing can be more foreign to a man in that situation than to try to argue with God about the significance of "dispositions," "environment," and training, or about the boundary of wilful, deliberate, and intentional sins and the point where guilt begins. When man finds himself "guilty," a debtor to God, it does not mean simply that he finds a certain act inexcusable, but that *just as he is*, because of his hostile and egocentric will which results in individual sins, he is "worthy to be cast away from the presence of God." In the judgment of religious self-consciousness man discovers that he is guilty, not only when he can determine that he has acted with "full freedom"—if it were ever possible to do so—but also that he is responsible and guilty because sin cannot be separated from his will. Sin *is* an expression of and reflects the actual disposition of a man's will. It makes very little difference to religious consciousness of sin whether our sinful acts were more or less dependent on the solidary interrelationship of sin. No dependence, however strong, can remove the volitional element from personal sin, or obscure the fact that I—precisely I—am unworthy to stand before God. It is noteworthy in this connection that those who have spoken most frankly about the guilt of sin have also spoken most emphatically about the bondage of the will. If my consciousness of sin were to be made dependent upon the higher or lower degree of conscious freedom and intention with which these sins have been committed, it would lead directly to a casuistry which would destroy *all* responsibility and *all* profound consciousness of sin. That which is essential in the judgment of the religious self-consciousness is simply this—that my will, such as it actually is, and that I, just as I am, are unworthy before God. With his clear insight Luther expressed the heart of the matter when he places these two alternatives before us: either man is responsible for nothing, or else he is responsible for his life as a whole. This is true, since the judgment of religious self-consciousness always refers to the ego as a whole, is always absolute and never seeks to excuse itself.

Since the consciousness of guilt is thus practically identical with the consciousness of sin, it is in reality not concerned with the question as to whether and to what degree individual sins (actual sin) are dependent upon the solidary interrelationship of sin. When it is a question about the religious self-consciousness and that judgment which God pronounces on our sin, it is misleading to draw a sharp distinction between sin and guilt, which was so often done in the theology of the nineteenth century. It was asserted at that time that we could speak of guilt only in regard to those sins which have been committed wilfully and deliberately; but that there could be no question of guilt if individual sins were dependent on and the result of the solidary interrelationship of sin. If this were the only valid conception of sin, it would inevitably lead to the casuistry mentioned before, and would in reality dissolve the concept of guilt, since in every situation it would be possible to seek protection behind the solidary interrelationship. This approach ignores the fact that religious self-knowledge can never regard the individual sinful act as an isolated deed, but on the contrary understands it as a reflection of the actual condition of the ego. It also overlooks the fact that the judgment pronounced is absolute and does not recognize any relative excuses. As soon as the total viewpoint characteristic of Christian faith is noted, it becomes absolutely impossible to justify the guilt rationally by a division of responsibility. To the man who stands face to face with God, guilt is an inescapable fact.

We may add here that, if the idea of the solidary interrelationship of sin is to become meaningful for religious self-appraisal, this interrelationship must be allowed to impose an increased responsibility and a greater guilt on the Christian man. It makes our responsibility and our guilt more acute and convinces us that our guilt is not simply the guilt of our own sin, but a guilt of that solidary interrelationship in which we participate and to which our own sin has been added.

2. Religious Consciousness of Guilt Knows of No Degrees of Guilt

It is clear from our previous presentation that religious consciousness of guilt cannot differentiate between higher and lower degrees of guilt. Since the concept of sin always refers to man as a whole, and furthermore, since God's judgment on sin is always an unconditional and radical rejection, it is meaningless, as far as man's stance before God is concerned, to differentiate between serious sins which entail serious guilt and lesser sins which entail lesser guilt. Consciousness of guilt and awareness of our own unworthiness do not become weaker because a sin, according to human estimation, is less serious. In this connection there is in reality no place for a gradation of sins as greater or lesser. Religious self-appraisal is indifferent to all such endeavors. Our unworthiness before God, as the Sermon on the Mount unequivocally declares (Matt. 5:22, 28), is the same whether sin expresses itself in the most secret thought or in the most hideous act, whether it is a question of omission or commission, and whether it is a question of an unconscious act or one committed deliberately and on purpose. However "small" a sin may appear according to a human estimate, to religious consciousness awakened by the divine judgment it gives evidence of that disposition which is hostile to God's loving will and renders us worthy to be cast away from his presence.

Consequently there disappear all the casuistic distinctions of scholasticism intended to determine the degree of peril and guilt connected with various kinds of sin. Such a graduated catalog of sins serves only to obscure the Christian concept of sin and guilt. The distinction of scholasticism between "mortal" and "venial" sins has no justification. There is no sin which is not "deadly," but neither is there any sin which, as far as the divine will is concerned, is not forgivable.

If, therefore, God's judgment on sin is unconditional and radical, there is from the point of view of sinfulness no distinction between men. Instead, the word, "all have sinned and fall short of the glory of God" (Rom. 3:23), is valid here. From the religious point of view the difference lies in men's relation to the saving and gracious will of God; it is a question of their receiving or rejecting the divine grace. When this line of demarcation is established, two things must be noted: first, the line cannot be drawn so that it becomes visible from an external point of view, in reality it is known to God alone; and second, the line must in reality be drawn, so to speak, within man, since sin does not cease under the conditions of this earthly life and since fellowship with God exists only as forgiveness and as a struggle against that which is opposed to the divine will.

When Christian faith speaks of a state of "hardness of heart," it understands thereby a definite rejection of the divine and gracious will characterized by the suspension of the consciousness of guilt. This state is designated in the New Testament as "sin against the Holy Spirit." When this sin is defined as "unforgivable," it is not because God ceases to be willing to forgive, but because divine love does not operate through external coercion but through inner conviction, and the conditions making such a conviction possible have ceased to exist in the state of hardness of heart. But whether a person has committed this sin or not, God alone knows. *One* thing is certain: where there is any consciousness of guilt, the sin has not been committed.

3. The Relative Point of View

When man stands face to face with God and permits His judgment to fall upon his own ego, he becomes conscious that he is really guilty and unworthy in the sight of God. Here there is no graduated scale of guilt. But it does not follow that it is impossible to speak of different degrees of guilt, or greater and lesser guilt. Guilt can be understood in different senses. The central, religious conception of guilt which we have hitherto discussed is not the only one. We *can* speak of "guilt" also in a narrower, purely moral sense. The failure to distinguish between these two meanings has been the cause of much confusion. It is, of course, possible to use the concept of guilt with reference to the specific conditions of individual acts and to adopt an empirical and psychological point of view, provided it is made perfectly clear that the concept is not understood in its deeper, religious meaning. "The problem of guilt" in this narrow sense appears again and again in intercourse with our neighbors, when we adopt the viewpoint of *coram hominibus*, as Luther calls it. Man *coram deo* can no more reckon with relative standards than he can avoid doing so *coram hominibus*. In this respect we must take into account the influence of such things as heritage, environment, and so on, and even the connection between individual guilt and the solidary interrelationship of guilt. Here the idea of different degrees of guilt has a place. If, however, it is evident that our judgment in reference to our neighbors, and our own judgment in reference to our relation to them, is dependent upon the connection between individual evil and the solidary interrelationship of evil, it is just as evident that the judgment we pronounce is *relative* in character. The problem of guilt is from this point of view insoluble. The more we try to penetrate its mystery, the more clearly it becomes impossible to review all the pertinent factors and to make a satisfactory division of guilt.

If we then distinguish between a purely religious point of view (man *coram deo*) and a moral point of view (man *coram hominibus*), the distinction between these two cannot be so defined that in the former case we deal with the "person," disposition, and the inclination of the will, and in the latter case, with actual deeds and the moral conduct as such. In the first place, through such a distinction the *coram deo* point of view would be unduly restricted. *Coram deo* it is *also* a question about deeds, about human life in its entirety, and about both the disposition and the acts. Neither is it possible on the basis of the moral point of view to ignore the disposition and regard it as irrelevant; both external acts and disposition must be considered. It must be established that we are not concerned with a delimitation which would place a certain area of human life in the "religious" and another in the "moral" sphere, but rather that we are dealing with human life from two distinct points of view. As the two Latin expressions which we have borrowed from Luther indicate, in one case it is a question of man's relation to God, and in the other, man's relation to society. This may also be expressed in another formula: in one case it is a question of man *in loco justificationis,* and in the other, man *in naturalibus.*

When in relations between men the different degrees of "guilt" must be taken into account, this gradation can be motivated from two points of view. To some extent the degree of guilt can be measured by the quality of the act. A certain act can imply a greater degree of evil in human society than another, and can be the result of greater or less malice. But at the same time it is necessary in the appraisal of all these human acts to take into serious consideration the conditions under which these acts have been performed. From this point of view the guilt increases the more man has been surrounded by conditions favorable to a moral life, and the more his training, disposition, environment. and the like, have placed him in a favored situation from a moral point of view.

When we pass over to the religious point of view, *coram deo,* these relativistic considerations lose their validity. The scholastic casuistry which has had such baneful influence on the conception of the relation between God and man is the result of a confusion of these two points of view. *In loco justificationis* nothing else than a total view of man has any place; here nothing matters except on the one hand human sin and guilt, and on the other, the grace of God alone.

33. Divine Fellowship Is Realized Through Forgiveness

1. *The concept of forgiveness.* When forgiveness is designated as the way whereby fellowship with God is realized, it must not be understood as a unique act of God, but rather that which constitutes the fundamental basis of the Christian life of faith. The forgiveness of sin is the act of God through which his sovereign love subdues sinful man and incorporates him into fellowship with God.

2. *The miracle of forgiveness.* The unfathomable and miraculous character of forgiveness is expressed in the fact that divine love, which stands in unmitigated opposition to sin, receives sinful man into its fellowship. Man thereby becomes *simul iustus et peccator.*

3. *Forgiveness does not nullify God's opposition to evil.* If forgiveness supersedes all purely ethical points of view, it implies also the strongest possible expression of God's opposition to evil. It is especially in forgiveness that divine love appears as a radical judgment of sin and the fellowship of forgiveness makes more acute the consciousness of the distance between God and man.

4. *Misinterpretations of the concept of forgiveness.* The Christian concept of forgiveness presents, therefore, a threefold antithesis. Forgiveness cannot be rationally motivated through a *legalistic* interpretation of Christ's work of reconciliation. Nor can it be *moralistically* motivated by citing as a condition of forgiveness some quality possessed by man as such, or some human attitude, or the future results of the act of forgiveness. Finally, it cannot be motivated through *humananizing* or *hyperevangelical* conceptions which imply a minimizing of the act of forgiveness as a judgment. Faith discovers that the basis of forgiveness is found only in God's spontaneous and inscrutable, saving and condemning love, as this realizes itself in the act of God in Christ.

1. The Concept of Forgiveness

With our discussion of the Christian concept of sin in the three previous chapters we have noted the factor which separates man from God. In this and a few of the following chapters we shall investigate the Christian view of the realization and the nature of fellowship with God. The presentation will naturally center around two chief words: forgiveness of sin and faith. Fellowship with God is realized in and through God's act of forgiveness, and it exists as a relationship of faith.

Forgiveness of sin is used here as the principal word in setting forth how fellowship between God and man is realized because this expression is so rich in content and so easily comprehensible. "Forgiveness" stems from the area of the most intimate personal life and indicates, therefore, that it is a question of nothing less than the re-establishment of the fellowship and filial relation with God which was broken through sin. This concept, therefore, is much more suitable for our purpose than all those taken from the juridical sphere, since it sets forth the fact that here we are dealing with an act of *God's love.* Forgiveness does not imply simply a remission of "punishment." As long as the relation between God and man is conceived of in juridical terms, the question is principally about acquittal and freedom from punishment. The law is the only connecting link between the judge and the accused: they have no personal connection with each other. The question is only whether the accused can be acquitted according to the law. Even if a "pardon" is granted, it need not imply a more intimate personal relation between the accused and the presiding judge. What happens is simply that the punishment is remitted and the accused is set free. It is quite a different situation when it is a question about a purely personal relationship, for example, a friend's relation to a friend, and a child's to his father. When these relations are disturbed, the question is not simply whether legal action is to be taken and punishment meted out; what is now at stake is the elimination of that which separates and threatens to destroy old ties of affection. The question is whether the former confidential and intimate personal relationship can be re-established and continued anew. This can be done in only one way—forgiveness. The juridical categories prove to be inadequate when it is a question of interpreting the inner character of the relationship to God. Just because the relationship between God and man is so intimate and personal, "forgiveness" becomes the most immediate and expressive word for that act of God's love whereby he vanquishes and subdues sinful man and incorporates him into a fellowship with himself. The divine fellowship is realized through forgiveness—the only way possible, because God is love and man is a sinner.

Although the concept of forgiveness, therefore, is extremely useful in the presentation of the act of God through which fellowship between God and man is established, it is also subject to certain misinterpretations—which would, of course, be true of whatever concepts might be used. According to the testimony of the history of Christian thought the principal danger is that forgiveness might be interpreted negatively as simply a remission of punishment. Such an interpretation is not satisfactory and does not exhaust the rich content of this idea. The essential element is the positive re-establishment of broken fellowship. When Luther so consistently uses forgiveness as the principal word in his Catechisms and elsewhere, he pours into it this full positive significance: where there is forgiveness of sins, there also is life and blessedness.

Among the expressions which might be used in this connection the word "justification" occupies the chief place. From a positive point of view, when this word is used in its deepest meaning, its content is the same as "forgiveness of sins." It might well be said, however, that the word justification does not possess the naturalness and intimacy of the word "forgiveness." "Justification" is in reality a technical theological word originally used in a polemical situation which must be clearly understood if the connotations of the word are to be appreciated. This is true with regard to both Paul and Luther. It is not, to be sure, subject to the danger of being interpreted negatively, as forgiveness has been; it has a positive connotation. But "justification" *can* easily be interpreted in a sense foreign to Christian faith, since it is unquestionably easy to understand it as implying that man in a real and positive sense becomes righteous and free from sin. Under all circumstances the history of theology after the Reformation indicates that the concept of justification readily loses its Reformation meaning and is misinterpreted in various ways. It has been difficult to utilize and preserve the insights contained in the Reformation's interpretation. The word has therefore largely become more or less meaningless and strange. Its positive content has been expressed much more effectively by the term "forgiveness of sins."

Finally, it should be stated emphatically that forgiveness of sins cannot be restricted merely to the beginning of Christian life. Forgiveness is not an act that occurs only once, at a certain time, and establishes once and for all the basis on which the Christian life exists. On the contrary, forgiveness belongs to the whole of Christian life, since this life depends on the fact that "the grace of God is new every morning." If forgiveness is the basis of the realization of fellowship with God, it means that forgiveness is both the essential foundation of the Christian life and its continually active power. We cannot, therefore, divide the Christian relationship to God in such a way that forgiveness should belong to the beginning of Christian life and faith to its continuation. If we distinguish between forgiveness as representing the realization of fellowship with God and faith as representing its continuous existence, it must be made clear that this is not a distinction between different stages of the Christian life, but a conceptual differentiation intended to present forgiveness as the principal foundation of Christian faith in the sense that faith owes its existence and its content to the divine act of forgiveness.

2. The Miracle of Forgiveness

The divine act of forgiveness appears to faith as an inscrutable miracle. It does not occur in accordance with human thinking and expectation, but contrary to all that we may expect or think. It can therefore be said that in a certain sense forgiveness has a miraculous character. This appears in the fact that *God* meets the sinful and *unworthy* man with *full* forgiveness. 1) The one who "forgives" is the God who stands in an unmitigated and implacable opposition to sin. He does not forgive on the premise that to understand all is to forgive all. He cannot pass by, ignore, or condone sin. The opposition is irrevocable, and the judgment is radical. *This* God now enters into association with sinful man and receives, not the "worthy," but the unworthy and condemned man into fellowship with himself. If we listen to the testimony of Christian faith where it is given in its deepest and clearest form, it is abundantly evident that the essential element is just this: God's forgiveness is given, not to one who is sufficiently qualified to receive it, but to one who is entirely unworthy. 2) Another factor in the matter emphasizes even more strongly the strange and unexpected activity of divine love. God's forgiveness does not appear to faith, like so much of human forgiveness, as a half-measure, a forgiveness which has an element of suspicion and remembrance of the offense. It is a *full* and therefore a restoring forgiveness which unites man with God. God's forgiveness meets us as a forgiveness through which the old has passed away, has been erased, and all things have become new. Just because forgiveness has this character faith can say that "where there is forgiveness of sins, there is also life and salvation." Because God's act of forgiveness implies that he receives unworthy man into fellowship with himself, the act appears to the eye of faith as an inscrutable miracle contrary to all human calculations and expectations. Its character is supra-ethical. It transcends everything merely moral; it is the inmost and deepest mystery of religion. 3) The inexplicable element in the divine act of love is enhanced still more by the fact that faith well knows that sin and unworthiness do not disappear so long as earthly conditions obtain. If freedom from sin were the immediate or gradual result of the fellowship with God established by forgiveness, the inexplicable character of forgiveness would at least to some extent be removed. But this is so far from being the case that man's incorporation into this fellowship with God rather makes the consciousness of sin more acute, and even, from one point of view, expresses itself as a much keener consciousness of sin and guilt. Luther illustrates this situation by his famous statement that the forgiven sinner is *simul iustus et peccator*.

When we speak here of the forgiveness of sin as an unfathomable miracle, it is not a question of a paradox in the sense of two logically opposite ideas, but rather of something "paradoxical" in the original sense of the word, i.e., something that is contrary to what we might "intend" or expect. This is true both of the nature of the divine act of forgiveness and of the phrase, *simul iustus et peccator*. God's act of forgiveness is an impenetrable mystery because God's love, which meets us here, cannot be rationally motivated. Every attempt to assign a cause for the divine act of love as it meets us in the event of Christ obscures its essential character. Nor does the clause, *simul iustus et peccator*, contain a logical contradiction. That would be the case only if the word *iustus* were interpreted to mean that man has been made just in the sense of sinless perfection. But this is not the meaning. The man who has received God's forgiveness carries on a continuous and unceasing struggle against sin. Man during his earthly life is and remains completely *peccator*, but he becomes at the same time completely *iustus* in the sense that he is *propter Christum* accepted and approved by God. *Simul iustus et peccator* expresses, therefore, the inexplicable fact that in spite of man's sin God receives him into fellowship with himself through forgiveness.[1]

3. Forgiveness Does Not Nullify God's Opposition to Evil

It is clear from the preceding that the divine act of forgiveness cannot be contained within the order of justice, and that in reality it transcends all merely ethical points of view. The forgiveness of divine love cannot be motivated by ethical considerations. Faith *cannot* find any other basis of forgiveness than unfathomable divine love itself. In this sense God's love is "uncaused" (cf. § 14). But this must not be interpreted to mean a discount or a weakening of God's opposition to evil. No approach could be more foreign to faith than the assertion that forgiveness has the character of laxity and palliation. Even though human forgiveness often may have this character, divine forgiveness is immensely different. On the contrary, it is clear to faith that forgiveness does not weaken or cancel God's opposition to evil, but that this is expressed most emphatically in the very act of forgiveness.

This becomes evident in various ways. In the first place, reconciling and forgiving love has adopted the way of self-giving sacrifice in its

---

[1] Cf. Anders Nygren, "*Simul iustus et peccator hos Augustinus och Luther,*" in *Till Gustaf Aulén* (Lund, 1939), pp. 257 ff. "The justified man is according to Luther *completely* just, but at the same time *completely* a sinner; *totaliter iustus* and at the same time *totaliter peccator*. This conception of Luther has often been characterized as paradoxical. It must appear such to one who attempts to solve the problem by division. In that case *iustus sum* must mean *peccator non sum*, and if one should insist on keeping the two propositions *iustus sum* and *peccator sum*, this could be done only by interpreting it to mean *partly* just and *partly* a sinner. The propositions *totaliter iustus* and *totaliter peccator* seem to be mutually exclusive. But the situation is quite different in the case of Luther. From his point of view there is no contradiction between these two propositions. If man's righteousness before God should consist in his own works or inner quality, he could never be designated anything but a sinner. In justification man does not receive forgiveness for his past sins so that he can subsequently live on the righteousness which he has thus received. On the contrary, the justified person must live by forgiveness just as much in the present as in the past. There is *nothing* in man to which he could point and say: in this respect I do not need forgiveness. And yet he is entirely just, but this righteousness is a *iustitia aliena*. Christ is his righteousness, and this righteousness received in faith is perfect. To assert that this righteousness is not whole and perfect, but fragmentary, would be to despise and blaspheme Christ."

struggle against evil. Exactly because the way of divine love is the way of Christ and the work of Christ bears the mark of the cross (cf. § 26), it is inescapably clear to faith that God's forgiving love has nothing in common with laxity and extenuation of evil, which we human beings so often put in the place of forgiving love, but which is nothing but a caricature of forgiveness. In the second place, God's unmitigated opposition to evil is expressed in the fact that forgiveness also contains a judgment. No judgment strikes deeper than the judgment of love that subdues through forgiveness. Consequently God's act of forgiveness is inseparably connected with man's remorse and penitence. Forgiveness comes to man in this particular way. It must be underscored, however, that forgiveness is not dependent on remorse and repentance *in the sense* that these are the causes of the divine act of forgiveness. They are, on the contrary, created by forgiving love. Just because forgiveness has this character of judgment at the same time that it creates fellowship, it strengthens the consciousness of the distance between God and sinful man. In the third place, the opposition between God and evil is apparent in the fact that forgiveness becomes a regenerating power in human life (cf. § 34). Since forgiveness is the establishment of fellowship with God, it implies that divine love becomes the ruling force in human life and reveals its renewing power. *Iustificatio* is inseparably connected with *sanctificatio*. But this inseparable connection cannot be understood in such a way that regeneration should be the cause and explanation of God's act of forgiveness. Forgiveness cannot be explained on the basis of regeneration, but is caused solely by divine love and includes regeneration.

4. Misinterpretations of the Concept of Forgiveness

The Christian conception of forgiveness has often been obscured and misinterpreted. In regard to what has happened in this respect in the history of Christian thought the concept of forgiveness as defined in the previous sections must be differentiated from three common misinterpretations. These three have one thing in common. They seek in one way or another to explain it rationally and to assign a certain *cause* or causes to the divine act of forgiveness. In the first place, the nature of forgiving love has been obscured by a *legalistic* interpretation of Christ's work of reconciliation. In the second place, the idea of forgiveness has been reinterpreted in a *moralistic* and ethical direction by trying to find in man certain conditions which could be interpreted as causes of divine forgiveness. In the third place, the miracle of forgiveness has been eliminated by *humanizing* the conception of God and weakening the radical opposition of divine love to evil.

The essential character of divine love becomes obscured when, on the basis of the scholastic theory of the atonement, the work of Christ is interpreted as a compensation given to divine righteousness (cf. § 26, ¶ 4). Even if one does not go so far as the nineteenth-century theologian Philippi, who drew the conclusion that man was entitled to receive "forgiveness" after God had received the compensation, the scholastic theory contains an apparent tendency toward a rational explanation of the possibility of divine forgiveness. The compensation is understood as a logically possible compromise between the demand for punishment and its remission. The chief element in the idea of forgiveness is thereby obscured, namely, the "uncaused" and unfathomable character of the forgiving love directed toward sinful and unworthy men. That God forgives is no longer the inscrutable miracle of divine love, since he has already received due recompense for the transgression. But the positive content in the idea of forgiveness, the establishment of fellowship between God and man, is also obscured. When the gift of forgiveness is understood in an external and juridical sense, it loses not only its character as miracle but also its inner power. It is no longer clear that forgiveness includes both judgment and renewal. The real objection to this interpretation, however, is that the work of Christ is not understood as the work of divine love in its self-giving sacrifice. As long as we adhere to this fundamental idea of Christianity, it becomes impossible to incorporate the work of Christ in a moralistic context and to dissolve the miraculous character of divine forgiveness by an "explanation" of love's possibility.

In the moralistic and ethical misinterpretation of the concept of forgiveness we may distinguish three types. One can seek to motivate God's forgiveness by assuming that man has a certain quality, a certain given "value" which God takes into consideration. One can also fix attention on the attitude of man and interpret faith, remorse, and penitence as the conditions which motivate and explain the divine act of forgiveness. Finally, one can point to the effects of renewal and regeneration in human life which have their origin in forgiving love and assume that God forgives in view of these effects.

We meet the first of these three types wherever idealistic thought has influenced Christianity. Whenever this happens, the conception always appears that man is in possession of a certain "divine" quality, a certain "infinite value" which belongs to human nature as such, and that this value is in reality the reason that God "forgives" man. From this point of view sin belongs to the external part of man and does not affect his inner life because there lies the "core of personality" God values. We find an example of this in recent literature in F. C. Krarup's book. The fundamental theme to which he returns again and again is that forgiveness implies God's recognition of our personality in spite of our failings. Forgiveness is regarded as an evaluation of the whole being on the basis of the personality. Forgiveness implies God's recognition of the inner core of human personality, an acknowledgment of man "as he is in himself." [2] Such a conception is contrary both to religious consciousness of sin (cf. § 30) and to faith's consciousness of forgiveness. Christian consciousness of sin does not regard sin as something external or incidental, with the core of personality untouched, but, on the contrary, sees it as a corruption of the will, and consequently as something that touches precisely the "core" of the personality. The sinner cannot approach God and say: "You know that I have many 'faults' and 'imperfections,' but do not look at these, but to my personality as a 'whole,' to the inner 'core'." He must say rather: "I, just as I am in the inner recesses of my personality, am unworthy to be called your son." It is for this reason that the Christian concludes that forgiveness cannot be based on anything else than God's *unmerited* love.

The second moralizing type points to certain attitudes of man as the condition and cause of divine forgiveness. Lutheran scholasticism moved gradually in this direction, as it maintained that God justifies man *ex praevisa fide*. In contrast both to the Reformation and to its own real intentions, this scholasticism was compelled to regard faith

[2] F. C. Krarup, *Livsforstaaelse* [*The Understanding of Life*], p. 97.

as the human condition of the divine act of justification. That man's attitude is designated by the word *praevisa* and that it is seen under the aspect of God's foreknowledge do not alter the fact that it is a question here of a human cause of divine forgiveness. Another variation of this type occurs often in Pietism, especially in its "legalistic" form. In this case the divine act of forgiveness is motivated, at least to a certain extent, by man's remorse and penitence. The questionable element in this conception does not consist in the fact that remorse and penitence are inseparably connected with the act of forgiveness—that viewpoint is essential to Christian faith—but that remorse and penitence inevitably comes to be regarded as human accomplishments which furnish an acceptable motivation for the divine act of forgiveness.

The third of these moralistic and ethical types appears in the conception that the forgiveness of God can be at least partially explained on the basis of the results which divine love will produce in human life. When God forgives, he supposedly does so with a view to what the forgiven man will become through divine grace, he looks forward to the time when the person will stand forth as righteous in the actual meaning of the word, because of the divine powers at work in him. In the last analysis this would be the cause of the divine act of forgiveness. When Luther is cited in support of this view, it is because he makes justification include sanctification. But in the measure that this sanctification is conceived of as the cause of justification, the most profound and purely religious view in Luther's interpretation is lost. The matter can be expressed in this way: it is not sanctification that "explains" justification, but God's unfathomable justification which explains sanctification.

Finally, the meaning of the Christian idea of forgiveness has been obscured by a weakening of the radical opposition of divine love to evil. We will consider here especially two types: the so-called hyper-evangelicalism and the humanistic interpretation of Christianity during the eighteenth and nineteenth centuries, which was based on idealism. These two are in many respects quite different, but in relation to our present discussion they exhibit a certain kinship.

"Hyperevangelical" pietism was generally opposed to the legalistic trend in pietism. In contrast to the tendency to prescribe a certain amount of remorse and penitence as a condition of forgiveness, hyper-evangelical pietism was concerned that no humanly constructed hindrances should be placed in the way of divine love. The slogan was: "Come, just as you are." Its weakness does not appear in this slogan, which in reality is taken from the very heart of the gospel, but in the difficulty it encounters in combining the idea of judgment with forgiveness. This is partly explained by the fact that this kind of pietism is closely connected with a legalistic interpretation of the work of Christ. The humanistic and idealistic interpretation of forgiveness likewise weakens the opposition between the divine will and sin.

In contrast to all these misinterpretations of the Christian idea of forgiveness, Christian faith finds the basis of forgiveness only in God's spontaneous and unfathomable, saving and condemning love. Forgiveness is not based partly on something human and partly on God; its "possibility" and *reality* depend entirely on God's love. But this "possibility" cannot be either rationally explained or motivated. Every such explanation would in reality deprive Christian faith of the foundation on which rests faith in the forgiveness of sins. In regard to the human "possibility" Christian faith can say nothing more than: "With men this is impossible; but with God all things are possible" (Matt. 19:26). Forgiveness is entirely God's work, a gift of God. But this does not mean that in this fellowship with God we cannot speak of human "activity." Christian faith speaks without hesitation about man's seeking and receiving, of his turning toward and committing himself to God, and his bold *yes* to divine love. But this does not in the least imply that forgiveness is *based upon* man's attitude. From the point of view of faith this human activity is only the result of the divine activity in human life (cf. § 35, ¶ 2). According to the viewpoint of faith salvation is entirely God's way to man.

34. Forgiveness of Sins, Life, and Salvation

1. *The miracle of the new life.* Sin as separation from God means *death*. Forgiveness of sins, being received into fellowship with God, means *life*, participation in the eternal life of God.

2. *The new life as conflict and service.* The fellowship with God established in and through forgiveness contains within itself regenerative power. This expresses itself negatively in a struggle against sin and positively in the fact that man is commissioned as the servant of divine love. The works of love have their source in the power of God's love.

3. *Salvation and peace.* Forgiveness of sins as fellowship with God includes salvation. Even though this blessedness cannot be fully experienced in this life, it appears nevertheless as peace.

4. *Note on the meaning of spontaneity.* The ethical perspective referred to in ¶ 2 is misinterpreted if the spontaneity of divine love working in man is interpreted psychologically as something belonging to man in himself. It must be pointed out that here we are speaking of the work of the Spirit, and that the "freedom from the law" mentioned in this connection means in reality obedience to the commandments which through the Spirit becomes real and meaningful to man.

5. *Note on a false idealization of the Christian life.* A false idealization of the Christian life appears when the fact that the Christian is at the same time *iustus et peccator,* "new" man and "old" man, is not sufficiently emphasized. The Christian, as "old man," lives continually under the law.

6. *Note on a false idealization of the Christian's relation to the world.* A false idealization of the Christian and his situation in the world appears also when it is assumed that God can realize his will only through the regenerated man.

1. The Miracle of the New Life

We may begin with the frequently cited words of Luther: "Where there is forgiveness of sins, there is also life and salvation." We must first note the word "life." For Christian faith salvation implies *life.* Salvation is deliverance from bondage to the powers of sin and death. Just as sin not only leads to death, but *is* death, since it is separation from God, so also the fellowship with God established through forgiveness not only leads to life, but *is* life.

There are good reasons for emphasizing this aspect of salvation. It cannot be denied that this aspect has often been unduly ignored, especially by the leading theology of the nineteenth century. It is characteristic that the representatives of this theology looked with suspicion and a certain air of superiority on the thinking of the early church which was concentrated around this idea of salvation as life.

The fathers were accused of holding a "naturalistic" or "physical" conception of salvation. It seems almost to have been assumed that to ignore the idea of life in favor of the idea of forgiveness was a sign of an evangelical and purified Christianity. It was maintained that the emphasis of the ancient church on "life and immortality" indicated that the interpretation of salvation was not sufficiently "ethical."

These accusations leveled against the ancient church by nineteenth-century research into the history of Christian thought are to a large extent unfounded and based on misinterpretations. In reality it is not a question of ignoring the idea of salvation from sin while emphasizing exclusively the idea of immortality. It is characteristic rather that salvation is conceived of as a salvation from both sin and death. Sin and death are inseparably connected, and, as Irenaeus says, are really two aspects of the same thing, namely, separation from God. If we object to the strong emphasis on Christianity as "life," we would have to object to the point of view represented in the whole New Testament. A few of the many examples will suffice to indicate this. The narrow way of salvation is "the way to life" (Matt. 7:14), to participate in salvation is to "enter life" (Matt. 19:17; Mark 9:43) and to "inherit eternal life" (Mark 10:17). It is well known that the Johannine writings are filled with references to this idea. "In him [the Word] was life" (John 1:4); Christ is "the bread of life," "the light of life," "the resurrection and the life," he that believes on him "has life" and has "passed from death into life" (cf. John 5:24; 6:33, 35, 53; 8:12; 10:10; 11:25; I John 1:2; etc.). But this is not a theme peculiar to John; it is one of the fundamental ideas in all the other New Testament writings. Justification "leads to life" (Rom. 5:18); Christians "have been brought from death to life" (Rom. 6:13); they have life "by the Spirit" (Gal. 5:25), who himself "is life" (Rom. 8:10); the names of the Christians are written "in the book of life" (Phil. 4:3); those who have "been raised with Christ" have died and their "life is hid with Christ in God" (Col. 3:1-3); death has come into the world through Adam, but life has come through Christ (Rom. 5:12-21); death has been conquered: "O death, where is thy sting?" (I Cor. 15:55); the choice is death or life (II Cor. 2:16). Christ is "the Author of life" (Acts 3:15): he has "abolished death and brought life and immortality to light through the gospel"

(II Tim. 1:10); in the Book of Revelation we read repeatedly about "the crown of life," "the book of life," "the water of life" (cf. 2:7, 10; 3:5; etc.). We have not tried to give a complete list of the passages referring to this subject. But the passages quoted show clearly how vital to the New Testament is this idea of salvation as life.

Christian faith cannot ignore this aspect of salvation without distorting its perspective. The antithesis between a "naturalistic" and an "ethical" conception of salvation is not germane to this discussion. It is not a question of a choice between these two. The Christian idea of salvation is certainly not "naturalistic," but neither is it merely "ethical." The conception of salvation, like the conception of sin, is entirely religious. Two factors seem to have been the cause of the neglect of this idea of salvation as life. In the first place, the starting point has generally been the idea of "the immortality of the soul" as a quality belonging to the "nature" of man, an idea foreign to faith. It is easy to understand that from this idealistic point of view the idea of salvation as life would be minimized. Death in this sense has lost the profound seriousness it has in Christian faith. The passing from death to life has become something natural and self-evident. In the second place, this tendency represents a negative conception of the forgiveness of sins. The insight that forgiveness implies primarily the establishment of fellowship with God is not recognized.

When Christian faith conceives of the salvation obtained through forgiveness as life, the meaning is not that "life" is something added to forgiveness, that we might speak of two separate "gifts." On the contrary, fellowship with God established in and through forgiveness is *eo ipso* life, a participation in the eternal life of God. This life is an unmerited gift, it is not a self-evident, human prerogative. But under historical conditions this life is "hid," "hid with Christ in God," and is not yet "revealed." "When Christ who is our life appears, then you also will appear with him in glory" (Col. 3:3-4). When salvation is understood as life, it means that the eschatological perspective of faith is given due consideration both as something present and as something yet to come (cf. § 36, ¶ 2).

2. *The New Life as Conflict and Service*

The new life of forgiveness implies fellowship with divine love.

This means that divine love itself becomes a power in human life. It exercises this power in a twofold manner: in struggle against evil, and in making man an instrument for the activity of divine love.

We have already indicated (§ 33) that forgiveness implies a judgment on sin and that the consciousness of sin becomes more acute in the presence and through the activity of divine love. But God's forgiving love is not only a discoverer and judge of sin, its power is revealed also in a continuous struggle against evil. Christian faith does not reckon with a condition of sinlessness during this earthly life (I John 1:8), nor does it conceive of the Christian life as a continuous progress toward such a goal. When Schleiermacher speaks of salvation as consisting in both a continuous strengthening of the consciousness of God and a corresponding diminishing of the consciousness of sin, such reasoning appears to faith as unrealistic and as a false idealization of Christian life and its situation. His incorporation of the Christian life into a monistic and evolutionistic world view has led Schleiermacher to suppress faith's point of view, that fellowship with God increases the consciousness of sin. The Christian perspective is decidedly dramatic. All idealizing of human life is foreign to faith. It recognizes only a lifelong struggle against that sin which would always separate us from him and which continually places us before him as unworthy. The old man must daily die from sin, and the new man daily come forth and rise. Fellowship with God is not a permanent treasure which we possess and with which we can settle down in peace; it can be possessed only by being continually obtained anew. As Luther so often says, *Der Christ steht nicht im Sein, sondern im Werden* [The Christian is not in a state of being but in one of becoming]. The "new man" is not something finished and perfect; under the conditions of human life on earth he is continually becoming. The active presence of divine love in and through forgiveness signifies for the Christian life a continuous struggle against what would destroy the fellowship again, but its presence means also that this struggle is not hopeless, since an inexhaustible supply of power is given to the Christian by the sovereignty of divine love.

But this activity of divine love in human life expresses itself not only as a struggle against evil, but also as a realization of its own intentions and purposes. In the measure that divine love subdues man,

it makes him an instrument for its own activity. God's love finds its
way out into human life through human instruments. The man who
has been subdued by God through forgiveness is called upon to reveal,
i.e., realize, God's loving will in relation to the neighbor. No one in
Christendom has spoken more emphatically and profoundly about
this "vocation" of the Christian than Luther. The Christian is to be
"a Christ" to the neighbor, and Luther even says that he is to be
"God" to him. "*Gotte sind wir durch die Liebe, die uns gegen
unseren Nächsten wohlthätig macht; denn gottlich Natur ist nicht
anderes denn eitel Wohlthätigkeit.*" [We are "Gods" through the
love which makes us benevolent toward our neighbors; for the divine
nature is nothing else than pure benevolence.][1]

This very radical statement would be entirely misinterpreted and
the conception of the life in faith would be thoroughly misunderstood if it were assumed that this involves a surreptitious apotheosis
of human life and human love. This manner of speaking certainly
does not imply that the man of faith is able to point to and rely upon
his own love. It is never a question of any other love than the love
of God, whose "power is made perfect in weakness" (II Cor.
12:9-10).

From this point of view the celebrated words of Luther that "salvation is necessary for good works" are seen in their true meaning.
When Luther enunciated this proposition, he had in mind the poison
which is deadly both for salvation and for the works of love, namely,
the securing of personal "merits." He wanted to maintain, not only
that salvation cannot be gained through "meritorious works," but also
that constant concern with self, precisely this poisonous egocentricity,
paralyzes and frustrates man's opportunity to become an instrument
in the service of divine love. As E. Billing has conclusively shown,
however, Luther's radical proposition did not have simply a contemporary significance, but is universally valid. The "peace" which
forgiveness affords signifies participation in a power which cannot be
obtained in any other way. So long as enmity rules in the depth of
the human heart, or so long as man is selfishly inclined toward self,
"everything that happens to us serves only to intensify this selfish

[1] *WA*, 10^I, 1, 100.

inclination." Man is compelled to hunt continually for new substitutes for the lack of inner blessedness. Peace is the only remedy.
"Only when we are conscious of inner riches which surpass everything else, which not even death can take away from us, and about
which we need not contend with others, since they are given to us
strictly by grace and increase by being shared with others, only then
has the heart something to hold, something that sets it free from its
convulsive grasp on itself. Where peace and salvation really are present in the heart of man, he finds that he has power to spare, not only
to defend himself against the unclean powers, but also to share with
others." [2] In order to underscore the chief thought in this quotation
from Billing, and in order to guard against a rather obvious misinterpretation, I add here a few words by Anders Nygren: "Only when
we have understood that Christian love, according to Luther, is God's
own love which through the Christian finds its way out into human
life, can we understand the deepest meaning of the frequently quoted
statement by Luther that a man must be saved in order to perform
the good. This is commonly interpreted exclusively in a eudaemonistic
direction. When a man is saved and his own interests and affairs are
secure in his assurance of God's grace, only then is he rich and free
enough to be able to serve his fellow-men in love. The truth in this
interpretation is that "salvation" delivers a man from his egocentric
activity, not in the sense that all egocentric interests are satisfied but
rather because they are vanquished and destroyed. For Luther salvation means fellowship with God. But consequently only one who by
faith lives in this blessed fellowship is able to receive that supply from
above which enables him to dispense it in love." [3]

The ethical perspective expressed here is fundamentally different
from all "legalistic" ethics, since it is a question here simply of love
working spontaneously. It is different from all "utilitarian" ethics,
since it is not a question of any other motive than that contained in
love itself. Since, furthermore, the decisive element is the activity of
divine love itself, this "ethic" is differentiated from "intuitionalism"
which regards the ethical quality as inherent in human nature. The

---

[2] Einar Billing, *Herdabrev* [*An Episcopal Letter*], pp. 22 f.

[3] Anders Nygren, "Den kristna kälekstanken hos Luther," *Svensk theologisk
kvartalskrift* (1930), p. 29.

radicalism of the Christian perspective appears most clearly in the fact that it is not a question of human "merits," nor of human obligations of one kind or another. We are dealing here with a kind of ethics which implies that the human ego recedes, man is "removed away from himself" and becomes an instrument in the hands of God's love. To use New Testament vocabulary, it is a question of nothing else but "the fruits of the Spirit" (Gal. 5:22; cf. Rom. 7:6; 8:4).

3. Salvation and Peace

We have already touched on this theme: forgiveness as salvation and peace. If it is true for Christian faith that where there is forgiveness there is also salvation, the reason is to be found in the positive and unifying significance of forgiveness. Fellowship with God is "salvation," and salvation is fellowship with God. Though the connotation of the word salvation is primarily eschatological, it nevertheless appears in the present as peace. We might say that peace is the specific category of forgiveness. Forgiveness overcomes that inner anxiety found in the heart of every man as long as he is inclined toward self (incurvatus in se), or as long as the tyranny of egocentricity is intact. As sin is a continuous source of inner anxiety, so forgiveness is an inexhaustible source of inner peace. Forgiveness creates peace. Christian faith from the beginning and down through the ages testifies unanimously that the peace of God is the incomparable gift received through forgiveness. Paul gathers together all his wishes and prayers for his congregation in the word about "the peace of God, which passes all understanding" (Phil. 4:7), and in the Gospel of John the work of Jesus is summed up in the word "my peace I give to you" (John 14:27). Everything the disciples have received is comprehended in the word peace. It is significant that the apostolic greeting reads: "Grace to you and peace from God." Peace is the central content of the Christian life received through forgiveness. But it is necessary to emphasize in this connection that the significance of this fact is not that the Christian life is always characterized by strong and continuous feelings of peace and salvation, nor that peace disappears when these feelings subside. The gift of peace through forgiveness is not simply a variation in feelings.

When Schleiermacher interprets "salvation" in a more or less stoic sense and understands it as a certain uninterrupted harmony, or a feeling of being at home in the cosmos, it is a misinterpretation of the viewpoint of faith that depends on his general, monistic world view. But for Christian faith life in this world is neither a harmony nor an idyl. Peace does not depend on the fact that everything appears to faith in the last analysis as "harmonious," it is a peace "in spite of all," a peace in the midst of conflict. Because the forgiveness which brings peace is an act of God received and held by faith, or, in other words, because peace depends on fellowship with God, it can exist in the midst of darkness and tumult, and it can dwell in a human heart filled with storm and stress. Peace, as Einar Billing says, is "not a tender treasure which we must anxiously guard in order to protect it against the world, but that mighty power which guards us and in whose company we may pass securely through the world; not a perishable sentiment which comes and goes, but the secure and objective reality which surrounds us wherever we go, from which we cannot in a sense escape; not the last, final and highest in the Christian life, but the first, the basic—and the highest." [4]

4. Note on the Meaning of Spontaneity

In and through justification man is received into a new fellowship with God. This new fellowship based on forgiveness is a relationship of grace and adoption, the opposite of the legalistic relationship to God. As long as man's relationship to God rests on law, he strives to secure righteousness before God and to produce in himself that religious quality which will win God's favor and be acceptable to him. When God's act of forgiveness becomes the sole basis of fellowship with God, all these endeavors on man's part to qualify for this fellowship are eliminated. This is the significance of the statement that the legalistic relation to God has ceased to exist for the Christian. But this release from the way of self-righteousness does not mean that the Christian is passive in reference to the demand of love and the works of love. Rather the opposite is true. The release implies that man is received into the sphere of divine love and becomes an instrument used by God's love in the service of his neighbor.

When we speak of the spontaneous activity of love, it can easily be

[4] Billing, op cit., p. 17.

misunderstood in a psychologizing manner. It might seem that the Christian life, from a purely psychological point of view, should be characterized by a free and unhindered spontaneity and that there would be no opposition to overcome. Such an interpretation is a false idealization of the Christian life. It must, therefore, be underscored that this spontaneity is not a newly acquired human trait, attribute, or act; but is connected exclusively with divine love itself with the Spirit which subdues man and is active in him.

Freedom from the law, which we speak of in this connection, is described in the New Testament as a freedom of the Spirit. "Where the Spirit of the Lord is, there is freedom" (II Cor. 3:17). But this freedom signifies at the same time obedience to that which is demanded by this Spirit, or, in other words, to those commandments of God which become real and meaningful to men through the Spirit, as he introduces man into the continuous, creative activity of God. Freedom implies being free to serve and in obedience to God to render to the neighbor that service which love demands in the given situation. "The command does not disappear when legalistic relationship with God is left behind. On the contrary, when conscience finally comes to repose in trust in the gospel of God, man understands that he has hitherto not asked simply what God wants and commands; he has constantly been driven from one vain act to another in his pains to become adequately religious. But when he has come to faith, there lies a single command before him." [5]

5. Note on a False Idealization of the Christian Life

What we have said about spontaneity and obedience is complemented and made more acute when we note that the Christian man in this world is not only "the new man," but continually remains also "the old man," *simul iustus et peccator.* No interpretation of the Christian life could be more unrealistic than that which ignores this fact and speaks of everything "old" as having passed away when man was received into the new fellowship with God. The old has indeed disappeared in so far as the forgiveness of God is complete and unconditional and man stands before him *totaliter iustus.* But this

[5] Gustaf Wingren, *Luther on Vocation,* trans. Carl C. Rasmussen (Philadelphia: Muhlenberg, 1957) pp. 199-200.

change does not imply a change in the nature of man in the sense that he is now able to do God's will completely and thereby can point to his changed life as provided access to and security before God. On the contrary, he cannot point to one single act which is without sin. He can speak with gratitude of the power of God that is active in his life, but he is also conscious of the fact that this power of God is made perfect in his weakness, as Paul says (II Cor. 12:9). Sin clings to man's life as a whole, and he cannot point to a single act for which he must not ask God for forgiveness. The Christian therefore stands continually under the demand and discipline of the divine commandments. But this does not imply a return to a legalistic relationship. The law in question here is the law which Paul calls "the law of the Spirit of life" (Rom. 8:2), which obligates us "not to live according to the flesh" (Rom. 8:12). This law of the Spirit of life becomes actual and concrete in and through the vocation given him by God and in the demands which love places upon him in reference to the neighbor.

6. Note on a False Idealization
of the Christian's Relation to the World

The idea has sometimes been advanced that the will of God can be done only by those who have received the Gospel in faith, and that it really is done by them. This idea is deeply rooted in the pietistic conception of Christianity. Such a point of view can lead to various consequences in regard to the relation between the Christian and the world. On the one hand, the result may be that the world is regarded as entirely profane, as an area in which the will of God is not done. In this connection there arises a tendency to isolate Christians from the world. This approach has contributed momentum to the secularizing process which has been going on during the last centuries, even though the real causes of this process have been of another kind. On the other hand, the conclusion has also been drawn from this premise that all the problems and difficulties of the world would be solved if all men became Christian and as such did God's will.

If we examine the thesis that the will of God can be done only by those who have received the gospel in faith, and that it really is done by them, it must be stated that neither of these propositions is valid. The latter statement is, as we have seen, a truth which must be qualified, since the Christian is *simul iustus et peccator*. The first proposition, however, is not true, since God has other means which he can use to realize his will. Here we must remind ourselves of what was stated in § 21 in regard to the law of creation. There we advanced the thesis that the tasks and orders of this world are not profane, but are given by God and are the bearers of his law, and that the vocation and the functions which belong to men are given to them by God. In these vocations and functions the divine law operates and its purpose is to suppress evil, subdue the recalcitrant, and thereby to realize God's will. God's will may be done also by those who do not confess his name, and often in such a manner as to put professing Christians to shame. His will is done as men oppose brutal and ruthless oppression, struggle to maintain a just and orderly society, and manifest a general concern for the welfare of humanity. Such attitudes have found frequent expression in modern times.

Under these circumstances it is plain that Christian life must not be isolated from the world. Christians too have temporal functions which they must carry out in accordance with the vocation given to them. But it would be just as misleading to assert that all earthly tasks and problems would be solved if all men became Christians. Such reasoning does not agree with the conditions in the world or the situation of the Christian life. It would indeed involve a monstrous arrogance on the part of Christians. This insight does not imply a denial of the fact that when the gospel is received in faith, it supplies new demands and possibilities in regard to the vocation, nor of the fact that the gospel extends and enriches the content of this vocation (cf § 48, § 1).

35. Divine Fellowship Exists as a Relationship of Faith

1. *The relationship of faith.* Fellowship with God which is based on forgiveness exists as a relationship of faith. Its content and character are determined solely by the activity of divine love relative to man. On man's part it is therefore characterized by unconditional trust

and obedience. Since God is the Sovereign in this relationship, all eudaemonism is excluded from the life of faith. And since divine love radically condemns sin, the idea of an identity which blots out the distance between God and man is excluded.

2. *Faith as the work of God and as human activity.* The activity of divine love is the sole foundation of faith; therefore faith is completely a work of God and a divine gift. This does not exclude, but rather includes, the fact that faith involves the whole volitional activity of man. From this point of view faith is a turning and a commitment to God. The slogan "by faith alone" (*sola fide*) is a genuinely Christian watchword, since it rejects the thought that this activity implies "human merit" or service and that it therefore is rooted in something other than God's subduing love (*sola gratia*).

1. The Relationship of Faith

The fellowship with God established on the basis of forgiveness has its continued existence as a relationship of faith. Faith is, as we have already stated (§ 2), the characteristic word of the Christian relationship between God and man. Christian life exists as a life "in faith." Fellowship with God is a fellowship "in faith." This expresses both its riches and its limitations under the conditions of life here on earth (cf. II Cor. 5:7).

We must first emphasize that both the content and character of this fellowship of faith are determined and defined by the activity of divine love relative to man. The idea that faith may be regarded as a human condition for divine fellowship is thereby excluded. Faith is not a human achievement or quality that can be isolated from the activity of divine love. By its own estimate faith is *nothing* in itself. It is what it is through the divine and loving will that calls it into being. The relationship to God is created, maintained, and determined by divine love. In this sense God is the subject of faith.

But this does not exclude the fact that faith is a phenomenon which belongs to human life. Faith as a creation of divine love implies that man is received into a definite relationship with God. From this point of view God appears as the sole "object" of faith, and man's relation to this object is then characterized by an unconditional trust. In so far as faith rules in and characterizes the life of man, man stands in a relation of unconditional trust to that divine and loving will which has subdued and subdues him. This relationship of trust implies also an unconditional obedient *yes* to the God who reveals himself. From this point of view it is meaningless to distinguish between trust (*fiducia*) and "assent," as if it were a question of two different things. Trust involves an "assent" to the content and message of the divine relevation. On the other hand, "assent" has the character of full and complete trust (cf. § 2, ¶ 1).

We have spoken of faith as a creation through the act of forgiveness on the part of divine love, and as an unconditional trust on man's part. Now redemptive love is at the same time a condemning and sovereign divine will (cf. §§15, 16). This gives the Christian relationship of faith its character. In this relationship God is the Sovereign, the Lord. Faith implies that man is placed under divine government. There is nothing more essential to this relationship of faith than that it involves the sovereign dominion of the divine and loving will which breaks down that human will which is separated from God and ruled by the ego. A fellowship with God cannot exist in the sense that the divine will would enter human life as a fact or coincident with other factors. Wherever a fellowship with God is established and exists, it implies that the divine will dominates and exercises the sovereign authority which belongs to divine love. When the relationship of faith is realized, it means that God breaks down and overcomes egocentricity. While sin as unbelief is egocentricity and inclination toward self (cf. § 30, ¶ 2), the relationship of faith is characterized by the fact that the ego has ceased to be the center around which man revolves in selfish bondage, and that God has become man's center and Lord.[1] Faith "removes us out of our own line of vision" (§ 10, ¶ 4). Christian faith conceives of the relationship between God and man as a relationship of adoption; man has become a "child of God" (cf. Rom. 8:14, 16; Gal. 3:26; 1 John 3:1, 2, 10; etc). But this "adoption" would be misinterpreted in the direction of a profane familiarity that is foreign to faith, and of an egocentric eudaemonism if the fact were even slightly obscured that God "the Father" is also the sovereign

[1] Cf. William Temple, *Fellowship with God* (New York: Macmillan, 1921), pp. 73-74. "You cannot have salvation as long as you want it. Only when God has so drawn you into the embrace of his love and into obedience to his will that in devotion to him you cease to care about yourself, can your self be saved."

Lord and that this relationship of faith implies that life is placed under his sovereign government. To live in faith means, as Paul says, a crucifixion of the selfish ego and a liberation from the slavery of self (Gal. 2:19-20). *In the measure that* man lives in faith, he is not *incurvatus in se*, selfishly contained within himself. In the realm of faith everything has its center in God as the Lord of human life.

As the relationship of faith is defined by the sovereignty of divine love, it is likewise determined by the condemning activity of this love. The man of faith stands also under judgment and under God's unconditional condemnation of sin. The Christian relationship of faith is, therefore, radically differentiated from those conceptions which tend to interpret it as a relation of identity between God and man. Since all pure mysticism tends in this direction, there arises a twofold contrast to the Christian faith: mysticism destroys both fellowship with God and remoteness from God. It might otherwise seem that mysticism would surpass Christian faith in regard to the emphasis on fellowship when it speaks of man's immediate entrance and absorption into the divine. But in reality the relationship ceases to be a fellowship. The "god" whom man reaches on this way and the "infinity" into which he is plunged do not carry him outside the charmed circle of egocentricity. Just as the God of mysticism becomes simply the unfathomable, about which nothing can be said, so this "god" loses the power to lift man out of himself and to "remove him from his own line of vision." Absorption into the divine becomes in reality nothing but absorption into self. But at the same time, in spite of its talk about man's "negation of self," mysticism removes the distance between God and man which is a fundamental fact for Christian faith, and which *increases* in and through this fellowship with God, as we have had occasion to point out several times. Since divine love also includes judgment, and since man here on earth never ceases to be a sinner, Christian life in faith is characterized by a peculiar twofold perspective. Fellowship with God is obtained in and through the divine act of forgiveness, but this fellowship is not an inalienable possession; it exists rather as *becoming* and perdures in a continuous struggle against that which is hostile to God (cf. § 36). Faith speaks of the existence of "the new man." This is not empty and meaningless talk. The new man is not, as has been said (Gogarten), only *ein Fabelwesen*. "If any one is in Christ, he is a new creation" (II Cor. 5:17). Denying the existence of "the new man" would be the same as denying that act of forgiveness of divine love which creates fellowship with God. This would be to wound faith in its inmost heart. But to regard "the old man" as vanquished and gone would be from faith's point of view the most terrible arrogance. During this earthly life man stands in all respects under the judgment of God, and "the new man" of which faith speaks is not an ego separated from "the old man." The words of Luther are here valid: "the old man shall daily be drowned and destroyed, and the new man shall daily come forth and rise."

The Christian faith is, therefore, characterized by a peculiar twofold perspective. Faith includes both conflict and peace, self-denial and assurance of victory. It makes man conscious both of his unworthiness before God and of his participation in "that victory which overcomes the world." In faith man is at the same time nothing before God and "a lord over all things." "If God is for us, who is against us?" (Rom. 8:31). But this confident consciousness of victory which is characteristic of Christian faith is the very opposite of egocentric arrogance. It would be entirely misleading to characterize faith's consciousness of victory as exaltation of self. Faith knows of nothing else than an "exaltation of God"; its "self-consciousness" is *ein vollkommen selbstloses Selbstgefühl*[2] [a completely selfless self-consciousness]. It trusts God above all things.

2. Faith as the Work of God and as Human Activity

We have already pointed out in our preliminary definition of the concept of faith (§ 2) that faith can be considered from two points of view: on the one hand, God subdues and dominates man, and on the other, man turns toward and commits himself to God. This problem, which we touched upon then, must now be analyzed in more detail. It is clear from what we have already said that the most fundamental and vital viewpoint of faith is that its origin and exist-

[2] Holl, "Was verstand Luther unter Religion?" *op. cit.*, p. 84.

ence depend entirely on the loving will of God and on nothing else. Faith knows that it exists as a work of God and as his gracious gift. The relationship of faith exists as a relation of complete dependence on the God who overwhelms and dominates man.

It is the glory of evangelical Christianity that by its watchword, *sola fide, sola gratia*—by faith alone, by grace alone—it turned with determination against all who would obscure this fundamental character of the life of faith. But it cannot be denied that in maintaining this watchword of faith as altogether a work of God, theology, and not least Lutheran theology, has obscured the fact that faith also, from one point of view, exists as human activity. Theology has thereby given a quietistic character to the life of faith, which in reality does not agree with its nature and threatens to paralyze its power. This theology assumed that it was possible to assert the viewpoint of grace and the *sola gratia* of the Reformation only by avoiding as much as possible any reference to activity on the part of man. The divine and the human were considered as two factors which would balance each other. Whatever was added to the human would then detract from the divine. Under these circumstances theology was driven into a hopeless dilemma from which it could not escape. If God really "does everything," then, of course, man "does nothing." If it be assumed that man can do something toward his salvation, then it could not be interpreted in any other way than as "co-operation," and this implied a "synergistic" or "semi-Pelagian" conception which is opposed to the "by grace alone" of the Reformation. Since no one was willing to say that God works in men by means of an external force as a power of nature, it became necessary to grant, however unwillingly, a certain degree of receptiveness in man, which naturally implied a certain amount of human activity. This activity had to be reduced to the smallest minimum, when it was not possible to eliminate it entirely. But however severely it was limited, as soon as any activity on the part of man was admitted, the principle at stake had to be surrendered, according to this understanding of the matter.

The proposition of Lutheran scholasticism that God justifies *ex praevisa fide* is significant. Faith in this case is understood as a human condition. It was a hopeless situation, for it was impossible even to maintain that principle which it was most important to affirm, namely, the Reformation principle "by grace alone"; and at the same time it was considered necessary to avoid everything which might be interpreted as a challenge and an appeal to man. The words of Paul must appear very strange to such a theology: "Work out your own salvation with fear and trembling; for God is at work in you, both to will and to work for his good pleasure" (Phil. 2:12-13). Here the idea of faith as throughout a work of God does not stand in opposition to an appeal and an unreserved challenge.

It is clear, however, that the quietistic approach with its fear of everything that suggests human activity is not in accord with the actual situation of faith. It is very significant that the "activistic" aspect of faith has found a much stronger expression in preaching and in hymns than in theology. This aspect could not be suppressed in the practical life of piety, even though it could be done more or less successfully in theological theories. The Gospel's injunction to seek, pray, and knock re-echoes in the direct and immediate expressions of the Christian life. Faith appears from one point of view to be activity; it even places the greatest possible demands on man's spiritual energy. Faith implies a choice, a decision, a venture, perhaps a timid but at the same time a bold *yes* to God. And as faith in its origin has an active character, so its whole existence is activity. The heroes of faith have testified to it in all ages. Luther, at the same time that he speaks of faith as a work of God, has also described faith as a continuous and persistent struggle, and has spoken of its bold *dennoch*, its "nevertheless." Faith exists as a militant and praying faith which can exist and continue only by being constantly won anew. There is always something of this element in faith: "Lord, I will not let you go unless you bless me."

But is not the watchword of the Reformation, *sola gratia*, disclaimed when such references are made to the activity of faith? It may appear so but only as long as God is conceived in terms of an extra-mundane being separated from the world. Such a conclusion is not possible when God is seen from the viewpoint of faith as the one who is seriously involved in current events and who, in order to establish his dominion of love, contends with those forces which are inimical to his will. From the point of view of this active conception of God's work of redemption everything is seen in a new light. It is no longer possible to talk about the choice of faith and its *yes* to God as a human activity apart from God. This whole problem with which an older theology struggled fruitlessly and to its own detriment simply vanishes. It is perfectly clear to faith that what we call our seeking is nothing else than the *Father drawing* us to himself, and the bold *yes* of faith is nothing else than *God's subduing* of man. Faith knows that here if anywhere it is necessary to seek, pray, and watch. But in the midst of this activity nothing is more certain to faith than that all this is God's work and his unmerited gift. Our "conversion" implies that we are overwhelmed by God and are "born anew" through his loving will. When faith turns to God in prayer, it means that God is about to prepare a way for his dominion (§ 45). "We do not know how to pray as we ought, but the Spirit himself intercedes for us with sighs too deep for words" (Rom. 8:26). God "draws" us unto himself, he subdues us, in "forgiveness" he removes that which separates us from him and assumes dominion over us. That which we call the struggle of faith is nothing else than the struggle of the living God to realize his dominion. This struggle continues through the ages, and in the midst of it stands Christ as the great Victor whose struggle and victory are on our behalf, and of whose fulness we all receive—grace for grace (John 1:16). "Salvation" is entirely the creative act of divine love; we are redeemed *sola gratia*, through God's love alone.

The watchword of the Reformation remains, therefore, as the principal word of Christian faith in complete agreement with the testimony of the New Testament. But the human activity of faith is not obscured. *Sola gratia* does not lead us into passivity and quietism; it presents rather, as Paul indicates in Philippians, the strongest appeal to men to work out their own salvation "with fear and trembling." The significance of the watchword of the Reformation is that it irrevocably stands guard against all attempts to separate human activity from God's own activity and to consider it as "merit." The deadly poison lies in this idea of merits. Even if it appears in a sheltering disguise, as so often happens, it remains a deadly poison to the life of faith. To speak about human merit in the presence of God introduces an irreligious element into the religious life. God and our merits are like fire and water. But guarding against the idea of merit is at the same time a protection against all egocentric "piety." As long as we are concerned with our own ego and its "merits," there is no possibility of obtaining that freedom from the tyranny of the ego and that withdrawal "out of our own line of vision" which constitute "salvation." *Sola gratia* is a watchword not only against the idea of merits, but against all conceptions which pretend to find the cause of divine love in human efforts or value (cf. § 33, ¶ 4). It stands guard against all attempts to conceive of the way of salvation as man's way to God. It tells us that here is no other way to God than God's way to man. In this sense the term *sola gratia* is eternally and universally valid. It was not significant simply for a certain period of Christian history when it was so strenuously emphasized; nor is it a self-sufficient word of evangelical Christianity. It is rather a touchstone for Christianity as such. The principle, *sola gratia*, stands guard against all tendencies to make the ego and personal blessedness the central concern in the realm of faith, against all *Selbstbehauptung*, etc. It maintains unceasingly and irrevocably the theocentric character of faith. In the realm of faith everything has its center in God and his dominion, and faith originates and lives in that loving will of God which realizes itself in the human world.

36. Faith as Possession and as Hope

1. *Faith as "possession."* When man in faith receives the unmerited gift of divine love, faith implies a present "possession" of this gift. Since the life of faith here and now is lived under the conditions imposed by sin, this "proprietorship" is radically distinguished from self-confidence and can exist only by being continually received.

2. *Faith as hope.* Since fellowship with God exists only as a becoming, in struggle against opposition. Faith appears as hope in that consummation which occurs when all that is "partial" passes away. From this point of view fellowship with God in the present appears as an earnest of what is to come, and the expected consummation as something "wholly other" than the present.

3. *Relation between faith as "possession" and as hope.* These two aspects of faith lend mutual support to each other. Faith rejects both the emphasis on the present which obscures the future perspective,

and that metaphysical eschatology which obscures the eschatological present reality.

1. Faith as "Possession"

Just as faith may be defined both as a work of God and as a human activity, so it may be seen also from another twofold viewpoint. It is, on the one hand, fellowship with God established on the basis of the act of forgiveness of divine love, and, on the other hand, a living hope (I Pet. 1:3, 4).

If faith means that man is incorporated into fellowship with God, it possesses a richness which cannot be overestimated. Faith has "the pearl of great price." "He who believes, *has*," says Luther. Faith receives the gift which is God's own love, or God himself. Everything that faith "possesses" is included in this one thing. Christian testimony has from the very beginning given the strongest expressions to this fellowship and "possession" of faith. The life of faith is a "life in the Spirit," "in Christ," a life of God and in God. Faith does not live in anxiety, but in undaunted trust, as Paul says: *nothing* can separate us "from the love of God in Christ Jesus" (Rom. 8:39). And John says: "Our fellowship is with the Father and with his Son Jesus Christ" (I John 1:3); "we have confidence before God" (I John 3:21; cf. 4:18; 5:4; etc.). The matrix of this confidence of faith is the fact that the fellowship rests on God's love and on nothing else. If this foundation is weakened and the existence of faith is made dependent on something else in addition to divine love, the boldness and confidence of faith are undermined. In the common piety and theology of the Middle Ages the Christian life appears, therefore, as a balance between hope and fear. When the Reformation brought back the confidence of faith, the reason was that divine love became again the sole basis of faith. The emphasis on the "possession" of faith was renewed. "Where there is forgiveness of sins, there is also life and salvation."

The new age has come in Christ. "Eternal life" is not only in the future, it is something which the man of faith enjoys even now under the conditions of earthly life. Where God is, there is salvation and eternal life: "He who hears my word and believes him who sent me, *has* eternal life; he does not come into judgment, but *has* passed

from death to life" (John 5:24; cf. 3:36). Eternal life is something
which already exists in and through faith's fellowship with the eternal
God. It must be added, however, that faith's eschatological present
must not be separated from hope's future perspective.

But if this relation of faith to divine love exists in the present, this
"possession" about which faith so boldly speaks is not a secure and
permanent property. The confidence of faith is radically distinguished
from *securitas*. All self-confidence is excluded. Such an attitude
would imply a self-exaltation which would be diametrically opposed
to the humility of faith. Faith itself exists as a becoming. The "possessing" of this gift on the part of faith must be constantly and continually renewed. The life of faith is a life in constant peril, an unceasing struggle against opposing forces. Consequently the boldness
of faith is accompanied by fear and trembling. The opposition of the
Reformation to the mixture of hope and fear of the Middle Ages does
not derive from the fact that the Reformation knew nothing of "fear"
—to stand face to face with God is to fear him—but from the fact
that this fear is now fused with trust and ceases, therefore, to be a
timor servilis. Trust itself includes a trembling which does not cease
during this life, because man is man and God is God.

2. Faith as Hope

Faith is directed not only toward the present and active God, but
also toward that which does not yet exist. It is essential to faith that
it stretch forward to "what lies ahead" and "press on toward the
goal" (Phil. 3:13-14). Faith exists as *hope*. The hope of faith is rooted
in the act of divine love, it arises from the contrast between the cost-
liness of the gift and the imperfections of life. As we have already
pointed out, the life of faith is a constant struggle against the powers
of sin which intend to destroy the fellowship of faith with God and
rob it of its inner peace. Christian life is a constant becoming, and it
has the character of that which is imperfect and unfinished. This
imperfect and unfinished state does not disappear during this life;
rather it becomes more apparent as faith grows strong and vigorous.
The more faith perceives and understands what fellowship with God
means, the more clearly the unfinished character of life here on earth
appears. But at the same time faith emerges as a living hope. The inner

riches of the life of faith and fellowship with the exalted, living, and eternal God transcend the framework of earthly life. Faith cannot be contained within a this-worldly perspective nor within the boundaries of this life, since God cannot be contained within these limits. Christian hope is, therefore, throughout the hope of *faith*. It does not rest on any theories of the indestructible nature of man or on "the immortality of the soul," but entirely on faith's encounter with God. If the God of faith is a living God, then life with him is a life that cannot be enclosed within the narrow confines of the conditions of this early life. Faith looks beyond that which is "partial" toward a consummation, the content of which is the undisturbed and pure life with God, exalted above all opposition and imperfection, where God's dominion is unrestricted and unhindered (cf. § 52).

If we note more closely how faith speaks about this hope, we encounter two lines of thought which strangely contend with one another. On the one hand, "that which is to come" appears as the completion of what now is what is to come is, so to speak, in line with the present, i.e., the "possession" of faith is to be exalted to a higher dignity. The present is an outer court of "the life of the world to come" and an earnest of what is to be. On the other hand, the present appears as only a faint shadow of the future. The future is understood as a new creation (Rev. 21:1), as something "wholly other" than what now is, and as something about which faith can speak only in groping figures. "It does not yet appear what we shall be" (I John 3:2). It is not simply a question of a perfection of what now is, and not only a liberation from the limitations of the present life of faith, but of something that is in the essential meaning of the word "wholly other." This twofold perspective of hope and the conflict between these two lines of thought indicates clearly that the content of Christian hope appears to faith as an unfathomable mystery which lies outside the capacities of human thought.

3. The Relation Between Faith as "Possession" and as Hope

The life of Christian faith is characterized by a certain inner tension between these two aspects, which reflects the inner rhythm of faith. At certain times in the history of Christian thought this tension has turned into an antithesis in which faith as "possession" has been emphasized to the exclusion of faith as hope, or vice versa. In other words, faith has sometimes been understood as exclusively this-worldly and sometimes in terms of exclusively future eschatology. Both of these misconceptions are due to the fact that the inner richness of faith has not been fully understood.

When faith is conceived of as exclusively this-worldly, the intention is to emphasize as much as possible the present ethical functions of the Christian life. The danger is that faith may be understood as a relation to the world rather than as a relation to God. The theology of the latter half of the nineteenth century furnishes many examples of the tendency to reduce "the kingdom of God" to an ethical and cultural ideal. The defect of this line of thought is not that it takes the present into account, nor that it emphasizes that the life of faith exists for the purpose of spending itself in love. This emphasis is a sound counterbalance to the eschatology that issues in quietism and passivity. But the danger is that the essential element of faith is obscured, namely, that faith is committed to a kingdom that is not of this world. Without this eschatological perspective fellowship with God becomes limited and the power of faith paralyzed. When faith becomes concentrated on temporal goals, it becomes unable to accomplish its work in the world. If faith is to be active in the world, it has to be "free from the world"; it must live in God and be anchored in the hope of his eternal kingdom.[1]

If the exclusively temporal perspective has a certain optimistic view of the course of this world as a constant progress, which does not conform to the actual situation, the view of an eschatology concerned exclusively with the future represents a pessimism which results in quietism and passivity in reference to the affairs of this world, and conceives of faith as a flight from the world rather than a victory over it. Faith here closes its eyes and dreams of being separated from the world "that is in the power of the evil one." The reason for this attitude is also its failure to appreciate the inner richness of faith. If faith is in reality fellowship with God, it cannot avoid relating the

---

[1] Cf. Temple, *Fellowship With God*, p. 69: "The man who will do most to move the world is not he who concentrates all his attention upon the needs of the world and dedicates all his energy to reforming labours. The man who will do most to move the world is he who truly dwells with God; for through him there will operate in the world the sources of omnipotence."

divine will to the affairs of this world, and cannot, therefore, sink into inactive pessimism. It knows that fellowship with God implies responsibility and at the same time inexhaustible possibilities. It "hopes all things," because fellowship with God means submission to the government of the sovereign power of existence.

The more faith appears as unconditional trust in the loving will of God, the more closely possession and hope of faith will be united. These two aspects of the life of faith will then no longer exclude each other. There is, to be sure, a tension between them. Faith lives in the present. If God is near and with us, then we live now in the Father's house. Life here on earth is not something indifferent and of less value; it is filled with significance and responsibility in the service of the heavenly Father. Every passing moment becomes from this point of view filled with eternal meaning. But faith places us also as "strangers and pilgrims" in this world, and it speaks of "those who deal with the world as though they had no dealings with it" (I Cor. 7:31). Faith has "its citizenship in heaven" (Phil. 3:20). Faith is at home in this earthly sphere, because God is there, effecting his loving will; and faith is a stranger in the world because sin is there. But this inner tension does not mean that one of these viewpoints must curtail the other. These two aspects of faith strengthen each other. When faith "possesses" in a rich and full measure, its hope rises triumphantly. And conversely, when the hope of faith is living, its light penetrates into the present and transforms it so that the treasures of faith appear in a new and transfigured form.

Part III

THE CHURCH OF GOD

The Nature of the Church

37. The Church as the Dominion of Christ

1. *The dominion of Christ on earth.* The finished work of Christ is the foundation of the church; in and through the exaltation the church appears as his continuing work. The church is, therefore, the dominion of Christ on earth (*regnum Christi*), as it is exercised and perdures until the consummation.

2. *The church and Christ.* The church and Christ are correlative. Christ has become embodied in the church. Various biblical expressions illustrate this relationship: the church is "the body of Christ," "the vine," "a holy temple in the Lord."

3. *The church as a fellowship created by the Holy Spirit.* The church is, therefore, a creation through the act of God in Christ. This may also be expressed in this way: the church is the fellowship created by the Holy Spirit. Since the church is a divine creation, its nature cannot be comprehended within sociological categories, but only in the context of faith.

1. *The Dominion of Christ on Earth*

In the previous part we spoke of the work of God in Christ. This work of God is accomplished in and through the church. The chapters which discussed the questions of God's act of forgiveness and his act of creating faith are therefore in a certain sense an introduction to the following discussion of the church of God and its work.

The problem of the relation between Jesus and the church has long been a subject of discussion. There has been a wide difference of opinion. The exegesis which flourished at the beginning of the present century within the Reformed communions generally assumed a negative attitude. The church, so it was said, is a later creation which has no relation to the historical Jesus. But the attitude of present-day exegesis is different. The reasons for the attitude of the older exegesis were rooted in an unhistorical misjudgment of Jesus' messianic claims

and their significance, and a similarly unhistorical interpretation of his
work on the basis of personal points of view. The problem of the
measure in which the church has its foundation in the teaching and
work of Jesus, and the measure in which it corresponds to his intention, is a complicated question which cannot be discussed fully in this
work. If we listen to what exegetical research of the present has to
say, it should be underscored that the solution of the problem does
not depend entirely on the interpretation of those passages in the
Gospels which speak directly of the church. It is much more important to note how frequently the idea of the establishment of a new
fellowship, a new *koinonia*, occurs in the Gospel reports of Jesus'
words and work, and how this idea characterizes the Gospels as a
whole.

It was Jesus' desire to gather and "organize" a new people, a true
Israel of God, a *koinonia* prepared for the kingdom of God. Among
the great number of passages in the New Testament which deal with
this subject we call attention to the following: Jesus as the bride-
groom, the prepared wedding feast, the temple to be built, the cornerstone which is laid, and so forth. Some of his acts reveal the same
intention: the call of the twelve, the commissioning of the disciples,
the feeding of the five thousand, the last supper, and so on. The idea
of the church as a communion and fellowship gathered around the
Messiah is inseparably connected with the messianic idea. From this
point of view it can hardly be denied that the church which appeared at Pentecost not only had its historic roots in Jesus' teaching
and work, but that it is also consistent with his intention. The continuity between Jesus and the apostolic church is unbroken.[1]

But however significant these historical questions may be, it is in
principle much more important to note how inseparably the New
Testament associates Christ and the church. The decisive point in the
question of the relationship between Jesus and the church is in the
final analysis the fact that the foundation of the church is the finished
work of Christ and that the church appears as a living reality in and
through the exaltation (cf. § 27). The Christian church is the church

[1] Cf. Anders Nygren (ed.), *This Is the Church*, trans. Carl C. Rasmussen
(Philadelphia: Muhlenberg, 1952), especially the articles by Anton Fridrichsen,
Hugo Odeberg, and Olof Linton.

of Easter and Pentecost. If the exaltation is the starting point of the continuing work of Christ, this continuing work is directly connected with the church, and the church is in the final analysis nothing less than this work continuing through ages and generations. We might state the matter thus: the church is the result of the finished work and is identical with the continuing work of Christ.

The church may therefore be defined as the dominion of Christ, *regnum Christi*, as this obtains under the conditions of life here on earth. In § 27, ¶ 3 we remarked that according to the viewpoint of the New Testament the kingdom which Jesus accepted in and through the exaltation was of a universal character, but that it is concentrated in the church as far as life here on earth is concerned. When this reign of Christ is established, it means the eschatological breakthrough of a new age, a new aeon, the new "time of fulfilment." The old age remains, but in the midst of this old aeon the church as *regnum Christi* represents the new age. The church lives in this world, but is not of the world. It participates in two worlds. It is the messianic fellowship, the true Israel, the new covenant, *Christus-Kyrios* united with his own in the world. The church thereby becomes an eschatological reality and has its eyes focused on the consummation to come when the old aeon has definitely passed away and the glory of the kingdom of God will be revealed. But even though the future perspective is essential for the church, this does not remove or minimize the significance of the fact that the church already here on earth lives in that new age which has come in and with the victory of Christ over those destructive powers which have kept men in servitude. To participate in the *regnum Christi* is to live in that new age which because of the victory of Christ is the new age of life.

2. *The Church and Christ*

The church and Christ belong together. They constitute an inseparable unity. The church exists in and through Christ. But neither does Christ exist apart from his church. Just as the church cannot be conceived of without Christ, so neither can we think of *Christus-Kyrios* without his dominion, without connection with that fellowship which belongs to him. Where Christ is, there is the church. This proposition can also be reversed: where the church is, there is Christ. Fellowship with Christ is a fellowship with him in and through the church. In that he lives and works in his church. Christ has become embodied in his church. Under the conditions of this earthly life the church is the mode of the living and active revelation of Christ. There he meets us and deals with us.

The inseparable unity between Christ and his church finds expression in the description of the church as "the body of Christ" which occurs so often in the New Testament. This figure, which to Paul is in reality much more than a figure, reveals in a concrete way the inseparable unity between Christ and the church, and tells us that Christ lives in and gives life to his church. When Christ in Ephesians and Colossians is called "the head"—"he is the head of the body, the church" (Col. 1:18)—the intention is not to designate what separates him from the church, as has sometimes been suggested. "To designate the Church as the body of Christ and Christ as the head of the Church is not to imply that *one* part is allocated to Christ and another to the Church; on the contrary, it emphasizes their indissoluble relationship and unity. Christ is not the head pure and simple, but he is the head of his Church. Similarly, the Church is not a body in itself, viewed apart from the head, but it is just the body of Christ. The body of Christ is Christ himself." [2]

We find the same fundamental view of the relationship between Christ and the church in a number of other biblical expressions such as the vine and the branches (John 15:5), and the church as a holy temple in the Lord: "Christ Jesus himself being the chief cornerstone; in whom the whole structure is joined together and grows into a holy temple in the Lord" (Eph. 2:20-21). In both of these passages the church is one with Christ, and he is at the same time the Lord and unifying power of the church. The vine and the branches: the power of life from Christ. The temple: Christ the foundation of life. It may be added that all three of these figures express both the inseparable unity of the church with Christ and the Christian fellowship within the church. The body has various "members" which have different functions (I Cor. 12), but they all belong to one and

[2]Anders Nygren, *Christ and His Church*, trans. Alan Carlsten. (Philadelphia: Westminster, 1956) p. 95.

the same body. The branches belong to one and the same vine and therefore have fellowship one with another. The stones of which the temple is built do not lie separated from each other. "As living stones" they are joined together, each set into its own place. These figures speak, therefore, of the inner fellowship in the church. But everything depends on fellowship with Christ. Fellowship with him is at the same time fellowship in the church.

We may add a marginal note to what has been said here about the unity of Christ and his church. There is nothing more essential to be said about the church than that Christ is one with his church, and the church is one with him. But this "identity" has its origin exclusively in the activity of Christ. The church has life in his life. The statement about "identity" is true as long as the starting point is Christ and his work; but it becomes a misinterpretation if the church is made the starting point. The church is what it is through the activity of Christ; but Christ is not what he is through the church.

3. The Church as a Fellowship Created by the Holy Spirit

The church, as the dominion of Christ, is the church of God. Its origin is in the finished work of God in Christ, and it perdures as the creation of the continuing work of God in Christ. On the basis of what we have already said about the relation between the Spirit and the continuing work of Christ (§ 28), the church as the dominion of Christ is at the same time the *fellowship created by the Holy Spirit*. These two definitions of the nature of the church must be considered as parallel. The gift of the Spirit and his work are the sign of the coming of the new age and of the fulfilment of the promise to the fathers. The Spirit is also the earnest of the coming consummation. That the church is a fellowship created by the Spirit emphasizes the future perspective inseparably connected with the church.

The Spirit is, therefore, just as inseparably connected with the church as *Christus-Kyrios*. The Christian confession relative to the church in the third article of the Creed is a confession of faith in God the Holy Spirit who "calls, gathers, enlightens, and sanctifies," and thereby establishes a temple of "living stones" and creates that spiritual fellowship which is "the communion of saints." The confession of faith in the church does not imply, therefore, that it is a confession of faith in something in addition to God; or, in other words, that the church stands as some intermediate reality between God and man, or an entity coincident with God, so that faith would be directed in part to God, Christ, and the Spirit, and in part to the church. The confession of faith in the one, holy, catholic church expresses an essential and precious element in our Christian faith in God, because it confronts us with that activity of God which is accomplished in the continuing work of Christ, and with that Spirit who calls, gathers, enlightens, and sanctifies.

Under these circumstances it would be misleading if, with Schleiermacher, we were to conceive of the Spirit as a kind of *Gemeingeist*. This would mean that faith is no longer concerned with the Spirit, but with the human spiritual life. The church is distinguished from all other "spiritual fellowships" because everything in it depends on the creative and sanctifying activity of the Holy Spirit. The church originates and grows in the measure that the Holy Spirit through the Word and the sacraments (cf. §§ 41-47) accomplishes the work of sanctification in the souls of men; or, in other words, as the forgiving and condemning love of God realizes itself. In this fellowship of the Spirit everything depends on the fact that God's love is allowed to rule. Luther describes very pointedly the inner life of the church when he calls it "a kingdom of grace," a *regnum gratiae*, and when in the Large Catechism he asserts that the life of the church is characterized by "a continuous and unceasing forgiveness of sins, both that which we receive from God and that which we exercise mutually in forbearing and edifying one another."

According to this analysis the primary viewpoint of Christian faith relative to the church is that it exists as a divine creation in the world of men. Under such circumstances it is clear that one cannot rightly understand the nature and function of the church as long as one follows a sociological approach. Such sociological points of view are legitimate in their own sphere and context, but they cannot elucidate the nature of the church. The church about which the third article of the Creed speaks is something entirely different from a mere human organization, or a human society and association for the satisfaction of certain religious needs and interests. Only the eye of faith can discover the innermost and deepest nature of the church. The church appears as a living reality only when faith directs its attention to Christ and discovers the inseparable connection and unity between him, his finished and continuing work, and his church. From this point of view the historical communions are seen in their true light. But this will not lead to an idealization of these churches, nor to a romanticism which deifies frail human reality and is blind to its defects. Faith's clear view of the nature of the church condemns unreservedly everything within the historical communions which does not bear the stamp of the activity of the Holy Spirit. But it knows also that it is not a question of organizations and associations of men, but, in spite of and in the midst of all frailty and human weakness, we stand here in the presence of the dominion of Christ and the fellowship created by the Spirit—the Church of God.

38. One Holy, Ecumenical, and Apostolic Church

1. *The living church.* The one, holy, ecumenical, and apostolic church is the church which appeared as a living reality in and through the exaltation of Christ, and which since that time has perdured through ages and generations.

2. *The unity of the church.* Since the church is the dominion of Christ, and since it has, therefore, only *one* Lord, there is only one church. The unity of the church is manifested in the Word and the sacraments. Consequently this unity is not a uniformity of organization, doctrine, or life. The various church communions are different expressions of the one, ecumenical church.

3. *The holiness of the church.* The holiness of the church rests on the finished and continuing work of Christ, which is the power sanctifying the church. It is not dependent on the subjective "holiness" of the members. The church is "a communion of saints" only through God's act of salvation.

4. *The ecumenicity of the church.* The church is ecumenical because the act of God in Christ has a universal significance and purpose. This universality is expressed in the great commission: "Go and make disciples of all nations." The church exists as continually becoming. Its boundaries, which are continually shifting, are defined only by the extent of the activity of Christ, the Spirit, and the gospel among men. They cannot be fixed in such a way that definite limits are drawn around certain qualified individuals.

5. *The apostolicity of the church.* The church is called apostolic because the gospel by which the church is built was given to it as an apostolic message, and because this message is continually proclaimed anew by other messengers following in the footsteps of the apostles.

1. The Living Church

In the preceding sections we spoke of the church as a church of God, a divine creation in history and in the life of men. That church which the old confession describes as the one, holy, ecumenical, and apostolic church is not an abstract idea, or an "invisible" church, or the "essence" of the church, in contrast to another, concrete, actual, and historical church. It is not strange that such a distinction has been attempted. Men have looked at the various denominations and have found it difficult, not to say impossible, to apply to them the exalted predicates which the confessions ascribe to the church. The church ought to be one, but in reality it is separated into many denominations which have often fought bitterly with one another. The church ought to be holy, but its defects, weaknesses, and sins are only too apparent. The church should be inclusive and characterized by the open arms of the Father, but its actions have often been narrow and exclusive, and it has drawn limits which belie the claim to universality. When all this has been taken into consideration, it seems natural to distinguish between two kinds of churches, and to place the ideal and essential church in contrast to the concrete, empirical, and historical denominations. The former would then be an invisible church, and in contrast, the latter a visible and tangible reality. This approach has been fairly common among Protestants during latter centuries, not least under the influence of pietism, and the claim has sometimes been made that this represents a simon-pure "protestant" point of view.

These theories have had baneful results. They have served not to clarify but rather to obscure the problem of the church. But the most serious result of this division has been the dissolution and destruction of the consciousness of the church. The more "important" church, the invisible church of the essence, became nothing more than a pale and flimsy ideal, an abstraction; and the so-called visible church, the historical denominations, came to be regarded more and more as human institutions and organizations. This meant that the "visible church" lost (one could say was deprived of) more and more of its religious content and its character as a church. The most evident result of this supposedly higher spirituality, which regarded it as unspiritual to apply these high predicates to actual churches, was that these churches came more and more to be regarded as profane. The spiritual and "invisible" church had no living reality, and the "visible" church was no church at all.

The idea that these speculations about the church can find support in the Reformation is entirely false. Luther and Calvin would have rejected them at once as spiritualistic errors. When Luther spoke about an invisible church and about the church's visibility, his meaning was something entirely different.[1] His view of the church was infinitely more realistic and absolutely free from such a depreciation of the actual, historical church. However sharply and violently he criticized Rome, he nevertheless said that the Roman church is "holy," because in this church there still remain "baptism, sacrament, the words of the gospel, the Holy Scriptures, the churchly offices, the name of Christ and the name of God."

Neither does this theory of division have any support in the conception of the church found in the New Testament. Primitive Christianity knows nothing about two kinds of churches. It knew no other church than that of Easter and Pentecost, in which the apostles were the authorized messengers of the Lord and which brought the message of *Christus-Kyrios* out into the world. This church is "the body of Christ" and "a holy temple in the Lord." We have every reason to hold fast to the testimony of primitive Christianity. On the first Pentecost the church appeared as a tangible reality, and its tangibleness has not been lost. This primitive conception of the church corresponds accurately to the viewpoint of faith in general: faith finds the superhistorical and the revelation of God in history (cf. § 4), and it finds, therefore, also the dominion of Christ and the fellowship created by the Spirit in the church which was born at Easter and Pentecost and has perdured through ages and generations. Faith knows of no other church. This does not imply an idealization of

[1] Cf. Herbert Olsson, "The Church's Visibility and Invisibility According to Luther," in Nygren, *This Is the Church*, pp. 226-42.

the church and its life (cf. § 37, ¶ 3); but it means that faith does not lose sight of what belongs to the real nature of the church.

2. The Unity of the Church

The church is one. Its unity rests on the fact that the church is the dominion of Christ. The unity is a unity in Christ because the church is the body of Christ. The body of Christ cannot be more than *one*. The unity is given in the very existence of the church; it is, in other words, an existential unity. There may be different forms of Christian fellowship, but these do not destroy the existential unity of the church. This could be destroyed only if the church had several Lords. Since the church has only one Lord, *Christus-Kyrios*, and one Shepherd (John 10:16), the unity of the church rests on a secure foundation.

It is a different matter that this unity has been only partially achieved in the church. It has been hidden and damaged by schisms and contention. It is, therefore, the inescapable duty of the church to overcome these differences and to realize more and more fully the actual unity inherent in the church (cf. § 50). This twofold view of Christian unity meets us constantly in the New Testament; on the one hand an actual, inescapable reality; and on the other hand, exhortations to realize and preserve this real unity. Thus the Letter to the Ephesians exhorts the members of the congregation to "preserve the unity of the Spirit in the bond of peace"; and it does so on the basis of the unity which actually exists: "*one* body and *one* Spirit, just as you were called to the *one* hope that belongs to your call, *one* Lord, *one* faith, *one* baptism, *one* God and Father of us all, who is above all and through all and in all" (Eph. 4:3-6).

The unity, an indestructible unity in Christ and his Spirit, manifests itself in the gospel entrusted to the church by which it is edified. This gospel appears in different forms, as Word and as sacraments. The reference to the gospel as the basis of unity in the church does not imply, however, that another basis has been found in addition to Christ and the Spirit. The gospel creates unity because Christ and the Spirit are active through the Word and the sacraments as "means."

The Word and the sacraments are the bearers of the unifying and homogeneous message which centers in *Christus-Kyrios*. This message can indeed be perverted by men, and such perversions cause schisms, injury, and havoc. But the gospel remains. It cannot be changed by men and made into something else. It is and remains "a sure saying" (I Tim. 1:15), and it appears, therefore, as the bearer of the unity of the Christian church.

Consequently, the unity of the Christian church is a unity in and through the Word and the sacraments. It is, however, not a unity consisting in organizational uniformity. The unity does not demand that the Christian church should at all times and in all places have identical forms and orders of organization. Even if this were the case, it would not in the least guarantee the unity which is essential and decisive for faith. On the contrary, *this* unity may exist under different external forms. This means only that the Holy Spirit can accomplish his creation of fellowship under various forms. To maintain the opposite would, according to faith, mean that we place the forms above the Spirit. The organization is important, but it is important only in so far as it serves as an instrument of the Spirit. The office of the ministry is one of the instruments of the activity of the Spirit through the Word and the sacraments, and because of this function it is one of the constitutive factors of the church (cf. § 47). As an instrument of the gospel it certainly belongs also among those factors which create unity in the church. But this does not mean that a demand may be made for uniformity in everything that belongs to the organization of the church, nor that the organization of the New Testament congregations should be regarded as some kind of ideal and as legal authority for all time to come. The organization of the church must rather have a certain amount of elasticity to adapt itself to changing conditions. The principle is then always that the organization must be of such a character that under various conditions it serves in the best possible manner as an instrument of the gospel for the establishment of the fellowship.

The unity of the Christian church is not a uniformity in doctrine either. The gospel is the unifying factor of the church, but it is not a finally formulated, doctrinal authority. If a finally and irrevocably fixed system of doctrine were proposed as the basis of unity, it would lead to an intellectualized orthodoxy and a false objectivity. But such false objectivity invariably turns and becomes the exact opposite (cf. § 50).

Finally, the unity of the Christian church is not a uniformity of life. It is not a purely subjective matter. It is true that the nature of the life which God bestows upon men in and through the church is determined by God's act of forgiveness, and participation in this new life is, therefore, a participation in a common treasure. But this does not mean that the unity of the church demands an identity of experience and practice, or a fixed religious and ethical quality. As the light passing through a prism breaks into a variegated system of colors, so "the new life" appears in a variety of experiences and patterns of life. It cannot be imprisoned in a legal straitjacket. The demand for uniformity in life is contrary to the variety of human life in the world and would serve to disrupt rather than to unify the church.

3. The Holiness of the Church

As dominion of Christ, the church is holy. This holiness rests on the finished work which Christ makes effective through his continuing work. The holiness of the church is not an external, hierarchical, and institutional holiness, nor does it consist in the character of the members of a closed and limited society whose claim to "holiness" rests on their own qualifications. The holiness of the church depends entirely on that Holy Spirit who is active in the church. If faith is to be certain that there is "a communion of saints" in the world, this certainty cannot be based on the existence of a relative degree of human holiness, much less on any human perfection. Such a conception is contrary to the fact that the justified man possesses no subjective holiness of his own; from the subjective viewpoint he is at the same time *iustus* and *peccator*. Just as faith's certainty of fellowship with God rests entirely on his forgiving love, so its certainty about the holiness of the church cannot rest on anything else than the saving power of divine love, i.e., God's act of forgiveness. With intuitive insight Luther saw that what is determinative here for the individual life of faith is also determinative for the church. In the large commentary on Galatians he declares that the confession of faith in a "holy" church is a confession of faith in the victory of Christ. Luther

vigorously distinguishes between the view of faith and empirical perception. Only faith can see the holiness of the church. "Reason and
the eyes" perceive the imperfections of Christian life and conclude
that the church is unholy. But, says Luther, "I deny the truth of
this conclusion. If I look at myself or my neighbor, the church would
never appear holy. But if I look at Christ who reconciles and
sanctifies it, the church appears as entirely holy, for he has taken
away the sin of all the world." [2] We may add another word from the
same source, where Luther says that the reason for the holiness of the
church is that we "have God's work among us, i.e., the Word and
the sacraments, and these make us holy." [3] It is not a question of a
"holiness" of our own, but of the fact that there are powers which
sanctify us.

The holiness of the church derives from the fact that the Lord
himself is present in his church and there realizes the work of redemption which he finished once for all. He leads men out of
bondage to the evil powers and translates them into the new context
of life which has come in the new age of the resurrection. The
church exists in the interval between the resurrection and the consummation. It is an instrument of that kingdom which now struggles
against the demonic powers, but which in essence belongs to the age
to come.

The conclusion of what we have said about the holiness of the
church is that the church is at the same time *sancta et peccatrix*. This
is inevitable because the members of the church are at the same time
iusti et peccatores. We cannot say that the church is free from sin
when the members are not. Such a claim would really imply that
the members of the church did not belong to it. This claim would
be in conflict not only with what "reason and the eyes" perceive,
but even more so with the understanding of faith. It would also be
contrary to the significance which the term "the saints" has in the
New Testament. "The saints" is a designation of those who belong
to God, who have been incorporated into life in the new covenant,
and who by the grace of God have become members in the body
of Christ, the church. But there is no "perfection" implied here

[2] *WA* 40^I, p. 445.
[3] *Ibid.*, p. 70.

(cf. § 39). The church is *peccatrix*, but at the same time, as the chosen bride of Christ, it is *sancta* through Christ's own *sanctificatio* (John 17:19).

If the church is holy, it implies that it is "not of this world." "Holiness" places us in the presence of the otherworldly perspective. The church lives and works in this world. But it is not of this world. "Holiness" stands guard against all tendencies to confine it within this world and transform it into a power coincident with other earthly powers. The temptation to do this lies near at hand. Intentions may be most generous, pointing to the many earthly tasks which confront the church of Christ. The temptation is for the church to become absorbed in and limited to the affairs pertaining to this world. But the "holy" church cannot be merely a society for the promotion of better social conditions, and the like, or a proponent of a future social utopia. That holiness stands guard against such tendencies does not mean that the pressing problems of this world are not important for the church. It is rather connected with the insight that the ability of the church to serve the purposes of divine love and righteousness here on earth depends entirely on the fact that the church is "not of this world" and that its "citizenship is in heaven."

4. The Ecumenicity of the Church

The church is *ecumenical* or *catholic* because the finished work of Christ is universal. "God was in Christ reconciling the *world* to himself" (II Cor. 5:19). Both the finished work and the continuing work of Christ are universal in character. This is seen clearly in "the great commission" according to which Jesus sends out his messengers to make disciples of all nations. The Spirit working through the Gospel wants to penetrate as far and as deeply as possible into the human world, and his activity does not stop before any boundaries of time or space. He is no respecter of persons. "There cannot be Greek and Jew, circumcised and uncircumcised, barbarian, Scythian, slave, free man, but Christ is all, and in all" (Col. 3:11). The ecumenicity of the church expresses the universal scope of the victory of divine love in Christ, of the reconciliation of the world, of the free access to forgiveness, and of the open arms of the Father.

"You are all one in Christ Jesus" (Gal. 3:28). When, therefore, all boundaries of race, denominational affiliation, and social status are eliminated it means that there is a universal brotherhood in the church. "You have one teacher, and you are all brethren" (Matt. 23:8). "Through him we both have access in one Spirit to the Father" (Eph. 2:18). The gift is the same for all. Access to the Father is the same for all. All are called to the family of God. No one has preference over the other. No one has any occasion for boasting. It is true of everyone that he possesses nothing which has not been given to him as a gift of grace alone.

Since the ecumenicity of the church implies a universal purpose which does not cease as long as life on earth lasts, it means that the church is continually in a state of becoming and of change. Christian faith therefore, cannot draw any boundaries around the church. About this problem of boundaries Christian faith can say nothing more than that the church extends as far as the activity of Christ, the Spirit, and the gospel reach, that the church of God is being established where the Spirit of Christ is active, and that because of this work of the Spirit the boundaries of the church are continually changing. It might seem that the result of this conception would be the blotting out of the boundaries of the church, but in reality this definition is the only one which does *not* erase these boundaries. All other boundaries are imaginary. If an externally fixed boundary is substituted for what is fixed by the activity of the Spirit through the gospel, faith would interpret this as a removal of the actual and decisive boundary.

The church therefore, cannot be defined from below, as it were, on the basis of the individuals who belong to it. Such a point of view which fixes certain human qualifications as prerequisites for the formation of the church have lost sight of that which according to faith is the creative and constitutive factor of the church as a creation of God. This conception assumes, consciously or unconsciously, that the church is a society, an association, an organization of certain qualified persons. Their right to membership in the church would rest on their own qualification. In principle it makes no difference whether these qualifications are understood in one way or another. One may, for instance, say that the church is the sum total of all true believers, and thus make the Christian confession the principle governing the formation of the church; or the boundary may include all who have been baptized. In the first case the qualification is "true believers," and in the second "baptized." [4] In either case this represents a conception of the church different from that which came into being at the inception of the Christian church. In both cases limitations are imposed which encroach on the universality of the church. Just as it is true to say that everything in the church has its center in faith, because the center is Christ, so it is false to assert that the church can be built on the human qualification of personal faith, or that the church may be defined as the sum total of all true believers. Just as it is correct to say that baptism is an act of God through which he creates the church and that we become members of the church through baptism, so it is wrong to say that the church is the sum total of all baptized. The church is not the sum total of the believers, nor of the baptized. It is the dominion of Christ on earth and the fellowship created by the Spirit (cf. § 40, ¶ 2, regarding membership in the church).

We may add here a remark about the word catholicity. The "catholicity" of the church is the classical Christian expression for the universality of the church. But in evangelical usage the word "catholic" has unfortunately become associated exclusively with the Roman church. That this glorious appellation of the church has been reserved for the Roman communion represents a certain danger in view of the power of language over thought. It has tended to weaken the consciousness of evangelical Christianity as being an expression of that which is universally Christian. That the Roman church cannot claim to be the sole representative of the universality of the church is perfectly clear. The various denominations are all members in the one, holy, catholic, and apostolic church, because and in so far as the constitutive factors of the church are active in each one.

5. The Apostolicity of the Church

When the ancient confession calls the church "apostolic," it refers to a constitutive element of the Christian church. This name implies first of all a reference to the significance of the apostles as the

---

[4] Cf. Ruben Josefson, "The Church and Baptism," in Nygren, *This is the Church*, p. 243 ff.

authorized messengers of the Lord and of the fundamental work they accomplished. The sure and unchangeable gospel which has been entrusted to the church and by which the church lives was given to it as an apostolic message. But the word apostolic tells us also that the gospel needs messengers for its activity. It is not accidental, or simply a matter of convenience, that the church has a ministerial office in the service of the gospel. Such a service is essential for the church and belongs to its nature (cf. § 47). The apostles were the first messengers of the Lord. But the message must thereafter be proclaimed anew by other messengers following in the footsteps of the apostles. When the church is called apostolic it implies a twofold perspective. It means that the Word is a living word, proclaimed by ever new messengers; and the apostolicity emphasizes also the continuity, the unbroken connection in the life of the Christian church.

39. The Communion of Saints

1. *Communio sanctorum.* The church as the body of Christ is a *communio sanctorum.* The fellowship implied in this term is both a *koinonia* with Christ and a mutual fellowship among the members.

2. *The cloud of witnesses.* This mutual fellowship is not limited to the church as it exists in the present. It is at the same time a *koinonia* with those who through the ages have been witnesses to faith.

1. Communio Sanctorum

We have spoken already of the church as a communion created by the Spirit. The use of the word communion is not intended to designate the church as an "institution" or a "corporation." It is true that the church has an institutional character, and we will discuss this aspect of it later. But primarily the church is a fellowship, a *koinonia.* The members of the church are members of the body of Christ. They are branches of the true vine. They are living stones in the temple. The chief characteristic of this *koinonia* is that it is a fellowship with Christ and a mutual fellowship among the members. From the point of view of the membership the church is "the new people of God," "the new Israel." In the New Testament members of the church are consistently designated "the saints."

As has already been said, when the word saints is used for the members of the church, it means that they belong to God. To belong to the church of Christ is to belong to God. The members belong to him by virtue of his call and election. "You did not choose me, but I chose you" (John 15:16). The "holiness" they have is not their own holiness. God alone is holy (Rev. 15:4). Christ alone is the Holy One of God (John 6:69). The Spirit of God alone is the Holy Spirit. The holiness of the members is a participation in this holiness of God and a communion of the living and active Spirit (Eph. 1:13).

But the holiness of the members does not imply some kind of perfection, either complete or partial sinlessness. The insistent and often harsh counsels and admonitions addressed to "the saints" in the letters of the apostles bear abundant witness to the fact that the members of the church participated in the sinfulness that belongs to humanity. Paul writes to the Corinthians, for example, that he cannot address them as "spiritual" but as "men of the flesh." But at the same time he does not question the fact that they are God's people and the temple of the Holy Spirit. These apostolic exhortations bear witness also to the obligations involved in membership in the church of Christ. The church is a fellowship in which salvation is available for every individual, and in which the members participate fully in all the blessings procured by Christ, as well as in the consequent obligation to live lives "worthy of the gospel of Christ" (Phil. 1:27).

The significance of *communio sanctorum* in the third article of the Creed has been the subject of considerable discussion. Does it mean, as traditionally translated, "the communion of saints," or fellowship in "holy things," i.e., the means of grace? The majority of modern scholars prefer the latter meaning and can present very good reasons for their opinion.[1] But we can also say that in principle there is no

---

[1] In addition to the reasons which are generally presented and which we cannot enumerate here I would call attention to the parallelism between the Apostles' and the Nicene creeds. There is an evident parallelism between them. But at the place where we read *communio sanctorum* in the Apostles' Creed, the Nicene Creed says, "I acknowledge one Baptism for the remission of sins." Everything indicates that the parallelism ought to obtain at this place also. While the Apostles' Creed points to the fellowship *in sacris* and very likely refers to the Lord's Supper, the Nicene Creed points to baptism as that fundamental sacrament through which men become incorporated into the church, receive the forgiveness of sins, and participate in the resurrection and the life of the world to come.

real contradiction between these two interpretations. In reality they speak from two different points of view about one and the same thing: the *koinonia* in Christ. Through the fellowship *in sacris* this *koinonia* becomes a present and living reality.

Communio sanctorum is both hidden and visible. What is hidden is our fellowship with Christ: "Your life is hid with Christ in God" (Col. 3:3). But this does not mean that *communio sanctorum* exists as some kind of "invisible church." It appears in many ways as a tangible reality: as a fellowship *in sacris,* in Word and in sacraments, in worship and prayer, as a fellowship in the service of Christ, in bearing one another's burdens, in "the mutual conversation and consolation of brethren"—this last being regarded in the Smalcald Articles as one aspect of the activity of the gospel in the church.

2. *The Cloud of Witnesses*

The *koinonia* of the church is not limited to the church as it exists now in the present. Death does not constitute a boundary. The fellowship of the church includes the witnesses to the faith in all ages. When the Letter to the Hebrews in the eleventh chapter has enumerated a long line of witnesses from the time of the old covenant, it continues in chapter twelve to stress the significance of the fact that "we are surrounded by so great a cloud of witnesses," and especially that we look "to Jesus the pioneer and perfecter of our faith" (Heb. 12:1-2). In these words the author of the letter has disclosed the true perspective of the relationship between the many and the One. Just as the old covenant had its heroes of faith, so the new has "so great a cloud of witnesses." For the church which now lives and struggles, these witnesses are a precious heritage and a source of help and encouragement. But these witnesses do not draw attention to themselves for their own sake, but rather point to him who is the Pioneer and Perfecter of faith. The Christian attitude to the heroes of faith does not involve a personality cult.

There is a tragic aspect to this chapter on the heroes of faith. The attitude of evangelical Christianity has to a very large extent been determined by the opposition to the Roman doctrine of the saints and to Mariology. The opposition has been and continues to be inevitable. But the evangelical attitude has remained purely negative

and has therefore lost something of that living and life-giving relationship which unites the faithful in all ages. This negative attitude
is not found in the twenty-first article of the Augsburg Confession,
on the subject of "The Saints," nor in Luther's treatise on the Lord's
Supper of 1519, where he speaks repeatedly about the fellowship
"with Christ and all his saints."

The opposition of evangelical Christianity to the Roman doctrine
of the saints and to Mariology is obvious. In regard to the doctrine
of the saints we call attention to the following points. Through its
fixed rules for beatification and canonization the Roman hierarchy
determines what persons have the necessary holiness to be declared
saints. From an evangelical point of view this is a usurpation of judgment which belongs to God alone. The idea of "a treasury of merits"
which the church has authority to dispense is foreign to evangelical
faith. Of course it is true that official Roman theology exercises a
certain restraint in these matters, but popular piety readily translates
respect and honor into a real worship of the saints, often with the
tacit approval of the hierarchical authorities. The widespread use of
relics has also played a fateful part in Roman piety.

The situation is similar in regard to Mariology and the worship
of the Virgin. After the church council in Ephesus had authorized
the designation *theatokos* for Mary, Mariology became extremely
popular during the Middle Ages. Its popularity has grown immensely in modern times as is evident from the dogmas of
the Immaculate Conception (freedom from original sin) of 1854, and
the Assumption of the Virgin Mary of 1950. These dogmas, which
define what originated in popular piety, have no biblical foundation,
nor does the practice of veneration of the saints. When the attempt
is made to find authority for these dogmas in the New Testament
ideas and viewpoints are read into the words of Scripture which are
foreign to the biblical authors. Developments in these areas of doctrine and cult shows how little the tradition is dependent on the
witness of Scripture. This is equally true in regard to the tendencies
to emphasize Mary's part in the work of redemption.

But in spite of the many objections that may be raised against the
Roman doctrine of the saints and Mariology, the Christian faith cannot be satisfied with pure negation. Such an attitude does not do

justice to the position which Mary holds as *the Mother of the Lord* and to the honor which belongs to her: "henceforth all generations will call me blessed" (Luke 1:48). Luther frequently expressed this honor in strong terms, as for example in his exposition of the Magnificat (1528). Nor is it proper to ignore those who through the ages have born witness to the living God and to their Lord Jesus Christ, and who, in the expressive words of the apostle, have been "fellow workmen for God" (I Cor. 3:9). But if we speak here about "saints" and celebrate All Saints' Day in their honor, we commemorate not only certain prominent and powerful witnesses, but also those who have labored in obscurity and silence, but who nevertheless within their own sphere have been witnesses to the living God. The words of the Lord in the Sermon on the Mount may serve as a guide for us in this matter: "Let your light so shine before men, that they may see your good works and give glory to your Father who is in heaven" (Matt. 5:16).[2]

40. The Church and the Christian Life

1. *"The mother who bears and fosters every individual Christian."* The Christian life exists in and through the church. The individual Christian is not isolated, nor is he antecedent to the church. The church is "the mother who bears and fosters every individual Christian."

2. *Membership in the church.* Membership in the church rests on the call of God, not on human qualifications. It is realized and actualized in the measure that man becomes what God's call intends him to be: a living member of the body of the church.

1. *"The Mother Who Bears and Fosters Every Individual Christian"*

All Christian life has its roots in the fellowship created by the Holy Spirit, or, in other words, in the church. The church is, therefore, according to Luther's well-known words in the Large Catechism, "the mother who bears and fosters every individual Christian." This statement expresses in a forceful way the dependence of the in-

[2] Concerning this entire discussion, compare K. E. Skydsgaard, *One in Christ* (Philadelphia: Muhlenberg, 1957), pp. 185-220.

dividual Christian on the church and the antecedence of the church in reference to the individual believer. Whether we are concerned with the beginning of faith or its continued existence, the relation to the fellowship created by the Spirit is of fundamental importance. The Spirit's work is carried on in the church. The church meets and enfolds the individual as a *solidary interrelationship of blessing* (cf. § 31, ¶ 1) which is opposed to and struggles against the solidary interrelationship of sin. This interrelationship of blessing is, to use an expression from the Gospels, that holy fire which Christ has lighted and which burns unceasingly in the world. It is the Holy Spirit who creates this interrelationship of blessing by bringing man to Christ in order that man might find in him the One who continually realizes the redemptive activity of divine love. That the man of faith is dependent on the church is the same as saying that he is dependent on Christ who is active in the church. The church cannot be separated from Christ any more than Christ can be separated from the church. Faith does not find Christ *outside* of or coincident with the church as the interrelationship of the divine blessing, but rather *in* this interrelationship. There is no room here for a proposition that would compel us to choose between Christ and the church. It is just as meaningless to predicate Christ without the church as to affirm the church without Christ. The former would mean that we seek the living among the dead; and the latter, that we take the soul away from the church and thereby destroy its life.

The character of the church as "the mother who bears and fosters every Christian" has often been obscured by the so-called individualistic movements. It is understandable that such movements have appeared as a reaction to institutional and legalistic reinterpretations of the idea of the church. Against the institutional conception a subjective reinterpretation of the idea of the church has appeared, which places the individual Christian life as antecedent to the church and regards the church as an association of a greater or smaller number of individual Christians. In evangelical Christianity "individualistic" ideas have often appeared which obscure the actual significance of the Christian fellowship. It has even been asserted that the essential meaning of the Reformation was that the emphasis was shifted from the church to the individual. That this is a gross misinterpretation is clear from the words already quoted from the Large Catechism concerning the church as mother. That such a misinterpretation could appear may be explained in part as due to the varied meanings of the word individual, and also to the fact that "individualistic Christianity" has been interpreted to imply an assertion that in the relationship between God and man we are dealing with a relationship between "God and the soul," as Augustine expressed it, or, in other words, an immediate and direct relationship between God and man. If, however, the word individualism is used in its ordinary meaning and individualistic Christianity is made to imply that the individual is independent of the church, that he is isolated from the fellowship with others, and that he is antecedent to the church, such an individualism is unrealistic and contrary to the conditions under which faith lives. "Individual Christianity" is in reality a *contradictio in adjecto*. The Christian life in faith is not isolated from the fellowship; it lives and is nourished, "is born and nurtured," in that solidary interrelationship of blessing which the Holy Spirit creates through the ages. He who desires to separate himself from this relationship condemns himself to exist on a very restricted diet. In fact, such a course indicates an egocentric isolation, self-sufficiency, and "inclination toward self" which is the very opposite of faith. We may, therefore, state the following propositions as self-evident. If individualism means isolation of the individual, it is in reality that sin from which man is delivered in and through faith. If individualistic Christianity means that from the point of view of the individual Christian the church is something secondary, this conception is contrary to the conditions under which faith lives.

In view of this relation between the church and the individual it must be said that Schleiermacher's famous formula of the relation between "Catholicism" and "Protestantism" is not very illuminating. "The antithesis between Protestantism and Catholicism may provisionally be conceived thus: the former makes the individual's relation to the church dependent on his relation to Christ, while the latter, contrariwise, makes the individual's relation to Christ dependent on his relation to the church." [1] According to this formula

[1] Schleiermacher, *Christian Faith*, p. 103.

the church in Protestantism would be secondary in relation to faith, and the emphasis on the church as primary would be characterized as something specifically belonging to Rome. Much unrealistic, "Protestant" individualism has been dependent on this formula of Schleiermacher. That it is completely contrary to the words of Luther which we have quoted is apparent, and even on that basis we may assert that Schleiermacher has not expressed the relationship which is characteristic of evangelical Christianity. It is remarkable that his formula is really contrary to what he himself says in another place in his work. He asserts that the difference between evangelical and Roman interpretations of Christianity must not be stated so that the Roman emphasizes the priority of the fellowship and the Protestant stresses the individual life in faith, because the antithesis lies in the different conceptions of the nature both of the individual and the church's life.[2] The antithesis in regard to the conception of the church appears especially in the fact that Rome identifies the Christian church with the Roman Catholic church.

2. Membership in the Church

It is obvious that the conception of the church which holds that membership in the church is bestowed through God's call and election is of a different character from that which conceives of the church as an association of people with certain definite religious qualifications and achievements manifested in faith, confession, and conduct. Underlying these various notions are the intentions of producing as far as possible a "pure" church, a church made up of true believers and persons with a true Christian experience, in contrast to the church as "a mixed fellowship." Membership in the church becomes dependent on what can be determined in regard to a person's Christian life and whether this person's Christian experience is of such a character that it can be accepted.

It is clear, however, that this conception of the church is not consonant with but rather foreign to that conception of the church which we find in the New Testament. Here we do not meet the idea of a pure church in the sense previously indicated, nor the idea that certain distinct qualifications constitute the basis for member-

[2] *Ibid.*, p. 360.

ship in the church. In regard to the former it may be sufficient to refer to the parable of the weeds among the wheat, where the idea of establishing a congregation of only "sanctified" and "pure" members is definitely rejected. " 'Then do you want us to go and gather them?' But he said, 'No; lest in gathering the weeds you root up the wheat along with them. Let both grow together until the harvest' " (Matt. 13:28-30). We hear sometimes of the conception that the so-called pure church is the ideal, but that actual conditions are such that it cannot be realized. The latter part of this statement is undoubtedly correct, but according to the New Testament a pure congregation is not an ideal to be sought during this earthly existence. It is rather a utopia; and, what is worse, a utopia that is dangerous and fatal for the Christian church.[3]

Nor do we anywhere in the New Testament meet the idea that a person can qualify for membership in the church by any religious achievements. If we desire a really decisive proof of how foreign this idea is to the New Testament, we need only consider the account of Jesus' relation to the children and his word that to such belongs the kingdom of God (Mark 10:13-16, and 9:33-37). When Jesus admonishes the disciples to become as little children, it does not mean that he ascribes certain qualifications to children. On the contrary, it is perfectly evident that the children have no qualifications and that they receive their place in the kingdom only through the call of God. Consequently, the baptism of children is fully consonant with the whole spirit of the Gospels (cf. § 44). Jesus does not as a rule issue his call to those who are properly qualified; he had come to call, not the righteous, but sinners. A theory which would set human qualifications as the foundation for membership in the church is not only foreign to the New Testament, but contrary to the fundamental view of salvation which is presented there.

But what we have just said about the conception of the church and membership in the church must not be so interpreted as to obscure and depreciate faith, confession, sanctification, and a life of

---

[3] What we have said does not mean that the church should cease being a tangible reality. Its tangibility does not depend on the fact that "both grow together until the harvest." In other words, it does not depend on sin, but on the grace of God. It refers to the totality of means and instruments which the Spirit employs in his work, which obviously is not without result.

service in love. The idea is sometimes advanced that the conception of the church which makes membership dependent on definite religious qualifications places a stronger demand on the Christian life than the conception which starts with the call of God. But this represents a false statement of the problem. Through the call of God the Christian is incorporated as a living member in the body of Christ. He is called to realize and actualize this membership. The relation between the gift of membership and the obligation it imposes meets us in the words of John 15:16: "You did not choose me, but I chose you and appointed you that you should go and bear fruit and that your fruit should abide; so that whatever you ask the Father in my name, he may give it to you." The call of God and his reception of man into the fellowship of his church confront man with the most serious obligations. There is no challenge greater than that which comes from God's revealed will to receive man into fellowship with himself in the church (cf. § 48). To change the question of the conception of the church into a question of stronger or lesser demands is to bypass the heart of the matter. It is not a question of an antithesis between a stronger or weaker emphasis on faith, sanctification, and the service of love, but of something entirely different, namely, the foundation of our membership in the church and how this membership is obtained. This foundation, at least as far as the New Testament is concerned, is not based on human achievement, but on God's call and election in Christ through the Word and the sacraments.

The Constitutive Factors of the Church

41. "The Means of Grace"

1. *The constitutive factors of the church.* The activity of the Holy Spirit which creates the church takes place through "the means of grace." These constitutive factors of the Christian church are God's holy Word, the sacraments, and prayer.

2. *The means of grace as an expression for the immediate activity of the Spirit.* "The means of grace" must not be understood in a mechanical way as factors which as a third element stand between God and man. Anything which to the Christian faith is "a means of grace" is so only because and in so far as the love of God thereby enters into a direct relation to man.

3. *The elasticity and stability of the means of grace.* The conception of the means of grace possesses both elasticity and stability. On the one hand, the boundary of the means of grace cannot be externally drawn, and on the other hand, all means of grace are defined by the event of Christ.

1. The Constitutive Factors of the Church

Since in the previous chapter we dealt with the nature of the church from various points of view, our task now is to discuss those factors which are essential to the work of the Spirit and which therefore have a constitutive significance for the church. Theology has called these constitutive factors of the church "the means of grace." Several well-founded objections may be made against the use of this phrase. It is apparent that it has given rise to a certain mechanistic conception of the ways in which the Spirit of God works in the creation of the church. The very expression, *"means* of grace," easily leads to the view that we are concerned here with something separated from the divine Spirit, or something standing between the Spirit and man. But the phrase has also the merit of emphasizing that the purpose of everything in the church is the establishment of the "kingdom of grace" (§ 37, ¶ 3), a kingdom in which God realizes the dominion of his love. The phrase may be used, therefore, as long as it is clear that the Spirit is not separated from the means of grace, but constitutes their living power (cf. § 2).

In the second chapter of Acts life in the ancient church is described in these words: "And they devoted themselves to the apostles' teaching and fellowship, to the breaking of bread and the prayers" (Acts 2:42). The constitutive factors in this "fellowship," this *koinonia*, were the apostolic message, sacramental communion with the Lord, and prayer. These constitutive factors are the same for the church of Christ today as in the early church. The means of grace are: The Word, the sacraments, and prayer.

On the basis of the description of the church in Acts we designate prayer as a means of grace, although this does not conform to traditional usage. No one can deny, however, that prayer is an essential "mark" of the church, a center of the church's spiritual power—and thus a means of grace. In this respect we may join with Schleiermacher in *Der christliche Glaube*, when in the section dealing with "the essential, unchangeable, fundamental features of the church" he follows his exposition of the Word, sacraments, and office of the keys with a discussion of "prayer in the name of Jesus." The reluctance with which prayer has been regarded as a means of grace has doubtless been due to the fact that prayer has been interpreted as an exclusively human act in which man turns to God, and therefore, it is argued, prayer cannot have the character of a means of grace. It is quite evident, however, that this argumentation is not very cogent, since prayer is not only our turning to God, but also God's approach to us, and a mode through which God accomplishes his loving will (cf. § 46). Since this aspect of prayer is an essential part of its meaning, we are justified in speaking of prayer as a means of grace.

2. The Means of Grace as an Expression for the Immediate Activity of the Spirit

We have already stated that the expression, "means of grace," tends toward a more or less mechanical conception of the work of the divine Spirit. The means of grace are understood as a third element which stands between God and man; while in reality these means are nothing less than the modes of God's immediate dealings with man. In the history of Christianity we note a certain conflict between a mechanical conception of the means of grace and an opposition to the idea of any kind of means. This latter viewpoint asserts that the conception of means of grace tends to destroy the immediacy of the Christian fellowship with God. Man does not really come directly to God, but comes in contact with certain "means of grace" which take the place of God. Thus the question can arise: does God work immediately or through means? The fanatical, mystical, and spiritualizing approach holds to the first of these alternatives. It can easily be explained why this opposition to the "means of grace" has appeared again and again within Christianity. The cause is that hardened and mechanical conception of the means of grace which has appeared not only within the church of Rome but also in evangelical theology and which ultimately rests on a conception of God as an extramundane being who sits enthroned in exalted majesty and therefore can deal with men only through some intermediary means. But the Christian faith has had good reasons to reject a conception which gains immediacy for the relationship between God and man at the price of surrendering the means of grace. This way leads to a suppression of the living revelation, not to the desired immediacy. The danger is that the relation between God and man loses its content, and that we cannot escape from the charmed circle of our own ego. The mechanical conception of the means of grace cannot be replaced by negations, but only by a deepened insight into the character of these means. It will then become apparent that this problem is not real and that God works immediately precisely when he works "through means." The idea that the means of grace could be understood as an independent factor between God and man is completely foreign to faith. The means of grace are nothing but those modes through which God continually realizes his loving will. In the means of grace God does not merely give certain gifts, he gives nothing less than himself. Wherever faith encounters a means of grace, it encounters God himself, who is the immediately and effectively active God. The means of grace tell us that God is not only the distant and hidden God, he is the living God who is active in the present and works "immediately" wherever he works. Therefore Christian faith is opposed to a false conception of the means of grace on two fronts: it rejects a mechanical objectivity, and also a spiritualizing dissolution of the means of grace.

3. The Elasticity and the Stability of the Means of Grace

It is clear from the previous discussion that the concept of the means of grace possesses a relatively high degree of elasticity. Christian faith has no interest in circumscribing the compass of the means of grace. On the contrary, it must oppose all such attempts, inasmuch as it would inevitably eventuate in a diminution of the rich connotations inherent in the concept of the means of grace. In regard to the elasticity it may be said that there is a certain degree of difference between these means, since this elasticity is less marked in the case of the sacraments. But the means of grace also possess a definite stability. If they cannot be circumscribed by eternal boundaries, they can so much the more readily be identified on the basis of that inner character which distinguishes them as means of grace. The stability in the concept of the means of grace rests on the fact that Christ is the Lord of the divine revelation and that the establishment of the church by the Spirit signifies throughout a realization of the reign of Christ. The Christian faith knows of no means of grace which are not characterized and defined by the event of Christ. The Word as a means of grace, both Scripture and the oral word, has its center in him who is "the Word." The sacraments are also inseparably connected with the work of Christ. Baptism is a baptism in the name of the Father, the Son, and the Holy Spirit; and the Lord's Supper receives its content from that act of Christ in which divine love became victorious through sacrificial self-giving. Prayer as a means of grace is prayer in the name of Christ. As such it is connected with the answer to prayer; or, in other words, as such it is God's approach to the souls of men. Christ is, therefore, the ruling power of the means of grace. We have already stated this by saying that the means of grace are the modes of the activity of the Holy Spirit, since the Holy Spirit is also the Spirit of Christ.

42. The Word of God

1. *The Word as message.* "The Word" as a means of grace is the self-impartation of divine love in the form of *a message.* This message authenticates itself as the Word of God through the testimony of the Spirit. The criterion is not that man autonomously decides what is "the Word of God," but, on the contrary, that the Spirit in and through the content of the Word subdues man and places him under "the reign of the Word."

2. *The sure and living Word.* In and through its incarnation in Christ, the Word of God is something given once and for all; it is anchored in the holy Scriptures. But in and through the continuing work of Christ it is at the same time living and continually active in the present.

3. *Two misconceptions.* The Christian conception of the Word as a means of grace must be distinguished from two extreme viewpoints: in the first place, from that approach which through theories of inspiration and proofs mechanizes the Word and ignores the fact that the Word comes to us in the form of human testimony; and in the second place, from that approach which conceives of man as autonomous in relation to the Word, thus destroying the character of the Word as a divine message and separating the Spirit from the Word.

4. *Note on law and gospel.* The Word of God is in part law, in part gospel. Both of these are essential to the church. The church lives by the gospel. But it must also guard the sanctity of God's law.

5. *Note on the position of the Old Testament.* The position of the Old Testament is determined by its connection with the revelation of God in Christ. The Old Testament is the prerequisite for the New, and the New is the standard for the interpretation of the Old.

1. The Word as Message

When the Reformation through Luther emphasized the Word as the central means of grace in the church, this implied a new discovery as far as the theology of the Middle Ages was concerned. The medieval church conceived of divine grace as being completely associated with and active through the sacraments. The Word was significant only as doctrine and law. It is noteworthy that when the theologians of the older Franciscan school presented the idea of the Word as "prevenient grace," they were thinking of that law which produces a certain contrition in man and thereby prepares him for the "real" grace which comes through the sacrament. Luther regarded the whole medieval conception of the means of grace as a degradation of the Word. It can be asserted that the entire work of the Reformation is connected with the discovery that the Word which God speaks to men is the means through which his grace, i.e., his forgiving and life-giving love, comes to men. Even though this was a discovery of something that had been obscured in the Latin theology of the Middle Ages, it was nevertheless a rediscovery of what is essentially Christian and from the beginning had constituted the center of Christianity—since in the primitive church everything was concentrated in the message, the gospel, as it came in apostolic preaching *as well as* in the sacraments.

The Word as a means of grace signifies for Christian faith the self-impartation of divine love in the form of a *message*. It is not simply a question of the impartation of a doctrine which man could theoretically appropriate, or that certain subjective "religious experiences" are expressed in words. The Word appears as a divine message. It is important to emphasize this point of view in contrast both to an intellectualized reinterpretation of "the Word" and to a psychological dissolution of it.[1]

If the Word as a means of grace has the character of a message addressed to men, it must be further underscored that this message is to faith a direct expression of the voice of God speaking to men. It is not a question of an impartation of the divine and saving will through certain intermediaries; it is divine love itself which is active in this message and which in grace and judgment directly approaches men. The Word comes to man, not as a word from man himself, or

[1] During recent times the concept of the Word has been the object of much theological research. Dialectic theology has used the Word as a principal concept, and has strongly emphasized that the Word is God's direct word to men, *senkrecht von Oben*, which confronts man with the necessity of making a decision. It has turned its polemic especially against the psychologizing dissolution of the concept of the Word common in the theology of the nineteenth century (cf. Emil Brunner, *Die Mystik und das Wort;* Karl Barth, *The Doctrine of the Word of God*, trans. G. T. Thomson [Edinburgh: Clark, 1936]). As far as Swedish theology is concerned, these conceptions of the Word do not contain anything new. Long before the rise of dialectic theology Einar Billing, in his work, *De stiska tankarna i Urkristendomen*, and elsewhere had emphasized the character of the Word as a message. He conceived of the preaching both of Jesus and the apostles from this point of view. The view of Billing is preferable to that of dialectic theology, since in his conception the character of the Word as a means of *grace* is much more clearly expressed.

originating within himself, but as a strange Word, a voice "from above." It comes indeed in the form of a human word, but it is not the word of men but of God himself. Faith receives the Word not "as the word of men, but . . . as the word of God" (I Thess. 2:13; Gal. 1:11); it is God who in the Word does the speaking and acting. It authenticates itself as a divine word through "the inner testimony of the Spirit." "God must tell you in your heart: this is God's word" (Luther). The conviction does not come through any external demonstration. It occurs inwardly, because the Word comes with an authority which man cannot escape, and which captures and subdues man. The conception of faith in regard to what occurs here would be completely obscured if it were asserted that man himself according to his own pleasure decides whether or not he will accept the Word as the Word of God. According to the viewpoint of faith man has no standard whatever whereby he can presume to judge and decide whether or not a certain word is the Word of God. The "conscience" of man cannot be regarded as such a standard. Conscience cannot be the court of last appeal, nor can it render an infallible decision. On the contrary it must be said that conscience is captive "under obedience to the Word." The authority is not in man, but in the Word itself. The Word confronts man with an authority from which there is no appeal. If man submits to the Word and receives it as the Word of God, it is not on the basis of subjective discretion, but because he cannot escape its inner compulsion. The Word convicts through its own content and character. If faith says that the conviction comes as a result of the inner testimony of the Spirit, it is the same as saying that it occurs through the content of the Word and through its own inherent power. Because the Word is a direct expression of and actualizes the divine will, there is, in the words of the older evangelical theology, a *mystica verbi cum spiritu sancto unio intima et individual* [2] [an intimate and personal mystical union of the Word with the Spirit].

The old evangelical theology was guided by a correct intention, which agrees with the viewpoint of faith itself, when it rejected the idea that the word of Scripture contains God's will but not God's power, and that the power comes from the Spirit who works in the

[2] Hollazius, *Examen theologicum acroamaticum,* II, 452.

souls of men in conjunction with the Word. This was rightly regarded as undermining the conception of the Word as a means of grace. This conception obscured the inherent and convicting power of the Word. The *way* in which this older evangelical theology maintained the presence of the Spirit in the Word, by its doctrine of verbal inspiration and the idea that the Spirit dwells in Scripture even "apart from its use," was quite unsound and led to a mechanical conception of the means of grace. But the intention and purpose were legitimate. These theologians perceived that the character of the Word as a means of grace is intimately connected with the fact that the testimony of the Spirit cannot be separated from the convicting and subduing power which is inherent in the content of the Word and through which man is placed under "the government of the Word."

2. The Sure and Living Word

The Word which is active as a means of grace is at one and the same time a sure and a living Word. The sureness of the Word rests on the fact that "the Word" has become embodied and incarnate in Christ. "The Word became flesh and dwelt among us" (John 1:14). The Word is "sure" both in the sense that its meaning is clear and definite, and that, as given once and for all, it stands fast as the unshakable Word of God valid for all times and generations (cf. I Tim. 1:15; II Tim. 2:11; Tit. 1:9). The incarnate Word is at the same time a living Word, not only because it appears in a living person, but especially because "Jesus Christ is the same yesterday and today and for ever" (Heb. 13:8) or, in other words, because his finished work unceasingly becomes living and active in his continuing work (cf. §§ 27, 28). Both of these points of view, the sureness of the Word and its living character, apply to the word of Scripture as well as to that oral message which from the earliest times has been proclaimed in the church. The task of preaching is to make the message of Scripture living and relevant to every new generation, or to act as a herald of its living message. In so far as preaching fulfils its task, its proclamation is in itself a living Word of God, essential for the life of the church.

The Word incarnate in Christ is anchored to the Scriptures. Christian faith regards the Word of Scripture as the fundamental and normative Word of God. The message which is proclaimed through the ages is received from and determined by this Word of God. The dominant place Scripture occupies in the Christian life of faith does not rest on theories which attempt to demonstrate the divine authority of Scripture; its positive foundation is the fact that Christian faith is Christocentric, that Christ is the central content of Scripture, and that every message about the act of God in Christ is derived from and determined by the message of Scripture. To set aside the scriptural Word of God would be the same as setting aside Christ and the Word incarnate in him.

The Bible has throughout the ages abundantly demonstrated its right to this foremost place. It has authenticated itself as the incomparable and inexhaustible source of power of the Christian church; one might be tempted to add, as a source which has become richer because it has been active in each generation. There has been no renewal of Christian life which has not received its power from the Scriptures, and which has not *become* a renewal precisely because it received its power from this source. When Christian life has been removed from this center of power, it has been weakened and has lost its inner strength. This indicates more clearly than anything else the significance of the Scriptures as the center of spiritual power for the Christian church. When the message of the biblical Word of God is not isolated but is seen in its connection with every living Christian message, the Bible demonstrates its superiority as the Christian book of life above all others and as the central Word of God.

3. Two Misconceptions

The viewpoint of faith in reference to the Word as a means of grace must be distinguished from two misconceptions: a mechanistic objectivization and a spiritualistic dissolution.

The mechanical objectivizing of the Word appears as soon as the attempt is made to support or demonstrate the character of the Word as a Word of God by rational arguments, thus obscuring the fact that the Word always manifests itself in the form of a human testimony. We meet such a mechanical objectivizing in the theory of verbal inspiration, which originated in the Middle Ages and has been associated with all scholastic theology. But it appears not only in this special theory, but in all theories of inspiration in the measure that these involve a rational demonstration, and an obscuring of the human aspect of the Word. This mechanical objectivizing is contrary to the actual attitude of faith and to the real character of the Word. It is contrary to the attitude of faith, since faith does not submit to the Word because its divine authority has been demonstrated, but because the power of the Word itself compels submission, or, in other words, because of the inner testimony of the Spirit.

From the point of view of faith a completely foreign approach obtains when Melanchthon and later scholasticism add to the testimony of the Spirit a number of arguments which are intended to support and prove the divine authority of Scripture. Here things are joined which do not belong together. Where the testimony of the Spirit is found, all other arguments are superfluous and irrelevant; and where it is not found, no other arguments can serve as substitutes. Mechanical objectivizing is contrary also to the nature of the Word, since the Word always appears as a human testimony. From the point of view of faith the Word has a twofold character. From one point of view it is in its entirety a human testimony. Scripture is a collection of historical documents of religion. But in the midst of all the human and incidental, in these religious documents of man faith discerns the divine voice, the Word of God, speaking with unconditional and inescapable authority directly from God to man. The Word of God comes in the "form of humiliation." These conditions under which the Word of God exists cannot be improved or overcome by any kind of theories of inspiration, or by arguments that are designed to protect the Bible from its "humanity." Faith always discovers the revelation of God in "secret," in the human covering that hides it. This universal and fundamental rule applies also to the Word of God, both in Scripture and in preaching.

The point of view of Christian faith with reference to the Word as a means of grace must also be distinguished from a spiritualistic dissolution of the Word. This approach may appear in various forms: as mysticism, rationalism, and humanizing idealism. However much these types may differ from one another, they have in common the characteristic that in one way or another they separate the Spirit from the Word. When this occurs, the Word loses its character as a divine revelation. The Word becomes a human word. The boundary between "the highest human" and the divine becomes uncertain, and the human becomes autonomous in relation to "the Word of God." The supposedly higher immediacy of mysticism in the fellowship with God means in reality that "the divine" is sought and found in "the depths of the soul," consequently in "the highest human." In rationalism the eternal rational ideas inherent in the nature of man become the standard whereby "the Word" is measured and evaluated. Man appears as autonomous in relation to the Word also within the humanistic interpretation of Christianity influenced by idealism. There is no line of demarcation between the Spirit of God and the spirit of man. This is reflected most clearly in the fact that Christ is no longer regarded as the incarnation of the divine Word, but as the "religious archetype" of humanity, "the ideal man," who embodies in himself the religious and ethical ideal of humanity. The Word then ceases to be regarded as a strange word that comes to man and invites and compels him to submission.

4. Note on Law and Gospel

The Word of God comes to us as law and as gospel. The questions about the relationship of one to the other, and of the significance of the law, have been discussed in several sections of this book, especially 3, 21, 30-34, 48, and 49. Here we simply emphasize that the church is born of the gospel and lives by the gospel, and also that the church is under obligation to guard the sanctity of God's law. The church's relationship to God is of such a nature that all "legalism" has been overcome. But at the same time God's commandments and statutes remain sovereign as they reflect his struggle against and judgment of the evil powers. The gospel is the church's most precious possession. The proclamation of the church is primarily a proclamation of the gospel. It is, however, the duty of the church to maintain, interpret, and obey God's commandments and statutes, all of which have their source in his loving will and are concerned with human life as a whole.

5. *Note on the Position of the Old Testament*

The fact that the Christian church has received the Old Testament into the biblical canon implies that the Old Testament as well as the New must be interpreted from the point of view of the act of God in Christ (cf. § 3, ¶ 4 and § 7). The Old Testament is a prerequisite for the New. It describes the drama of revelation whose midpoint and climax is the event of Christ. Without the Old Testament the meaning of the New Testament could not be understood. Wherever the connection between the Old and the New Testaments was severed, as in Gnosticism and Marcion, the connection between creation and redemption was also severed, and the result was a misinterpretation of the meaning of redemption. The Old Testament receives its canonical significance for the Christian church as it is penetrated by the light which comes from the act of God in Christ.

43. The Sacraments

1. *The gospel in the form of action.* The sacraments are the self-impartation of divine love in the form of action. Among the holy rites which have been mentioned in this connection two are of special importance: baptism and the Lord's Supper. Their special position is due both to historical factors and to the fact that both in their own way fully embody the central content of the gospel.

2. *The significance of the sacraments.* The sacraments as means of grace do not mediate a different kind of grace from that received through the Word. Their significance lies rather in the peculiar form of these means of grace, in the certainty and concretion with which the sacraments actualize the gospel.

3. *Two misconceptions.* The Christian idea of the sacraments must be distinguished from two extreme views: a mechanical materialization, and a spiritualizing dissolution. In the former the grace of the sacrament becomes something other than the self-impartation of divine love, and in the latter the sacraments cease to be means of grace.

1. The Gospel in the Form of Action

In addition to the Word as a means of grace certain holy rites or sacraments must also be included among the centers of spiritual power of the church. These holy rites have occupied an important place in the Christian life from the very beginning. Exegetical research of the last few decades has emphasized this fact. When we come to determine which rites are to be included here, we must note that no unanimity on this question has been attained within Christendom. In the Orthodox as well as in the Roman church the number of sacraments has been fixed as seven: baptism, penance, confirmation, Lord's Supper, marriage, ordination, and extreme unction. We must note, however, that in evangelical Christianity all these holy actions also belong to the function of the church, with the exception of extreme unction, which in evangelical practice has been replaced by the Lord's Supper.

In this connection we must examine one of these actions more closely: i.e., penance—confession and absolution. The attitude of the Reformation to penance was to some extent uncertain, since at the beginning it was designated as a sacrament, although this designation was later discarded. But there was no uncertainty with regard to the significance of penance. This is emphasized strongly in the evangelical confessions. The Augsburg Confession contains an article on "Confession" in which is stated that "Private absolution ought to be retained in the churches, although in confession an enumeration of all sins is not necessary." In the Small Catechism there is a section on "how the common people are to be taught about confession." The Smalcald Articles speak about "the power of the keys" as one of the offices of the gospel. In the Small Catechism and in his sermons Luther emphasizes the significance of absolution, and that this should be received as God's own word of forgiveness. In contrast to this confession and absolution have been sadly neglected in later evangelical practice. As present there is, however, a growing realization of their importance in the pastoral care of the church.

The retention of baptism and the Lord's Supper as sacraments has generally been defended on the ground that these two sacraments were instituted by Jesus himself. Even though the word "instituted" has at present a meaning which cannot as such be identified with the usage in the Bible, it is clear that the biblical authors refer baptism as well as the Lord's Supper back to Jesus; but it should be noted that this is true also of "the power of the keys." Baptism is generally connected with "the great commission" in Matthew 28:18-20, and the Lord's Supper is associated with the narratives of Jesus' last meal with his disciples. Recent exegetical research has pointed out that the eucharistic pericopes must not be isolated from the important fellowship meals Jesus had with his disciples during his whole ministry. It cannot be denied that baptism and the Lord's Supper have from the very beginning been connected with the life of the church. The *koinonia* which is realized in the church has a distinctively sacramental character. "To live in Christ" is to participate in the church's sacramental fellowship with Christ.

What makes baptism and the Lord's Supper constitutive factors in the life of the church is not only their historical origin, but primarily their meaning. The criterion is that the sacraments in the form of action furnish a comprehensive expression of the central content of the gospel and are organically connected with the event of Christ. The sacraments appear to Christian faith as the self-impartation of divine love in the form of action. The two principal features which, as we have already indicated (§ 14), characterize this divine love, are concreted in baptism and the Lord's Supper. Baptism reveals the character of divine love as spontaneous and prevenient: it is the sacrament of prevenient love. The Lord's Supper reveals the self-giving of divine love in the event of Christ: it is the sacrament of suffering and victorious love. They are, therefore, not only historical "institutions," but rather actions of continuing divine grace.

2. The Significance of the Sacraments

When Christian faith regards the sacraments as means of grace it does not mean that the saving work of divine love could not be realized without sacraments. Such a point of view could be maintained only if the gift which is bestowed through the Word were regarded as a different kind and less valuable than the gift given in the sacraments. The assertion that the sacraments are means of grace does not in the least curtail other possibilities of divine love, a fact which the older evangelical theology clearly perceived.[1] But faith is not on this account led to despise the value of the sacraments.

---

[1] *Non defectus sed contemtus sacramenti damnat* [Not the absence but the despising of the sacrament condemns].

Faith is not interested in rationing the grace of God. It does not ask whether it is possible to dispense with one or the other of the means of grace; it asks rather what "means" the divine and loving will appears to use in order to realize its purposes. It finds that there is such a treasure in the sacraments as means of grace that the Christian fellowship cannot without detrimental effects neglect their use.

In this connection we must emphasize that the Reformation's concentration on the Word in no way implied a depreciation of the sacraments. Such a depreciation was entirely foreign both to Luther and to Calvin. The sacrament was not regarded as a secondary means of grace. Luther's fight against the Roman doctrine of the sacrifice of the mass was not in the interest of depreciation but rather for a restoration of the sacrament to its full Christian dignity. An evaluation of the sacraments in such a way that the Word would be given a higher rank was totally foreign to him. Christ himself is present in the sacraments as well as in the preaching of the Word. This conception excludes any evaluation as to rank.

If we are to define the significance of the sacraments as means of grace, we must first definitely assert that it does not lie in the fact that they mediate a special kind of "grace," or any other grace than that which comes to man through the Word. All attempts to attribute a special kind of grace to the sacraments lead to a weakening and disqualification of divine grace. Christian faith knows of no other grace than that which consists in the self-impartation of divine love, or, in other words, the fact that God gives himself. It is therefore clear that the sacraments could not be regarded as means of grace unles it is a question of the self-impartation of divine love, and that all notions about other gifts do not imply an addition or a higher gift, but rather a subtraction and something less. Faith cannot think of a greater gift than God himself. In that gift all other gifts are included, and without this gift all others are from the point of view of faith of no value. The legitimate element in the oft-repeated statement of the old evangelical theology, *idem est effectus sacramenti et verbi* [sacrament and Word have the same effect], lies in the fact that the gift of both the Word and the sacrament is nothing else and nothing less than the divine love which restores and unites men to God. If, therefore, Christian faith cannot credit the sacraments with bestowing a gift different from that received through the Word, it is clear that their specific significance for the Christian life depends on that special form in which the loving will of God here is expressed.

The question of the significance of the sacraments for the Christian life cannot at this point be discussed in detail; the final answer must be given in the discussion on the meaning of baptism and the Lord's Supper (§§ 44, 45). The general point of view, however, should be emphasized here—that the importance of the sacraments is connected with the fact that in baptism and the eucharist the central content of the gospel meets us *in a concentrated way in the form of an act*. The uniqueness of the sacraments lies in the peculiar form, an act, but this form is important because the sacramental act reveals the inmost nature of the Christian gospel. The significance lies in that certainty and concretion with which the sacramental act objectifies the gospel. The Word as a means of grace manifests its richness by presenting the gospel in the multifarious form of a personal testimony, but in the sacraments the loving will of God appears in the simple act, in a direct and certain form. This difference between the Word and the sacraments must not be emphasized too one-sidedly. If we say that divine love meets us as a message in the Word and as an act in the sacraments, these two forms must not be exclusively separated. In a certain sense the message of the Word is also an "act," and as a divine message it is the most powerful act of God. The sacramental act also has the character of a message. Precisely because this act reflects the inmost core of the gospel, it is the most concentrated gospel message which can be given. Word and sacrament are inseparably connected with one another in the service of the gospel. As pure actions the sacraments are nothing apart from the Word. But the sacrament serves as a guardian of the Word. When the fulness of the gospel meets us in the form of sacramental action, the sacrament protects the Word from becoming intellectualized into a "teaching," and from becoming decentralized.

Evangelical theology often speaks of the sacraments as a *verbum visibile*, "a visible word." The combination has the merit that it unites the Word and the sacraments, and emphasizes that the sacraments have the character of a message. It may be argued, however, that the formula, "a visible word," too strongly emphasizes the visual element, and that it does not call attention to the most essential character of the sacraments, namely, the action. In regard to the treatment accorded the sacraments by evangelical theology, it can be said that it reveals a certain monotonous repetition. The theologians have been satisfied to emphasize the very important fact that the gift received in the sacraments is the same as that received through the Word without trying to analyze the significance of the fact that here the gospel meets us in a concentrated way, in the form of an act.

It should also be noted that the sacramental act inseparably unites individual and congregational points of view. The sacramental act is always directed toward the individual, but it is at the same time a corporate act. These two points of view are also present in preaching, with sometimes one and sometimes the other point of view appearing more prominently. But it cannot be denied that this union of individual and congregational viewpoints is constitutive for the sacraments. Baptism is an act concerning the individual child, but at the same time an act through which the church is established. The Lord's Supper edifies and strengthens the church at the same time that it concerns the individual believer.

3. Two Misconceptions

The Christian conception of the sacraments must be differentiated from two extreme views: A sensuous mechanization of sacramental grace, and a spiritualistic dissolution of the sacraments as means of grace.

The history of the Christian sacraments indicates clearly that from the very beginning there have been certain dangers in the direction of mechanization connected with the sacramental idea. The most serious danger is that the sacraments come to be conceived of as working *ex opere operato*, i.e., through the mere performance of the act. Traces of this idea seem to meet us even in Paul (I Cor. 15:29). This conception is always more or less connected with the idea that the sacraments work in a physical way, or, in other words, that sacramental "grace" is reduced to a plane below personal and spiritual fellowship with God.

The mechanistic and materialistic conception of the sacraments arises when the sacraments are interpreted as "realistic" rather than "symbolic." Divine grace becomes a substance. The gift received is conceived of as something else, and therefore something less, than the self-impartation of divine love. A dissolution of the character of the sacrament as a means of grace occurs when the sacramental act is conceived of as "symbolic" in contrast to "realistic." The emphasis is then placed on human activity as such and the sacrament loses its character as a divine gift and an act of grace.[2]

The sacramental act is to Christian faith at the same time a symbolic act and a real deed of God. When the question is asked: are the sacraments symbols *or* are they real acts of God or of Christ? the question itself is entirely misleading. It is not a question here of an either-or, but of a both-and. The one does not exclude the other. To maintain the "symbolic" view in contrast to the "realistic" implies the abrogation of the sacraments as means of grace. To maintain the realistic in contrast to the symbolic implies a materialization of the presence of God. Neither of these approaches expresses the characteristic viewpoint of faith. Just as all our words about God have a symbolic character, it is clear to faith that the same is true also of sacramental acts. But this does not imply a denial of the *real and effective* presence of the divine will of love. As far as faith is concerned the essential thing is that the loving will of God realizes its purpose in these symbolic acts.

44. The Sacrament of Prevenient Grace

1. *Baptism as an act of God.* Baptism is the act of God's prevenient grace through which man is received into fellowship with the body of Christ, the church. Herein lie both the gift and the obligation of baptism.

[2] From this starting point it has been common to characterize all realistic interpretations of the Lord's Supper as "magic." The term was often carelessly applied in nineteenth-century theology, as if every thought of the presence of Christ in the Lord's Supper must be branded as "magical." But, as von Hügel rightly says (*Essays and Addresses*, p. 241): "Magic begins only when and where things physical are taken to effect spiritual results apart altogether from minds transmitting or receiving."

2. *The validity of infant baptism.* The validity of infant baptism rests on the fact that the grace of God is a prevenient grace. Infant baptism imposes upon the church an obligation and a responsibility toward baptized children.

3. *Misinterpretations of the Christian view of baptism.* The Christian view of baptism must be distinguished from a mechanical interpretation of the effect of baptism, as well as from spiritualizing interpretations which nullify the primacy of grace.

1. Baptism as an Act of God

In its treatment of baptism systematic theology cannot enter into the problem of its origin or analyze its history. Our interest is concentrated on the question of what is essential to baptism as a Christian sacrament, or, in other words, the question of the meaning of Christian baptism.

In elucidating the meaning of baptism, it might seem natural to start with the fact that it is an act through which the church incorporates new members into its fellowship. Baptism is, of course, just such an action of the church; but this does not reveal either the whole or the essential truth of its meaning. What is essential is that baptism is an act of God's prevenient grace, and that it is through God's grace alone that man is received into that church which is the body of Christ. Baptism is primarily an *actio* of God, with respect to which the church's act is a *re-actio*.[1]

The act of God in baptism is at the same time an act of Christ, an act through which Christ builds his church on earth. Because it is an act of Christ it is an act of God. Behind this act of Christ in the present stands his whole ministry from the incarnation to the cross and the resurrection. It is this work which he continues when, invisibly present in the Spirit, he receives new members into his church and makes them members in his body: "For by one Spirit we were all baptized into one body" (I Cor. 12:13). Christian baptism is therefore a baptism in the name of the Father, the Son, and the Holy Spirit.

The question whether baptism is a symbolic act, a "sign," or a real act of God is, in view of what we have said here, irrelevant. Baptism is both one and the other. It is not only a symbolic act

[1] T. F. Torrance, "Eschatology and the Eucharist," in D. M. Baillie and J. Marsh (eds.), *Intercommunion* (London: S.C.M., 1952), p. 31.

or a sign. Not even the expression, "an effective sign," states clearly what is involved. If we speak of baptism as a sign, it is a sign in the same sense as the works of Christ during his earthly ministry were "signs." Baptism is in other words really a divine "act of power."

The gift bestowed in baptism involves primarily membership in the *ekklesia* of Christ together with all the blessings and obligations inherent in this membership. Baptism is an incorporation into that *koinonia* in which Christ is the life-giving Lord. Thus the apostle can say: "For as many of you as were baptized into Christ have put on Christ" (Gal. 3:27). This membership depends entirely on God's prevenient grace. Baptism tells us that God's love toward us is the sole and secure foundation of the Christian life, that our freedom from "the power of darkness" and our fellowship with God is in his hand and originates in his gracious will. Baptism translates us into "the kingdom of his grace." In this sense baptism is "a new birth" (John 3:5 ff.), an incorporation into that new creation which has come in Christ: "If any one is in Christ, he is a new creation; the old has passed away, behold, the new has come" (II Cor. 5:17). This incorporation into "the new creation" does not involve a change in man, but a change in his situation, his status, and his conditions of life.

But although baptism primarily involves a participation in the body of Christ, it must not be understood simply as an act of initiation. Baptism does not look toward the past but to the future, both in regard to life in the church of Christ and in regard to the eschatological consummation. The intention of baptism is that man shall receive the gift in obedience of faith, and then grow "to mature manhood, to the measure of the stature of the fulness of Christ" (Eph. 4:13; cf. 4:16-19). Baptism means a new existence: to die with Christ, and to live with him; to die from sin and to live with and by Christ, to be "united with him" (Rom. 6:5). But this new existence is not something which the believer himself can create and develop through his own efforts. It is given to him in God's gracious act, and through the work of the Spirit it becomes his possession and the content of his life in the obedience of faith. This is the tremendous responsibility which is inseparably connected with baptism. It is possible to lose the grace of baptism, the gift of being incorporated into the body of Christ. But a situation can never arise where baptism can no longer be of any help, because baptism remains as an irrevocable expression of God's redemptive will.

It is clear from our discussion that this conception of baptism is inseparably connected with the doctrine of "justification by faith alone." Opportunity for a conflict between these two would arise only if "faith" were allowed to take the place of the grace of God. But "justification by faith alone" does not mean that man is saved by his faith as an achievement of his own power. The meaning is rather that man is saved by grace alone and by the unmerited love through which in Christ men become the children of God.

2. The Validity of Infant Baptism

Baptism in the Christian church is administered either to adults or to children. The legitimacy of infant baptism was not questioned until relatively modern times. From the days of the early church infant baptism was regarded as something self-evident. This fact is not at all surprising. If baptism is an act of God's prevenient grace, the validity of infant baptism is immediately established. Infant baptism proclaims with unmistakable clarity that membership in the church of Christ rests on nothing else than God's unmerited grace and love. The question whether infant baptism was practiced in the New Testament becomes, from this point of view of secondary importance. Everything indicates that infant baptism was administered also in the New Testament church. But the important consideration is that infant baptism is directly in line with the gospel proclamation of grace. The saying of Jesus that children belong in the kingdom of heaven could hardly have been understood in any other way than that children had equal right with adults to membership in the messianic community. If they did not have this right, they could not have belonged to the kingdom of heaven. The meaning and significance of the narrative in Mark 10:13-16 can be understood only if we accept it as a defense of infant baptism.

Attacks on infant baptism have no foundation in the New Testament. It is easily understandable, however, that opposition to infant baptism should arise when the conception of baptism became mechanized, when the action in the sacrament was conceived of as taking place *ex opere operato,* and when consequently the church was regarded as the sum total of baptized persons. But such an interpretation is foreign to the New Testament. The church is neither "the total number of the baptized," nor "the total number of believers." It is rather Christ in indissoluble union with the people belonging to him, the communion in which the Spirit is active, and where the new covenant is actualized in the mystery of the union with Christ. Those who question the validity of infant baptism must consider whether they do not deny the radicalism in the proclamation of the gospel of grace, and thereby also make God's gracious will dependent on human qualifications. When this happens, it indicates that a legalistic conception is making its way in.

As the creative factor of the church infant baptism removes all man-made hindrances out of the way to fellowship with God. It is the Magna Charta, which tells us that the membership of the individual in the church must not be made dependent on the examination and approval of men. No human caprice must be allowed to decide whether or not we may belong to the church of God. Infant baptism removes this guardianship and the heavy oppression it places on the spiritual life. It testifies that our membership in the church of Christ does not depend on the approval and acceptance of our fellow-men, but is founded on the loving will of God. We belong in the church of God on this basis alone, and we obtain what we possess in the measure that divine love subdues us and our fellowship with God is realized. It is possible that in our search and our spiritual struggle we may find the hearts of our fellow-men closed to us and the way of salvation obstructed by their precepts and ordinances. Then if we were dependent only on human judgments, we would stand on the outside, rejected. But infant baptism tears aside all these man-made hindrances, and testifies that we do not find the heart of God closed, and that even though faith is weak and the flame burns low, we nevertheless find room within the church of God.

But infant baptism is at the same time *the living conscience of the Christian church.* Infant baptism presupposes that it is possible to bring the baptized person into contact with the Christian spiritual life, and it stands as a living testimony of the obligation of the church to bring about this contact. Where this possibility is not present, baptism cannot be practiced in its highest form as infant baptism. The conditions under which infant baptism may be administered, therefore, are not only that a confessing church actually exists but also that the church has the possibility of caring for baptized children and providing them with Christian nurture.

3. Misinterpretations of the Christian Idea of Baptism

The Christian idea of baptism must be distinguished from two misinterpretations: the interpretation which speaks of the effect of baptism as mechanical and deals in ideas below the spiritual plane; and that which speaks of the human prerequisites for the reception of the grace of baptism in such a way that it abrogates the primacy of grace. We may add to this principal statement a few remarks about certain theories of infant baptism, which have appeared in the history of Christian thought.

At a relatively early time the biblical and early Christian conception of baptism became obscured. Instead of pointing eschatalogically toward life in the church of Christ and toward the consummation baptism was given a retrospective direction. The chief question was about the change in man which baptism was supposed to effect. In general the answer was given that baptism cleansed man from the inherited sinfulness inherent in human nature (cf. § 31). This was the effect of the grace "infused" in baptism. Grace was conceived of as an indefinable power, and the Spirit operating through this grace became an indeterminable potentiality separated from Christ. The contrast between this conception of baptism and that in the New Testament is obvious. Incorporation into the body of Christ through the redemptive act of God, which was central in the New Testament, was set aside in favor of a conception of a change in man through cleansing from the inherited sinfulness. The result was a false objectivity and a false subjectivity. When the rite of baptism by itself was thought of as producing this change, the result was a false, mechanistic objectivity. False subjectivity appeared because attention was drawn to the change which was supposed to take place in man. On the basis of this retrospective point of view the significance of baptism for the Christian life became obscured, and the way was opened for a doctrine of redemption which very subtly combined the idea of infused grace with a meritorious activity on the part of man.

In order to guard against all more or less mechanistic conceptions, the Reformers rightly emphasized that the gift of baptism is received only in and through faith. It was less fortunate when evangelical theology, in dependence on ideas which Luther at one stage of his life advocated, sometimes drew the conclusion that some form of faith must be present in the infant or given to him in order that the significance of the act might not be lost. The danger of this idea is that it leads directly back to those conceptions, below the personal and spiritual level, which it was intended to avoid—even in the most sensitive matter of all, namely the concept of faith itself. At the same time this talk about a faith given to or "infused" in the little child through baptism serves to undermine and obscure the real significance of infant baptism. It produces the impression that it concerns unrealistic and unverifiable assertion. If the value of baptism is inseparably connected with an ability on our part to discover some faith in the child, it cannot be said that its value rests on any sure foundation. In reality this discussion about "faith" in the little child obscures entirely that which to Christian faith is the very heart of the matter, namely, that infant baptism is the act of election by divine love through which the baptized person receives and is assured of his right to membership in the church. This is the "objective" gift of baptism which exists before and independently of faith. It is a different matter that this membership given and secured through baptism is realized only in the measure that the fellowship with God in faith actually is realized.

45. The Sacrament of the Lord's Supper

1. *Controversial theology and interpretation of the Lord's Supper.* There have been many sharp conflicts in the Christian church about the Lord's Supper. In seeking to elucidate the meaning of the Lord's Supper theology cannot ignore these controversies. But it would fail its purpose if it were to contribute to the maintenance of ancient battle lines.

2. *The Lord's Supper as an action of Christ.* The Lord's Supper is the sacrament in which the living Christ actualizes his once-for-all per-

fected and eternally valid sacrifice. As Christ on the last evening included his disciples in the sacrifice of love which was presently to be fulfilled, so now he includes his disciples in every age in the perfected sacrifice of the same love. In the bread of life and the cup of blessing he gives himself to his own and thereby renews the fellowship of the new covenant.

3. *The gift*. The gift of the Lord's Supper consists in this communion between Christ and his church. It includes forgiveness of sins, life, and salvation. The communion of the Lord's Supper is to faith a living reality in the present, but it is at the same time a living hope. Holy Communion is a pledge and an anticipation of the life of the world to come. Communion with Christ is *eo ipso* a communion between the members of the church.

4. *The Lord's Supper as an action of the church*. The Lord's Supper is primarily an action of Christ. From this point of view light is shed on the Lord's Supper as an act of the church. As such the Lord's Supper is a eucharist: the church's reception of Christ and his gift with thanksgiving, praise, and prayer. This eucharistic sacrifice is connected with the confession of Christ, and reminds the faithful of the obligation to give themselves sacrificially in service to the brethren.[1]

1. Controversial Theology and
Interpretation of the Lord's Supper

Hardly any article of faith has caused such sharp antitheses and so much division in Christianity as the doctrine of the Lord's Supper. Even within the New Testament there is evidence of conflict. Both Paul and John struggle against conceptions influenced by gnosticism. Conflict about the meaning and practice of the Lord's Supper was one of the chief causes of the great schism in the sixteenth century, first between Rome and the Reformation, and then between the churches of the Reformation. After the Reformation these antitheses became more rigid. Through the centuries there has been a conflict on three fronts. Each one has remained in his own chosen position and attacked the others with formulas developed at the time of the schism, polished and refined with the help of a scholastic theology. This polemic appeared unchangeable and sterotyped. Rome has given repeated evidence of its inability to understand the religious factors which caused the Reformation. Lutheran theology

---

[1] Cf. Gustaf Aulén, *Eucharist and Sacrifice*, trans. Eric H. Wahlstrom (Philadelphia: Muhlenberg, 1958).

repeated its polemic against the doctrine and practice of the mass as this appeared toward the end of the Middle Ages, and at the same time attacked the Reformed theology as a spiritualizing dissolution of the sacrament. Reformed theology, on the other hand, attacked Lutheran theology's so-called doctrine of consubstantiation, and called it a compromise solution, a holding to both sides.

When we look back over this confessional warfare from fixed positions, it becomes evident that the attacks on the part of all three were frequently directed against something which the attacked refused to recognize as characteristic of their own standpoints. It is also evident that the formulas used were seldom suitable for giving a clear expression of fundamental religious intentions. To some extent this old, unchangeable warfare has been replaced at present by fruitful conversations across confessional boundaries. Where this has taken place, the debate has ceased being a quarrel over stereotyped formulas and has become an attempt to discover the religious reality behind them. Ecumenical endeavors and associations have had a significance in this respect that should not be underestimated. However, the most important reason is the strong biblical orientation which more and more characterizes theology within the various communions. It has become clear not only that the Lord's Supper occupied a central place within the ancient church, but also that it stands in an inner, organic relationship to the whole biblical conception of salvation and the church. It is obvious that the latter must be determinative in any attempt to interpret the meaning of the sacrament. To be sure, theology cannot ignore the antitheses in regard to the Lord's Supper which have appeared in the history of the church. The divisions which occurred at the time of the Reformation have taught us valuable lessons. But this does not mean that theology is compelled to abide by the questions and formulations which characterized the controversial theology in the centuries following the Reformation. What is the peculiar characteristic of one group is significant only if it helps to elucidate what is genuinely Christian, and in that process it ceases to be peculiar.[2]

[2] Yngve Brilioth has made a valuable contribution to our knowledge of the celebration of the Lord's Supper within the evangelical communions in *Eucharistic Faith and Practice*, trans. A. G. Hebert (New York: Macmillan, 1930).

343

2. The Lord's Supper as an Action of Christ

The Lord's Supper is one of the holy actions of the Christian church and has always been a part of its life. The forms of celebration manifest great varieties from the most primitive simplicity to the most elaborate, liturgical action. But wherever Holy Communion is celebrated, it has retained its connection with the event which took place on the last evening of Jesus' earthly life. As the Lord distributed bread and wine to his disciples then, so in the celebration in the church bread and wine are given to the guests at the table (except that in the Roman church laymen receive only bread). Everywhere Communion is celebrated in accordance with the words: "Do this in remembrance of me."

What we have said now is a fact which anyone may verify: the Lord's Supper is an action of the Christian church which is continually repeated. But with this statement we have really said nothing about the meaning of Communion for the Christian faith. What is essential and primary is that *the Lord's Supper is an action of Christ,* an action of the living Lord who is present in the Lord's Supper. Nothing more essential than this can be said about the Lord's Supper. Its sacramental significance rests solely on the fact that it is an act of Christ. From this point of view light is shed on the meaning of the sacrament as an act of the church. But if the conception of the Lord's Supper as an act of Christ becomes obscured or eliminated, the sacramental action of the church would lose its essential content. It would then be reduced to a memorial of what once happened, a memorial service commemorating the martyrdom of the cross. This would become a "memorial" of character entirely different from that found in the New Testament. The anamnesis in the New Testament is a remembrance which moves what happened in the past into the present and makes it a "present reality." [3] It is none other than the living Christ himself who makes the sacrifice of the cross a living reality in the present.

The living Christ has always been present in the celebration of the Lord's Supper. It was so at the last meal in the upper room. It was so likewise at the meals which the risen Lord shared with his dis-

[3] N. A. Dahl, *"Anamnesis,"* in *Studia Theologica* (1947), p. 82.

ciples according to the narratives in the Gospels and Acts (Luke 24:30 f., 42 ff.; John 21:13; Acts 10:41) and which may be regarded as an introduction to the celebration of the sacrament in the ancient church.[4] This presence of Christ did not cease when the risen Christ no longer showed himself to his disciples. The religious significance of the ascension (cf. § 27) lies in the fact that now the living Lord was raised above the limitations of time and place, and therefore could be with his own "always, to the close of the age." The Lord's Supper is the particular place where he has promised to meet his own. In that sense the ascension is the presupposition for the celebration of Communion within the church.

The starting point for all interpretation of the Lord's Supper is the fact that the sacrament is an action of Christ. Christ himself meets his church and serves it. He is the real, the high priestly "Celebrant."

The Christ who in the Lord's Supper serves his church is the heavenly High Priest. But this does not mean that his earthly ministry and his perfected sacrifice on the cross are neglected or obscured. The living Lord who in Communion serves his church is none other than the Crucified. What happens in the sacrament is that here Christ actualizes the sacrifice which began with the incarnation and was completed on the cross. This sacrifice has been made once for all, but this does not mean that it belongs to the past. The exaltation of Christ is the testimony that God has received the perfected sacrifice of reconciliation. Through the exaltation God has set his seal to the atoning sacrifice. Therefore the sacrifice of Christ is valid for all times and for all generations.

When Christ in the sacrament actualizes this atoning sacrifice we are not concerned with a new sacrifice which might so to speak be added to and complement the sacrifice made once for all. Nor is it a question of repeating, but rather of *actualizing* that perfect sacrifice. Christ made the sacrifice "once for all when he offered up himself" (Heb. 7:27; cf. 9:25 f.). "He entered once for all into the Holy Place . . . thus securing an eternal redemption" (Heb. 9:12). Still less is it a matter of offering up Christ in some sense in the Lord's

[4] Cf. Oscar Cullmann, *Early Christian Worship*, trans. A. S. Todd and J. B. Torrance (London: S.C.M., 1953).

Supper in order to propitiate God. Such a conception would deny the sufficiency and perfection of the sacrifice made once for all. It would also imply that through some effort on our part we help to "propitiate God." In reality no man has ever offered up Christ. What happened at the crucifixion was that men committed an outrage against the Holy One of God. It was not men who offered up Christ, but Christ who offered up himself for us—and God gave his only Son and offered him up for us all.

The Lord's Supper is inseparably connected with the sacrifice of Christ. However, this does not depend on our action but on his. Here he actualizes the sacrifice on the cross in its eternal validity and effectiveness. The perfect, that which once took place, here becomes the present. The effective presence of the sacrifice is insepa- rably connected with the presence of the living Lord. His "real presence" and his sacrifice belong together. But the living Lord can- not be present without actualizing his sacrifice in its complete effec- tiveness. As in that last evening Christ included his first disciples in love's atoning sacrifice which was presently to be fulfilled, so now in the Communion service he includes his disciples in every age in that same atoning sacrifice of love—now perfected. When on the evening before his death Christ gave the bread and the wine to the disciples with the words, "This is my body, this is my blood," he made them participants in the reconciliation which was to be effected through his sacrifice on the cross. In the same way through the bread and the wine and the words, "given and shed for you," he makes his disciples in every generation participants in his eternally valid atonement. That he has attached his active presence to the bread and the wine means that the sacrifice of his body and blood becomes effectively present, and that in this Holy Supper he comes "with every spiritual blessing in the heavenly places" (Eph. 1:3).

From what we have just said it is clear that the significance of the Lord's Supper for Christian faith depends entirely on the real presence of Christ. It is well-known that in the history of Christian thought the real presence has been subjected to various interpreta- tions and misinterpretations. If interpretation is to agree with bibli- cal testimony to Christ's presence in the Lord's Supper, it must be guarded against two opposite theories: one, spiritualizing theories which obscure the fact that in the Lord's Supper the living Christ actualizes the sacrifice finished on the cross; the other, materializing theories which obscure the fact that the presence of Christ in the Lord's Supper is the active presence of the heavenly Lord. Briefly we might say: one obscures the cross, the other the resurrection.

As far back as in the New Testament the apostles had occasion to speak against both of these tendencies. Both Paul and John fought against Gnostic and Docetic ideas, which in the Lord's Supper considered only the heavenly Lord and ignored the incarnate Christ and his cross. Paul therefore points out that the Lord's Supper is inseparably connected with death on the cross. "For as often as you eat this bread and drink the cup, you proclaim the Lord's death until he comes" (I Cor. 11:26). John is concerned with the same problem when his Gospel begins with "the Word became flesh," and when Christ later says: "my flesh is food indeed, and my blood is drink indeed" (John 6:55). But this same John also rejects the idea of a physical eating of the god which was prevalent in the mystery cults. Against Docetic spiritualism he says: "Unless you eat the flesh of the Son of man and drink his blood, you have no life in you" (John 6:53). But against conceptions of physical eating he says: "It is the spirit that gives life, the flesh is of no avail" (John 6:63). These two statements are not contradictory. The statement about the flesh does not mean a materializing of Christ's presence, and the statement about the Spirit does not mean a spiritualizing of it. The activity of the Spirit takes place "in the flesh"; the flesh is the means. However, it is not the flesh but the Spirit who gives life. The presence of Christ in the Lord's Supper, according to John, is the presence of the living and life-giving Lord and his Spirit. But this heavenly Christ is none other than he who has "come in the flesh." The presence of Christ is therefore inseparably connected with the sacrifice as indicated in the words about eating the flesh of the Son of man and drinking his blood. This involves participation in the finished work of redemption. John means to say that the presence of Christ in the Lord's Supper is as real as his presence with the disciples during the days of his earthly ministry.

This combination of concrete realism without becoming grossly physical, and of clear spirituality without becoming immaterial is also characteristic of the ancient church. Gradually certain changes took place. The conception was changed when the chief concern became not the actively present Christ but what happened to the elements in the Supper. Theology sought to solve this problem with the help of the conception of substance. Gradually two theories developed: transubstantiation and consubstantiation. According to the former the bread and the wine were changed into the body and blood of Christ and ceased to be bread and wine. This change provided the basis for the medieval doctrine of the sacrifice of the mass. The transubstantiated elements could be presented as a sacrifice which the church controlled and could offer. But such a conception could not be reconciled with a conception of the Lord's Supper in which the essential element was the active presence of Christ. The weakness in the Roman doctrine of the Lord's Supper is not in its emphasis on the idea of sacrifice (this is rather its strength), but in the wrong conception of sacrifice developed on the basis of the doctrine of transubstantiation.

During the later Middle Ages the theory of consubstantiation was developed in opposition to transubstantiation. According to this theory the body and blood of Christ are united with the communion elements, but without the latter ceasing to be bread and wine. Even though this theory was less objectionable, the idea of substance was still present and obscured the active presence of Christ. The theory of consubstantiation later became a part of Lutheran theology in the centuries following the Reformation. It is significant, however, that the word does not occur in Luther's writings. His tremendous emphasis on the real presence of Christ as living and active was incompatible with the concept of substance. As medieval theology with its starting point in the concept of substance arrived at the theory of transubstantiation, so Zwingli with the same starting point tried to locate "the substance" of Christ in heaven. What Luther's admittedly speculative doctrine of ubiquity really meant was that he was able to break loose from this dilemma. He rejected the alternative of localizing Christ *either* in heaven *or* in earth which was inevitably involved in the scholastic theology of substance. The real reason for Luther's intensive opposition against a spirtualistic interpretation was that it obscures the sacramental character of the Lord's Supper. It obscures the fact that the Lord's Supper involves a gift, and that this gift of Christ is given in a tangible and visible manner. If we despise the manner in which the gift comes, the gift itself becomes obscured, and the Lord's Supper is reduced to a mere act of commemoration and confession. It becomes limited to ideas suggested by the symbols of the Supper. But Luther says: "The Lord does not say, your thoughts about me are in me, or my thoughts are in you; but he says, you are in me and I in you." Because Christ is present, the external things, bread and wine, become the bearers of the heavenly gift.

It is not necessary to discuss in further details the struggles and conflicts which occurred during the age of the Reformation. From what has been said it is clear what must be done in order to follow the biblical direction. The essential point is that in the Lord's Supper the living Lord actualizes the sacrifice once finished on the cross; and those who receive him he thus unites in fellowship with himself. Through the bread of life and the cup of blessing he gives himself to his own and thereby constantly renews the fellowship of the new covenant.

3. The Gift

Baptism is the foundation sacrament; the Lord's Supper is the sacrament of renewal. In the Holy Communion the Lord renews the fellowship of the new covenant. The gift he bestows in Communion is therefore primarily communion with himself. In this gift all others are included. Whatever might be said further about these gifts is simply an explication of the meaning of communion with Christ. The word "Communion," used frequently as a designation of the Lord's Supper, calls attention to this central gift.

What are the gifts included in communion with Christ? In a short and pregnant formula in the Small Catechism Luther has expressed what is a part of common Christian faith: the gifts of "forgiveness of sins, life, and salvation are given unto us in the Sacrament." The significance of these words has already been discussed in §§ 33 and 34 in the discussion of the miracle of forgiveness and the new life. Here we must add a few words in view of the changes in interpretation and emphases which have taken place in the history of the Sacrament.

Within the Reformed Communions the gift of forgiveness of sins has often been emphasized so one-sidedly as to constrict its meaning. The one-sided emphasis appears in the reluctance to speak of the gift of the Lord's Supper as "life." To some extent the reason for this is the reaction against the description of the Lord's Supper as "the medicine of immortality" in the ancient church. Even though this expression may lead to a certain obscurity in regard to the conception of grace, it cannot be denied that the emphasis of the ancient church on "life" pointed to an essential part of New Testament teaching. We need only recall the words quoted above from the Gospel of John.

The constriction of the meaning of forgiveness which has frequently characterized piety since the Reformation appears in the negative conception of forgiveness as primarily a remission of guilt and punishment. This conception had certain serious consequences in regard to the doctrine of the Sacrament as a whole. On the one hand, the Lord's Supper came to be regarded as an appendix to the preparatory service with its confession of sin and absolution. On the other hand, the celebration of the sacrament received a somber character, and the eucharistic joy which characterized the celebration in the ancient church (cf. Acts 2:46) was much less in evidence. In reality the forgiveness of sins and the new life in fellowship with God are inseparably connected with one another. We cannot conceive of forgiveness without the new life, nor of the new life without forgiveness. In this respect Luther's words are valid: "for where there is forgiveness of sins, there is also life and salvation."

The new life of salvation is a life which faith possesses in the midst of the conditions of sin and death which belong to life here on earth. But it is at the same time a life under the sign of hope. When the gift of the Lord's Supper is designated as "salvation," it emphasizes that the gift is an earnest and an anticipation of "the life of the world to come." The Lord's Supper is an eschatological sacrament. Here we encounter both a "realized" and a future eschatology. The new age has come in Christ (Heb. 1:1 f.; I Pet. 1:20; I John 2:18). The Lord's Supper is the bearer of that salva-

tion which belongs to the age to come. As the Letter to the Hebrews
says, we have tasted the heavenly gift and the powers of the world
to come (Heb. 6:4-5). But the eschatology of the Lord's Supper is
also characterized by waiting: "*Maranatha;* Our Lord, come!"
(I Cor. 16:22) is its constant refrain. The Lord's Supper celebrated
on earth is a foretaste of "the great supper in heaven."

The great, all-embracing gift of the Lord's Supper is communion
with Christ. But this communion implies also a communion among
the members of the church. One cannot be separated from the other
as surely as Christ cannot be separated from his church. The gift
is given to each one individually. But this does not imply at all
an isolating individualism. The Lord's Supper belongs to the church
as a whole. It opens the gates wide to the communion of saints.
The fellowship of Holy Communion is not only a fellowship of
those who at the same time kneel together at the table of the Lord,
but also a fellowship with those who generation after generation
among all peoples and tongues have belonged to Christ. When, as
has often happened both in Roman and Protestant piety, the Lord's
Supper was interpreted from an excessively individualistic point of
view, the reason was that the conception of the church as *Corpus
Christi,* as the vine and the branches, became obscured and truncated. In Luther's *Treatise Concerning the Blessed Sacrament* (1519),
which for all its brevity is one of the richest and most important
writings on the Lord's Supper, we find a living and comprehensive
view of the church in connection with the sacrament. Luther never
tires of telling us how "Christ and all his saints" meet us in the
Lord's Supper and enter into fellowship with us. When you realize,
he says, that Christ and his saints are present to share everything
with you, then "you will experience what a rich and joyous wedding-
supper and festival your God has prepared upon the altar for you." [5]
We need hardly add that this conception of the church is anchored
firmly in the New Testament. Paul asks: "The bread which we
break, is it not a participation in the body of Christ?" (I Cor. 10:16).
We should also remember in this connection the words in the Letter
to the Hebrews: "But you have come to Mount Zion and to the city

[5] *WA* 2, 750; *Works of Martin Luther* (Phila. Ed.), II, 20.

of the living God, the heavenly Jerusalem and to innumerable angels in festal gathering, and to the assembly of the first-born who are enrolled in heaven, and to a judge who is God of all, and to the spirits of just men made perfect, and to Jesus, the mediator of a new covenant, and to the sprinkled blood that speaks more graciously than the blood of Abel" (Heb. 12:22-24).

The Lord's Supper is, therefore, the sacrament of Christian unity, even though differences in theories and practices have caused divisions within the church. The unity is present because the Lord's Supper is communion with Christ. However men think, speak, and act, the Lord's Supper remains the sacrament of Christian fellowship and unity. But this character of the Lord's Supper involves at the same time the most compelling obligation on the church to manifest this unity in its life (cf. § 50).

4. The Lord's Supper as an Action of the Church

When we speak of the Lord's Supper both as an action of Christ and as an action of the church, obviously we are speaking, not of two actions, but of the same action from different points of view. When Communion is celebrated in the church of Christ, not only the minister and the guests are present, but One who is greater—who is the High Priest "for ever after the order of Melchizedek" (Heb. 6:20). It is he who makes the Supper a sacrament. He himself is, as we said above, the real Celebrant with his human servants as means. As an action of the church the Lord's Supper is a service of worship; a worship which receives its character from the action of Christ that supplies its content.

In the previous sections we have stated that in the Lord's Supper the living Christ actualizes his perfected and eternally valid sacrifice, that he makes his people participants in the reconciliation God made through him, and that he thus incorporates them into fellowship with himself. But just as the sacrifice is the center in the action of Christ, so it is also when we think of the Lord's Supper as an action of the church. When we receive Christ as he comes to us in the Holy Supper, this reception in faith is characterized by an "offering" of thanksgiving and prayer.

As an action of the church the Lord's Supper is thanksgiving and praise, *eucharistia*, a eucharistic offering. The thanksgiving and praise are directed to "the Lamb that was slain," the living Lord, who by virtue of his perfect sacrifice is worthy to receive blessing, honor, and glory (Rev. 5:12-13). Hymns of praise accompanied the celebration of the Lord's Supper from the beginning. They belong to the church's celebration of the sacrament. For the Lord's Supper is not a requiem mass. It is a sacrament, not only of suffering love, but also of victorious love. The light of the resurrection illumines the celebration. The Christ who is actively in the Supper is the living Lord. The church greets him with the ancient coronation hymn, "Blessed be he who comes in the name of the Lord!" The celebration of the Lord's Supper must be characterized by hymns of praise and by thanksgiving to the God who out of unfathomable love has in Christ reconciled the world to himself. The ancient preface in the Service strikes the right note: "It is truly meet, right, and salutary, that we should at all times, and in all places, give thanks unto thee, O Lord, Holy Father, Almighty, Everlasting God." The eucharistic hymn of praise has often been weakened and subdued. It is essential that it be sounded full and clear, otherwise the glory of the Lord's Supper becomes obscured.

The celebration of the Lord's Supper is a eucharistic act, but it is also the church's most important act of prayer. Here the prayers of the individual guests are united in the church's common offering of prayer. We pray because God's sacrificial act of love in Christ meets us in the Lord's Supper, and because we know our sin, our unworthiness, and our need. The offering of prayer in the sacrament is a prayer "in the name of Jesus" in the fullest meaning of that formula. We and our prayers are united in Christ's sacrifice of reconciliation and in his high priestly prayer of intercession. Modern Anglican theology has properly emphasized this connection between the prayers of the church and the intercession which the heavenly High Priest offers in behalf of the church for which he has given his life.[6] This connection is suggested in several passages in the New Testament: "We have an advocate with the Father, Jesus Christ the righteous" (I John 2:1); Christ "always lives to make intercession

---

[6] Cf. A. G. Hebert, "A Root of Difference and Unity," in *Intercommunion*.

for them" (Heb. 7:25); Christ now appears "in the presence of God on our behalf" (Heb. 9:24). In union with his church Christ takes its prayer and unites it with his own intercession. We must, however, add here two marginal comments. In the first place, if this intercession of Christ be spoken of as his continuing "sacrifice," what is involved is a "sacrifice of prayer," not a continuation or complement of that atoning sacrifice which he fulfilled once for all. The "sacrifice" of intercession depends on this perfected sacrifice. It is not intended to establish a new covenant, but to realize that which has already been enacted. By his intercession the Lord sanctifies, purifies, and unites his church (John 17:19 ff). In the second place, if we speak of the intercession which Christ as the High Priest offers "at the heavenly altar," it must not be assumed that Christ is not present and active at the altar on earth. The Lord's Supper is heaven opened. It unites heaven and earth. It testifies that God has "raised us up with him, and made us sit with him in the heavenly places in Christ Jesus" (Eph. 2:6).

The church's celebration of the Lord's Supper is praise and prayer. It is thereby also confession. When we speak of confession, we generally think of it in the form of words. But confession may also take the form of an act, as in the Lord's Supper. It may be said that this confessional character has become more prominent in our own day. The reason for this is that the more or less compulsory participation in the sacrament is not longer possible in the modern situation in which the church now exists. Participation in the Lord's Supper is a confession that we belong to the Lord who meets us in the sacrament. As such it is connected with self-examination. If we here speak of being "worthy and well prepared," the "worthiness" and the "preparation" consist in permitting God to judge our unworthiness and guilt.

Finally, in the Lord's Supper Christ brings to us the self-sacrifice of divine love. The gift he gives to his own involves also an obligation. In the Lord's Supper we encounter the sacrificial oblation of divine love; and it must involve, therefore, a consecration to a life in sacrificial service of love. Every participation in the Lord's Supper is a consecration to Christ and to a self-oblation of love. Our lives, too, are to be broken and given in the service of love (Rom.

12:1). The Lord who comes to his disciples in the Supper does not want to "take them out of the world" (John 17:15). He does not isolate them from God's created world; he sends them out instead to accomplish his purposes in willing service.

46. Prayer

1. *Prayer as a means of grace.* Prayer is a constitutive factor of Christian life. The character of prayer as a means of grace derives from the fact that prayer is not only man's turning to God, but more especially God's approach to man.

2. *Prayer as man's approach to God.* Prayer expresses both the militancy and the possessive character of faith. From the first point of view the most profound and dominant purpose of prayer is the realization of the divine and loving will: "Thy will be done"; from the latter viewpoint prayer is thanksgiving and adoration.

3. *Prayer as God's approach to man.* Prayer is the means by which God who answers prayer realizes his loving will; indeed, the most profound interpretation conceives of prayer as God's own act: "The Spirit himself intercedes for us" (Rom. 8:26); Christ "lives to make intercession for them" (Heb. 7:25; Rom. 8:34; I John 2:1).

1. Prayer as a Means of Grace

Prayer is an essential element in the Christian's spiritual life, and a vital condition of life for the Christian church. When prayer is excluded from the life of the church, the church ceases to exist. It is therefore eminently a constitutive factor of the church. The various means of grace, to which previous reference has been made, are indissolubly connected with prayer and become effective means of grace only in this connection. It is thus impossible to present the constitutive factors of the church, its spiritual centers of power, and omit from consideration the subject of prayer. In any presentation of Christian faith prayer of a necessity demands a place.

But if it is undeniable that prayer is an essential element in the life of the church, it is not on this account alone that prayer can and ought to be designated as a "means of grace." There has been a certain understandable reluctance to place prayer in this category. This reluctance has been motivated, as we have seen (§ 41, ¶ 1) by the tendency to conceive of prayer as entirely a human function. On closer examination this argument is found to be entirely untenable because, for Christian faith, prayer is combined with the answer to prayer, and because it involves not only man's turning to God but includes also an act of God. It may, however, be objected that the answer to prayer is a response, and does not necessarily prove that prayer itself is an act of God and therefore a means of grace. With reference to this objection it must be asserted that prayer is a means of grace not *only* because it is connected with the answer to prayer, but principally because prayer itself cannot be interpreted by Christian faith as simply and entirely a human act of turning to God. Prayer *is* indeed a human act of turning to God, but it is at the same time a divine act by which God draws man unto himself. As a matter of fact, prayer not only has its matrix in the quest of divine love for man, but in its inner nature it is an expression of this loving will as it subdues man. From this point of view prayer is indubitably a means of God's active "grace," a means of grace. It is noteworthy that when Luther speaks of prayer he maintains that prayer is evoked as God's benefactions are presented to the one who prays, and that prayer is thereby initiated and vitalized. According to this viewpoint the "benefactions" of God are not only conditional for the possibility of prayer, they also create genuine prayer. Prayer, in other words, is simply a means of grace, a way in which the divine and loving will realizes itself in the life of the Christian.

2. Prayer as Man's Approach to God

By an inner necessity faith expresses itself in prayer. The two-fold aspect of faith, which consists in the fact that faith is at once a present possessing and a constant becoming, that is to say, a militant faith (cf. § 36), is reflected in prayer. Prayer reflects both the militancy and the possessiveness of faith. Militant faith expresses itself in militant prayer which asks and seeks something from God; the prayer of possessive faith is the prayer of thanksgiving and in its highest form becomes adoration.

The ultimate purpose of *the prayer of militant faith* is the realization of the loving will of God. This is the constitutive element in all militant prayer. Whatever the prayer of faith asks for, its ultimate goal points in this direction. Faith cannot and does not desire anything else than the realization of God's loving will. Therefore the prayer of all prayers is always "Thy will be done." Prayer is a petition that God's will shall overcome all opposition and shall realize its unrestricted dominion. But this concern for the dominion of God's will on the part of prayer does not imply a spirit of resignation in the face of what happens. On the contrary, from this viewpoint prayer is seen as conquering prayer.

The purpose of prayer is not to effect a change in the divine will, but that the will of God *shall be done*. Since Christian faith conceives of God as pure love, and the purpose of the divine will is the realization of the aims of this love, it is meaningless to attempt to change God's will. Such a "prayer" would be nothing but an expression of a defective confidence in the divine and loving will and its wisdom. Since God is love, all prayer must be characterized by the desire to realize his loving will, and to realize it uncurtailed. Prayer, therefore, is principally a petition that we might grasp and understand fully and clearly this divine will and its purposes, and that this will shall entirely subdue us. Prayer becomes a means of perceiving God's will. The comprehension of the will of God is the condition on which it is realized in the experience of him who prays.

Prayer proposes to effect a change, not of God's will, but in ourselves and in the circumstances of life. It endeavors to open the doors to the power of divine love. It is indubitable, however, that the prayer, "Thy will be done," has often been interpreted in terms of resignation. This would imply that the purpose of this prayer is to express the petitioner's submissive resignation to surrounding circumstances, as if these circumstances were in themselves a direct expression of the divine will. In this way prayer loses its expansive power and its most profound content. Such a misinterpretation of the meaning of prayer occurs because of the tendency to accept everything that happens without further question as a direct expression of the divine will, ignoring the fact that existence comprises within itself much that is not expressive of God's will, but is actually in open conflict with it (cf. § 22). If this is inescapably clear to faith, then the prayer, "Thy will be done," cannot be uttered in the spirit of resignation. On the contrary, this prayer becomes in the highest degree a militant and conquering prayer of faith, a prayer which wages war upon all forces inimical to the will of God, and a prayer which calls down the sovereign power of God's love. It is precisely because everything in prayer is concentrated upon the accomplishment of God's will, that prayer is a power that overcomes the world.

The prayer of militant faith has a twofold background; on the one hand the fact of that evil which opposes the will of God, and on the other sovereignty of divine love even in relation to evil. When this antagonistic element is suppressed, prayer loses its militant character. Both Schleiermacher's position and Ritschl's in this connection are illustrative. When Schleiermacher inserts Christendom into the framework of a monistic world view, the result is that the only kind of prayer which he will accept as valid is that of submission and gratitude. As a matter of fact, in the final analysis, he conceives of the prayer of submission and gratitude as simply a corridor to that higher stage of existence distinguished by the characterization of Christian life in terms of an unbroken harmony and of perfect peace and joy in God. The unrealistic element in this conception is not that Schleiermacher designates Christian life as joy in God, but that he attempts to remove from the realm of prayer its essential tension and militancy. In this connection, Paul Althaus is right when he declares that this conception of Schleiermacher implies an unwarranted anticipation of the situation of the "church triumphant." "the conflict is swallowed up by victory *prematurely*, Christian dualism has been submerged . . . in a monistic conception of the world and of history." [1] As a matter of fact, militant prayer which opposes all evil can never be eliminated from Christian faith as it exists in the circumstances of life on earth. But this prayer is empowered by the sovereignty of the divine and loving will even in relation to evil.

Militant prayer must be distinguished from two misinterpretations: the transformation of prayer into passive resignation, and an egocentric orientation which makes man the master and God the servant

[1] Paul Althaus, *De yttersta tingen*, p. 83.

of his changing desires and demands. As has already been pointed out, prayer is concerned with the realization, not of man's but of *God's* will. This certainly does not exclude the fact that the one who prays, to use the words of Paul's letter to the Philippians, "in everything by prayer and supplication" [lets his] requests "be made known to God" (Phil. 4:6), and thereby commits his whole life with its needs into the hands of his heavenly Father. But egocentric importunity is certainly excluded from this militant prayer, and it is likewise clear to him who prays both that he does not rightly understand what is best for him and that what is best for him is decisively dependent upon his relationship to God.[2] Thus our petitions are dominated by all-inclusive prayer for the realization of the divine and loving will. This fact is also expressed when Christian faith speaks of prayer as "prayer in the name of Jesus Christ." This expression, which has reference primarily to prayer as a prayer of the Christian church, reveals at the same time something of the nature of Christian prayer. In every case Christian prayer is uttered with Christ in mind. The spirit of Christ is the power which deepens and sanctifies prayer, removes impure motives, and guards the direction of prayer so that it is in harmony with the loving will of God.

Because of an inner compulsion, the scope of militant prayer expands to include *intercession.* Intercession is therefore not a secondary or incidental element in the prayer of Christian faith. Christian prayer must of necessity become intercession simply because prayer is primarily concerned with the realization of the divine and loving will. When Christian faith is isolated, it withers. When prayer dwells in the presence of divine love, it cannot be concerned simply with me and mine; it becomes necessarily also a bearing of the burdens of others. Thus prayer expands into intercession.

As an *expression of the possessive character of faith,* prayer manifests itself as *thanksgiving and praise* to God for his unspeakable gift, which at its most profound level involves the gift of himself. In its highest and purest form this prayer of thanksgiving becomes adoration, *adoratio.* The one who prays bows in worship before the

²William Temple, "Prayer and Conduct," in *The Pilgrim* (1921), p. 337: "Prayer which is mainly occupied with a result to be obtained is comparatively powerless to obtain results."

unsearchable majesty of divine love which condescends to draw near
to those who are dust and ashes and are unworthy to dwell in his
presence. Faith worships him who alone is "worthy to receive glory
and honor" (Rev. 4:11; 7:12).

3. Prayer as God's Approach to Man

Prayer is not only man's turning to God, but is at the same time
and primarily God's approach to man. As far as faith is concerned.
prayer is not a transaction in which man alone is active; it is rather
a communication between God and man. Prayer is not simply man
speaking to God, but it is also God giving an answer. Luther has
characteristically put it thus: "It is a conversation; on the one hand
we speak to God, and on the other, *he* speaks to us. To speak to
him means to pray, and this is something great and glorious—that
the exalted majesty in heaven condescends to us who are miserable
worms, in order that we might be permitted to open our lips in
prayer before him and that he willingly hears us. But it is even
more glorious and precious that he speaks to us and that we may
listen to him. . . . What *he* has to say is much more comforting than
anything *we* have to say." [3] The viewpoint which is primary to
faith asserts that God hears our prayers and answers them. When
faith speaks in such terms about divine answer to prayer it does not
imply that all the "wishful prayers" which man may utter are to
be fulfilled by God, but rather that prayer is not without its answer, and that such answer to prayer always involves at its deepest
level the realization of the divine and loving will. According to
faith, God employs prayer as a means through which he accomplishes his purposes in victorious conflict against inimical forces.
And what is true of other means through which God works is also
true of the "means" of prayer, namely, that God works immediately
even when, according to man's viewpoint, he works through some
means. In and through prayer God draws man into subjection to the
dominion of his will; he enlightens man as to the purpose of this
will, how it wins its victories, and commissions man to be an instrument in the service of this will. Thus, from faith's most profound

[3] Quoted by Friedrich Heiler, *Das Gebet* (2nd ed.), p. 231.

point of view, prayer appears as God's own work in man's soul. The God to whom we pray is not merely a distant, extramundane deity, but the God who is living and active in the historical process and who precisely in prayer relates himself directly to us, indeed, who is nearer to us than we are to ourselves. Faith has expressed this conception of the effective presence of God in prayer by reference both to the way in which the Spirit of God makes intercession for us and to the intercessory prayers of Christ. "You have received the spirit of sonship, whereby we cry, 'Abba! Father!'" (Rom. 8:15). "Likewise the Spirit helps us in our weakness; for we do not know how to pray as we ought, but the Spirit himself intercedes for us with sighs too deep for words" (Rom. 8:26). But the Spirit who prays is also the Spirit of Christ. From this viewpoint, therefore, the continuing work of Christ appears to expectant faith as a continuous prayer of intercession. Prayer in the name of Christ is at once a prayer in which Christ continually realizes his work and one in which the intercessory prayer of divine love is mighty on our behalf. "Since the labors of all men in the service of God's kingdom are directed by the work of an eternally active God, therefore the presentiment emerges that even the prayers of men in the final analysis are directed by a deeper, never-ending intercession, borne and evoked by it." [4]

47. The Christian Ministry

1. *The ministry as a commission given by Christ.* The Christian ministry also belongs to the constitutive factors of the church. It has its basis in the commission of Christ and is a necessary instrument in the activity of the gospel that establishes the church. The primary function of the ministry is the preaching of the Word and the administration of the sacraments. In this respect it is a ministry of reconciliation.

2. *Misinterpretations.* The religious point of view of the ministry as a service under the divine commission is obscured when the ministry is misinterpreted in an objective or a subjective manner.

1. The Ministry as a Commission Given by Christ
In the previous chapters we spoke of the means of grace as the

[4] Billing, *Herdabrev*, p. 103.

constitutive factors of the church. But the Christian ministry must also be included among these constitutive factors, since the ministry is a necessary instrument in the activity of the Word and sacraments that establish the church. It has sometimes been discussed whether the ministry belongs to the *esse* or only to the *bene esse* of the church. In the latter case it would be assumed that the ministry is an appropriate and practical institution, but that it is not "essential" for the church and does not belong to its constitutive factors. The idea has sometimes been added that this represents the evangelical viewpoint in contrast to the Roman. This is incorrect, however, in the measure that Luther's conception of the matter is of guiding consequence. There is, to be sure, an antithesis between Luther and Rome in regard to the ministry, but this lies, as we shall see later, on an entirely different plane. It does not touch the question as to whether or not the ministry should be regarded as a divine institution. In reality Luther has emphasized even more strongly than Rome that the ministry is a divine ordinance which rests on a divine commission. He motivates the ministry on the basis of the saving work of God in Christ. The service of the ministry, he says, is "a service which goes *from* Christ, not to Christ, and which comes *to* us, not from us."

The ministry has the same secure position in the New Testament. Its fundamental point of view can be summarized in a few propositions. The ministry is inseparably connected with the church. Its basis is the commission of Christ, and it is consequently a divine commission. It possesses, therefore, an authority given to it by Christ, but this authority is not a personal possession of the minister. The ministry is a ministry of service, a *service* in the church. Its function is to serve the brethren by serving the gospel.

That the ministry implies a commission from God is emphasized in the whole New Testament, in the Gospels as well as in the letters. The Lord sent out his disciples with the message: "As thou [God] didst send me into the world, so I have sent them into thy world" (John 17:18; cf. 20:21). The messengers are invested with authority by the Lord. They have authority to forgive sins in his name. "Whatever you bind on earth shall be bound in heaven, and whatever you loose on earth shall be loosed in heaven" (Matt. 18:18; cf.

THE CONSTITUTIVE FACTORS OF THE CHURCH §47 ¶1

Matt. 16:19; John 20:22-23). But their authority is not a personal authority. They are entirely dependent on Christ, they are his instruments and servants. Everything depends on the fact that they serve. "Whoever would be great among you must be your servant . . . even as the Son of man came . . . to serve" (Matt. 20:26-28). The function is to make disciples of all nations, and it is done in his name. "He who receives you receives me, and he who receives me receives him who sent me" (Matt. 10:40). In Acts and in the letters we see how this ministry developed in the church. But the religious viewpoint is the same. The decisive element is the commission which has been given and which is to be faithfully administered. We find that Paul, often in the strongest terms, emphasizes the commission, ministry, and service which have been given to him. But he emphasizes just as strongly that the authority is not his, and that he is nothing in himself. "What then is Apollos? What is Paul? Servants" (I Cor. 3:5). He wants to be known as "a servant of Christ and a steward of the mysteries of God" (I Cor. 4:1). His confidence does not come because "we are sufficient of ourselves to claim anything as coming from us; our sufficiency is from God" (II Cor. 3:5). His boldness rests on the fact that the ministry has been given to him by God's mercy. "Therefore, having this ministry by the mercy of God, we do not lose heart" (II Cor. 4:1). The ministry is entirely a service of Christ. But for that very reason it is at the same time directed toward the service of the church, the congregation. The ministry can serve the church only by being entirely a service to Christ. "If I were still pleasing men, I should not be a servant of Christ" (Gal. 1:10). Service to the congregations consists in this: the messengers bring forth the message about Christ. "We preach . . . not ourselves, but Jesus Christ as Lord, with ourselves as your servants for Jesus' sake" (II Cor. 4:5). The messengers thereby contribute to the joy of the congregations. "Not that we lord it over your faith; we work with you for your joy" (II Cor. 1:24).[1]

When we consider the ideas of the ministry expressed in these quotations, it is clear that the starting point with reference to the ministry is the commission. The Lord himself has given this com-

[1] Olof Linton, "Church and Office in the New Testament," in Nygren, *This is the Church*, pp. 100-135.

mission, in the first place to his apostles who thus have a special position, but also through them to all those who during the centuries have been authorized as the messengers of Christ in the footsteps of the apostles. This means that the commission of Christ is continually given through the church, and that, from the point of view of faith, the ministry is maintained in the church through the activity of the Holy Spirit. From this point of view it becomes quite misleading to ask whether the commission comes from the church (the usual word in this connection is the "congregation") or from the Lord himself. From the point of view of faith this alternative is meaningless, since a commission from the church cannot be such unless it is a commission from the Lord who is the Head of the church.

Paul defines the ministry of the church as a *ministry of reconciliation*. Its significance can hardly be expressed in a more vivid manner. "All this is from God, who through Christ reconciled us to himself and gave us the ministry of reconciliation; that is, God was in Christ reconciling the world to himself, not counting their trespasses against them, and entrusting to us the message of reconciliation. So we are ambassadors for Christ, God making his appeal through us. We beseech you on behalf of Christ, be reconciled to God" (II Cor. 5:18-20).

That the ministry of the church is a ministry of reconciliation implies that it has its foundation in the finished work of Christ, in the atonement. If the reconciliation is a work of God from above, then the ministry of reconciliation is also a gift from above, a ministry given by God. The atonement demands a ministry, not because it needs to be complemented or repeated. It has been done once and for all. It remains for all times and generations. But the atonement demands a ministry because it addresses itself to every new age and every new generation. The victorious act of reconciliation must be carried out in new struggles. The victory of self-giving love does not mean that the struggle has ceased. The ministry of reconciliation is a ministry of struggle and conflict. As God's act of reconciliation in Christ was carried out in a struggle against the destructive powers, so the messengers of reconciliation are called upon to participate in this struggle. It is carried on in the consciousness that human power does not avail anything here, for "everything is from

God," but also in the consciousness that Christ is the victorious Lord and that his messengers go forth under his authority.

The ministry of reconciliation must proclaim the message of reconciliation. All the tasks which may belong to the ministry are gathered together in this one essential function: the word of conciliation has been entrusted to us. This aspect must be carefully noted. The message which has been entrusted to the messengers must be proclaimed as it really is. Attention must be drawn to the message, not to the messenger. The messenger serves the cause whose servant he has become. The messenger is an instrument, nothing else, but also nothing less than an instrument. It is the cause itself that is to speak, *majestas materiae* [the majesty of the matter]. The Word and the sacraments are the bearers of the message of reconciliation. The ministry belongs to the constitutive factors of the church because the Word and the sacraments are the constitutive factors of the church. This means likewise that the activity of the ministry has its center in worship life. It has been thus from the very beginning in the Christian church, and so it must remain. Ordinances and forms may change, but the church is the same throughout the ages. The fellowship of the church is a fellowship in the Word and the sacraments, a fellowship which expresses itself in worship life. Worship is the center of the church, because the decisive element is fellowship with Christ, and because this fellowship is realized in worship life. "Where two or three are gathered in my name, there am I in the midst of them" (Matt. 18:20). This fellowship with Christ is especially connected with the Lord's Supper, which is the seal of the new covenant. The function of the ministry appears, therefore, as something secure and irrevocable, however the forms of activity may change. There is no other church than the historical, actual, and concrete church which stems from Christ and his apostles, and which is founded on the Word of God and the sacraments in whose service the ministry of the church is engaged.

The office of the ministry has its own distinctive task and function in the church. This special office is not rendered unnecessary even though the New Testament declares that all Christians are called to be "a royal priesthood" (I Pet. 2:9), "a holy priesthood, to offer spiritual sacrifices acceptable to God through Jesus Christ"

(I Pet. 2:4). God has called all who believe in Christ "out of darkness into his marvelous light." Here there is no distinction and no difference in rank. All are members of the body of Christ in the fullest sense. But this equality does not mean that a special office of the ministry becomes superfluous. The duty of every Christian, as Peter says, is to "offer spiritual sacrifices." But the members of the body of Christ have different tasks and functions. The Lord calls and consecrates some of them for the special office of serving his church in the pastoral ministry.

2. Misinterpretations

Misinterpretations of the significance and status of the ministry arise when the religious point of view is not preserved pure and inviolate. Such misinterpretations have either an objective or subjective character, and lead to either a mechanical or a spiritualizing conception.

The first of these types appears both in the Roman and in the evangelical tradition. That the ministry in the Roman church is understood in a mechanistic way is to a large extent due to the theory of the sacrifice of the mass. The priest stands as the representative of humanity in the repeated sacrifice of the mass. Through the cultic rite he presents an achievement to God which is intended to benefit men. The ministry thereby becomes a mediator between God and man. In and through this mechanical conception of both the sacrament and the ministry, the ministry of reconciliation has been interpreted in a way that is foreign to faith. In spite of the fact that Christ's act of reconciliation is the unique sacrifice through which all human "sacrifices" intended to influence God are abrogated, the priest here appears as a "sacerdotal priest" in a sense which belongs to the pre-Christian period. It was not an accident that Luther's criticism of the Roman mass was concentrated on the sacrifice of the mass. By this criticism he struck also at the Roman perversion of the office of the ministry.

An objective and mechanical interpretation has at times appeared also within evangelical Christianity. While the Roman interpretation was attached to a mechanization of the sacrament, the evangelical viewpoint was attached to the mechanization of the Word as a means of grace. The change appeared as orthodox theology began to identify the Word with pure doctrine. It is significant that in regard to the function of the ministry the emphasis came to be placed on doctrine and its impartation rather than on proclamation, message, or kerygma in the primitive Christian sense of that word. By this intellectualization of the Word the purely religious aspect of the ministry was weakened and obscured, and the way was opened for a conception which was closely akin to institutional bureaucracy.

It is not strange, therefore, that a reaction begins in connection with pietism. Here the pendulum swings to the opposite extreme. The question about the ministry and its status now became a question of the personal and religious qualifications of the minister, and resulted in a dissolution of the concept of the ministry. When the emphasis is placed on personal piety, the function of the ministry to proclaim the message is obscured, and a burden is placed on personal piety which it is not able to bear. This subjective tendency which occurred in pietism received a curious development in romanticism and its cult of personality. In this connection it is interesting to see what Schleiermacher has to say about the ministry in *The Christian Faith* to be sure, the chapter is entitled "The Ministry of the Word of God," but the central point is the distinction between a stronger or weaker religiosity: the stronger influences the weaker through self-communication. This occurs through *Selbstdarstellung* [self-presentation]. "There can be no self-communication except through self-presentation acting by way of stimulus; the imitatively received movement of the self-presented person becomes in the receptively stimulated person a force that evokes the same movement" [2] Once we have noted that Schleiermacher looks at the ministry from this point of view, it is of less interest to mark that with customary skill he later seeks to combine this idea with the title of the chapter. But one does not need to be in doubt about the real meaning of his approach, especially since his idea about the Holy Spirit as *Gemeingeist* constitutes the mediating link between his talk about the

[2] *The Christian Faith*, p. 612.

ministry of the Word and the "self-presentation" of stronger religiosity.

The Christian conception of the ministry is misinterpreted and perverted when the minister is regarded as a sacrificing priest, when his task is restricted to the impartation of certain fixed doctrines, or to a sharing of personal religious experiences. The idea of the ministry is delivered from all these objective and subjective misinterpretations when the essential element is that commission of Christ given in and through the church, and when the function is completely defined by that message which is to be faithfully proclaimed in the service of the Word and the sacraments. Here there is no room for the pendulum to swing between an objectivism which places the messenger apart from his message, and a subjectivism which substitutes for it one's own personal religious experiences. The message, the living Word of God, contains an appeal directed to the messenger as much as to those who may hear it through him. Nor can it be accepted that the function of the ministry is a certain religious "self-presentation." If the messenger places himself in the foreground, he offends the "majesty of the matter." Everything depends on the fact that the message is proclaimed as the living Word of God it actually is.

CHAPTER SEVEN

The Church in the Present Age

48. The Obligations of Church Membership

1. *Living members in the body of Christ.* The goal of the one who has been called by God to membership in the Christian church is to become more and more a living member in the body of Christ and to serve Christ by serving the neighbor in love, being nurtured and strengthened through the means of grace.

2. *The activity of the church.* The two principal forms of the church's activity are evangelism and social missions. In relation to society the activity of the church is designed to prepare a way for the influence of Christianity within the various areas of life.

1. Living Members in the Body of Christ

The church of Christ is not of this world, but it has its existence in this world. The church belongs to the new age, but it lives at the same time in the old. This means that the church is a contending church, an *ekklesia militans*. Its life is characterized by the unceasing struggle between the loving will of God and those destructive powers which in this age oppose God's will. Membership in the church must be seen from this point of view. To be a member in the church of Christ means to be incorporated into that new solidary interrelationship in which the Spirit is active. Under those circumstances the meaning and goal of the membership are perfectly plain. This new man who has been incorporated into the new relationship of the Spirit shall more and more become a living member in that church which is the body of Christ. What this implies has already been described in those chapters which dealt with Christian fellowship with God as existing on the basis of God's act of forgiveness and as expressed in the life of faith (§§ 33-36). In our resumption of the discussion of the meaning and obligation of this membership, the intention is to clarify the matter further from the point of view of membership in the church militant.

The meaning and purpose of membership, therefore, is that man shall become a living member in the body of Christ. The necessary condition is that man receive nourishment for his spiritual life from those means of grace which are offered in and through the church. Faith is a gift of God; it is the living form of that new life which is given by God. No one can compel himself to believe. But the use of the means of grace may be regarded as an obligation which accompanies membership in the church, even though it must be added that this "obligation" is at the same time the great privilege which the church offers. The Christian life of faith is edified, purified, and strengthened through the use of the Word, the sacraments, and prayer as means of grace. There is no rivalry between the individual use of the Word and prayer and the congregational usage of these means of grace and the sacraments in the worship life of the church. On the contrary, these two mutually assist each other. Since the Christian life in principle is a life in the fellowship of the church, the significance of the worship life of the church with its climax in the Lord's Supper is of highest importance for every member in the church.

Because the membership in the church rests on the call and election of God, it involves the strongest challenge to man. He must prepare himself for the struggle against those destructive powers which intend to bring this membership to nought. The apostolic watchword is relevant in this connection: "Work out your own salvation with fear and trembling; for God is at work in you, both to will and to work" (Phil. 2:12-13). The Christian life is never, under the conditions of earthly life, a secure and inviolate possession. What has been won can be lost. But the armor which man must put on for this struggle is, as the Letter to the Ephesians says, the armor of God. "Therefore take the whole armor of God, that you may be able to withstand in the evil day, and having done all, to stand" (Eph. 6:13).

Membership in the church, therefore, imposes an inner obligation on man himself which directs him to use the means of grace whereby the Christian life is nurtured, disciplined, and strengthened. But

370

there is at the same time an outward obligation, which concerns man's conduct and appears in the demand that he shall "bear fruit." This is the practice of love in relation to the neighbor. The whole "Christian ethics" is characterized by the dominant directive of a service in love on behalf of the neighbor in the struggle against the destructive powers. This Christian view of life is misinterpreted if in its place the ennobling and perfecting of one's own personality is regarded as the principal ethical task. This has often been the case especially under the influence of romanticism. But to place sanctification under this aspect means in reality to concentrate on egocentricity. The goal sought in this way is just like happiness, which escapes the one who tries to capture it. It is not a question of developing one's own personality into an ideal, but of walking in the new order of love into which man has been placed, and of obeying and following the commandments which God gives in the various situations in life and which are intended to serve the neighbor.

In the measure that man discovers and obeys God's will in the various situations in life, his calling, which is connected with those ordinances of life given in creation and connected with the law of creation, is deepened and enriched. The calling receives a richer content and becomes free and flexible. Man becomes more personally concerned in the call, and new possibilities are opened for works which do not lie within the framework of the law.[1] What the Sermon on the Mount says about the works of love is not to be interpreted as "a new law" with a multitude of fixed ordinances for every circumstance in life, but is rather an expression and an example of what the Gospel can accomplish in various situations.

2. The Activity of the Church

In a previous chapter we discussed the Christian ministry. What we said there does not imply that the ministry alone should represent the activity of the church, and that the church can be divided into an active and a passive part. The ministry has its particular task, but the demand for activity on the part of the church applies to just as great a degree to all the members of the church. It is not a demand addressed to certain qualified groups among the mem-

[1] Cf. Wingren, *Luther on Vocation*, p. 66.

bers. Not even in this way can the church be divided into an active
and passive part. The demand for activity applies to all members
on all levels. But it is perfectly natural that this demand is met more
fully as the members more and more become living members in
the body of Christ.

The meaning of this demand for activity is evident from what we
have said about the twofold obligation of membership: the inner
and the outer. In this connection we are concerned especially with
the latter, which has its basis in the new order of love. From this
point of view the activity of the church expresses itself in two chief
forms: evangelism and social missions. Both of these must be
understood in their widest sense. Evangelism is directed toward non-
Christian peoples. But it must at the same time be concerned with
the non-Christian and secularized multitudes within Christendom.
Social missions includes the Christian service of love in all its forms.
It must be carefully noted that it is not a question here of simply
eternal works, but of an activity which has its foundation in and is
characterized by love. The inmost character of the activity of the
church is revealed in Luther's statement that the Christian is to be
"a Christ to his neighbor." The cure of souls is a function which
does not belong solely to the ministry, even though the minister
has his special task when under the seal of the confessional he
hears confession and in accordance with the command of Christ
pronounces absolution.

The activity of the church directed toward society is designed
to bring Christian influence to bear on various areas: in legislation,
in social life, in the education of youth, and so on. The people who
belong to Christendom have all been subject to these influences
since the day Christianity came to them, and this has to a large
degree determined their social life. What this has meant and means
can best be seen when we note what happens in a land where Christian influence is eliminated and the state maintains principles contrary
to Christianity. The present time furnishes fearful examples of this.
Membership in the church involves an obligation to guard the
Christian social and political heritage. In reality it cannot be preserved except by being cultivated and by gaining new victories in
the struggle against opposition.

49. Church and State

1. *The function of the state.* According to Christian faith the state has a function given to it by God. Its primary function is to maintain the order of justice. In this function the state is the bearer of God's law.

2. *The functions of church and state must not be confused.* Church and state each have their peculiar functions which must not be confused.

3. *The church and the order of justice.* Since it is the function of the church to guard the sanctity of God's law, the church must function as the conscience of the state in case the state violates this law.

1. The Function of the State

The Christian view of the state and its order of justice is radically different from the secular and profane point of view. Even though there have appeared tendencies within Christianity to consign earthly functions to the realm of the secular, this has only demonstrated a lack of appreciation for the meaning of the Christian faith in creation and for the universality of divine law. From the Christian point of view there is in reality nothing that is "secular." Life cannot be divided into two parts, the secular and the spiritual. God's will and law meet man in all the situations of life.

If we note what the New Testament has to say about "government" and its function, it is clear that Christian faith from the very beginning has placed what we call the state in direct relation to the will of God. The state has a function given to it by God. It exists in order to serve God. It is, in other words, an expression of a divine demand, i.e., God's law has been embodied in this order of society. To be a citizen of a state means to encounter in a specific form the demand of divine law and to be subject to its compulsion. The obligation of citizenship is at the same time a divine obligation.

According to the Christian view, the primary function of the state is to preserve justice and order, which is a basic condition for the accomplishment of its many other tasks. As the bearer and preserver of the order of justice, the state is an expression of the creative will which desires order in contrast to chaos. The order of justice exists primarily to prevent violence and unrighteousness. It is, therefore, that foundation on which all secure human intercourse must be built. It is the means God uses to war against the evil, demonic forces and to establish peace and justice in society. Where the order of justice prevails, there the will of God is realized in accordance with the demands contained in his law. It is realized whether the demand is met willingly or under compulsion. The question of spontaneity is not germane in this connection. Spontaneity has reference to the gospel, while the state operates within the area of the law.

If the state is to maintain the order of justice, it must possess power. The power of the state is the protection of the order of justice. At this point the state appears as the organized power which does not hesitate to use force when necessary. Justice and power are from this point of view very closely related. Power is a prerequisite for the state to function as a state of justice. But at the same time there is a demonic temptation included in this power, a temptation to set aside the perspective of justice and to use power for selfish ends. The state has then failed in its function. Everything depends on whether the state upholds an order of justice which serves the law of God and its purposes. If this is not the case, that power which was meant to serve God by capturing and destroying the demonic powers enters instead into the service of these powers.

If the question is asked which divine law is connected with the state and its order or justice, we refer to the discussion in § 21 concerning the law of creation. We stated in that connection, among other things, that the law of God is always the same, and always in its inner essence a law of love. The question whether the law of love can be related to the state has occasioned much confusion. The reason for this has been that in the interpretation of the law of love the starting point has been the Sermon on the Mount. When we read here that we are not to oppose an injustice, we evidently encounter a statement which cannot be applied within the area of justice, since the function of the order of justice is to oppose evil. One may then be tempted to draw the conclusion that the law of God cannot be related to the state. The alternative seems to be:

either a desperate effort to apply the propositions of the Sermon on the Mount to the order of justice, or a radical refusal to apply the law of God to it at all. In the latter case the result is a purely secularized conception which maintains that the state has its own laws, and that these have nothing to do with the divine law.

But this whole approach must be definitely rejected. Such a statement in the Sermon on the Mount that evil is not to be resisted does not belong to the sphere of "the secular government." Neither does it belong to the realm of law. It belongs rather to the sphere of the gospel, and its presupposition and possibility lie in that kingdom of God which is established and exists where the gospel rules. If such a proposition were applied to the sphere of the state, it would mean a confusion of law and gospel. But one must not draw the conclusion that the law of God with its demand of love is not concerned with the order of justice of the state. If the state is an expression of God's will, it must be animated by that purpose which inheres in God's law. This purpose is *a positive caring for the neighbor*. The intention is not that the fixed rules of law which belong in the state's order of justice shall be taken directly from God's law. When the New Testament states that the law is fulfilled in "one word," the commandment of love to the neighbor, it expresses a fundamental principle which in practical life and in the actual order of justice may be applied in a great variety of ways. The important element is that this fundamental principle be allowed to determine the order of justice in a positive manner. If this is not the case, the positive fellowship, which is the prerequisite for human life even in the sphere of the state, cannot function. Without a positive concern for the neighbor no real fellowship can be established and maintained.

2. *The Functions of Church and State Must Not Be Confused*

According to the previous paragraph, the state has a function entirely different from that of the church. The primary function of the state is to maintain order in contrast to chaos within human society. The function of the church is to establish upon earth that fellowship in which Christ is the Lord, through the means of grace to build up the body of Christ. This differentiation between the two functions meets us already in the New Testament. This has been further developed with energy and clarity by Luther, who maintains that the two diverse "kingdoms," the spiritual and the secular governments, must not be confused. The function of secular government consists primarily in maintaining the order of justice. It exercises its authority by force and compulsion if necessary. The spiritual government is occupied entirely with the salvation of man. It rules only by means of the Word. It uses no secular instruments of power. But though Luther maintains the mutual independence of these governments in terms of their independent functions, this does not mean that there is no relation between them. Nor does it mean that the church should remain passive in situations where the state violates the law of God for human society. The church must speak when the law of God is transgressed.[1]

The relationship between church and state has assumed many different forms through the ages. This is purely an organizational matter which does not affect the nature of the church. In reality there must be some regulations governing the relationship between church and state—it is only a question of what kind. A close association may further the work of the church, but it may also prove a hindrance because of the pressure the state is able to exert. But there is no guarantee that a separation of church and state will provide the freedom essential for the life and work of the church. The situation of the church in modern Communist countries furnishes ample proof of this fact. A closer connection between church and state presupposes that the state recognizes the significance of the work of the church. It presupposes also, not only that the ecclesiastical organization must be given a form that enables the church to perform its work, but especially that the state leaves the church free to accomplish its work in accordance with the commission given to it by the Lord of the church. There is nothing about which the church is more sensitive than the attempt of the state to give directives for and establish limits to the preaching of

[1] Many German theologians, especially during the Nazi regime, failed to observe this aspect of Luther's thought. As a result they have misinterpreted Luther's doctrine of the state. Cf. Gustaf Aulén, *Church, Law and Society*, and G. Hillerdal, *Gehorsam gegen Gott und Menschen, Luthers Lehre von der Obrigkeit und die moderne evangelische Staatsethik* (1954).

God's Word. "The word of God is not fettered" (II Tim. 2:9).

Conflict between church and state must arise, both when the church exceeds its function and encroaches upon the function of the state, and when the state takes over churchly functions and seeks to appear more or less as a church. A conflict of the latter kind arises when the state enlarges its "sovereignty" to include all areas of life, and when it thus advocates a world-view and conception of life which is foreign and hostile to Chrisian faith. History bears witness to many such conflicts from the earliest time down to our own day. During later centuries men have attempted to avoid a conflict between church and state by the theory that the state should be neutral in religious matters. History, however, gives no confirmation that such an attitude is possible. It confirms rather the words which Harold Hjärne wrote in his book, *State and Church*: "The government must always in one way or another assume a friendly or a hostile attitude to the church, either Christian or anti-Christian."[2]

3. The Church and the Order of Justice

The functions of both the church and the state are given by God. The primary function of the state is to be the bearer of God's law as the preserver of an order of justice. It may fail in this respect. Ordinances may be established in the name of justice which grossly violate the elemental requirements of God's law. Power may become the master of justice instead of its servant. This self-contained and egotistical power appears as a demonic power hostile to that order which the will of God intends and demands. Under such circumstances the church must function as the conscience of the state. It cannot avoid this obligation, because it is its duty to watch over the sanctity of God's law.

The role which the church maintains in this kind of conflict must be characterized by its own function. The struggle must be carried on entirely with the church's own spiritual weapons. It must seek to awaken insight into what an order of justice really requires, and a sense of responsibility over against love's demand to care for one's neighbor, a demand which cannot be violated without unleashing

[2] H. Hjärne, *Stat och kyrka*, p. 209.

the powers of destruction. The testimony of the church must be just as clear whether it is a question of an open violation of the law of God, or whether the opposition is hidden behind a disguise of Christian phrases used as a cloak for selfish usurpation of power. Everything depends on the fact that this testimony to the sanctity of God's law does not fail even if the trials be ever so difficult and testimony results in persecution and martyrdom.

When the church through its witnessing to the law of God thus functions as the conscience of the state, it does not exceed the responsibility given to it, nor does it claim superiority in relation to the state.[3] The church does not regard its function as superior to that of the state. According to the Christian viewpoint it is a question of essential functions which God has given. Since both originate in the will of God, the obligation of the state in reference to the order of justice is just as essential as the function of the church is in its sphere. When the church finds it necessary to oppose violations of God's law, this means simply that the church performs that service which has been imposed upon it, and which consists in this—that it reminds the state of its own high function and the obligations which this entails. The church does this in the conviction that no more essential directive can be given for the order of justice than that it be developed and maintained in accordance with the principle indicated in the law of God.

50. The Unity of the Church and the Disunity of the Churches

1. *The basis and purpose of the ecumenical movement.* The ecumenical movement rests on the presupposition of the actual unity of the

[3] Such claims to superiority seem to be involved in Barth's exposition of the relationship between *Christengemeinde* and *Bürgergemeinde*. According to him the impulse to right conduct within the *Bürgergemeinde* can come only from the "knowledge" which the *Christengemeinde* possess in the gospel. This "Christological conception of the state" rests on the fact that Barth derives the law from the gospel. Contrary to what the Bible teaches, his position means that God can work only through the gospel and through the law derived from *it*. Cf. Karl Barth, *Christengemeinde und Bürgergemeinde* (1946); Hillerdal, *op cit.;* and Gustaf Wingren, *Theology in Conflict* (Philadelphia: Muhlenberg, 1958), pp. 126-28.

church given through the fact that the church is the body of Christ. This is a perfect unity. The purpose of the ecumenical endeavors, therefore, is not to perfect this unity but rather to manifest this unity in the life of the church. It must be noted that the *skandalon* of Christianity is not its multiplicity (this is rather an asset), but the sin connected with schism.

2. *Ecumenicity and theology.* It is the duty of theology to make its contribution to the manifestation of the unity of the church. It will make this contribution in the measure that it penetrates into and elucidates the nature of the unity given in Christ, and the consequences of that unity for the life of the church.

1. The Basis and Purpose of the Ecumenical Movement

This chapter is intended to elucidate a few of the principal questions connected with the ecumenical movement. It is not a part of our task to narrate the history of the ecumenical movement, but a few introductory remarks are still necessary.

Ecumenicity is an idea which has appeared in the twentieth century. It is true that we may find many examples in the past of attempts to establish fellowship across confessional lines, but these were individual explorations rather than actions of the churches. The modern ecumenical movement plays a large part in the life of the churches. There are many reasons for its appearance: among them especially world missions and the present international situation with all its complications. But the chief reason is the gospel itself and the inescapable obligation which the gospel imposes on the church. The ecumenical movement became active immediately after the First World War, and proceeded at first along two lines. The one, Life and Work, sought to promote cooperation between the churches in the interest of Christian world service without regard for the existing differences. The other line, Faith and Order, took as its aim the overcoming of antitheses and strengthening the Christian fellowship in confessions and orders, but without working for any organizational uniformity. Both of these tendencies developed a lively activity, manifested especially in a number of ecumenical conferences, which were the first of their kind since the great separation in the sixteenth century. After the two lines merged, the ecumenical conference in Amsterdam, 1948, established "The World Council of Churches," which serves to promote and continue the ecumenical work. While the evangelical communions (with very few exceptions), the Orthodox, the Old Catholic, and the Oriental churches are all represented, the Roman church stands officially aloof, although individual Roman theologians show a vital interest in ecumenical questions.

We must also note in this review that in addition to these ecumenical negotiations a number of different communions have come closer together and in some cases have effected an organizational union. The most prominent example of such a union is the Church of South India, established in 1947, a union of Anglicans, Presbyterians, Methodists, and Congregationalists.[1]

When we examine what has happened in ecumenical affairs during the present century, it becomes obvious that a turning point has been passed in the history of the church. The direction is no longer as in the past toward greater fragmentation, but rather toward growing understanding and fellowship. In this case the most important thing is not the direct result but the change in what might be called the Christian atmosphere.

As we examine a few of the chief ecumenical problems from a systematic point of view, we must emphasize that all ecumenical endeavors rest on the basis of the actual unity of the church given through the fact that the church is *corpus Christi*. The unity is not something to be created through ecumenical conferences. Nor can it be said that this unity is defective or imperfect. The actual unity described in such biblical expressions as "the body of Christ," "the vine and the branches," is a perfect unity which need not and cannot be complemented or made more perfect. If this unity did not actually exist, all attempts to establish Christian unity would be doomed to failure. But it is also true that this actual unity in Christ imposes the most sacred obligation on all Christian communions, which live under the sin of division and are daily conscious of their consequent weakness. The demand is that this actual unity should be *manifested* in the life of the church.[2] This is not a matter

[1] Cf. Bengt Sundkler, *Church of South India: the Movement Towards Union* (London: Lutterworth, 1954).

[2] We may properly use the Lord's Supper as an example. "The *skandalon* of Christendom consists, not in its lack of fellowship in Holy Communion,

which the church may choose to neglect. It is essential that the unity which is given and which cannot be destroyed by human actions should find tangible expression in the life and work of the church. It is not sufficient to speak about "the unity in spirit" which exists in spite of all conflicts. If the ecumenical conversations were to be satisfied with such an intangible unity, it would indicate that the real nature of the church's actual unity and the seriousness of the obligation that unity imposes on the churches had not been understood. It would also show that the *skandalon* connected with schism has not been taken seriously.

The *skandalon* is not the multiplicity within Christendom, but the sin connected with schism. Here we encounter a number of very complicated problems. It is obvious that unity does not demand uniformity in life, doctrine, or organization (cf. § 38, ¶ 3). Even if this uniformity could be achieved, it would make Christendom poorer, narrower, and weaker. Multiplicity in and of itself is a great asset; it bears witness to the tremendous, creative power of the gospel in manifold human situations. Everything indicates that this multiplicity will become even more prominent as the church becomes more firmly established in such areas as India, China, Japan, and Africa. It is, of course, also evident that the schisms within Christendom have been connected with much sin and produced inestimable damage. However, this is not to say that every act which has led to separation can be judged as sin. If this act served the gospel and reasserted a truth which had been concealed and corrupted, it must be accepted as legitimately Christian. But even when this has been true and it has resulted in a sorely needed religious renewal, the schism as such cannot be declared free from sin. Every schism which has occurred within Christendom has been connected with sin. There has been not only a salvatory renewal, but also tragically harmful effects for the parties concerned and for the whole of Christendom. The serious question which Paul directs to the Corinthians can be asked in all schismatic situations: "Is Christ

for this exists and can never be broken, but in the fact that this fellowship is not made manifest in the life of the Church. That the unity exists, but that we ourselves retard and hinder it from being expressed, this is our *skandalon*." Nygren, *Christ and His Church*, p. 123.

divided? Was Paul crucified for you? Or were you baptized in the name of Paul?" (I Cor. 1:13). We could substitute here for the name of Paul the names of all the great men of God who have been connected with the schisms within Christendom.

In ecumenical conversations it has often been said that the divided churches should confess and repent of their sin and guilt. This suggestion is no doubt justified, but it must be clearly understood what is implied. The demand is directed to the communions now existing in the present. It is not a question of trying to divide the sin and guilt between the parties originally concerned in the separation. Nor are we called upon to make a confession of sin on behalf of the fathers who lived and worked at the time of the schism. Such a confession would be both meaningless and hypocritical. It would mean that we minimized or tried to escape the confession of sin incumbent upon us. Our present confession must involve the mutual suspicions and rivalries which are so evident a part of our separations. We must be conscious of the injury thereby done to "the fellowship of the brethren" (Acts 2:46). No church can claim to be fully innocent in this respect. All have tendencies toward self-sufficiency and arrogance in relationship to others. This attitude becomes very serious when one branch of the church sits in judgment over others, and even goes so far as to deny to others membership in the body of Christ. This is to usurp a right of judgment which belongs to God alone. No communion has a right to regard itself as the exclusive representation of the church of Christ on earth. Such a claim is pure arrogance. But a communion which does not make such exclusive claims is not thereby free from guilt. *Every* communion is called upon to confess its share of guilt for the injury and suffering inflicted on the body of Christ.

The divisions bear unambiguous witness to the sinfulness of the church. But this insight does not in any sense invalidate our certainty as to the holiness of the church (cf. § 38, ¶ 3). On the contrary, knowledge of this sinfulness is a prerequisite for a right understanding of the nature of holiness. When sinfulness is denied, holiness is conceived of either from a purely institutional point of view: the church as a holy institution; or else from a purely subjective point of view: the church as the sum total of all properly qualified peo-

ple. But a denial of the holiness of the church would imply a denial
of the unity given in Christ and of the possibility of actualizing
that unity in the life and work of the church.

2. Ecumenicity and Theology

The work within the ecumenical movement is not concerned only
with theology, but theology does have a very important task in this
connection. The ecumenical movement has placed theology in a
novel situation. It is true that even in former times theological conversations have been held across confessional boundaries. But it is
only in this century that permanent and continuous conversations
between theologians from different denominations have been arranged for the purpose of furthering ecumenical endeavors. In view
of this fact it is possible to speak of a new theological era.

The theological history of the ecumenical movement covers only
a few decades, but even in that short time a remarkable development has taken place. It was natural that the first stage of the theological discussions should have had the character of a confrontation
in which an attempt was made to discover the extent of differences
and similarities. In reality this was only the presentation of the
problem without furnishing a constructive program. The Faith and
Order Conference in Lund, 1952, marked a new departure in the
ecumenical discussions. If theology is to have any significance for
ecumenicity, it must endeavor to explicate the nature of that unity
given through the fact that the church is the body of Christ, and
the consequences involved in this conception of the church. It is
obvious that such a procedure must have a biblical foundation.
Such a fruitful study of the biblical material has been made possible
by the fact that modern biblical research has had more of an inter-
confessional character than in the past, and has led to fruitful contacts across confessional lines.

When we say that the theological task is concerned primarily
with the unity given in Christ, it must be emphasized that the
reference is not to some kind of "unity in the spirit" which exists
above and beyond all conflicts. To be sure we are concerned with
a unity in the Spirit, i.e., the Spirit of Christ. But this is not a unity
"in the wide blue yonder," but a unity which appears in concrete

forms as the Spirit creates the church through the means of grace, and their instruments, that is, through the constitutive factors of the church (cf. §§ 41 and 47). When the New Testament admonishes us "to maintain the unity of the Spirit in the bond of peace," it also indicates immediately the elements which are essential for this unity: "*one* body and *one* Spirit, just as you were called to the one hope that belongs to your call, *one* Lord, *one* faith, *one* baptism, *one* God and Father of us all" (Eph. 4:2-5).

An "ecumenically-minded" theology works on the basis of two important premises: the actual unity of the church given in Christ, and the actual differences represented by the various confessions. It would be a mistake to assume that the second of these is completely negative. A theology indifferent to its own confessional standpoint cannot serve the ecumenical cause. It takes the false position that the Spirit who leads us into all the truth has had nothing to do with the conflicts within the church. An "ecumenically-minded" theology would become meaningless if it should seek to gain results by disregarding the truth which may have been expressed in the various confessional statements. The question of truth is decisive. The words of Paul are valid in this connection: "For we cannot do anything against the truth, but only for the truth" (II Cor. 13:8). Superficial and ambiguous formulas are of no value. Ignoring the demand of truth will prove fatal.

What then is an "ecumenically-minded" theology? It is the will to encounter, the will to learn to know one another and to learn from one another, the will to critical self-examination, the will to complete honesty in all dealings with others, and above all the will to obey the Spirit who, according to Jesus, "will guide you into all the truth" (John 16:13). Two positions must then be rejected: on the one hand, the self-sufficient confessionalism which refuses to listen to other voices, refuses a critical self-examination, and assumes the right to judge everyone else; on the other hand, the kind of ecumenicity which seeks to gain results by smoothing over the differences or by uncritically uniting conceptions which are inherently incompatible. Positively stated we may say that the theological task is the same as always: to elucidate the meaning of the Christian faith as it is defined by the Christian message concerning the redemptive act of God in Christ (cf. § 1). Thereby the opposition between the confessional and the universally Christian is transcended. The confessional is significant in so far as it contributes to an explication of the meaning of the common Christian faith.

The Church in the Light of the Christian Hope

51. The Living and the Dead

1. *The Christian fellowship and death.* The Christian fellowship is not limited to this earthly life. Fellowship with God includes an indestructible fellowship with those who belong to God. Christian faith knows of no relation to the dead except in and through God. This viewpoint is decisive for all affirmations of faith relative to the relationship between the living and the dead.

2. *Two misconceptions.* Therefore all those conceptions which are based upon the idea of merits are invalidated. Likewise, spiritualistic attempts to effect an external connection with the dead are foreign to Christian faith.

3. *The perspective of faith.* The attitude of the Reformation involves a wholesome concentration upon the decisive importance of the present period of grace through its emphasis upon the seriousness of death. This has resulted in a cleansing of the life of faith by the removal of foreign speculations. But there has sometimes been a tendency to associate this attitude with a weakening of the idea of life after death, which has obscured the communion of saints which transcends the boundaries of life on earth. As far as faith is concerned, however, the character of this communion is given in and with the sovereignty of divine love.

1. The Christian Fellowship and Death

The church lives in this world, but is not *of* this world. It is the child of the new age. Therefore the life of the church in its totality has an eschatological character. Everything which has previously been said about the church must be understood from the viewpoint of eschatology. Two principal ideas of faith are finally decisive, the one has reference to the relation between Christians now living and those who have died, and the other concerns the perfecting of the church (§ 52).

The Christian relationship between God and man does not isolate the individual Christian, but establishes him in that living spiritual community in which the divine and loving will realizes itself in conflict with inimical forces. Because faith is a living fellowship with God, it likewise expresses itself in fellowship with the brethren. This fellowship cannot be confined within the limits of life on earth. Just as faith, because it is fellowship with the *living* God, cannot be circumscribed by life on earth (§ 36, ¶ 2), so the fellowship of Christians, based upon and characterized by the relationship between God and man, cannot be restricted to life upon earth. Those who are united with God are united with one another, and this union is indestructible because it is rooted and perdures in the Eternal God.

A variety of ideas about the Christian fellowship which transcends the limits of life on earth has emerged within Christendom during the ages. These have not all been organically connected with Christian faith. In treating the subject of the relation between the quick and the dead, the task of theology is to establish the premises by which faith can enter this area of inquiry and thereby to guard against those postulates which are so foreign to faith that they either imply an actual dislocation of faith's perspective or simply have nothing whatsoever to do with faith. The basic and regulative principle governing this problem must be this: the relation between the living and the dead, of which faith ventures to speak, must be established in and through God. If "immortality" is not simply a rational idea for faith, that is to say, does not have its basis in idealistic theories about the indestructible nature of man (cf. §§ 18, 34, and 36), and if instead "eternal life" is based entirely upon the relationship between God and man, in the creative and life-giving work of divine love, then faith can make no assertions about the relation between the quick and the dead which are not entirely determined by the Christian concept of the relationship between God and man.

2. Two Misconceptions

From the basic principle which maintains that the relation between the quick and the dead must be rooted in and through the relationship between God and man, it follows that faith must be critical of those ideas within the Roman church which are based upon the strange and foreign concept of merit. The Roman church speaks of

a very far-reaching connection between the living and the dead.
On the one hand, the dead who exist in an "intermediate state" are
said to be subject to the influence of the church of the living; and
on the other hand, the dead intervene very extensively in the affairs
of the living church. The chief character of this mutual influence
in both cases is its dependence upon the strange doctrine of merits.
In the first place, the living church acquires merit by the saying of
masses, etc., which are of benefit to the dead; in the second place,
the merits earned by the departed "saints" are of great benefit to
the living. In the measure that such ideas of merit are projected,
the relation between the quick and the dead is established by the side
of and apart from the relationship between God and man. And
when this occurs the way is open for a lively and unrestrained
vegetation in this sphere, because there is no longer any regulating
and guarding principle to curb the imagination.

While Christian faith must oppose all such Roman conceptions
based upon the contaminating idea of merits, which is foreign to
the Christian relationship between God and man, it must also unequivocally oppose all spiritualistic attempts to establish a direct connection between the living and the dead. Faith has, of course, no
reason for expressing itself on the possibility or impossibility of
actualizing such connections. Faith does not generally express itself
with reference to the scientific investigations of those phenomena
with which spiritualism is concerned. To undertake an examination
of this field is not the responsibility of theology but that of psychology. Theology must only maintain that these spiritualistic endeavors do not belong to faith. Christian faith finds no religious
interest in the attempt of spiritualism to materialize the departed
spirits and the like. The approach of faith to the living and the dead
is fundamentally different from that of spiritualism because faith
can conceive of no relation except that which is included in the
fellowship between God and man. Any connection between the
quick and the dead which is not conditioned by the divine fellowship, but seeks to establish itself apart from this fellowship with
God, lies entirely outside the sphere of Christian faith. Therefore,
when spiritualism attempts to become the representative spokesman
for religion, Christian faith is compelled to repudiate it, for spirit-

ualism leads away from that which is absolutely decisive for faith, namely, the relationship between God and man.

3. The Perspective of Faith

The religious awakening of the Reformation was characterized by a struggle against the intermingling of human merits in the relationship between God and man. It was natural, therefore, that evangelical theology should oppose the development of the idea of a relationship between the quick and the dead based upon merit which had occurred in the Roman church, and also turn against the dominant position which these ideas enjoyed in popular piety. Evangelical theology instituted a war of extermination upon all ideas which were not legitimately Christian, and thereby achieved a purification of the church which was desperately needed. A chaste temperance followed the former multifarious preoccupation with these matters. Men began at least to perceive that, relative to this aspect of eschatology, it was a matter which eye has not seen and ear has not heard. But most important was the fact that in contrast to the prevailing laxity in thought, the decisive gravity and obligation of the present period of grace and the unconditional seriousness of death were energetically inculcated.

It may be questioned, however, whether this process of purification, while it accomplished much that was good and inalienable, was not at the same time foreshortening the perspective of faith and restricting its hope. It is not without reason that E. Rodhe has written, "It cannot be denied that his process of purification has cost something. It is indubitable that for many the eternal and spiritual world has become distant and unreal. The memory of the departed has paled, reverence for death and the dead has declined. It is not easy to suggest how these lost values shall be recovered and new ones obtained, for under all circumstances care must be taken that the austere soundness and honest temperance which is our heritage from the Reformation is not lost."[1] The question is, therefore, whether this soundness and temperance can be united with the more meaningful, less negative approach to the relationship between the

[1] E. Rodhe, *Livet efter döden*, p. 35.

quick and the dead; that is to say, whether we can find room for
those hopes and presentiments which are actually in harmony with
the Christian relationship between God and man. In fact, the restriction of the perspective of Christian fellowship seems to imply
a curtailment of those possibilities which are available to the sovereign love of God. In the measure that this sovereignty emerges in
all the majesty which it has for Christian faith, the Christian fellowship also emerges inescapably and dynamically as transcending all
circumstances of life on earth. Those who have been claimed by
divine love are not severed from fellowship with the church militant.
Indeed, faith cannot, without being presumptuous, maintain that physical death marks the boundary line of the possibilities of divine love
(cf. § 19, ¶ 3). To be sure, faith cannot employ this conception
as a quietus for the purpose of abridging the decisive importance
of the present period of grace, but it is entirely free to use it as a
motive for that love which "hopes all things."

If these viewpoints are in harmony with the Christian relationship
between God and man, then a twofold perspective is given to the
presentiment of faith, namely, a twofold prayer of intercession.
When the eye of faith is raised to those who have been lifted beyond
this life with its sin, tribulation, and need, it perceives them as a
praying host and surmises that even intercession has its place in their
prayers, along with thanksgiving, praise, and adoration. Furthermore,
when faith recalls the departed ones and thinks of the inexhaustible
possibilities of divine love, such thoughts easily pass over into intercessory prayer.[2] Love is not halted by death. No speculations about
the scope of such prayers are able to diminish their outreach. They
have their Christian legitimacy because the communion in question
here is entirely dependent upon the relationship between God and
man, and because all impure and foreign ideas about merits are now
excluded. In other words, such prayer is genuinely Christian simply
because its matrix is love, and everything motivated by love is legitimately Christian because God is love.[3]

[2] It is noteworthy that the present Swedish Prayer Book has made a place
for such prayers again (cf. prayer for Easter Day and prayer for the occasion
"when someone has departed in death"). The Prayer Book has in fact made
connection at this point with the tradition of the earliest times of the
Reformation.

52. Regnum Gloriae

1. *The church and regnum gloriae.* Christian faith looks forward in hope to that consummation in which the will of God is no longer obliged to realize its purposes through conflict with inimical forces as has been the case in the circumstances of life on earth. "The kingdom of glory" appears, on the one hand, as the result of the continuing and creative activity of the Holy Spirit in the present. On the other hand, it appears at the same time as a radical and revitalizing transformation of the existential conditions and circumstances of the church. Faith's hope of a final consummation stands therefore in opposition both to that pessimism which curtails the task of the church "militant" and to that optimism which in one way or another apotheosizes the earthly.

2. *The content of Christian hope.* When the consummation appears to Christian hope as the kingdom of God in which the divine and loving will is at once realized and continues to actualize itself in ever greater degree, blessedness receives an inexhaustible and ineffable content which is completely distinct from all egocentric ideals of bliss.

1. The Church and Regnum Gloriae

The Christian hope is altogether a corporate hope.[4] Since Christian faith exists only as participation in the body of Christ, the church, the Christian hope is a hope of the ultimate perfection of the church in the kingdom of glory. The background of this hope is the contrast between the church's abundant resources and its imperfection, its holiness and its sinfulness. But it is against precisely this background that the hope which is firmly rooted in the encounter of faith with sovereign divine love is delineated. Since divine love is a sovereign love, the spiritual fellowship of faith cannot be circumscribed by the narrow and cramped boundaries of earthly

[3] Cf. Rodhe, *op cit.*, pp. 36 f. "Nothing can be more natural to the Christian than to connect his thoughts of the dead with his religious thought-world. Memories of the departed linger on even when one comes into the presence of God. Supposedly this is legitimate as long as it is a question simply of religious meditation. But when this meditation is transformed into prayer, then the memories of the departed are supposed to be banished, for prayer for the dead is not supposed to be made. The result is that just when the Christian begins to live most profoundly and seriously, he must banish from his mind the thought of the ones with whom he has been united in love."

[4] Cf. C. H. Dodd, "The Communion of Saints," in *New Testament Studies* (1954), I.

life. The horizons of this life are lifted, and the eye of faith perceives in expectant hope that kingdom wherein the loving will of God reigns unchallenged and in which all that is "in part" has passed away.

The emergence of *regnum gloriae* is apprehended by faith from two viewpoints (cf. § 18, ¶ 2). From one point of view the kingdom of glory is based upon the church militant. The struggling church is transformed into the finished dominion of God. This is the result of the creative activity of the Holy Spirit in the circumstances of life on earth. But on the other hand, the relationship between these two entities is not one in which the church is gradually developed and purified until it finally merges into the heavenly glory; nor does the opposition to the creative activity of the Holy Spirit steadily diminish until at last it ceases entirely and the church thus reaches the level of perfection. On the contrary, the opposition of inimical forces is indissolubly connected with the circumstances of earthly life. Therefore faith is compelled to look forward to the accomplishment of God's perfect dominion as being effected by an act of God's power which involves a radical transformation and re-creation of things as they are. The consummation implies not only a continuation, a development of what now is, but also a thorough, total transformation of the existential conditions and circumstances of the church. This transformation is connected with Christ's second coming, the judgment and final realization of the kingdom of God.

The twofold viewpoint with which faith thus apprehends the relation between the church militant and *regnum gloriae* confronts faith with a twofold antithesis. On the one hand, faith opposes that pessimism which regards the idea of transformation in such a way that the connection disappears. On the other hand, it opposes that optimism which asserts the idea of continuity and development at the expense of the concept of transformation. False pessimism curtails the task of the church militant and obscures the significance of history as being the laboratory of a universally purposeful divine will. False optimism labors under the illusion that the divine will can be completely realized in the circumstances of life on earth, with the result that it ends by apotheosizing the earthly. False pessimism underestimates the power of God which lives and works in the church militant; false optimism underestimates the opposition which in the circumstances of life on earth constantly renews its hostility to the struggling will of God, and ends therefore in utopian dreams. Faith is too much aware of the actual situation to fall into such an unrealistic optimism. But it is also too conscious of the actual resources of power available to the church militant to embrace a pessimistic asceticism. Faith perceives that the divine and loving will realizes its dominion through bitter conflict with inimical forces; therefore it knows of no unrealistic optimism. But at the same time it perceives that it is *God* who wages the warfare; therefore it knows of no pessimism.

2. The Content of Christian Hope

The great consummation appears to Christian hope as the kingdom in which the divine and loving will is at once realized and continues to actualize itself in ever greater degree. The content of that selection to which Christian faith looks forward is determined by the unbroken fellowship with God and by the fact that this fellowship is realized in the form of the kingdom of God. Fundamentally, however, this does not imply two complementary viewpoints; there is no fellowship with God which does not thereby involve participation in the kingdom where he reigns. Just as the character of Christian faith is theocentric, so also Christian hope is theocentrically determined. All egocentric ideas of personal bliss are excluded from that kingdom where the divine and loving will reigns. The fellowship of love determined by God is diametrically opposed to all egocentricity.

Two viewpoints are indissolubly connected with faith's conception of *regnum gloriae*, namely, that on the one hand here the domain of the divine and loving will is unopposed and perfect, and on the other that this will continues to actualize itself in ever greater measure. The latter viewpoint has often been excluded from faith's consideration of eternal life. But when this has occurred and faith has been inclined to interpret eternal life in terms of mere rest and blessed peace, then in the final analysis eternal life has ceased to be eternal *life*. The state of salvation has taken on the character of an inert immutability which is completely foreign to dynamic life. But such an interpretation of salvation actually has no vital connection with faith's conception of God. It is by inner necessity, therefore, that the two viewpoints of Christian faith are thrust into the foreground, namely, that, in the first place, eternal life is a final goal, the character of which is rest with God, eternal peace; but, in the second place, that the divine and loving will is continually active and that eternal life is therefore characterized by a divinely motivated activity. The inexhaustible content of salvation is given in and with the indissoluble union of these two viewpoints. But at the same time, the content of life eternal is so ineffable that faith is unable to speak of it in any other terms than groping figures. Meanwhile, every attempt to define the content of eternal life in rigid concepts eventuates either in passive stagnation or in unfulfilled becoming. This circumstance does not imply, however, any diminution of the assurance or richness of Christian hope. For Christian hope receives both its assurance and its richness in the encounter of faith with the sovereign, creative love of God.

INDEX

Messiah, 206, 293
Metaphysics, 2, 9-12, 41, 44-45, 48, 58-59, 60, 78-82, 85, 87, 104, 110-11, 124, 132-35, 142-43, 146, 155-56, 158-59, 237-38
Ministry, 302, 361-68
Miracle, 84
Missions, 30, 372
Modalism, 56, 191
Monarchianism, 190
Monism, 123-24, 171, 176, 178, 358
Monophysitism, 191
Monotheism, 53, 226-27
Monotheletism, 191
Morals, moralism, 49, 91-92, 102-04, 147, 156, 211, 232-33, 254-55, 263-66
Mysticism, 21-22, 40, 43-46, 102, 105-06, 116, 134, 200, 280, 327-28; of infinity, 45-46, 136-37; of the Middle Ages, 45-46

Nature, 26-28, 126, 164, 170; kingdom of, 152; as related to revelation, 26-28
Neo-Platonism, 186, 190-91
New age, 52, 144, 201, 286-87, 294
Newman, Cardinal, 76
New Testament, 31, 33-34, 36, 42, 51-52, 64, 66-67, 72, 74-75, 83, 104, 109, 112, 117, 120, 192, 198-99, 204-05, 219, 244, 253, 268-69, 275, 284, 293-95, 300-01, 315-16, 322, 329, 338-39, 342, 362-63, 373, 375-76
Nicaea, 185, 191
Nicene Creed, 72, 195, 224, 309
Niebuhr, Reinhold, 208
Nietzsche, F. W., 120
Nominalism, 85, 122
Nygren, Anders, 113, 190, 261, 272, 293, 295, 381

Obedience, 235, 275, 278
Old Testament, 26-27, 32-37, 54, 66-67, 104, 117, 120, 205, 322, 329
Olsson, Herbert, 300
Opus alienum, 112, 118, 146, 150

Opus proprium, 112, 118, 146, 150
Ordination, 330
Orthodox church, 69-70, 73, 75, 330, 380
Otto, Rudolph, 83

Pantheism, 44, 125, 128, 131-35, 229
Parseeism, 176
Paul, 23-24, 30, 46, 61, 66, 112, 130, 199, 201, 203, 222-23, 258, 280, 283, 295, 347, 363
Peace, 267, 271-74
Pelagianism, 236, 241-42, 247
Penance, 330
Penitence, 265-66
Pentecost, 293-94, 300-01
Perfection, 140, 144-45, 161-62, 236, 260-61, 304-05
Philippi, F. A., 263
Philosophy, 5, 42; Greek, 128, 133, 190-92; of religion, 2, 7-12, 14
Pietism, 60, 117-18, 265-66, 276-77, 299, 367
Pope, 75
Pragmatism, 87, 89-92
Prayer, 172, 318-19, 321, 352-61, 370, 390
Preaching, 3, 325, 327, 334, 361
Prenter, Regin, 227
Priest, 366-67
Propter Christum, 196-97, 204-10, 216, 260-61
Protestants, 299, 314-15
Providence, 161, 167, 172-74
Psychology, 60-61, 64; of religion, 2, 12-13
Punishment, 145, 147, 149-51, 155, 177, 205, 207-08, 257-58

Quietism, 154, 282-84, 289

Race, 242-43, 306
Rationalism, 43-44, 58-60, 85, 102, 105-06, 110-11, 113-14, 116, 327-28
Real Presence, 223, 346-49
Realism, 347
Reconciliation, 39, 98, 128, 131,

Teleology, 27
Temple, William, 179, 279, 289, 359
Testimonium spiritus sancti internum, 94-95
Theocentricity, 6-7, 52-57, 87
Theodicy, 177
Theologia crucis, 217
Theologia gloriae, 217
Theology, 2-18, *et passim;* of ancient church, 5, 11, 30, 39, 46, 50, 56, 72, 133-34, 185-94, 227, 350; Anglican, 193-94, 353; dialectic, 323; and ecumenicity, 379, 383-85; evangelical, 16, 23, 70, 75-76, 320, 324-25, 331-34, 341, 389; experiential, 60; Lutheran, 282, 342-43, 348; of Middle Ages, 58-59, 122, 124-25, 286-87, 322-23, 348; natural, 11-12; of nineteenth century, 33, 38, 47, 104, 109, 134, 192-93, 251-52, 265-68, 289, 323, 335; orthodox, 367; post-Reformation, 59, 108, 258; Scholastic, *see* Scholasticism; systematic, 2-19
Theophany, 185, 190-93
Time, 127-28, 213, 218
Torrance, T. F., 336
Tradition, 68-78
Transcendence, 84, 122, 132-35
Transubstantiation, 348-49
Trinity, 225-30
Tritheism, 227-28

Trust, 22-23, 277-79

Ubiquity, 348-49
Unbelief, 231, 233-35
Unitarian, 135, 229
Universe, 27, 134, 146, 150-51, 156

Virgin Mary, 195-96, 310-12
Virtue, 43, 48
Vocation, 271, 276-77
Voltaire, 117
Von Hügel, 335

Wallin, J. O., 27-28
Wells, H. G., 123
Will, 231, 236-38, 245-46, 250-51
Wingren, Gustaf, 275, 371, 378
Word of God, 297-98, 301-02, 304, 308, 317-19, 321-29, 331-34, 361-62, 365-68, 370, 376-77; inspiration of, 322; visible, 333; *see also* Scripture
Work-righteousness, 92
World, 160, 167-74, 197-98, 201-02, 208, 221, 276-77, 289-90, 294, 305, 358, 369, 386
World Council of Churches, 379-80
World view, 27, 38, 41, 80, 82, 84, 109, 123, 156, 169, 171, 176, 178, 358, 377
Worship, 359, 365, 370

Zwingli, Ulrich, 348

Type used in this book
Body, 10 on 13 and 9 on 10 Janson
Display, Garamond
Paper: White Standard Antique